First Church of the Brethren
1340 Forge Road
Carlisle, Pennsylvania 17013

A
Dynamic Psychology
of
Religion

A
Dynamic Psychology
of
Religion

PAUL W. PRUYSER

HARPER & ROW, PUBLISHERS
1817   NEW YORK, HAGERSTOWN, SAN FRANCISCO, LONDON

Grateful acknowledgment is made to the following:

Dr. Albert C. Outler, for quotations from his translation of *Augustine: Confessions and Enchiridion,* Library of Christian Classics, Vol. VII, Philadelphia, Westminster Press, 1955.

The University of Chicago Press, for quotations from the author's article, "Some Trends in the Psychology of Religion," *Journal of Religion,* 40:113–129, April 1960.

The Westminster Press, for quotations from *Western Asceticism,* Library of Christian Classics, Vol. XII, edited by Owen Chadwick, 1958.

The editors of *Theology Today,* Princeton, New Jersey, for quotations from the author's article, "Anxiety, Guilt and Shame in the Atonement," *Theology Today,* 21:15–33, April 1964.

First Harper & Row paperback edition published in 1976.

ISBN: 0-06-06701-X

LIBRARY OF CONGRESS CATALOG CARD NUMBER: 68-17589

76 77 78 79 80 81 10 9 8 7 6 5 4 3 2 1

To the memory of my mother
Elizabeth Pruyser–van Dingstee

Contents

Preface

Portions of this book were first given as the Lyman Beecher Lectures at Yale University's Divinity School in the spring of 1968. When Dean Robert C. Johnson invited me to lecture in this famous series, I was told that its concern was no longer with preaching. Since I was given much leeway in selecting my own topic, I decided to bring to completion a project that had occupied my mind for several years: to write "my" psychology of religion. The possessive pronoun indicates much personal involvement, a deep sense of conviction, and an awareness of uniqueness about the material that is now being presented in book form. Offering it to the public cancels the possessive implications of the pronoun.

The book was written in the conviction that the psychology of religion, once a respectable preoccupation of some leading psychologists, has been for some years in an intellectual cul-de-sac. To put it very concisely, nearly all the classical texts in this field use religious phenomena as their ordering principle. Thus, they focus selectively on prayer, mysticism, worship, conversion, cosmic consciousness, or religious development. They also tend selectively to ignore some very important religious products, such as doctrinal formulations and theological systems. Furthermore, not many of them are addressed to the common, simple, pedestrian manifestations of religion in the gray mass of ordinary believers who are neither great saints nor prominent sinners, who have never had a conversion experience, who pray rather tritely, and for whom the word "cosmic" is only an academic nicety.

In contrast to this approach I had teased myself and my students for some years with the idea of a psychology of religion which would order its data in terms of psychological categories, use normative and clinical observations with appropriate fluidity, assess theological propositions as products of religious concept formation, and take into account the inconspicuous, everyday features of the religious life. The word "dynamic" in the title is a short term for the theoretical orientation used: a clinical, psychoanalytic psychology which includes considerations of ego psychology and does not shy away from appraising the phenomena it encounters.

I have received much encouragement for this project from friends and colleagues, which encompass psychologists, psychiatrists, theologians, and the proverbial "intelligent laymen," including a good many women. Three friends are to be thanked explicitly for their labors of love in reading the manuscript critically and making valuable suggestions. These are: Dr. Seward Hiltner, Professor of Theology and Personality at Princeton Theological Seminary; Dr. Kenneth R. Mitchell, Director of the Training Program in Pastoral Care and Counseling at The Menninger Foundation, and Dr. Philip Wollcott, staff psychiatrist in the C. F. Menninger Memorial Hospital. Sheer work and much inventiveness have come from Mrs. Kathleen Bryan, my secretary, who made the completion of the book a pleasure.

But the most valuable support, emotionally and practically, has come from my wife Jansje, and my children Henriette, Herman, and Pauline. That the book is not dedicated to them, but to the memory of my mother, is only due to the fact that my mother was first in introducing me to the world of religion.

Unless otherwise indicated, scriptural quotations are from *The Holy Bible*, Revised Standard Version.

A

Dynamic Psychology

of

Religion

I

Orientation

"ABOUT THE year of the Lord 1581, in Germany, at a place called Alden-
burgh, it happened that a Baker, the master of a very untoward Boy, upon
some great provocation, fell upon him with his fists, without mercy; upon
his head especially; so that the Boy fell sick upon it of an Epilepsie: whereof
he had divers terrible fits, and was twelve dayes speechlesse. Yet after a
while those fits abated, and by degrees vanished quite away. But then instead
of them, he fell into ecstasies, in which he would continue two, three, four
hours, without either sense or motion. As soon as he was out of a fit, the
first thing he would do, was to sing divers songs and hymns, (though it was
not known that he had ever learned any,) very melodiously. From this singing he would now and then passe abruptly to some strange relations, but
especially of such and such, lately dead, whom he had seen in Paradise: and
then fall to singing again. But when he was perfectly come to himself, and
had left singing, then would he sadly and with much confidence maintain,
That he had been, not upon his bed, as they that were present would make
him believe; but in heaven with his Heavenly Father, having been carried
thither by Angels, and placed in a most pleasant green, where he had en-
joyed excessive happinesse, and had seen things that he could not expresse
–&c. The same Boy when he foresaw his fits coming upon him, he would say,
that now the Angels were ready to carry him away. There were divers relations made of him at that time: but that which I have here, I have from
Joh. Coboldus, a Doctor of Physick of the same Town . . . his opinion there
is, that they were *symptomata morbi melancholici*, occasioned by the
Epilepsie. For that it is natural to those that have been epileptical, to fall
into melancholy, besides his own experience, he proves out of *Hippocrates*.
But because this Boy besides his visions, was also reported, and believed
commonly, to prophesie many things: the Doctor doth acknowledge himself
posed in that, and professeth to doubt, that besides Nature, there might
be some operation of the Devil concurring. Wherein nevertheless he seemeth
afterwards to have altered his opinion, and to adscribe all partly to Nature,

1

(Ecstasies and Visions,) and partly (Prophecies,) to Art and Imposture: not only because the Boy had alwaies been an arrant Rogue, (for his age,) and very subtle and cunning; but also because when he was removed to another house, and more carefully watched, his prophesies did vanish; yea and his ecstasies too, (after a while) as he seemeth to intimate."[1]

This passage was written in a psychiatric treatise by Meric Casaubon, published in London, 1655, under the title "A treatise concerning enthusiasme, as it is an effect of nature: but is mistaken by many for either divine inspiration, or diabolical possession." It is quoted here because it contains, in a nutshell, an astoundingly large inventory of religious behavior. In the first place on the part of the narrator: he uses the rather pious phrase *year of the Lord* where a simple date would have been enough. But then consider all the religious items he describes regarding his patient. The boy has epilepsy, for centuries called the *sacred disease,* and in this case strangely related to *ecstasies,* a religious emotion of great renown. He sings hymns, which means that he engages in overt religious action. There is even a hint that his knowledge of such hymns may come from a *supernatural source* for it was supposed that, as an arrant rogue, he had never learned any. He is reported to have had *visions of the dead,* to have made *visits to Paradise,* and to have looked around in *heaven,* with its pleasant greens (the story is German!). He had been with his *Heavenly Father,* the primary religious object, to whom he was carried by *Angels.* It is unclear whether these were actually visions, i.e., hallucinations, or fictitious thoughts, i.e., delusions, asserted as real. He seems to have experienced the religious emotion par excellence: *excessive happiness* or bliss. The patient *interprets his own fits religiously,* when he attests that his premonitory symptoms signal that Angels are ready to carry him away. He engages in *prophecies,* an ancient religious habit, but the observers, using their own religious framework, wonder whether this is not better seen as *demon possession.* The observers also question the *genuineness* of the boy's religious behavior and ascribe his acts to Art and Imposture, undoubtedly assuming that a rogue can hardly have genuine religious convictions! There is the final hint that the boy's religious behavior was an *adaptation* to his circumstances.

The two Doctors of Physick struggle with some interesting questions about the case. Is this boy's religiosity health or illness? Is it madness? Is it sincere or just a bit of mockery? Is it supernatural or natural? What is the connection between brain disorder and enthusiasm? Is his prophecy a gift from God or a visitation from the Devil?

The distinction between supernatural and natural causes of the boy's symptoms is Casaubon's. He must have been quite religious himself, and a scientific child of his time as well, for he wrote elsewhere in this dissertation:

... as the disease is cured by natural means, so the Enthusiasms go away, I will not say by the same means, but at the same time. ... Many such we might find perchance in the lives of reputed Saints.

One could hardly be more cautious: "not ... by the same means, but at the same time." What shall one make of such cases of religious behavior—both in the patient and in his doctor? Indeed, what shall one make of religion?

One way of approximating an answer to these questions is to take recourse to a certain perspective on religion and survey systematically its profuse manifestations. This is what any psychology of religion proposes to do. To be sure, the psychological perspective is by no means the only way of looking at religion systematically. One can look at it historically, sociologically, politically, and philosophically, through art and architecture, by way of literature and poetry, and even in pharmacological perspective.

This book is a psychology of religion, and as such it stands in a long line of similar works. Since it does not purport to be a history of the psychology of religion, I must refer readers with historical interests to other sources, for instance the excellent *Readings in the Psychology of Religion,* edited by Strunk.[2] But I feel obliged to sketch out first some major trends in the psychology of religion, so that some of the peculiarities of the psychological perspective be clarified from the start and my own clinical viewpoint within the larger psychological perspective be understood.[3]

More than fifty years ago the leading academic psychologist in America at that time was asked to give the Gifford Lectures in Edinburgh.[4] What William James said on that occasion probably still constitutes the most important single psychological work on religion. He made some excellent propositions: (a) that religious phenomena are continuous with other psychic phenomena; (b) that in religion, as everywhere else, the sublime and the ridiculous are two poles of a continuum, with many ordinary, drab and hackneyed happenings in between; (c) that in religion, as in other human endeavors, feelings tend to be more important than thoughts; (d) that there is not one single psychic wellspring for religion in the form of a special instinct, sentiment, or disposition; (e) that religion has a human and a divine side and that psychology can study only the former; and (f) that people do not simply *have* a God but that they *use* their God and that religion is known by its fruits in behavior. A little later, psychoanalytic investigators would repeat this last statement with more vigor and with a more precise knowledge of the kind of use people make of their God. James added a simple typology and had a keen interest in the medical side of religion, not only diagnostically, but also in terms of mental hygiene. That latter interest is again rearing its head in our day.

I believe that James's fourth point—that religion cannot be delegated to one special psychic function—is of major scientific importance. Before and after him many people have asked whether the essence of religious experience is to be found in a feeling, act, attitude, value, cognitive state, drive, or whatever. They sought an element, a *prima materia,* of religious experience. James's answer is the parallel in religion to the debunking of the old and outworn phlogiston theory in chemistry. *All* the psychological part processes may participate in religious experience, and *none* of them is specific to religion. Instead of raising the wrong question about specificity, let us inquire what the preponderant part processes are in the religious experience of certain people or in certain systems of religion; in other words, let us set forth the *varieties* of religious experience.

But, as soon as that inquiry has been made, one must raise the next question: whether the gist of religion really lies in part processes or whether it has to be sought elsewhere. If religion claims the whole man, as some of its spokesmen say, by what sort of process does it achieve its holistic, integrative character—if it ever does? James answered tentatively that this would involve a shift in the center of energy, but he could not pursue the matter in further detail.

There is some reason to wonder whether James's most lasting legacy, which led to the phenomenon known as the "James tradition," was not at bottom a political as well as a scientific contribution. Since James, the term "religious experience" has become an expression for a somewhat cagey way of dealing with certain aspects of the psychology of religion. Its premises seem to be: (a) some people have subjective experiences, of one sort or another, called "religious"; (b) psychology, as an empirical science, deals with experiences of people; therefore, (c) the psychology of religion, if it is to be empirical, deals with the subjective experiences of people called "religious."

There is nothing wrong with this conclusion, except that it is based upon too narrow a premise. For James, subjective experience meant feelings, and the best empirical data were to be found in the feelingful expressions of feelings. This emphasis on feelings and utter subjectivity cuts down on the importance of cognitive states, decisions, and acts—on the very things in which systematic and moral theology is interested. Hence the work of James and his followers did not have to be taken too seriously by the theological disciplines. After all, *this* psychology of religion dealt only with the very subjective, all-too-human side of religion —it did not deal with God, with doctrine, or with the nature of the redemptive community. It did not even deal with the nature of faith, for James had used a more naturalistic term for it in his "over-belief." To be sure, it touched upon the nature of man, but only so lightly and so humanly that it necessitated no change in churchmen's thoughts about God and his relation to man. Moreover, even James's pragmatism was sufficiently palatable to the prevailing theological climate of the time to prevent all too vigorous skirmishes.

My thesis is that James set up too narrow boundaries to the field of the psychology of religion and that many of his successors held to those limits without giving the matter much thought. Perhaps they found the limitation tactically useful. Some exceptions must be noted, but they had little influence. The Wiemans, for instance, deplored the restrictions.[5] A few of James's contemporaries, notably Coe[6] and Leuba,[7] were more daring on this point, but most students take no recourse to their original works. Leuba must be credited with having faced the question of the existence and the nature of God; he took the viewpoint that religion deals with an illusory reality. Freud would have more to say about that later.

Religious life involves images, intuitions, concepts, and the human history of all these about God. But, above all, it involves an object relation with God, and psychology must be interested in all these aspects. I am not sure whether psychology can or should waive the ontological question, as, by the way, some theological systems do, but I am sure that it cannot stop short of man's thinking about God and the forming and obtaining of his image. Beside the feelingful renditions of religious feelings stand the thoughtful renditions of religious thinking. Diary pages, such as James used, may be excellent sources to get at feelings; it would seem to me that theological treatises are the appropriate sources for religious thoughts in an articulate form. In the interpretation of dreams, psychoanalysts make distinctions between the primary and the secondary processes of thinking, between latent dream thoughts and the manifest dream content. Students of religion also face phenomena which are highly stratified, like dreams. They can apply analogous distinctions to the material that interests them, e.g., prayer activities.

The method of the James tradition consists chiefly, if not exclusively, in nonexperimental fact-finding and description. Use is made of biographical materials, questionnaires, and simple or complex (but mostly simple) correlation techniques. Much work has gone into correlating incidence of conversion, frequency of prayer, loyalty to parental beliefs, etc., with global personality traits. There were others besides James, of course. An interesting psychologist of religion is R. Müller-Freienfels, who in 1920 published two little volumes in German.[8] His work is broad and helpfully systematic but not always deep. Of particular importance is his description of the field: individual forms and institutional forms of religion are put side by side, and much attention is paid to myths, liturgy, and such religious acts as prayer and sacrifice. He uses no special methods of investigation but works, as many students of religion do, from his desk, using a simple Kantian scheme which emphasizes feeling, willing, and thinking. Under "thinking" are included all possible cognitive aspects of religion: the acquisition of knowledge, contemplation, the exercise of logical functions, and the use of symbols. I believe that this latter emphasis is of importance.

Müller-Freienfels' contribution also contains a helpful schematization of historical trends in the psychology of religion. He considers the following six tendencies or schools of thought:

1. Theological schools of thought which try to give psychological underpinnings for a given theological system. An example is Schleiermacher, who defined religion in its subjective aspects as the feeling of utter dependence.
2. The ethnopsychological school produced by English and French positivism, exemplified in Wundt's work.
3. A school of differential psychology particularly strong in America, with its traditional interest in individual differences. Examples: Leuba, James, Starbuck.
4. A psychopathological school, particularly strong in France. Examples: Delacroix, Flournoy.
5. An analytic school aiming at an independent analysis of traditional religion, knowing that its psychological roots are often purposely hidden from scrutiny. Examples: Feuerbach and perhaps Nietzsche.
6. The psychoanalytic school, which emphasizes the role of unconscious motivation, of drives, and of the function of the superego.

We will come back to some of these schools later and consider psychoanalysis first. Psychoanalytic studies of religion started early in this century. One of Freud's first case studies, that of the wolf man,[9] contained some interesting notes on the role of religion in psychopathology. In addition to Freud's *Totem and Taboo*[10] and *The Future of an Illusion,*[11] the works of Pfister[12-13] and of Jones [14-16] must be mentioned here. Because of the general hostility to psychoanalysis in the early decades of our century, there was at first very little carry-over of the analysts' observations and theories into the main body of religious studies, with the seeming exception of Reik's study of ritual.[17]

Psychoanalytic studies of religion have a special character, conceptually as well as methodologically. They are basically studies of motivation for religion, and the person's set of beliefs and practices are approached from the point of view of wish fulfillment, drive control, primary- and secondary-process thinking, object relations, the genesis of conscience and the ego ideal, and the economics of libidinal and aggressive urges. Because the word "symptom" in psychoanalysis covers an almost infinite range of possibilities, religion can be approached as a symptom. Psychoanalysis said more forcefully what James had said earlier, namely, that people *use* their God.

The mechanics of the psychic household, the defense processes of the ego, and fundamental psychosocial constellations, such as the Oedipal conflict, were all brought to bear upon religion, phylogenetically as well as ontogenetically, individually, and collectively, within a genetic-dynamic formula. This formula added an entirely new dimension to the methodology of the psychology of religion in that it demanded longitudinal assessment of the individual in the network of his object relationships. It also holds that personal documents, which were the mainstay of James's studies, cannot be taken at face value but must be approached with analytic sophistication. And since for practical reasons such studies nearly always coincide with the process of psychotherapy, an excellent opportunity is here provided for evaluating the significance of religion in relation to other pursuits, preoccupations, values, and needs of the individual. In other words, here is one place where one can study how religion "fits" into life.

An interesting feature of psychoanalytic study of religion is its shortening of the psychological distance between gods and men. Note that I speak here of psychological, not of ontological, distance. God's names, as Jones has remarked, such as Father, Maker, Sustainer, and Provider, are relevant to the family drama. To me, the statement that a god is a father figure may also imply its complement that biological fathers have numinous qualities. In other words, psychoanalysis has established a new affinity (not identity) between gods and men which cuts across the technical distinction between the divine qualities of transcendence and immanence.

As to the old dispute on psychology's relation to the ontological question about the deity, I would like to make a second comment. It is a perfectly psychological question to ask why and on what grounds some people answer the ontological question about their god vigorously in the affirmative, why some deny it, and why a third group of people say that they do not know. Particularly since the matter cannot be decided logically, as even some theologians admit, the psychology of knowledge, like the sociology of knowledge, may have some important contributions to make. The ontological question with capital letters is one thing; but every individual's way of coming to grips with it is quite a different thing.

Freud's term "illusion," denoting the formal psychological status of religious beliefs, has given rise to bitter opposition, particularly from those who have only read the title of his book. The book itself clarifies the meaning of the term: religious beliefs are illusions in the sense that they are not pure products of experience or end results of rational thinking but fulfillments of the oldest, strongest, and most urgent wishes of mankind.[18] An illusion is not a mistake. Rather it is like Columbus thinking he had discovered a new seaway to India, while he had actually discovered America! An illusion is not necessarily false, that is, incapable of realization or contradictory to reality. The great question is: If illusions are needed, how can we have those that are capable of correction, and how can we have those that will not deteriorate into delusions?

I can find little fault with Freud's definitions. They bring to my mind Paul's admonition to the Corinthians: "For now we see in a glass darkly, but then we will see face to face" (1 Cor. 13:12, AV). Knowledge of any god is always approximate and always full of distortions. Our psychic organization, our perceptions, our thoughts, our wishes, our moods participate in the shaping of our beliefs. We knew this before the "new look" in perception and before the concept of perceptual defense. As theologian Paul Tillich has pointed out, our doubts codetermine the dynamics of our faith.[19] The divine purpose is never completely known by mortals, and, because of this, they find themselves making guesses about it. The guesses may not be unaided; they may be wise and inspired; but they remain guesses. Moreover, as Jones has remarked, "what one wants to know about the divine purpose is its intention towards oneself."[20] It is exactly because religion deals not with abstractions but with realities by which people live that psychoanalytic formulations must be taken seriously.

Perhaps the most significant contribution of psychoanalysis to the psychology of religion is its insistence upon the role of conflict in religion, and of religion in conflict, personal as well as social. Religion can now no longer be seen as an isolated item or parcel of experience but as a quality of an individual's experiencing the world and himself; it can be defined as a way of problem-solving. This point had already been made in 1911 by a nonanalytic psychologist, George M. Stratton,[21] who saw the source of religion in man's being entangled in all kind of conflicts, stemming from inner and outer polarities. I believe that this position is heuristically of great importance to the psychology of religion. Several questions come to mind right away:

1. Which problems have been solved or can be solved by religion?

2. What kind of religion can solve a given problem?

3. To what extent are problems really solved by religion, or, which problems are refractory to religious solutions?

4. Can a man fall back on traditional religious thoughts and beliefs, or must he look for religious innovations?

5. Which new problems are in turn posed by attempts at problem-solving through religion?

6. Does religion, as it is used in problem-solving, remain itself problem-free or does it become conflict-laden?

Some of these latter questions seem particularly relevant to certain

developments within Protestant theology and to recent thinking on the problem of mental health. Both Christianity and mental health seem to require
some degree of tension and of "considered non-conformity," to use Shoben's
beautiful phrase.[22]

At any rate, within such a framework the concept of religious experience
as a state has to give way to the concept of religion as a process. Problem-
solving takes time, and it always involves a future, that is, the unknown.
Phenomenologically, it may even mean a preoccupation with the unknown.
The person who is engaged in problem-solving proceeds by hypotheses—
one after another. How are his hypotheses corrected under the impact of
experience? How does he draw, and modify, his cognitive maps?

With psychoanalysis the psychology of religion should have undergone
a change in concepts, in orientation, and in attitude toward the material
studied. Instead, it underwent a change in personnel. For psychoanalysis
is also a branch of psychiatry and, through it, of medicine. Within psychology, its impact was felt mostly in the specialization of clinical psychology, which has had relatively little contact with the psychology of
religion—the latter has remained more closely in the fold of academic
psychology and educational psychology. The psychoanalytic impact on
psychiatry is great. Its impact is also felt keenly in pastoral education, and
in pastoral theology. I believe that this selective spread of the influence of
psychoanalysis has altered the status of scientific concern with religion in
a major way.

First of all, it has meant a shift from pure science to applied science.
Second, it has meant a shift from the traditional academic department to
the professional training program. Third, much if not most of the activity
in psychology and religion has moved from the university campus to the
psychiatric clinic, the hospital, and the parish. Indeed, the combination
"religion and psychiatry" is now more popular than the psychology of
religion, and pastoral theology is rapidly becoming also a pastoral psychology.

Many of these changes seem to depend on the emergence of a new professional specialty, that of the psychotherapist, and on the uncertainty about
the prerequisites for his training. But whoever he may be, and whatever his
academic background, it is important to note for our purposes that his role
implies both a marvelous opportunity and a profound ambiguity in relation
to the possibility of an advancing psychology of religion. The psychotherapist admittedly combines science and art, and he combines them in
unsteady proportions. On the one hand, he is in a unique position of near-
ness to deep and subtle processes, just at that level of depth which many
have surmised is the level at which religion has its significance in a person's
life. Certainly, he reaches a stratum of personality functioning by which
the psychology of religion could be immensely enriched. But the deeper he

goes with his patient, the more difficult it becomes for him to maintain the cool, objective, and detached attitude of the traditional scientist. Moreover, the psychotherapist's endeavor to help (and "helping" is one of the foremost definitions of his profession) is matched by his patient's desire to obtain health, and this may place the observational data about the patient's religion, if any, in a distorted, or at least very limited, perspective. For, despite the intriguingly deep level at which observations about an individual's religion may be obtained in such a setting, the purpose of "helping" and "being helped" tends to give rise to cheap superficialities about religion as a mode of, a vehicle for, or a criterion of adjustment, or to the tedious attempts at establishing correlations or even equations between religion and mental health.

This perhaps is as good a place as any to mention the works of Jung,[23-27] though it is nearly impossible to do justice in a few paragraphs to this penetrating but imprecise thinker. Since his extensive writings cover many borderland areas among psychology, psychiatry, medicine, history of religion, theology, and cultural anthropology, it would be tempting to confine ourselves here to Jung's contribution to the psychology of religion proper. However, his own demonstration of the interweaving among so many diverse themes, constructs, observations, and symbols makes such a restriction intolerable. They are all relevant to the psychology of religion, though some more peripherally than others.

One will search in vain for the classical chapter headings of psychology of religion in Jung's works. There are no systematic treatises on the religion of adolescence or on conversion. There is very little material on individual differences in religion. All these and many other topics are scattered throughout his works, sometimes in relation to religion, sometimes in connection with nonreligious aspects of living. But there is an abundance of rich, searching, and sometimes daring propositions from which the psychology of religion could benefit.

While several thinkers have stated that people *use* their gods, there is probably no one who has come so close as Jung has to saying that people also *make* their gods. Lest one be frightened or repelled by the implications of this position, it should be noted that Jung was one psychologist who did not shrink away from the word "soul," which he at times even seemed to prefer to the more neutral and technical term "psyche." Added to this is his conception of human life as a process of individuation in which the self and its destiny are actively sought and nurtured. The journey of the self is described as a road toward salvation—indeed, the soul and the self (though objects of empirical study) have by postulate been given a sacramental and pseudodivine status! Hence Jung was able, from this position, to study the psychological side of the whole process in which man lives with his God and God with "his" men, in terms of the religio-psychological borderline concept of "archetypes."

God is here no longer an abstraction, no mere Prime Mover or *Summum Bonum,* but something to which people feel related *in tension.* In other words, psychology of religion can be a psychology of interaction and interpersonal relationships with supernatural beings in which not only man but also God, as well as the dialogue between them, become objects for analysis. For God is not the projection of a thought or idea onto another person (as the paranoid patient may project some quality of himself onto someone else), but he is projected *as a person.* Thus he is within reach of personality theory. In his *Answer to Job* Jung was indeed consequent enough to describe God as a changing, developing Being who learned to respond to one man's exemplary morality. He also discussed the difficult problem of God's sexual identity.

But psychotherapy is only one area in which the hand of dynamic psychology and psychiatry is shown. There is another, and perhaps much wider, field of professional endeavor in healing relevant to the psychology of religion. I think that the development of modern hospital psychiatry, as distinct from mere custodial care, has also some important implications for the psychology of religion.

The modern psychiatric team shows division of labor and specialization of functioning with the preservation of a common goal—healing. But the division of labor is not radical; there is indeed much overlap between the functions of the team members and considerable unity in basic scientific theory. Psychiatrist, psychologist, social worker, nurse, and chaplain, to mention only typical team members, all work together in the evaluation and the treatment of the patient. The modern mental hospital is also a social institution which maintains many intimate ties with the community. It interacts, more or less intensely, with many professional and social groups: local physicians, judges, ministers and priests, civic groups, welfare agencies, and various religious organizations such as churches and councils of churches. Many different persons and forces are marshaled on behalf of "total care" for the patient. Some of these groups or individuals have an obvious and direct concern with the religious welfare of the hospitalized patient before, during, and after his temporary isolation. Much of this activity has become channelized and epitomized in a new professional specialty—the mental-hospital chaplain. And this is the place to highlight one more trend in the psychology of religion represented by Anton Boisen.[28-30]

In his profound book *The Exploration of the Inner World,* Boisen put a new stamp on psychopathology and religion by placing both in the framework of the life crisis. Mystical experience can best be understood if it is seen in the same order of intensity and depth that attaches to severe mental illness. Both are processes of disorganization and reorganization of personality, of transformation, dealing with man's potentialities and ultimate loyalties. I think that this is a position which places religious experience functionally and experientially most clearly at the nexus of holistic, integrating tendencies of the organism. In this theoretical framework, religion is not an adjuvant to integration; it *is* integration. It is one way of solving problems, sometimes successfully. Religion and mental illness, and of course by implication also mental health, are to be approached as existential conditions. Specific categories of experience obtain the focus in mental illness and in religion: world catastrophe, death and rebirth, the feeling of cosmic importance and of personal responsibility and mission. Religious language is close to the primary-process language known from psychoanalysis.

Whatever one may think of Boisen's propositions in detail, they certainly stress a dimension that is much needed in the psychology of religion. The concept of the mental-hospital chaplain with special clinical-pastoral training as a part of the psychiatric team is chiefly Boisen's creation. This chaplain has a unique function: he represents religion in all its aspects on the psychiatric team and to the patients. We must ask what implications this has for the psychology of religion.

The chaplain is first of all a pastor, not a theologian. His task lies in shepherding, co-ordinate with the healing goal of the psychiatric team, which goal he shares. For our purposes the most significant part of his function is that it brings him into contact with persons who have met with utter failure in problem-solving, with or without religion or pseudo-religion. Some may have met with failure in earlier attempts at religious problem-solving, which has resulted in specific resistances to even the faintest religious allusions. If Boisen's thesis is correct, the chaplain is forced to *seek* religion in psychopathology; and he finds it—sometimes in obvious manifestations of psychopathology *of* religion, sometimes in seemingly nonreligious processes, and at other times nowhere. I believe that this has some major consequences. While James and the traditional body of the psychology of religion focused on the more obviously and indisputably religious experience—on the "pure cases," so to speak—the chaplain is, as all ministers of the faith are, broadening the range of religious data immensely by including all potentially religious phenomena. The old question was: *Which are the significant data of religious experience?* The new question is: *Which data of experience are of religious significance?*

Now let us look at the clinical psychologist on the psychiatric team. Can he assess and evaluate the religious experience of his patients, if any? My personal experience as a member of such a team has been enigmatic, perhaps even shocking. I have been intrigued by the paucity of spontaneous religious references in test responses and interviews, even among ardent churchgoers. Some of our tests seem able to tap fairly deep levels of personality functioning, and yet we rarely encounter a clearly religious response to our Rorschach and Thematic Apperception tests. Patients say many things and sometimes indulge in a large amount of moralizing; they may even see a church steeple in an inkblot, but this appears on further scrutiny to be purely an architectural or a scenic-idyllic item. Where in the tests do we find their religion? Is it a failure of our tests, or is it proof of the negligible role of religion in the life of many people, admitting that we actually deal with a selected group? Or is it perhaps the result of the patient's social perception which compartmentalizes all encounters with people in terms of specific roles? Does the patient seek out the chaplain to talk about religion, only to ignore this dimension of his life in his meeting with other team members? I do not know the full answer to these questions, but I surmise that they can all be answered with a partial affirmative.

For the psychology of religion this situation means that the clinical psychologist will not readily be able to furnish new data from tests. As a matter of fact, the first datum is negative: there is not as much religion as we might have thought.

But here again we have to heed the question: Which data of experience are of religious significance? Could it be that the patients are giving us religious responses without our knowing it? And perhaps without their own conscious knowledge? There was a time when sexual references in language, action, and fantasy went by unrecognized, because the power of sex and the role of symbolism were not understood. At that time sex was delegated by the civilized to a separate and remote chamber of the mind or, rather, the body. Perhaps we are in the psychology of religion in the same stage at which sexology was in the days of Havelock Ellis and Richard von Krafft-Ebing.

A second comment about psychologists may be in order. In several of my colleagues who are articulate, introspective, and sensitive people and who subscribe to an integrated set of religious propositions, the reading of standard texts on the psychology of religion elicits disappointment. I have always shared their reaction; we sense keenly that the heart of the matter has not been reached. In the same vein there is, even among some writers of books on this subject, a hardly hidden overtone of hopelessness with regard to the relevance of their own works. Does it mean that they feel psychology is still too young to tackle such a formidable task? Or must we think of the possible role of repression which handicaps even psychologists in coming to grips with religion? Perhaps we can learn something from that mighty prescientific psychologist Feuerbach,[31] who put all his emphasis on the given existence, that is, the sensing, thinking, and self-actualizing person, and who had the temerity to say, "Theology is anthropology," because in the object of religion nothing but the essence of man is expressed. Of course, Feuerbach's "nothing but" is dogmatic and to that extent unscientific, but his temerity, rigor, ardor, and immense curiosity are to be envied to this day.

The effectiveness of hospital psychiatry depends in very large measure on the adequacy of the case study. What is psychiatric case study? Books have been written on the subject, but the essence of it lies in what psychiatrists do, which is, according to Menninger, "try to understand their patients."[32] The case study is a formulation of that understanding. It is written purposefully, with the double aim of communicating the understanding to others and of marshaling all the available forces and knowledge to change the patient's condition. A good case study usually involves all the specialists on the team, but in the end it depends on the synthesizing ability of the psychiatrist.

A good many psychiatric case studies begin with phrases like this: "This is the case of a white, thirty-five-year-old, prim, Methodist, Midwestern housewife," only to omit any further reference to the religious dimension in this person's life, except perhaps for a note on the role that the choir or the Sunday School played in getting her acquainted with her husband. Meanwhile, the phrase itself is a perfect stereotype and sets up all kinds of expectancies which may help channelize possible interpretations. On the other hand, some books on the psychology of religion make use of the case-study method (as, e.g., P. E. Johnson did quite effectively[33-34]) only to emphasize all possible aspects of experience relevant to religion, but with a neglect of the person's sexual history, his infantile and childhood experiences, his economic history, etc. I think that in both instances the psychology of religion does not really profit from the clinical case-study method, and this judgment stems from my ardent belief that it could profit so much if the case study were done with care, holistically, existentially, and following the natural articulations of the patient's subjective and objective reality. Nor should my allusion to the phrase "prim, Methodist housewife" be taken as a persiflage of the writing of case studies. I admit— nay, I am even proposing—that the psychiatric assessment of the religious dimension in the life of a patient is a difficult business. Casaubon's vignette with which I opened this chapter shows how easily one can go astray.

But psychiatrists must make an attempt, and their procedures must be fair to the reality which they want to assess. They need not assume that everyone is deeply religious, but neither may they assume that religion is a compartmentalized area of a patient's life and, consequently, delegate its assessment to the chaplain or some other specialist, or simply ignore it. To be sure, in some people religion *is* compartmentalized, but that is psychologically an interesting phenomenon which merits special mention and interpretation. Above all, it seems to me that one can in no case expect "religious data" just to pop up. Strictly speaking, there are no religious data, ready to take, just as little as there are any sexual data. Rather *all* data —events, processes, actions, objects, and object relations—may have either or both a religious and a sexual significance for the patient, or for the examiner, or for both. An excellent demonstration of such polydimensionality of meanings is given in Erikson's masterful *Young Man Luther*.[35]

There is still a different angle on this problem. Even in well-documented and well-integrated psychiatric case studies religious references are often missing. We shall discuss this in Chapter III. Sometimes this may be because of the examiner's lack of interest, but sometimes it happens despite attempts at obtaining religious relevancies from the patient. I cannot quite explain this, except that I have a hunch that the faith of many people may be completely inarticulate, and in others it may rarely reach a level where explicit references to it can be made. I also surmise that in some patients, and perhaps in many normal people, specific religious qualities and numinous values have shifted from traditional and suitable objects to what theologians would call idolatrous objects,[36] concerns, pursuits, and values. The chromium-plated car, articles from the mail-order catalogue, the life style of suburbia, the pursuit of conformism, the aspiration to orgastic potency, and the zealous search for mental health are cases in point. If there is some validity in this speculation, the psychology of religion may be greatly enhanced and enriched by a meticulous study of people's idols and idolatries. The scientific study of religion must include *all* gods, *all* numina, *all* ultimate concerns, even those that may turn out to be false ultimates. I know of no better way to accomplish this than by a thorough application of the clinical method in psychiatric case study—a method which attempts to portray and conceptualize "what men live by." Why not assess, as part of the case study, what a person considers holy?

If we are indeed concerned with all gods, we must also deal with *all* the ways of man in worship, prayer, and ritual. Books on the psychology of religion have usually emphasized the diversity of styles and types of such religious actions. But there is a conspicuous limitation of approach in relation to prayer. Entirely typical is the following statement in W. H. Clark's textbook: "In studying prayer we have the additional difficulty of surveying an area of the inner life of which the average person is loath to speak. If one prays at all, the matter is apt to concern his very dearest wishes."[37] The conclusion drawn from this observation is that the psychologist's curiosity should therefore be tempered by his reverence; in regard to prayer, he must content himself with "soft techniques" such as questionnaires and gentle interviews.

I am entirely at odds with such a policy. Prayer has been widely considered as "the heart of religion." One of its best expositors, Heiler,[38] has said that it is the most spontaneous and the most personal expression of religion. If this is so, the psychology of religion must look for ways of coming to grips with it. And again I believe that the chaplain, the psychiatrist, and the clinical psychologist are here in a unique position to contribute, because of their rich knowledge of, and total concern for, their charges. Meanwhile, the psychologist of religion can learn another lesson from the history of psychoanalysis: if observations on others are difficult to make, he can observe himself. Freud analyzed his own dreams and published them in order to advance the science of dream interpretation. I would invite the religious ones among the curious scientists of religion to study their own prayers, including just these "dearest wishes" about which the "average person is loath to speak." Science knows no taboos, and *noblesse oblige*.

So far, I have stayed within the framework of the psychology of religion in the formal professional sense. I mentioned psychiatry and the mental-hospital chaplaincy only in terms of how they contribute to the process of assessing and evaluating the role of religion in life, the nature of an individual's faith, and the possible distortions thereof. The aims of psychiatry, and particularly of the chaplaincy, do not coincide with the aims of psychology. This review cannot be brought to a conclusion without considering at least one more discipline, the aims of which are widely different from those of psychology, but from whose matrix of observations, theories, and speculations exceedingly important contributions to the psychology of religion have been made. That discipline is theology, or the body of divinity.

We cannot go into the problem of how this vast body is internally articulated and how it relates to the arts and sciences. (In his book on pastoral theology, Hiltner has offered an interesting schema of these relations.[39]) Nor can I venture here to review all the psychological relevancies of theological studies, although I am convinced that there are many. This would be beyond the scope of this book and perhaps beyond my competence. I say "perhaps" because I feel that it would take a *psychologist* to establish such psychological relevancies, but I also realize that this is a formidable task. Systematic theology usually contains more or less elaborate doctrines of man; moral theology presents values and goals for human behavior and includes admonitions and adhortations; pastoral theology presents aims and methods of shepherding. In all these there is at least an implied psychology, dealing with the actual and ideal conditions of man, with origins, alienation, motives, values, conscience, goals, conflict, repair, and learning. It would take us too far afield to examine here any of these psychological implications of theology, but I think that it can and should be done for the advancement of the psychology of religion.

Some theologians have been quite explicit on psychological matters.

While Schleiermacher[40] formulated his thesis on faith as the feeling of "utter dependency" still with a clearly apologetic aim, later theologians have attempted to give precise descriptions and analyses of psychic conditions in faith for their own sake. Two of them, Rudolf Otto and Paul Tillich, must be mentioned because of their immense value to the psychology of religion.

Otto's celebrated phenomenological study *The Idea of the Holy*[41] and his later work *Mysticism East and West*[42] have left a deep impression on readers in many different professions. His two-pronged approach to the subjective and the objective poles of the core experience in religion, that is, the idea of the holy or numinous corresponding in each of its aspects with specific moments of human experience, is a masterpiece of synthesis. The emphasis is not on individual differences, although some striking differences are portrayed, but on the "common good" of religion, on the generalities that govern religious experience. But experience is related at every step with its object; the science of man as *Homo religiosus* and the science of the *Numen* are not divorced. Otto's phenomenological analysis is a convincing answer to the fallacious assumption that the psychology of religion deals only with man—it must deal with God, for religion is the establishing, experiencing, and nurturing of a relation between man and his gods. There is no psychology of the artist apart from the artistic work and beauty that is given form; neither can there be a psychology of religion apart from the idea of God and the forms in which holiness becomes transparent. Just as theology deals also with man, psychology must deal also with the numinous.

Allport has stated: "A narrowly conceived science can never do business with a narrowly conceived religion. Only when both parties broaden their perspective will the way to understanding and cooperation open."[43] Psychology cannot be theology or philosophy, but neither can it behave like the ostrich with its peculiar technique for shutting out fearsome objects. The truth of a religious assertion is a substantial part of the religious experience, for *Homo religiosus* is passionately involved in it and ultimately concerned with it. When a truth turns out to be disappointing, when it lets us down, we must reorganize our lives and seek a better truth, else we become ill. Whether God-in-general is real or not, the God-in-particular of this or that believer must at least be realistic. Not sensually and concretistically, in that "He walks with me and He talks with me" (this is Whitehead's "fallacy of misplaced concreteness";[44] or what Woodger labels the "finger and thumb philosophy"[45]); neither as a loose thought or even as a concept, but in the psychological sense that gods are loved and responded to by people who live with them. Freud's definition "illusion," with the specifications that I mentioned, is not such a bad term after all.

A psychology of religion without some evaluation of gods is a narrow undertaking. Though it is true that the reality of God cannot be asserted or denied by psychology, it is also true that a miserly and unimaginative attitude on the part of the scientist cannot do full justice to the nature of the experience of God in believing subjects. I would hold that a humorless scientist cannot write a full psychology of humor; nor can the dreamless psychologist ever write the rich scientific text of dreams that Freud wrote. To know what aspects of experience have religious significance for a person presupposes some familiarity with the possibilities and perplexities of religion in the investigator.

I think, then, that the psychology of religion may assume an attitude of naïve realism toward the object of religious beliefs. All sciences take this attitude toward their direct and indirect objects. The philosophical critique of this position is a matter for the philosophy of science, not for the sciences themselves. To assume this attitude is not to place psychology in the service of religious apologetics. If, as Whitehead[46] holds, religion is one of the strong forces which influence man, and if the believers place one source of this force in God, the psychologist must study gods *for the sake of studying man*. I use the plural form here to indicate, moreover, that what is relevant to the believer is God's attributes *in relation to himself* rather than the general idea of God. And these are exactly some items of difference between various theologies. In some way, the problem of God's existence is to be approached as an individualized and particular, rather than a general, question. Woodger has remarked that it is difficult to distinguish existing from existing *for someone*.[47] Its parallel in the psychology of religion is that God is never a simple object, one among many, but always a *love* object to the devout person. Now love objects have a plus factor to the lover which outsiders cannot observe. To me, my spouse has attributes which my neighbors will never perceive. That is why my relationship with her is more dynamic than my neighbors'; it involves commitment, loyalty, exaltation, and a highly particularized order of reality. Again, Woodger states that it is impossible to know that something exists without knowing something else about it.

Existentially oriented thinkers have had less trouble with the ontological problem than classical theologians have had. They have seen that the arguments for God's existence are less relevant to religious vitality and truth than had been assumed. They have seen the profound but sublime irrationality of all religious propositions. They have noticed, moreover, that God-centeredness is not necessarily the opposite of man-centeredness. The various Cartesian splits between being and knowing, subject and object, natural and spiritual realms, are only some possible options of human thought. It is unscientific to take them as dogma. Hebrew genius produced another possibility: that the knowledge of man and the knowledge of God are co-variants. To the extent that some religious men proceed on this premise, the psychology of religion may accept it as a postulate and knowingly assume the implied ontological position. I do not think that it will stop being a science for that matter.

Much affinity with the existential mode of thought is present in the works of Tillich. In *The Courage To Be*[48] and *Dynamics of Faith*[49] he stands in part on the shoulders of Otto. His expressions "ultimate concern" and "centered act of the personality" have a strong appeal to dynamic psychologists, for they reach the motivational depths, the urge character, the directional qualities, and the forever conflict-laden ways of human problem-solving. Tillich's emphasis on the cognitive process in religion, epitomized in his definition of faith as including the dynamics of doubt, offers much to the psychology of religion. Religion can now be seen as exploratory behavior, driven, among other things, by man's curiosity and by his perpetual attempts to maximize contact with a maximal environment to the full deployment of his potentialities. The psychology of learning is interested in such propositions. Tillich's specifications of anxiety, and his emphasis on the dynamics of courage, have aroused considerable interest in psychological and psychiatric circles. I believe that the pursuit of just these subtle psychological processes implied in the terms *faith, courage, doubt, concern*—and I would like to add *hope* and *love*—will in the long run considerably enrich the psychology of religion.

We are now nearly ready for our journey into the psychology of religion. A few remarks are needed to alert the reader in advance to some idiosyncrasies of this text.

Unlike in most works on the psychology of religion, no attempt will be made to provide a definition of religion at the outset. The previous sketch of trends has already revealed that there is considerable variability in definitions of religion which have been made for purposes of psychological study. There is even more variability in definitions which have been offered for religious purposes. I want to approach the subject broadly, so that there is ample opportunity for clarifying distinctions and divisions within the large framework. I wish to remain responsive throughout to the tension generated by the apposition of the two questions I alluded to earlier: Which are the significant data of religious experience (and thus a sure and safe ground for the psychology of religion)? and, Which data of experience are of religious significance (and thus an imaginative challenge to the psychology of religion)? But, since definitions of very weighty matters belong more properly at the end than at the beginning of a study, I promise to take up the issue of defining religion again in the last chapter.

The psychological perspective in which we will consider religious phenomena is a clinical perspective. Clinical psychology is at home with fluid concepts, low-order abstractions, and *ad hoc* theoretical constructs.

It deals with complicated and at times very untidy situations. Therefore, clinical psychology is loath to impose a conceptual order so neat that the real disorderliness of experience fades out of the picture. It perceives continuities where others would only see discontinuity; conversely it sees distinctions where others would hold out for sameness. A case in point is the relation between health and illness. There was a time when these two were sharply distinguished. Despite the striking phenomenological differences, clinical psychologists are wont to note the impressive dynamic similarities between the two. Another case is diagnostic nomenclature. Just at the time that "neurosis," "psychosis," and "schizophrenia" have become household words taken to mean very specific ailments, many clinicians are ready to abolish them for lack of accuracy. What is more, their work is beginning to convince them that such words, and the images they conjure up, are little more than pseudoscientific monstrosities which impede man's progress in understanding human woes.[50]

The manner of organization and presentation in this book will follow psychological, not religious, categories. One will look in vain for a chapter on prayer, mysticism, or worship. There will be no chapter on types of religious experience. Though prayer and worship are indeed outstanding specimens of religious behavior, it entails serious risks to take them as organizing principles in a psychological work. One is the writer's temptation to equate religion with any of these behaviors and take it as a presumed "essence" of religion. A second risk is that the psychologist may lose his own ground if he employs religious categories, since they are not germane to his psychological enterprise. Psychologists think in psychological terms which are germane to the psychological perspective on all things: art, management, school learning, and religion. A third risk is that one can easily get too exalted a view of religion by taking its most pregnant manifestations as principles of organization. Few people are religious heroes or spiritual geniuses. Most devout people know little of mystical experience. I am not sure that praying is as popular as some religionists think it is. Much of religion is quite simple, habitual, and pedestrian, even trite. These features too must be taken into account.

Finally, this is an American book by a middle-class author, a European immigrant, who is affiliated with a mainline Protestant denomination. It thus has an inevitable focus on the author's own tradition, which he knows best. Religion at large is infinitely broader than what meets the eyes in the mainstream of the white Western world. Consequently, there is no pretension to cover *all* religion, nor apology to those who may feel that some faith group or denomination has been slighted.

II

Perceptual Processes

in Religion

PHENOMENOLOGISTS are fond of saying that through perception man becomes related to the world and that both parties to the perceptual act are active participants. The world "opens up" or "gives itself" to the perceiver; the perceiver "takes what he sees and hears and touches for such and such" and thereby makes the world *his* world. This proposition is trite enough and in a way so completely natural and self-evident that one is likely to forget how positive an attitude toward perceiving is implied in it. Perceiving is joyously greeted as an opportunity for both man and nature to come to know each other.

Such a joyful attitude toward perception is not shared by everybody. Vast numbers of people have been taught to distrust their senses and the world they reveal. Many religious movements have a deep prejudice against perception, claiming that it brings man in contact with the "wrong world" and that the senses lead him to sensuality and sensuousness. This negative attitude can take many forms. The accent can be, as with the writer of Ecclesiastes, on the vanity of sensing and sensate things. Or it can be, as in Platonism, on the fragile and evanescent quality of the world of perceiving, in which nothing endures. It can emphasize, as Stoicism does, the futility of the perceptual world, an attitude which made Samuel Butler exclaim that life is one long process of getting tired. Some belief systems have gone further by holding that perceiving is not only lascivious, vain, unstable, or useless but actually false and deceitful. The soul, asking for real bread, is given the stones of perception from which it gets indigestion.

Another attitude toward perception is exemplified by the three little monkeys who cover their eyes, ears, and mouth to indicate that they see, hear, or speak no evil. In this evaluation not all perception is discouraged or curbed, but only an "evil" part of it, in the hope that selectivity is

21

possible when some moral ground rules are followed. But the fact that such moral knowledge about "good perception" and "bad perception" is projected back onto man's simian progenitors suggests that it derives from an ancient taboo on perceiving. There is indeed much evidence that ancient and modern men have not always been so comfortable with the optimism of the phenomenologists about the harmony of man and world in the act of perceiving. In opening one's eyes one can see horrible things, awesome appearances, dangerous beings, indeed even the gods themselves! Demons or fairies may be heard in the whispering winds; the hand can touch slithery things too quick to grasp and thus of mysterious substance and habitat; wafts of odor hint at the presence of invisible spirits. Even those things which seem stable and clear at first sight, like the astral bodies, appear to behave with puzzling and ominous movements. Nature is both delightful and horrific, attractive and repulsive, trustworthy and suspect. Perceiving puts man in touch with the numinous, be it holy or unholy, good or evil. And since seeing is partaking in the reality of that which is seen, the act of perceiving itself may become regarded as inherently numinous, charged with magical qualities, powerful energies, and dreadful consequences. If this position is taken, the perceptual process needs to be regulated by taboos or religious rites. Moses was not allowed to see God on Mount Sinai; the hoods of nuns provide only a sort of tunnel vision which is exclusive rather than inclusive; even today some Mexican-Indian women are not supposed to glance at any men who pass by on the road.

In Aldous Huxley's *The Doors of Perception*[1] one finds a fourth attitude toward perceiving. It may be described as an attempt to raise perceiving above the routine recognition of "this is a house" and "that is a tree" to the inspired, poetic, and emphatic affirmation of essences that may lead one to say "there is no place like home" or, in Rilke's words, "truly, thou art the tree."[2] This position advocates a renewal of perception, on the presupposition that ordinary perception is actually a deteriorated perception which has become functionally inadequate. This view too has a long religious history. In demanding that perception have maximal lucidity and in supposing that lucidity is the mark of the "really real," religious people have, solitarily or in groups, done everything they could to induce states of enhanced perception. Through demanding physical exercises, dietary experiments, regulated breathing, posturing, and dancing, through the ingestion of toxins, through sleep deprivation and exposure to noxious stimuli, through concentrated meditations or rhythmic shouting and hand-clapping, devout people all over the world have tried to change their ordinary perceptual acumen to that state of brightness of which can be said: "Behold, I make all things new."

Still, the bright vision that reaches perfect lucidity is not yet the beatific vision. To augment the mind's clarity, to accelerate the sense of time's flow, and to stretch the co-ordinates of space perception are fascinating exercises, but they remain indifferent to object choice. If lucidity is the goal, any object or stimulus will do: a rose, a gem, a bottle of ink, the scent of honey, or F-sharp on an oboe. But Dante wanted to see Beatrice, and the great mystics wish to see the invisible object of their desire, God. There is a difference between melting away in creation or uniting with any created thing and standing face to face with him or her whom one holds to be the creator. The former states are characterized by peer relations between the perceiver and some part of his world, the latter by relations between unequal powers, with one dependent on the other. From this point on one may desire to share in the greater autonomy of the other. In these mystical perceptions of the divine it is the value of the object that counts and not the perceptual acumen of the perceiver, although the latter is not negligible. And given a desirable object, be it Beatrice, Jeremiah's God, the Virgin Mary, or the energetic Dionysius, the mystical lover has at least two ways open for his strivings. He can aim at absolute unity with his object, at the price of his own and his object's identities, or he can strive for the most direct confrontation in which the lover and the beloved maintain their own identities but form a twosome. Those who seek unity are monists who are impatient with all differences; those who seek confrontation are dualists of a sort who may hold many differences to be superficial but who maintain respect for a last difference in scale between the ultimate and the contingent.

Evidently, then, one remarkable aspect of the role of perception in religion is that the act of perceiving is often itself religiously evaluated. We found that it can be encouraged or discouraged, sharpened or dulled, enhanced or thwarted. It can be ritualized, or placed under taboos and restrictions. It can be the vehicle of worship, and it can be banned from worship as a threat to piety. It can be seen as divine or demoniac.

It becomes then one of the first tasks of a psychology of religion to explore and describe the ways in which perceptual processes enter into religious experience. Though I hope not to go astray in a completeness compulsion, I certainly aim at sketching the immense variety of sensory experiences on which religion draws. Simple sensations as well as complex perceptual processes will equally demand our attention, for as I have indicated in the first chapter, our working definition of religion spans a spectrum from the simple to the complex and from the ridiculous to the sublime, without bias.

VISION

It is a telling comment on the religious significance of sensory processes that the word "vision," in addition to denoting mere sight, is used also to describe experiences in which the visual process manifestly does not occur. By "a man of vision" we mean a person with much imagination who has the ability to produce the hitherto unseen. In the statement "Juan Diego had a vision of Our Lady of Guadalupe," the word refers to a vividly projected image which bystanders could not see. A "seer" is a soothsayer, or a prophet who announces things to come. Saints who have reported visions "saw" exactly what the eye could not see; and priests, shamans, kings, and ordinary citizens from ancient times to the present have described some of their dreams as "visions." Similarly, apparitions have occurred to men and women in sleep or drowsiness—precisely at times when the visual apparatus is known to be dysfunctional.

In all these intensive uses of the word "vision" there is a numinous quality which refers to the greatness, powerfulness, or unusualness of the experience. All involve glimpses of the divine, caught by human mortals, sometimes with their eyes closed. These sights may be blissful or horrific, but they are always uncanny. They are sometimes described as revelations, special revelations that is, which reveal what people with eyes open fail to perceive. Whether extrasensory or supersensory, the transcendence from ordinary sight and down-to-earth reality testing to the special vision of metaphysical truth has always been subject to religious evaluation and appreciation. The very intensity of the visionary experience, regardless of content, the power of it and the deep emotions it engenders in the beholder, have given it religious significance in nearly all cultures at all times.

But this equation of intensity or rarity of experience with religion can have deceptive implications or deplorable consequences. It can blind us to the enormous role that ordinary visual processes play in the pedestrian details of the life of any religious believer. One entering almost any place of worship will note that something is happening to the surrounding light as one moves from the street into the building. The interior is usually darker, at least near the entrance, and as one moves forward into the sanctuary he observes that certain parts of the interior are placed under special lighting effects: altars, statues, pulpits, or decorative wall surfaces receive regulated light from well-placed windows, floodlights, or stained-glass windows. Sometimes the church interior is not darker, but more colorfully lit than the typical daylight gray. In certain worship services the lighting effects change with the liturgy: during prayers the light may be dimmed, during sermons it may be focused on the preacher, during sacramental administrations the whole building may be suffused by semi-darkness. The variations are of course endless and may take historical cues from ancient sun worship to Teutonic forest clearings, from mountain-top celebrations to the rites performed in kivas underground. Since gods have been traditionally placed either high above the earth or underground, light itself has certain archaic religious values which can be ritualized according to one's belief system. And with the values of light, the act of opening or closing the eyes, of squinting, peering, staring, looking up, or looking down can attain religious significance.

According to a Protestant cliché, meant pejoratively, the Catholic Mass is a "feast for the eyes." Churches in which the Mass is celebrated may vary widely in style, according to national cultures, but to most Protestants they abound in color in windows and on walls, in statuary, in vestments worn by the priests and acolytes, and in the ornamentation of various articles used in worship, with mosaics possible in ceilings and floors. The color-play of vestments changes with the postures of the celebrants, and the frequent turnings of the priest at the altar create for the congregation a visual impression that is similar to that of a crowd watching a dance of peasants in native costumes on a marketplace: the colors move and change and twirl so as to engage the eyes in perpetual movement. A truly overwhelming array of visual stimuli bombards the worshipers, many of whom have learned to associate not only the objects but even the colors themselves with special religious meanings. There are liturgical colors for each season and for many special occasions: purple, white, green, red, black, pink, and gold, each of which is supposed to evoke a knowledgeable response in the beholders. Special lights occur within the local light of the sanctuary: candles stand in particular niches to add not only a special hue to the general light diffusion, but also a brilliant sense of movement and thrill to the static quality of the larger surroundings.

At first sight, this feast for the eyes stands in marked contrast to the sobriety and starkness of the classical Protestant locale for worship typified in the Puritan churches in America and Western Europe. The Puritan rejected the color of Catholic worship and toned everything down to the bleak tones of white, gray, and black. Whitewashed walls, oak-stained or white painted pews, a black academic gown of the minister, and at best the edge of a red moroccan Bible which had to lie opened on the lectern, were all his eyes could feast on. As a matter of fact, his eyes were not supposed to feast on anything. His ears were to hear, and for this reason visual impressions had to be severely restricted. Even in his dress the Puritan had to tone down the color values to black and white, so that only the quality of the cloth and the expertise of the cut could faintly indicate status differences among the congregants. The Quakers combined stark surroundings with an appeal to a mystical, inner light.

Such striking differences in elementary sensory processes in two basic forms of worship in the Western world stem from different evaluations of the religious value of the senses and their use. As the differences became stylized and repeatedly practiced over the generations of believers, they became of course linked with further religious associations and value judgments. The eye seems distinctly favored in the Catholic tradition, the ear in the Protestant tradition, although both traditions abound in multisensory stimulus usage. Visions seem to be more frequently reported in the Catholic tradition or are at least more readily appreciated in that tradition than in the Protestant one. Catholics are more prone to pray with the eyes open or focused on the altar, while Protestants tend to close them in prayer. I remember worshiping during summer vacations in the staid Protestant churches in old fishermen's villages in the Netherlands, where one could see the men during prayer holding their caps or hats in front of their eyes, obviously to darken their visual fields should their eyes accidentally open during the very long pastoral prayers that were offered.

The point is that within a given tradition one not only learns to prize his own habits and customs, but tends to see the alternatives decidedly in a negative way. To Protestants of the Reformed mainstream, Catholic or Anglican sensory preferences are gaudy, worldly, regal, pompous, or simply satanic; to Catholics or Anglicans the Calvinist preferences are somber, stingy, impoverished, intellectual, or cheap. Theological works abound in attempts to rationalize personal positions, and between the articulate thoughts and the practical doings a style arises in which such seemingly simple and neutral psychological processes as sensation and perception attain complex religious meanings.

The use of stained-glass windows for lighting or dimming church interiors has become very complex in organized religion. I do not know its origin although I surmise that iridescent color surfaces without specific form were used in much the same way one would appreciate jewels: for the play of light itself. But they became eventually instructional pieces of art, teaching an illiterate congregation the things they ought to know about their beliefs by symbolic or concrete portrayals of the deity, portraits of apostles and saints, episodes from the life of Jesus, etc. They also could portray the life of the congregation itself: its leaders, episodes from its founding, memorials to deceased members or shrines to wealthy donors, complete with family trees and other accessories of social status. Some motifs are highly symbolic, others are startlingly concrete. With all these ancillary purposes, a window, rather than merely letting in or diffusing natural light, may come to act as a visual focus in its own right, and with that it can become an object of meditation. In this way, the history of light effects in places of worship may turn full circle from instrumental uses in the beginning via representational purposes to highly symbolic and at the end even metaphysical centers of meaning.

Such an evolution or cycle of meaning is not so strange when one remembers how much religious language abounds in metaphors of light and darkness. The Essenes called themselves the Children of Light and anticipated an apocalyptic war between themselves and the Children of Darkness. The association of God with light is ancient and widespread, and has maintained itself well beyond the stages of sun or moon worship. The Sol Invictus theme is still in use in certain Christian churches; offerings of light in the form of candles are still being made. A nimbus bedecks the head of deities and saints in instructional or representational church art. Renaissance paintings allude to the invisible creator God through fine rays of light emanating from the edge of the picture.

The divinity of light, which is described as the first act in the Hebrew creation myth, can take a somersault to become the divinity of the eye. God can be portrayed as the all-seeing eye, and the eye of man is in romantic literature taken as proof of man's eternal dignity or the divine origin of his soul. The numinous quality of the human eye may assume a negative value in the case of the "evil eye."

But the eye not only sees light and color spectra. It also is an organ through which one organizes and recognizes space. And space too has an enormous religious significance that can be regulated and ritualized in the space arrangements for worship, the locus of the divine, and all the hierarchical space orderings through which man becomes instructed to "know his place" in the universe. Such basic space dimensions as "high" and "low," "right" and "left," "above" and "beneath," are saturated with religious values which find expression in church architecture and in hidden assumptions that underlie many cultural customs.

Scholars in comparative religion have repeatedly pointed to the importance of sacred space in archaic and contemporary religious systems. The kind of spaces that are held sacred may vary with the culture and the physical environment, but in all cases one finds some bounded area near the tribal village in which or around which the religious life of the group is centered. It is linked with the most fundamental meaning of the word "taboo": the forbidden space onto which no trespassing is allowed. Such places, or the objects within them, have "mana." They are numinous space centers in which the gods dwell or into which they come when they visit the earth. The sacred spaces can be certain mountains, streams, meadows, forest clearings, valleys, or caves; they can be as concrete and specific as slits in rocks and as wide and formless as the sky. These elementary forms of the numinous qualities of space are easily recognizable when one turns to archaic or primitive religions, but one tends to overlook the fact that they are in our midst in the more developed forms of religion. Every place of worship testifies to numinous space, from the storefront assembly hall in a metropolitan area to the most splendid Gothic cathedral, from a worship area in the national parks to the most modern church building.

An excellent example of a thoughtful use of space, conscious of the inherent numinosity of space in the service of worship, is St. John's Abbey in Collegeville, Minnesota, built by Marcel Breuer for a Benedictine community. From some distance one sees first a gigantic banner of concrete, housing bells, appearing as if it were a triumphal arch. One mounts a few steps to pass under it to a stone platform, and upon opening the doors of the church enters a rather narrow, dimly lit, low-ceilinged space, and is greeted by a statue of John the Baptist whose posture is such that one feels invited to descend a few steps into a baptistery. In making this descent, visually or literally, one comes to another row of doors which open into the sanctuary, but in proceeding forward one first passes under a low-hanging large balcony, the farthest edge of which suddenly opens into a nave of enormous height and width, brightly lit by wide windows. In this building, space is organized to maximum liturgical advantage, and one feels himself almost literally sinking and rising, shrinking and stretching, darkened and lit, while moving through it. My point is that some such visual space experience is inherent in any arrangement for corporate worship, whether the architectural end result is successful or unsuccessful, purposeful or makeshift.

Arrangements for worship are for a major part space arrangements. So are arrangements for private prayer. Religiously speaking, space is hierarchically organized in levels, and in the transactions between man and his gods these levels are explicitly recognized and stylized. Priests are allowed to ascend to higher levels than the laity in their actual work at altars and in their various ceremonial tasks and stances. The people leave certain spaces for their priests and for their gods, allowing for themselves only the lower or narrower spaces which are becoming to them as mortal men. Architectural design of houses of worship creates a spatial focus on the spots where the dynamic-religious acts take place: altar, pulpit, baptismal font, or the central clearing in a Quaker meetinghouse. Endless debates have taken place about the proper place for an altar in the Roman Catholic rite: whether in the middle so that everybody can be on all sides of it, or at the end of the nave so that the congregation sees only its front; whether high on a platform or dais, or low at the seating level of the congregation. Similar arguments are being brought to bear upon the ideal place for the communion table in Protestant worship, and even on the height and locus of the pulpit from which preaching is to be done. Height itself was celebrated in the great Gothic cathedrals; the view upward was indeed the dominant space motif in all Gothic architectural art. Visitors to the temple ruins at Teotihuacán in Mexico are impressed by the absolute dominance of horizontal lines and space divisions in the Aztec rituals, despite the height of pyramids and conical mounds, and the long stone stairways. The dominant view is lateral, the dominant lines are horizontal, the dominant structures are platforms and terraces.

Who dares to lift his head upward in prayer, when he is taught to cast his face down? Who dares to stand while praying, when his tradition demands that he kneel or prostrate himself? For the man of religious faith, the very glance of his eyes upward or downward is ritualized when he is involved in religious acts. Every departure from the norm that is taught is an act of liberalism, freethinking, protest, or defiance. When, at the dinner table, everybody "bows his head" except Junior, who keeps his high and mighty, there is a daring tinkering with the basic numinosity of ritualized space dimensions. And Junior "will have to come down on his knees" some day!

Again, religious language abounds in spatial metaphors to describe the realities of God and man. God is high; man is low or of a lowly nature. Divine wisdom is deep, on a different plane from the superficialities of man. God keeps certain saints on his right side and puts the damnable ones on his left. Or he throws them into the pit. Pious people admonish each other to lift up their hearts or to look on high from where their salvation will come. In the three-story universe of the New Testament writers, man, God, and Satan each has his own distinct plane. In the face of such linguistic oddities one could argue that all life is lived in space and that the religious life finds no escape from that basic reality. Such an objection misses the central point that in the religious perspective space itself is numinous and spatial dimensions are ritualized. Hence, space perception and movements in space have certain rules and values over and beyond the physical inescapabilities. The numinosity of space is psychically real for believers and has drastic behavioral consequences. It determines burial rites and sets rules for burial underground, above the ground, on stakes, in tombs, in pyramids, or in vaults. It determines whether one is to be buried standing upward or lying down, with arms and legs drawn up or lavishly stretched out. It determines whether one's remains are to be placed in holy ground or in a public cemetery, or scattered over land or sea. It determines the notion of so-called church property with exemption from taxation and certain zoning privileges. It determines whether and where one's home shall have a shrine for worship, a niche for a religious statue, or a place for a religious picture, crucifix, candle, or text. It determines the proper locale for the mezuzah on one's doorpost. It determines whether one's Bible is to be kept among the paperbacks on the family bookshelf or in a special place. It creates shrines by roadsides, tabernacles for holy books or scrolls, natural or artificial settings for meditation. The numinosity of space forces one to stand up, kneel, sit down, or prostrate oneself. It prescribes whether one shall put a hat on or take it off.

All the visual experiences thus far described are in principle normal perceptual processes. Even when they sometimes involve much symbolism and all kinds of surplus values, they usually occur with adequate reality-testing and social conformity. But what about abnormal visual experiences? What about religious hallucinations? Does not religion abound in abnormal or marginal visual phenomena, in the so-called "visions"? I will postpone the discussion of abnormal perceptual processes until the end of this chapter. We should first consider other perceptual modalities such as hearing, tasting, smelling, and touching, which also have their normal and abnormal ways of functioning.

AUDITION

Gods allegedly make noise, and their worshipers listen and make noises in turn. The gods roar in thunderstorms, howl in whirlwinds, rustle in the leaves of sacred oaks, sing in the zephyr, gurgle in brooks, whisper in the leaves that drop in the fall. They are capable of an astounding array of formless or organized sounds. Sometimes they raise their voices and speak words. They say "Hark" or "Stop and listen" or "Hear my word." When that happens, certain men attune their ears and forget everything else around them. Indeed, they may so identify themselves with the divine voice they hear that they in turn start to speak, presumably in God's voice. They say things like "Hear, O Israel" and "Thus says the Lord." Or they utter nonsense syllables and sputter and gargle strange noises in states of frenzy.

But since the world is full of sound most of the time, gods may be hard pressed to find a hearing in the buzzing confusion. They then resort to a unique and especially numinous auditory stimulus: silence. It is indeed sometimes hard to judge which is more divine, sound or silence. For the religious mind both are numinous, depending on the context in which they appear. Similarly, it is a religious question where the sound is, in the noisemaker or in the hearer. Said Emily Dickinson:

> To hear an oriole sing
> May be a common thing,
> Or only a divine.
>
> It is not of the bird
> Who sings the same, unheard,
> As unto crowd.
>
> The fashion of the ear
> Attireth that it hear
> In dun or fair.
>
> So whether it be rune,
> Or whether it be none,
> Is of within;

The "tune is in the tree,"
The sceptic showeth me;
"No, sir! In thee!"[3]

Magic abounds in the auditory sphere. In addition to the divine noises, there are special religious noises made by humans: incantations, chants, drawnout and unctuous speechmaking with nasal tone qualities, hymns, instrumental music, furtive whisperings, and ritualized periods of silence. Moaning and groaning are not uncommon. And just as Emily Dickinson said, there may be great confusion about the origin of all these noises. Though most of them come manifestly from men, many religious noise-makers claim that their sounds come from God or from spirits. It seems that in religious appreciation, sounds tend to assume a certain thickness or corporality so that both the sound maker and the sound perceiver partici-pate in its reality and feel equally enveloped by it.

Hence, sounds and hearing are essential parts of worship and are powerful conveyors of the "participation mystique" which Lévy-Brühl[4] has described as typical of primitive societies. Sound and hearing establish the bond among believers. Catholics all over the world feel united in a joint response to church Latin, quite apart from anyone's ability to under-stand that language. Worship noises are numinous noises, and even the crying or cooing of babies presented for baptism, which may at first be perceived as a disturbance of the proper order of the service, soon be-comes a beatific sound which proves God's benevolence. United in song, congregations testify to their special traditions and heritage.

But not all sounds are numinous to the same degree for all religious people. There is a social stratification of sounds which delegates wild noises, moans, and groans to the lower socioeconomic Pentecostal groups. More stately hymn tunes and controlled silence belong in the mainline Protestant churches. Gregorian chant is absent from both, since it belongs distinctly to the Catholic tradition. Even musical instruments are subject to religious controls of great force. Many Mennonite groups allow only a cappella singing. Until recently, the singing in Catholic worship was strictly assigned to a choir, with male voices only. Lutherans and Calvinist groups prize the organ, choirs, and congregational singing. The classical reformed tradition created a great advance in church music in the six-teenth, seventeenth, and eighteenth centuries. The pietistic sects specialize in nineteenth-century tunes of mediocre quality or worse. Negro religious music is unique in every respect: its beauty, spontaneity, fervor, inventive-ness, ability to blur the boundaries between the sacred and the profane. Singing with piano accompaniment is typical of storefront missions and is barely acceptable in middle-class churches. Accordion music is felt to be distinctly secular, if not vulgar, by all highly developed traditions, but for Southern snakehandlers it is the instrument of choice during the great religious festivals. The sonorous sounds of great bells in steeples can have a haunting or festive quality all their own and are equally appreciated by Christians of many traditions. But the shrill sound of a bell during the Mass, or the noise of a wooden clacker which signals a "take notice" during consecration or elevation, are peculiar to Catholicism and would be disturbing to Protestants. There is something odd, perhaps even frivolous, in hearing recorded carillon music from a church steeple that is too puny to contain bells.

But for millions of religious people the religious sound par excellence is the word. In the Hebrew creation story, the word is the creative process itself: when God calls, he calls forth. For Christians, already reared in Hebrew preferences, the word is the capitalized Word, that was in the beginning and became flesh and dwelt among men (John 1:1-3). For some Greeks it is the *Logos,* the dynamic, everlasting, and creative word-thought. With roots in all three religious traditions, most modern Western believers find the supreme act of worship is hearing the Word. The divine presence that is celebrated in worship is the presence of the Word, audible first, but by synaesthetic richness also visible and even tastable. And the preferred or dominant religious sense organ for millions of people is the ear. One comes to church to hear: the Word, the minister's voice, or the still small voice of silence. It is possible to take in a whole service with the eyes closed, at least in most Protestant worship services.

It follows that for those with an auditory preference in religion, there is a large amount of speaking to be done or to be listened to. Protestant ministers are indeed speakers, preachers, lecturers, scholarly expositors, hortatory taskmasters, or inspiring messengers. While officiating, they do very little with their bodies, they make few ritual gestures, they move little, but they speak. Many of them have had to take lessons in speech, so important is their speechmaking function. Similarly, young children in the congregation spend years in learning to listen, so important is the auditory role of the worshiper.

Words play an overwhelming role in prayer, whether corporate or private. In praying, one speaks, softly or aloud, or sometimes completely inaudibly. The words and phrases uttered may be highly stylized and proceed according to learned rituals, or entirely spontaneous and private, without any normative form. Prayers may be lengthy or short; sometimes a single word or expletive has the meaning of a complete phrase. In praying, the roles of speaker and listener are reversed from those ordinarily observed in worship. God is placed in the listener's role, and he "gives ear" to people's words.

With the prominence given to hearing and sound in many forms of worship and prayer, it is understandable that the total world of sound tends to become highly regulated in religious practices. All sounds have to be modulated and well chosen in order to fit the occasion. Except when one is leading a group in corporate prayer, one cannot pray too loudly: the voice must show modesty and an awareness of one's station vis-à-vis the divine. Praying too loud becomes arrogance or borders on swearing. During services, a hushed atmosphere is demanded, which is broken only by the voice of the worship leader or the responsive readings and singing of the congregation. The practice of silence in Quaker meetings, until a sincere and meaningful word can be said, is an indication that the "noises of the world" must die before the divine presence can be felt.

Staid middle-class believers read of "joyful noises" to be made "unto the Lord," but they can hardly tolerate the noisiness they hear in lower-class churches. Conversely, more emotive people consider the auditory stimulation of middle-class churches far too tame and dreary. It is obvious, then, that the rules for proper sound-input are classbound and have much to do with such values as dignity, orderliness, and propriety. There is a remark in Augustine's *Confessions* which suggests that orderly hymn singing was introduced in the Western church in order to combat the prevailing disorganized noises of shrieks and moaning.[5] Synagogues "sound" disorderly to disciplined Christians. The family ritual of silent prayer before meals is one way to impose silence in the cacophony of voices clamoring for recognition, in order that the right hierarchy of parental control can be re-established when such important favors as food are to be distributed.

THE TACTUAL SENSE

When young children go through a department store, their parents are in constant worry that they will touch everything instead of using their eyes for scanning the wares on display. "Look, don't touch" is the parental watchword. It is utterly unconvincing to the children, who come to the store to touch everything in the first place. It takes considerable growing up and self-discipline to stop touching and start looking, and when one really wants to know something very well, one starts touching again, at any age. Museum guards know all about this propensity even among sophisticated, grown-up people, who come to enjoy the visual arts but whose fingers are powerfully drawn to what they have already seen. Somehow, believing and touching are close together. We wish to touch and need to touch those we love. It is this knowledge of the fingers which finally convinced the apostle Thomas about the reality of the resurrected Jesus, whom he had already seen and to whom he had already talked.

But touching is also placed under strict taboos, for touching can have numinous powers. A touch can be intrusive, it can defile, it takes away the privacy of what is touched. Among the many attributes of God, his finger has some prominence and it is a sign of his all-knowing, all-uncovering, all-intruding power. The finger accuses, it "pricks" conscience. The man who is "touchy" feels fingers all around him. The human finger is also sensuous to the highest degree; it may feel the unmentionable, the unthinkable, the private parts, the organs of lust. If touching is a primitive sense, as some people hold, it is also a powerful sense and therefore needs social and religious regulation.

The numinosity of touch is clearly demonstrated in the Johannine passage in which the resurrected Jesus says to Mary "Do not touch me" or "Do not hold me" (John 20:17). It is the *noli me tangere* motif of the untouchability of the sacred. It comes back, with modifications, in the social concept of the untouchables, the lowest level in the Indian caste system, where it is a mixture of disdain, fear of contamination, and the quasi-sacredness of the poor. In another passage about the life of Jesus, touch conveys the magic *fluidum* that transfers power, in this case healing power, from one person to another. This aspect of touching as conveying powerful substances or emanations lies at the heart of the religious-medical practice of the laying on of hands, which plays such a large role in faith-healing rituals.

With all these examples of the numinosity of touch it is surprising to notice how little satisfaction the sense of touch finds in most modern forms of worship. In primitive societies, people wore amulets in the form of rings, pendants, beads, or figurines which had magical significance to the wearer. The nearest thing to directing the sense of touch purposefully in worship is the rosary, which keeps the fingers busy on a special object during prayers, and is clearly intended for sacred activity alone. I have often wondered whether the carrying of Bibles or hymnbooks among Protestants is not in part done to gratify the sense of touch or to direct tactile perceptions safely to a sacred thing. Otherwise, there is little tactile stimulation offered, except for kneeling which exerts pressure on the knees and elbows, and the feel of the hard wooden seats one sits on.

We should not underestimate the role of learning whereby certain tactile impressions may become associated with religion or religious practices. The singularly uncomfortable design of most church pews, the hardness of cushions even when they are covered with velvet, or the feel on the skin of one's "Sunday best"—all may become special tactile features of worship or prayer. Whatever the outward aspect of Sunday clothing may mean, its inside aspect is not to be neglected. The ancient Jewish and Near Eastern preoccupation with changing of clothes, laying off of old robes for new or fresh ones on religiously significant occasions, and putting on of sackcloth on mournful occasions, testifies to a basic relation between tactile sensations and a religious view of life. The same is true for the wearing of hairshirts and other distinctly uncomfortable or prickly and chafing garments in doing penance. A faint echo of this remains in the present church life of millions of people: the clothes to be worn in church cannot be leisure clothes, but must have an appropriate degree of uncomfortableness and stiffness.

The taboo on touching is strikingly demonstrated in some of the minor episodes of organized church life. In the ordination ceremony of elders in the Presbyterian tradition, fellow elders are admonished to place their hands on the head of the new elder to be ordained, who is knelt in front of them. The fact is that those standing around rarely touch the man in front of them; their gesture stops short just a few inches from actual skin contact. One can make similar observations on the delicacy with which sacral objects, such as communion plates and cups, are handled. They are rarely grasped with any degree of firmness. Pieces of bread are often cut in such minuscule cubes that they are barely perceptible between the fingers. Small wonder then that tactile stimulus hunger forces people to do a considerable amount of fidgeting with purses, eyeglasses, books, papers, and clothing, even in very staid and proper worship ceremonies.

KINESTHESIS

The internal perception of one's joints and muscles, stomach and bowel contractions, facial innervations, and postural shifts or pressures accompanies us under nearly all circumstances and is at times used for religious ends. The primary example of such directed use is the practice of yoga, a technique of muscular and postural discipline pursued to attain a special state of consciousness, of concentration, of physical healing, or of salvation. Milder forms of it in Western religion occur in the various forms of asceticism which demand postural exercises or deprivation of the distant senses such as vision and hearing. Still milder forms of it remain in such worship customs as kneeling, supplication, pronation, and the folding of hands in praying. Though these activities are probably not direct descendants of planned physical exercise, they do have their kinesthetic impact which is or may become associated with religious acts.

Perhaps the most common kinesthetic impression in modern worship stems from the mere act of sitting still, solemnly, in hushed silence and with decorum, in an uncomfortable seat and position for the duration of a service. Particularly when the mind begins to wander or when the hearing becomes too strenuous or boring, we become aware of many internal body sensations such as tingling, a feeling of stiffness in the joints, a peculiar internal warmth in the thighs or the lower back, or a sudden uncontrollable itch in a local patch of skin. Along with these feelings, there is often a hypnotic effect or a feeling of drowsines, which tends to increase the kinesthetic sensations even further. "Sitting still" and "being reverent" in dim light with a constant drone of auditory monotony is a significant part of the weekly religious experience of millions of people. I am stating this without sarcastic or denigrating intentions, but merely to record an incontrovertible psychological fact. I am sure that for many people the occasion of corporate worship in their religious community is the only time they can reach such a state and accept it as a value. It can be euphemistically described as "restfulness" or "peace" or "a quiet moment for meditation," but the fact is that the mind is often in a blank, perhaps a blessed blank, when that state ensues.

Rembrandt's paintings of an old woman with a book in her lap and eyeglasses in her hand (one in the Hermitage, Leningrad, and one in the Mellon collection in Washington, D.C.) portray this quiescent state with great precision and succeed in conveying a deeply religious atmosphere. The woman's eyes are open, but the glance is dull and seems turned inward; the posture is upright but relaxed, as in slight drowsiness, and the fingers hold the sacred object of a churchbook.

I was once told by a minister that one of his parishioners, a young girl, described a religious conversion experience she had recently had as "stepping out of a warm bath." That is a wonderful description, in kinesthetic terms, of a religious process.

The postural customs in quiet middle-class Protestant churches, which do not make much use of kneeling or standing up during singing, enhance kinesthetic sensations. When children observe their parents in church, they will see that the heads are slightly bowed down, that the arms are kept close to the body, and that the hands tend to be held folded in the lap. It is the classical, quiet, somewhat passive church posture. If this is the norm one perceives or the model that one tries to follow, what startling discovery it can be for the child to lift up his head and to justify this by acting as if he were looking at the ceiling! It is not only a beautiful small defiance of the parental form of religiosity, but it may mean a novel attitude toward the divine. I remember vividly that during my childhood, men customarily stood up during prayers. Only women and young children remained seated. Thus, for a boy of six or seven years it was important to stand up with the men so that one could take pride in one's sexual identity. But a few years later there were signs that the custom waned, which left considerable ambiguity in the situation. For a boy of twelve or thirteen to remain seated during prayers was then an act of modernity, tolerated to be sure, but requiring some daring decision. Still a few years later it became an act of self-assertion or defiance to stand up during prayer. Whatever practice one followed during these years had not only a social significance, but was somehow linked with the idea of taking a position vis-à-vis the divine. That simple act had religious meaning.

Indeed, how shall one place and posture oneself in the house of the Lord? Should one sit in his presence, throw oneself down, stand up before him, kneel, or do all these things alternately and in quick succession? Liturgy capitalizes on just such questions from one angle; the psychological art of leading a worship service gets to them from another vantage point. There are risks in both extremes; the perpetual standing up, sitting down, and kneeling that characterizes some services can deteriorate into sheer work and "business," whereas a long uninterrupted period of sitting may deteriorate into drowsiness or worse. In either case, kinesthetic impressions are rich and far more intense than most psychologists of religion have recognized.

PAIN

Pain can be like an old friend. I have seen patients with severe intractable pain, as in trigeminal neuralgia, who underwent a severe depression the moment they were surgically relieved of the facial pain they had had for so long. With the disappearance of the pain, some drastic personality change had to occur to secure the person's adaptation to his conscious and unconscious wishes, self-concept, and values. Such cases show that pain, despite its horror, can assume meanings which are an integral part of the individual's vital balance.

In the history of religions, pain has always played a central role, and it continues to do so in modern religious experience. Gruesome sacrifices have been made of animals and men, even children. Terrible wounds have been inflicted for the placation of angry gods. People have not only been butchered by priests and fellow believers, but have lifted their hands against themselves, cutting off ears, nose, or tongue, ripping out eyes, castrating themselves, inserting pins or scraping objects into their skins. They have walked barefooted on hot coals, swallowed painful poisons, stared into the glaring sun for hours, dangled from ropes that were sewn through their own muscles.

Considerable progress has been made in eliminating these crass forms of pain infliction as parts of worship or personal devotion. But the principle continues, publicly or in private. The casual tourist who visits the square in front of the cathedral of Our Lady of Guadalupe north of Mexico City will see devout persons painfully hobbling on their knees from one end of the square to the other, just as at one time, or perhaps still today, penitents might crawl or walk up to Rome's St. Peter's Church with peas or gravel in their shoes. While one does not see any more public processions of flagellantes, the practice of whipping oneself is still being continued in monasteries and seminaries in the most civilized countries. (Flagellant penitentes are reported to be active today in New Mexico, in defiance of state law.) Kneeling for long times, beyond the call of duty, in uncomfortable postures, soon gives way to actual pain in the knees. Long fasts can elicit pain in stomach or throat. Long walks, on pilgrimages, produce painful fatigue. Bites from rattlers and other poisonous snakes are not only a daring risk taken by those who engage in herpetological liturgies, but actually occur with regularity among members of snake-handling sects.[6]

Intense degrees and large amounts of unnecessary physical pain are borne, for the glory of God and for the sake of man's value systems, by people who suffer diseases while refusing to avail themselves of medicines and analgesics. Aside from persons with heroic stoicism who succeed in no longer being bothered by pain, and those with an optimistic "grin and bear it" attitude, much pain is borne because the sufferers accept it as a form of penance, as a deserved infliction, or as a demonstration of their god's inscrutable purposes. While some of these may try to combat the actual pain sensations by psychological means such as prayer, suppression, or denial, others accept it in the raw as pain without seeking to modify or lessen its impact.

Much more will be said in later chapters about mental pain, anguish, and suffering as parts of religious experience. These imply a more metaphorical use of the word "pain" as opposed to pleasure, tranquillity or happiness, and do not usually involve the delicate sensory nerve endings with which we have dealt in this section. But before we leave the topic of pain sensation we should pay attention to the demonstrated possibility that physiological pain thresholds can be altered by states induced by religious convictions. Shamans, fakirs, and laymen of various religious traditions can through autohypnosis reach states of frenzy or ecstasy which entail such drastic body alterations that they sometimes welcome opportunities to be hurt and wounded in order to "prove" to themselves or an audience that theirs is really a numinous state in which they are invulnerable to ordinary stress.[7] In these rapturous states, in which they seem to be "beside themselves" or possessed by something not their own, the pain thresholds can become so high that cuts, burns, blisters, sores, or longheld muscle contractions no longer hurt. In such cases, pain is not the desired religious goal, or a burden carried for penitential purposes, but a quasi-scientific demonstration of the gross alterations the individual has undergone. Some allusion to phenomena of this order is implied in the arguments that led in the first three centuries of the Christian Church to the docetic heresy. In short, this argument was that Jesus was too divine to have actually suffered on the cross. Gods, precisely because they are not men, cannot suffer or have pain. Neither can they die. If Jesus, therefore, according to the narratives about him, appears to have been in pain, this was only seemingly so; he "went through the motions" as a faithful actor.

TASTE AND SMELL

In the poetic imagination of the Psalmist, the word of the Lord is declared to be sweet to the taste (Ps. 119:103) and a priestly codex says of God that he will not smell the pleasing odor which the people have prepared for him (Lev. 26:31). Behind the poetry and the prophecy lie concrete perceptions of taste and smell which have a long association with religion. Like all other perceptions, they can be avenues to the divine and they can assume numinous qualities of their own which signal the divine presence or seal some of the contractual arrangements that man makes with his gods.

And why not? Gustatory and olfactory experiences lie at the very beginning of human life and are associated with the most primordial form of knowing: the act of eating. When a baby really wants to know something, he puts it into his mouth and in this way partakes of its substance and qualities. His like or dislike of the thing that is being explored becomes quickly manifest in his taking it in or spitting it out. When he takes too much of a good thing or something noxious he will vomit it back through the same mouth. Delight, pleasure, and gratification in their early forms depend heavily on processes in the oral cavity, and so do the experiences of loathing and nausea. It is small wonder, then, that the rituals of primitive religion abound in the giving of good-tasting foods and good-smelling scents to the gods, and in establishing or confirming the religious community of men through joint eating, drinking, or smoking ceremonies. And because of the lasting importance of oral desires and gratifications throughout life, it is to be expected that taste and smell, eating and drinking, continue to play a role in more developed religion as well.

The sacred repast, the holy meal, the sacramental banquet, the Lord's Supper, and even the traditional American church breakfasts, congregational suppers, and ladies' lunches in church basements furnished with elaborate kitchen facilities, all share in the conviction that "tasting together" is "knowing each other" and "loving each other." These rituals affirm implicitly, sometimes explicitly, that eating together means being of one household with one head, a common father. But convivial eating and drinking are complex acts and in this section I will confine our attention to the perceptions of taste and smell as such, leaving the symbolic and social aspects of these acts for later discussion.

In Madame Guyon's religious poems, her felt mystical union with Christ is described in gustatory terms: she recalls and still exalts in "the taste of Christ" in her prayers.[8] Other great mystics have recalled heavenly scents which concretized the divine presence for them. But mystical experiences are not everyone's religion for every day. For ordinary devout people "religious smells" mean the scent of incense burnings in their churches or of candles, scented or plain, whose odors fill their houses of worship or their shrines at home. For others it may be the smell of old scrolls or books for sacred purposes. It may even be for some the unique stuffiness of a particular church building where they have worshiped for years. For most churches have indeed a particular odor, unlike that of other large buildings where crowds gather. Tobacco smoke residues, so conspicuous in theater foyers, are strikingly absent from church buildings. Instead there is a faint smell, even on days of inactivity, of flowers, dusty curtains or wall hangings, incense, burnt wax, old wood, mortar and chalk, citric acid from fruit juice preparations, and an abundance of people, old and young. And above all, there is a striking absence of fresh air. In my own childhood, the older women used to eat small soft peppermints during the long sermons and kept the children quiet by an occasional handout of these little candies. As a result, the smell of peppermint acquired a definitely churchly association for many youngsters of my age. Perhaps the impression of vulgarity made by seeing people use chewing gum in church is largely a matter of lack of specificity: since chewing in public occurs almost anywhere it betrays a lack of dignity to do it at worship also. But if a specific food item could be found, like small candies in the form of a dove, or buttons of peyote, taste stimulation during worship ceremonies might be quite acceptable.

OTHER SENSORY EXPERIENCES

Among the minor senses is vibration experience. Resonances in the ribs and chestbone and in the skull add substantially to the enjoyment of music in normal persons and may give compensations for the loss of hearing in the deaf. There are at least two contemporary aspects of religious worship which give an abundance of vibratory sensations which leave no mean impact: the ringing of heavy church bells and the sonorous sounds of long organ pipes. Whatever drums and brass bands may achieve in the military or on occasions of state, church bells and organ sounds achieve on religious occasions. They arouse people to a state of solemn receptivity, they make them "keyed up" to participation in corporate acts.

Though bells and organs, like all musical instruments, are public in the broadest sense so that nobody can lay a special claim on them, there is nevertheless something hallowed about both, from their long association with church buildings and religious activities. The organ is not only the queen of musical instruments, but it is also considered the most divine. Most organ music is sacred music, if not by design, then by a historical process. Large organs can only be corporately owned because of their costliness and space demands, and the church was for many years the only organization that could acquire and maintain them. Gigantic strides in polyphonous music in the Western world were made through organists and the demands of congregational singing or choir performances. Small wonder then that organ music tends to have a numinous character, even when heard in dignified orchestral halls. Small wonder also that transfer of the organ to completely secular and popular settings such as theaters and movie houses required odd adaptations in which the classical tonal qualities of the divine or queenly instrument shifted to tinny, clangy, or toylike noises that imitated every known musical instrument except the organ! On the other hand, the family organ or harmonium has been used so exclusively in the rendition of nineteenth-century evangelical hymns that it has acquired an air of piety all its own, which is now nearly a curiosum of a bygone era.

Vibration sense is also produced in that ancient religious act of beating one's chest in grief, remorse, or repentance. The capacity of chest vibrations to evoke tears may well lie at the heart of the evocative power of an organ bourdon. The rhythmic clanging of large church bells seems to have an even clearer connection with ritual chest-beating.

While the ideal human body temperature maintains itself around 98.6 degrees Fahrenheit, states of depression cause it to fluctuate somewhat below the optimum and states of excitement or exhilaration tend to raise it. Hence, heat and cold have not only a metaphorical, but also a physiological kinship with bliss and sadness. Some mystics who have reported intense states of religious bliss have described these in terms of waves of warmth spreading through their bodies. The feeling of awe, on the other hand, has something to do with "cold shivers" and shakiness. Temperature sense, then, seems to lie at the root of those primordial aspects of religious experience which Otto has described in *The Idea of the Holy:* on the one hand the tremblings and shudders that come from awe for the *mysterium tremendum,* on the other hand the gulfs of benevolent and blissful warmth that accompany the approach to the *fascinans.* An abundance of metaphorical expressions give further testimony to the numinosity of temperature. When love slackens, it is said to grow cold. Hosea said that compassion grows warm and tender (Hos. 11:8). According to the Hebrew Psalmist, the Lord's benevolence is like the hen who keeps her chicks warm under her wings (Ps. 91:4). And the most pernicious irreligiosity is held to be the state of being neither cold nor hot. It is recorded that gods will spew the lukewarm people out of their mouths.

PATHOLOGICAL PERCEPTIONS

According to Schelling,[9] everything is uncanny that ought to have remained hidden and secret and yet comes to light. This leads to the questions: How do secrets come out of their hiding places? And where are the hiding places of the uncanny? The first question is not difficult to answer. Secrets are simply discovered or uncovered. The uncanny is perceived, when somebody opens his eyes, attunes his ears, feels a cold shiver, or touches something strange. Gods and demons are discovered in ordinary aspects of perceptual processes: lights, colors, tones, vibrations, smells, tastes, or temperatures which seem to man powerful, awesome, strange, or fateful.

The question about the hiding places of the uncanny is more difficult to answer. Where is the residence of mystery? Insofar as it lies outside man, his perceptual processes may discover it. But could some mysteries reside in man himself, and if so, can perceptual processes discover them? The biblical question "What is man that thou art mindful of him?" (Ps. 8:4) is a profoundly ambiguous phrase which combines at once man's denigrating smallness under the starry heavens and his glorious greatness which is only "little less than God." Not only the gods, but man himself is a *tremendum* for whom one stands in awe. And precisely to the extent that his own *tremendum* has been hidden to himself and suddenly comes to light, he is the uncanny personified, a vessel of numinosity. In states where such a discovery is central, perceptual mechanisms begin to function in strange ways and reproduce the uncanny in sensory experiences with a subtle difference. One begins to see, hear, or smell things which "are not there." One hallucinates. The things "which are not there" are seen with great vividness and with convincing reality, but others cannot verify them and feel equally convinced that they are "not there."

In alcoholic hallucinosis or delirium tremens the patient will hurl objects at threatening monsters he perceives or will squeeze his skin to rid it of "bugs" or "worms" which he feels crawling over it. In these visual and tactile hallucinations the objective unreality of monsters or bugs is so patent that the patient is quite alone in his strange convictions. Yet the boundaries beween perceptual reality and unreality are not always as clearcut as the distinction between a normal and a hallucinated perceiver. Feeling the presence of the beloved, with vivid visual or auditory sensations, is not so uncommon when one is engaged in writing a love note or relishing a memory of a recent shared moment. In such moments of keen anticipation as getting out of bed on Christmas morning, one is likely to misperceive old accustomed objects for packages and new presents. When one is in a somber mood, the clouds may assume the features of mournful faces. When in a state of anxiety one finds himself alone in the woods after losing the way, white stems of birch trees in moonlight may appear not only spooky, but like ghosts. In daydreaming, especially when one sits in utter boredom in a lecture hall, the blank wall in front may easily become a screen on which one sees his own imaginations. In a word, there is a gradation of hallucinatory lucidity and there are degrees to which an outer reality is ascribed to the things seen, heard, or felt. Behind the statements in this and the preceding paragraph lie important epistemological and ontological questions to which we shall return in subsequent chapters. At this place, our concern is with description and only low-level explanations.

In clinical practice with mentally disturbed patients, auditory hallucinations are fairly common. The patient hears voices which tell him that he is no good, point out his failures to him, scold him, or incite him to revenge. Somewhat less frequent are visual hallucinations which come in infinite variety of content, but are often frightening. Tactile, gustatory, and olfactory hallucinations are rather rare. Sometimes complex hallucinations involving more than one perceptual modality occur. I remember a boy of eighteen, handicapped from birth by cataracts and mild mental retardation, and with a history of diverse epileptic seizures for which drugs could only give partial control. In addition to *grand mal* seizures he had been observed to lapse into sudden states of frenzy and fury, in some of which he had pushed his hand and arm through a glass window. The nurses tended to see these states as temper tantrums or acts of negativism and destructiveness, in which he allegedly made a sham of the manifestations of his "true" epileptic seizures, for ulterior purposes. In several interviews I was able to elicit the following "inside story" of these episodes, which constitute a series of hallucinations whose progression also makes good sense from the point of view of brain physiology. His story came in many fragments, at first only loosely connected, but finally recognized in the following sequence.

At sudden and unpredictable moments things would go dark before his eyes. He would then first perceive flashes of light which quickly turned into a formless redness which in turn gave way to red geometrical shapes such as circles and triangles with rotating movements. These soon turned into a panoramic vision of a volcano from which red-hot lava poured over a landscape. The patient saw himself in that landscape, threatened by a gulf of lava nearing him. He then felt himself running away, and during his frantic run forward he would hear bangs and other noises which he felt were part of the volcanic explosion. Still running, he dashed over rocks in a mountain stream into which he stumbled and fell until he found himself in utter panic swimming for his life, grasping for logs in a large, turbulent pool of water. Now nearly exhausted he would smell an ugly odor, as of something burning, after a brief flash of which he became totally unconscious. I had occasion to observe him in one of these atypical seizures in which his motor movements, which were far more pronounced on the left side than on the right, indeed resembled a frantic swimming stroke.

The episodes ended in comatose states of variable length, but usually longer than half an hour.

There are many interesting and enigmatic features in this case. It shows an intersensory "march" of hallucinations which parallel brain discharges that move from the occipital pole through the calcarine areas to the posterior parts of the temporal lobe, from which they proceed forward to the anterior portions of temporal cortex as far as the uncus, where smell sensations are organized. The patient's panic would be a natural reaction to the threatening content of his hallucinations, but it is very likely also the direct result of accompanying discharges in the limbic brain structures. But what accounts for the vivid and well-organized visual content of exploding volcanoes in a patient with such impaired eyesight that he could barely enjoy a movie or television program, and who had certainly never traveled to see a volcano erupting? What brings the fragmentary memories and images into some semblance of unity, so that the episode unfolds like a story? Does the affect of fright come from the hallucinated scene, or is the scene produced to fit the fright? Moreover, with eyes closed and being unresponsive to auditory and tactile stimuli from the outside, where does the patient really "see" and "hear" his hallucinations? Does he think they are inside his head, externally in front or in back of him, merely imagined or really real?

Many of these questions are as yet unanswerable. But to the bystanders who have no fits, who perceive adequately, and who maintain normal reality contact, the patient's vision and noises and smells are simply not verifiable. Indeed, they will protest that they are "not really there." The best they can do, in a moment of sympathy, is to try to remember the time they had a nightmare and then acknowledge that one can indeed be frightened to death by imaginary things. They can further assert, when in the waking state, that the things they saw in their dreams must have come from inside themselves rather than from outside stimuli, although they were "staged" so as to appear external to the center of their self-awareness as dreamers. During the dream everything was real; only in the waking state, when many features of the dream are forgotten or distorted, can one acknowledge that it was, after all, "just a dream," without external reality. But the memory of that episode is still a psychic reality, about which one can vigorously converse with others.

In the history of religions, much has been made of hallucinatory experiences, great dreams, visions, visitations, or appearances. Since the reality ascribed to them during the experience appeared as an external reality to which the visionaries reacted with feeling and perhaps action, it stands to reason that the experiences themselves were first interpreted as visitations from or possession by supernatural powers. These powers were already postulated, named, and acknowledged on other grounds by corporate religion within the cultural framework. With increasing scientific sophistication and the decline of magical thinking, one will come to assert that the universe is not like a great aviary in which spirit birds perch on trees or fly around, to visit or take possession of human beings. The invasion model will have to be modified, or abolished. Visions can be interpreted as forms of illness already known to produce with some degree of observed regularity vivid fantasies: fever, epilepsy, toxic delirium, or "lunacy." At a still later stage, when one begins to inquire into the causes and mechanisms of these diseases, the interpretation may be reduced to psychological aberrations, molecular changes in tissues or body fluids, biochemical processes, etc. One may even develop a new invasion model: infections, brought about by "bugs" or microorganisms. The invading monsters are no longer gods or demons, but they are still unwelcome visitors from the outside. In all these models of explanation the causes are found to be of the same order as the common, undoubted, and demonstrable external world which is shared by everyone who has intact sense organs. The demonstration may have to be aided by laboratory equipment, but the scales and dials and pointers are clearly "outside," in the real world. What was experienced in the hallucinosis as external reality, and which seemed at first belied by unaided objective perception, is finally explained in terms of something external again: nervous tissue, molecular substances, electrical discharges, enzymes, viruses.

But psychology has advanced another possibility—that causes can be completely internal, subjective, and private. Energies can be activated and body processes can be mobilized by wishes, longings, unavailable memories, and aspirations. And the manifestations of these psychic functions, i.e., what brings them to the subject's own awareness, can appear to him as something external, "out there," in the same class of reality as the chair on which he sits and the house in which he lives. What is objectively an inner reality turns subjectively into an outer reality, so that the sensory processes can lay hold of it. One sees it, hears it, and touches it as one does furniture, the other people around, the streets of the city, or the trees in the landscape. The internal becomes externalized. The wish becomes *projected* in the double sense of a projectile being shot out and a picture being flashed onto a screen from where it is distantly visible. The "shot" is not necessarily fired into empty space, nor is the "picture" always projected onto a blank screen; any bit of objective external reality can become a convenient medium on which the shooting and the flashing may occur, albeit only after some denial or distortion of its uniqueness.

If all hallucinations can be explained by the projection mechanism and the dynamics of wishing, are hallucinations with religious content an exception? I do not believe so. But since strange mental phenomena tend to be seen as numinous in their own right, those with religious content have a double reinforcement of religious meaning and therefore may be given special status by the hallucinator. A third reinforcement may come from the cultural group to which he belongs—he may be praised, seen as blessed, or given hallowed status, if not special priestly or prophetic functions. A triple series of awe is at work: (1) the awe of the uncanny perceptual changes which transpose one way of looking into another one; (2) the awe of the perceptual content, which may convey extraordinary beings such as divine persons, or heavenly voices, mysterious messages, lights brighter than the sun, and transcendent beauty; (3) the awe of the community by whom one is now set apart as a privileged vessel of divine revelation. All three forms of awe arise within a more basic set of assumptions designed to give impoverished status to the world of ordinary sensory experience while extolling a more ultimate, durable, or "really real" realm which is the abode of the divine. In whatever manner this abode is imagined, the point is that what seemed so paroxysmally real in the hallucination is now attributed to what one knows to be most supremely real—and not without logic, once the assumption of a hierarchy of realities has been made.

But how does one come to the idea of a hierarchy of realities, with some realities being less "real" than others, or contingent upon something more "really real"? To answer this question adequately would mean writing a history of ideas, a history of philosophy, or a history of theological systems. But a few less ambitious suggestions can be made. One argument for a hierarchy within reality has been an application of cause and effect relations: all that is can only have been made by something that has the power to make things. The artificer is greater than his handiwork. The creator transcends the created. Creation is contingent upon the creator. Another argument stems from observed differences in the durability of things: there is both permanence and change. From this observation one can go two ways. One can extol permanence or durability while decrying change, by subordinating change to "being." Or can one extol change and see permanence as encrustation or decay, which means subordinating "being" to "becoming." All these arguments can be buttressed by high-level fictions about "being" and "nonbeing," the "thick" and the "empty," the "one" and the "many," plus the assumption of various logical or dynamic connections between these pairs. For our purposes, the finer points of these distinctions do not matter much. The important point is that whenever a hierarchy of reality is affirmed, it may affect the importance and the type of reality which one ascribes to hallucinatory experiences, especially those which have religious content or religiously symbolic value.

In the meantime, we have already moved from perception per se to interpretations of the validity of perception and the status of the perceptual world. In fact, we have begun to consider thinking, which is a logical consequence of perceiving.

III

Intellectual Processes

in Religion

IN MARK TWAIN'S *Letters from the Earth* Satan comments in his epistle to St. Michael and St. Gabriel on the odd contradictions he has found in the human race. Human beings prize nothing better than sexual intercourse— yet their heaven contains nothing of it. Few people can sing or play musical instruments and most people abhor noise—yet their heaven is a place where everybody sings all the time! Few passions are as strong as nationalism, chauvinism, racism, or patriotism—yet man's idea of heaven is a place where all are brothers, without exception. Every man on earth has some intelligence and prides himself on what little he has of it—yet "this sincere adorer of intellect and prodigal rewarder of its mighty services here on the earth has invented a religion and a heaven which pay no compliments to intellect, offer it no distinctions, fling to it no largess: in fact, never even mention it."[1]

If the reader feels pleased with these words I remind him that they are satanic utterances. If he feels piqued at them, I suggest that he blame Satan. But Mark Twain was a shrewd observer of man and he was right in sensing some tension between the use of intelligence in one's daily pursuits and its uses in his religious endeavors. There is something odd about thinking for religious ends. Religious thought is unlike common sense, scientific thought, or wit. A devout man may consider his best intellectual work not a triumph but a sin. An eminently curious mind of great talent may decide to spend the rest of his life in focused meditation on divine things only. Luther called reason a whore. And yet the great universities of the Western world arose from "divinity studies" and the pursuit of theology as queen of the scholarly disciplines. Few rational propositions sound as clear and logically tight as religious doctrines, their premises excepted.

In the light of these apparent contradictions one may well ask whether there is such a thing as "religious thought," or what such a phrase may mean. The positions vary from one extreme to the other. Some will ascribe to religious thinking a highly specific content: God, salvation, sin, bliss, faith. Others are like the theologian J. R. Fry who holds that "the man of faith does not think about different things, but about the same things as any other man, but from a peculiar perspective, in a different way, and occasionally with a different outcome."[2] Some will say that the religious man must bridle his curiosity; others will advocate that he must exert it to the utmost. Some religious thought borders on willful or feigned stupidity; in other cases it seems to reach the acme of intellectual power.

James suggested that the uniqueness of religious thought might lie in its divorce from sensory experience whereby it approaches the realm of pure ideas:

> The more concrete objects of most men's religion, the deities whom they worship, are known to them only in idea. It has been vouchsafed, for example, to very few Christian believers to have had a sensible vision of their Saviour; though enough appearances of this sort are on record, by way of miraculous exception, to merit our attention later. The whole force of the Christian religion, therefore, so far as belief in the divine personages determines the prevalent attitude of the believer, is in general exerted by the instrumentality of pure ideas, of which nothing in the individual's past experience directly serves as a model.[3]

James used developed Christianity as an example. But if one looks back at religion's primitive beginnings, one is struck by the concreteness and physical specificity of many archaic deities, and the long view of history shows in many developing religions a progression from the concrete to the abstract, from the visible to the ideational, from the belief in external powers to inwardness. This phylogenetic progression is matched by an ontogenetic development: to the young child the deities seem bound to specific forms and definite times and places, but in the course of growth and learning quasi-perceptual immediacy gives way to conceptual representations. White-bearded grandfather gods become principles of goodness and truth and beauty. Behavorial account books in heaven are replaced by subtle divine intimations of people's intentions and their frustrating struggles with the powers of evil. Gods and demons lose their location on mountaintops, in heavens, or in pits to an abstract "everywhere" or "nowhere." Direct sensory impressions become more rare, and sensory language about divine things becomes ever more metaphorical.

Organized religion itself has often helped to bring about this shift from perceptual concreteness to conceptual abstractness. Precisely to the extent that it tried to posit a more durable and invisible reality behind the world of appearances and beyond the claws of death, it has tended to denigrate the importance of sensory experience. The ancient Hebrew rejection of all images of the divine and the ban on pronouncing the divine name are other forms of suspecting the validity of perception, even in a people with a genius for the concrete and situational.[4] The picture controversy that has beset the Eastern Orthodox and the Western Church for many centuries occurred in a context that was heavily influenced by Greek, particularly neo-Platonic, thought. The Orthodox Church solved it finally by an extreme concretization that was highly ritualized: if pictures were to be made at all, the painters had to follow precise prescriptions as to color, medium, choice of subject matter, etc. All doctrine tends to stress intellectual correctness in the formulation of belief systems precisely to counteract the mind's tendency to wander freely in the overrich world of perceptual stimuli.

In this chapter we will approach the intellectual processes in religion with the help of psychological categories. Whether religious thinking has a special object or a unique style, whether religious fantasy and imagination are *sui generis,* whether man has a special noetic sense or religious curiosity—these are questions which can be kept open for a while.

CONTENT, LEVEL, AND RANGE OF INTELLECTION

What do religious people think about? What occupies their mind? I am afraid these questions can only get a less than satisfactory answer, for a moment's reflection will show that they are compounds of vagueness. Consider some parallel questions. What do artistic people think about? Tentative answers may vary from how to meet last month's bills to whether the next painting is to be done in acrylics or by collage technique. And artistic people may also do much thinking about their spouses, errands to be done in grocery stores, and reserving next Saturday night for seeing a movie that may not have a shred of artistic ambition. What do poetic people think about? Answers may vary from "Where have all the flowers gone?" to "The coward does it with a kiss, the brave man with a sword."[5] And one will have to add that poetic people may think of the corns that are hurting their feet, the new schoolbooks to be bought for their children, or taking out a life insurance policy. Some poetic people may not think much about anything, for their minds, like everybody else's, may be quite empty at times. And some artistic people may be so preoccupied with urgently needed home repairs that they practically think, dream, eat, and sleep hammer and nails. So it is with religious people: they may think about new cars, the stock market, or their stamp collection so exhaustively that they barely have time to ponder anything else.

Let us try a better question. Do avowedly religious people entertain thoughts for which avowedly nonreligious people have little use? If one goes by behavioral clues, one may indeed find some differences between these two groups. Religious people read certain books, tune in to certain radio and television programs, and donate to certain causes and organizations which the irreligious ones ignore. Verbal clues might indicate that religious people use certain words and phrases with much greater frequency and with serious intonation: salvation, Almighty, the fear of the Lord, Rabbi, faith, synagogue, Father, Let us pray. Religious people may organize and spend their time differently, setting aside specified hours for worship and ritual, which gives another clue to what they may think about.

It has been noted by Woollcott[6] that in psychiatric case studies which purport to assess the prevailing thought content of psychiatric patients, statements about specifically religious thoughts tend to be rare. Woollcott therefore engaged a number of hospitalized patients, who had already been studied and whose diagnostic records had already been written up, in a supplementary interview focused on their religious interests, practices, and background. The interviewer made clear that he himself was a psychiatrist, not a clergyman or any other "specialist" in religion. He asked the hospital staff to select two groups, one containing particularly religious patients, the other containing irreligious or areligious patients, leaving the staff free to use for this distinction any criteria they deemed fit, from factual material to inferences, including intuitive estimates or hunches.

Here is an abstract of the interview material from a patient considered actively religious:

"I have had to search for my own faith and it was done against many odds. Father was an atheist but somehow I think he believed in something. Mother went to church mostly to see what people wear. Both ridiculed the Catholic Church as 'silly superstition.' The family was scientific, but in adolescence I began to think that there were some things that science could not explain. I felt a strong need for something and had a nebulous belief in God. But I did not get anything out of going to chapel at school." The patient read a great deal about religious history in her late teens and started going from church to church, all Protestant. After marriage and the first child "I started to question things, to wonder what life was all about." Her husband tended to become angry when religion was mentioned so she learned to avoid that subject with him, but she went to church with increased frequency and in later years joined the Catholic Church. She relies heavily on prayer when she is under stress and says "it makes me calmer and teaches me to rely on things other than myself." She sometimes goes to church only to meditate: "I always wind up after a period of meditation thinking how lucky I am. The things I find there are faith, hope and peace of mind." She feels the Church's teaching is that "the individual does matter—he is important to God and to himself. At church I can feel truly humble and at the same time feel big. I can revert back to childish wishes and feelings, I can yield to a strong need for protection in a way which can be accepted in the church but not by people. I can eliminate my false front." She pictures God as a kindly, firm, protective father who takes care of her, yet not without sparing her the ordeals of life.

This woman revealed that she thinks about many things of religious relevance: whether she shall join a church, and which one; whether there is any plan or purpose in life; whether she can cope with personal problems through prayer or ritual. She takes time to meditate, but we do not know exactly on what. Are her meditations focused on specific themes, or are they loose musings, perhaps daydreams, in a peaceful atmosphere? She thinks about her worth, in her own and God's perspectives. She ponders her feelings of humility and bigness; she knows that she can at times give in to childish wishes without being ashamed. She thinks that she can drop her "false front" and be more honest. Undoubtedly, she thinks of many other things besides: husband, children, transportation, food, science, recreation.

From the "irreligious, or least religious" group Woollcott reports the following fragments given by an intelligent young graduate student of Jewish parentage:

"Father had wanted to become a rabbi, but had given this up in favor of business ambitions. Mother took part nominally in some Jewish social and cultural events, without apparent feeling." When the parents nevertheless insisted that he take Bar Mitzvah the patient was very upset and furious at their "ethnocentricity and we-groupiness." During adolescence he was vehemently irreligious, but during a course of psychotherapy he began to read voluminously in religion and philosophy, "looking for answers." Without accepting any dogma he felt some need for dependence on God, and tried to develop a philosophy of life without supernaturalism. He feels he needs "positive support in the form of moral values which will help me take positive action. When I need this support I go to Church, usually the Congregational Church, in the same way that I might go to the swimming pool to swim if I need to relax. It also provides me with the feeling of group identity." He thinks that religious experience is essentially an aesthetic experience which may be compared in some ways to observing nature, a feeling of freedom, or "for me even sitting in a furniture store among pieces of furniture which I admire."

The striking thing is that this man also "looks for answers" and occasionally goes to church, without affiliating himself with any organized religious movement. His thoughts are full of curious questions about the nature of things; he wonders how moral values can be supported and how he may react positively to the stresses and opportunities of life. He has taken a keen intellectual interest in religious questions and propositions, as much to learn from them as to attack them. He links religion with the enjoyment of beauty, from art to literature, and from nature to muscle movements and even furniture. And undoubtedly too, this man's thoughts are at times filled with concerns for his academic studies, his entertainment, and the practical aspects of his living arrangements.

These two examples show something else: that it is extremely difficult to sort out "religious" from "irreligious" people. Both can talk about God, even with some warmth, including the "irreligious" young man. And both can think predominantly about themselves, including the "very religious" woman. Both can go in and out of churches, make and break affiliations with organized religious groups, and indulge in various rituals: praying for the one, observing nature for the other. One may have loose meditations in a church setting, the other may have sharply focused intellectual questions in a furniture store, on a river bank, or while writing a term paper. One goes to church in order to discover herself as an individual who counts, the other to discover a group-feeling.

Opening Augustine's *Confessions,* one reads:

> "Great art thou, O Lord, and greatly to be praised; great is thy power, and infinite is thy wisdom." And man desires to praise thee, for he is a part of thy creation; he bears his mortality about with him and carries the evidence of his sin and the proof that thou dost resist the proud. Still he desires to praise thee, this man who is only a small part of thy creation.[7]

This is straight God-talk. Augustine's words are of undoubted religiosity. Now take a page from a man of equal intellectual power, a master of words with great concern for all the vicissitudes of man, Goethe:

> Nature! We are surrounded and embraced by her; unable to get away from her, and incapable of going any deeper into her . . . For ever and ever she creates new forms. What is now has never been before; what was before never comes again. Everything is new, and nevertheless always old. . . . Life is her most beautiful invention, and death is her trick to have more life. She envelops man in a haze, and she always prods him toward the light. She stirs needs because she loves movement. . . .[8]

Whatever these beautiful words and stirring ideas are, they are not God-talk. They are not church ideas. Yet they speak of the creator and the created, the absolute and the contingent, meaning and purpose, life and death, newness and light. Who would dare call these thoughts irreligious? The same Goethe struck in his conversations with Eckermann a blow at Napoleon for classifying in his private field library the Old Testament, the New Testament and the Koran under "Politics." Just as Napoleon could see religious things in political perspective, Goethe could see natural things in religious perspective.

These illustrations show the correctness of Fry's remark that the man of faith does not really think about different things, but about the same things as any other man, from a peculiar perspective. A mere enumeration of a person's thought content adds little clarity to the question of what religious people think about. They think of all things, depending on their curiosity, intellectual powers, and stamina in problem-solving. But they may think in terms of special thought categories, special concepts, special language, special metaphors, and, as Fry says, at times with a different outcome.

Nevertheless, the degree of a man's curiosity and the use of his intellectual powers can be affected by religious considerations. There is a religiously motivated anti-intellectualism. Curiosity can be stunted by religious prohibitions. Inquiry into nature can be religiously interpreted as meddling in the mysteries of the divine. The realm of mystery can be kept unnecessarily large. The phrase "Blessed are the poor in spirit, for theirs is the kingdom of heaven" (Matt. 5:3) has been all too often misinterpreted as condoning dullness, or turning intellectual laziness into a virtue. In religious perspective, thinking and knowing themselves can take on numinous qualities, whether divine or demonic. The biblical story of the garden of Eden imposes a special ban on the use of intelligence: if the first man eats of the tree of the knowledge of good and evil he shall die. And it is the Adversary who adds that through such knowledge "you will be like God." Clearly, the intellect is described here in terms of the cardinal features of the *numen*: it is both attractive and repulsive, *fascinans* and *tremendum*.

Religious people and religious movements have always known the ambiguities of intelligence. Fear of thinking has led to censorship and the Index and the *nihil obstat* label, to the tragicomedy of the Scopes trial, and to exceedingly dull Sunday School teaching. It can promote closed systems which keep people in intellectual, if not physical, bondage. Admiration of thinking has led to scholarly work, a learned priesthood or ministry, the Talmud, and the daring dictum that the truth will set man free. It can lead to open systems, open-mindedness, and a very creative use of the religious perspective. Great political reforms, such as the civil rights movement in the United States, owe the sad necessity for, and the amazing power of their existence, to both sides of the ambiguity.

It seems then that the critical psychological issue is whether thinking in religious perspective broadens or narrows the scope of a person's thought, and whether it dulls or sharpens his wits. And if, for religious ends, a man's thought should be focused on certain questions or issues, the focusing should enhance clarity so that new insights can be gained, and creative responses made. Religious preoccupations which make thoughts go around in circles, without new knowledge and without freedom from the circular captivity, are just preoccupations; that is, faltering thoughts without outcome, with much energy wasted. They are not one whit more useful or adaptive by being religious.

MEMORY

Some years ago, I administered psychological tests to a fifty-seven-year-old patient suffering from presenile dementia. Whenever I asked questions requiring a historical proper name for an answer, such as "Who invented the airplane?" or "Who wrote *Hamlet*?" his invariable answer was "Jesus Christ." This was said seriously, after considerable mental strain, and not as a swear word. On a sorting test, after having grouped together some small metal objects including a lock which demonstrated his practical ability to sort things into reasonable groups, he gave the following rationale:

> Because you can lock things with it . . . belongs to the United States of America . . . and for which it stands . . . all nations . . . justice for all . . . in the name of the Father, the Son, and the Holy Ghost.

This patient had severe intellectual impairment, with considerable memory loss. In trying to justify and explicate his grouping of metal objects, which could have been done by saying "These are all metal things," his eyes strayed across the lock to which he associated the ideas of safekeeping and safety, then property and authority, which he summed up in "U.S.A." But from that moment a rote verbal memory took over: the familiar phrases of the pledge to the flag, learned in school, which in turn elicited another verbal sequence of great endurance learned in church. He was a product of the Bible Belt, had first been a farm hand and then a cemetery worker, and he labored under the delusion that he would be arrested for having improperly filled out his Army papers during World War II, which was twelve years earlier.

This case fragment puts in bold relief the tenacity of childhood memories and rote language sequences, learned in the early years of life. It also shows that under duress, when one gropes for answers and is aware of one's faltering capacities, the safe phrases and thoughts from childhood tend to take over. Other aspects of the case confirm Ribot's law of the decline of memory: when senile decline sets in, recent memories fade out more rapidly than the remote memories which have been available for many years.

It is not accidental that the patient's thoughts, under the circumstances of intellectual failure, produced the two memory nuclei of State and Church. They are the symbols of authority, power, order, and protection.

In the vicissitudes of life, these abide and for many people govern the great decisions between birth and death. They have a natural pull if the individual feels that he can no longer rely on his own authority, and the direction of that pull is often regressive. It is toward the familiar admonitions, the familiar phrases, the hallowed ideas, and the cherished satisfactions that were once obtained from father's care and mother's ministrations.

Memory plays an exceedingly important role in personal preferences for religious verses and religious hymns. Familiar tunes and familiar words are what congregations want to sing, and as a group they tend to become quite annoyed when they are asked by their worship leaders to learn new hymns. This is at first sight a strange phenomenon because many of the "old familiar tunes" are of very poor musical quality and some of the verses represent theological misconstructions that the denominations have worked hard to overcome or correct. Why would an intelligent middle-aged man, perhaps with a high academic degree, who is in touch with the best poetry and musical performances of his culture, deign to sing "Rock of Ages"? How could he, when he avidly reads in his spare time the latest publications in the "Honest to God" debate?[9-10] I think the most convincing reason is the hymn's familiarity which produces automatic recall of mother's voice and father's peaceful mien and the pleasant simplicity of his childhood's religiosity.

While memory dynamics are highly personal, we should not lose sight in this section of the basic conservatism that is inherent in all religions. This can be seen as a corporate reliance on memory. Religious forces are preservative and conservative for the most part, so much so that when a creative or progressive trend occurs within a given religious system its spokesmen will soon find themselves at odds with the vast majority in the congregations and often be forced to establish a new organizational unit. An enormous part of religious forms, creeds, and experiences finds its *raison d'être* in history, rather than in the exigencies of the present time. There is something awry in the idea of a "new religion." Every age has many new movements and new causes, but new religions are rare. In order for an idea or cause to be held religious it must be linked with a creedal framework, an ancient scripture, or a time-honored idea or practice that one can consider hallowed. But hallowing is like aging in man and cheese: only time can do it.

In practice, therefore, an essential part of religion depends on the functions of memory, the personal memories of each member of the community, and the corporate memories of the group. Church buildings, as we saw in the previous chapter, are cluttered with memories and memory props —in windows, stones, paintings, and all the hundreds of articles adorned with plaques, indicating that they were given "in loving memory of Mrs. Kirkbride."

Memory functions are the quintessence of the religiously so important condition of remorse. Listen to Emily Dickinson's formulation of it:

> Remorse is memory awake,
> Her companies astir,—
> A presence of departed acts
> At window and at door.
>
> Its past set down before the soul,
> And lighted with a match,
> Perusal to facilitate
> Of its condensed despatch.
>
> Remorse is cureless,—the disease
> Not even God can heal;
> For 'tis His institution,—
> The complement of hell.[11]

One could hardly add anything to this perfect grasp of the mechanism of remorse. "Memory awake" is the failure of repression, which is quite against the natural tendency to forget unpleasant experiences. The practices of confession, in whatever corporate or individual form, are religion's way of keeping unpleasant memories alive until forgiveness has been symbolized in some way, at the right time, and under religion's own auspices.

STORE OF KNOWLEDGE

Another question must be raised: What do religious people know, if anything, that is unique to them? Do they have data, information, attainments, or forms of erudition which are less commonly known to others? Let us start with some pedestrian observations, recently reported in the press, based on studies of the impact of parochial school education. A critical assessment, both by Roman Catholic[12] and Lutheran[13] (Missouri Synod) educators, using a variety of techniques, shows that pupils and ex-pupils of parochial schools excel matched controls from public schools in certain items of knowledge. For instance, far more of the Lutheran school products could identify the century in which Luther lived, more of them knew what the Pentateuch is, and more of them were familiar with names and deeds of biblical figures. Both studies also tried to ascertain whether parochial school pupils had different attitudes on ethical issues and knew how to make applications of the doctrinal verities in which they had been trained to today's problems. But in these respects the studies were disappointing.

What concerns us here is how well these two studies confirm the intimations of common sense. The store of knowledge of religiously educated people contains facts and data from books, history classes, charts and maps of Palestine, and geographical locations of the Kaaba, the Mount of Olives, the city of Geneva, the castle of Wittenberg, or the shrine of Lourdes. If the faith is biblical, the store of knowledge may be a compound of kings and prophets, battles, genealogies, creation and flood myths, dramatic literature, sayings of Jesus, stories of healings and wonders. Perhaps it holds some capsule "rules for living" and attitudinal guides, such as the Ten Commandments, the Beatitudes, the summary of the Law, or the Lord's Prayer. Whatever the faith or creed is, the store of knowledge of its members will also contain data about ritual and liturgy, for instance that women must wear hats in Catholic churches, but not in most Protestant houses of worship, and that men always take theirs off except in Orthodox synagogues. The same holds for knowledge about special footwear in Islamic worship services, the use of rosaries, the handling of collection plates, and the rules for standing up or sitting down.

It is to be expected that the breadth of all this factual knowledge will vary with the level of one's intelligence, the amount and quality of teaching that one is exposed to, the intellectual stimulation provided in families and church schools, the availability of good libraries, and all the other factors that affect knowledge in general. As a rule, bright people will know more about their religion than dull people know about theirs. I put it this way because in a pluralistic society the diversity of denominations and sects will itself reflect the stratification of intelligence levels in the population at large. Some denominations are intelligent, scholarly, or intellectual; others are of low intellectual power. But there are many exceptions to these general rules.

From time to time one is accosted by persons who, without being very bright and without social evidence of much education and learning, have a surprisingly detailed textual knowledge of biblical literature, particularly of the prophetic and apocalyptic books. They can cite lavishly, usually in the seventeenth-century English of the King James Version, a large number of verses and passages, often with aggressive or hortatory content, being able to identify them by book, chapter, and verse. They must have spent large amounts of time accumulating these bits of knowledge at the sacrifice of anything else. Indeed, it is not unusual to note a singular lack of general cultural knowledge in their lives. Their fanaticism recognizes only one source of things worth knowing, their Bible, and all other sources of knowledge and information are held to be suspect. But one also finds the reverse condition: an amazingly large number of people with above-average intelligence and good schooling constantly defy the scholarly ambitions of their denominations by remaining ignorant of religiously relevant data that schoolchildren can easily master. In some of these cases the contrast between their general knowledge and their intellectual ignorance about their own religion is so striking that one may speak of a negative fanaticism. For these, religion and "unknowing" seem to be equivalent. They resist the use of their intellect in matters religious, persist in a nebulous childhood faith, and desist acquiring the knowledge whereby their faith might mature. They may be clever stockbrokers, graduate engineers, or widely traveled socialites with college degrees, but they are prone to think that Moses was one of the disciples, or that John the Baptist and his family settled Canaan.

Such striking disparities within the store of knowledge must be explained by specific resistances rather than laziness. Even the omnipresent variety of interests among people is too weak an explanation of the gaps in religious learning among intelligent church members. Variety of interest may explain the differences in knowledge between religious and irreligious groups, but the striking lag in knowledge among affiliated and intelligent church people is better attributed to a block on learning. It is a dynamic process resulting in unknowing, not merely a slothful lack of something. We have seen in previous sections that anti-intellectualism is sometimes fostered in religious groups, and that the general store of knowledge may be affected by it. But it can also be turned against the group's own special resources of faith, so that a member becomes loath to study his own scriptures, creeds, doctrines, or history. The resistance to learning may also be due to a desire to leave pious childhood impressions in their pristine naïveté. In other cases it may be an active rebellion against the adhortations of parents and teachers, a rebellion that does not go far enough to lead to a severance of membership with the home's religious affiliation. More positively, the resistance against religious knowledge may come from different conceptions of religion per se: if one defines religion as emotion and pursues it in emotional experiences of one sort or another, it behooves one to keep the intellectual grasp weak. Cloudy knowledge is more prone to yield the stage to emotional upheavals. Others equate religion and beauty, which induces them to seek in worship and ritual the supreme aesthetic moment which reasoning would defile. Those who see in religion mostly moral control of divine origin may resist subjecting their cherished "eternal" codes to the relativism that any historical study engenders.

All these resistances to knowledge are time-honored. Centuries before our own era the writer of Ecclesiastes had preached that "he who increases knowledge increases sorrow" (Eccles. 1:18) and that most of the pursuits of man are vanity. But there is a subtle difference: this particular preacher had first spent a lifetime gathering knowledge and exercising his curiosity and then gave his verdict. It is very likely, moreover, that he was depressed during these sermons, at that stage of life. Those with resistance to knowledge do not even gain the wisdom of the sad, ancient sage.

IMAGINATIVE PROCESSES

In 1489 two Dominican priests published a book called *Malleus Male-ficarum* (The Witches' Hammer)[14] which was intended as a guide to exorcists in the differentiation of sick people, bad people, and those possessed by demons. As late as 1959 a book under the title *Evidence of Satan in the Modern World*, by Msgr. Leon Cristiani,[15] appeared to address itself basically to the same theme. Both books affirm the existence of a Prince of Evil, not metaphorically but literally, who has the capacity to lay hold of people, use their bodies for the desecration of God's handiwork, speak and act through them, and sometimes change the possessed individual's personality so thoroughly that he is unrecognizable.

What kind of thinking is it that produces such fanciful entities? We can indignantly turn away from it and cry: superstition! Or we can play with it, half-bemused, and say: myth! Whichever of these two courses we take, we are agreed that we have here to do with a kind of thought that turns mental images into things or beings, unlike the products of memory which turn things or beings into thoughts.

This type of thinking is, however, not confined to medieval Dominican friars and a few outlandish contemporary monsignors. Here is a fragment of the writing of a scientist, founder of a scientific journal, expert in mining engineering, mathematician, and politician:

> It has been said that in the spiritual world, just as in the natural world, there appear to be spaces, consequently also distances, but that these are appearances according to spiritual affinities which are of love and wisdom, that is, of good and truth. From this it is that the Lord, although everywhere in heaven with the angels, nevertheless appears high above them as a sun. Furthermore, since reception of love and wisdom causes affinity with Him, these heavens appear nearer to Him in which the angels are, from reception, in closer affinity with Him, than those in which the affinity is more remote. From this it is also that the heavens, of which there are three, are distinct from each other, likewise the societies of each heaven; and further that the hells under them are remote according to their rejection of love and wisdom. The same is true of men, in whom and with whom the Lord is present throughout the whole earth; and this solely for the reason that the Lord is not in space.[16]

Thus wrote Swedenborg, whose work was greatly admired by the father of William and Henry James. Superstition? Myth? Abundant imagination? How did he know the number of heavens and hells—and what certainty could he have about angels?

Some thoughts are far removed from the reality that is presented to the sense organs. As thinkers, men not only reproduce what the senses have taught them, but produce their own novel images, albeit often with some help from the building blocks that experience has collected. There are many kinds of images, playfully produced or faithfully reproduced, concrete or abstract, richly detailed or sketchy. There are images of things and images of relations between things. There are images of words. And some thoughts seem to have no imagery at all, but consist only of "sets" or "directions." In each twenty-four-hour cycle, all of us move in our thinking on a spectrum from reality-oriented, sensory-based thoughts to the private and highly "unreal" dream thoughts, through the intermediary stages of hypnagogic and hypnopompic thinking just before falling asleep and while waking up which have their own peculiar free play of imagery. And while awake we may drift off into daydreaming, reverie, or fantasy, or decide to engage in deliberate and active imagination and speculation. We can postulate a few "as ifs" and erect whole castles in the air upon them, with fine logical deductions and inferences. Or we can be stingy and take nothing for granted that cannot be felt between finger and thumb—but even then we are prone to do some dreaming at night.

If we place, as McKellar[17] does, all thinking on a spectrum that ranges from R-type thinking (reality-tested) at one end, and A-type thinking (autistic) at the other end, it is clear that a very large part of all thought processes are mixtures of R and A. The global word "fantasy" would designate a fairly large portion of the spectrum and include the products of dreams, poetic imagination, artistic playfulness, fabrication, and delusion. It would include all myths and many religious ideas. Indeed, it would include both the assertion that man is made in God's image and Feuerbach's reversal of it that God is made in man's image. While it is popularly held that the imagination is boundless, it is much more useful to note that there is some structure to the richness of imaginative processes. This conviction underlies the psychoanalytic theory according to which thinking moves developmentally from type A to type R. But that movement is not simply giving up the one in favor of the other: it is a dialectic process in which A/R ratios change toward R/A ratios with a preservation of A-forces and R-forces. Indeed, A and R arise from perennial psychic structures which determine the dynamics of thinking. A-thinking denotes the "primary process" in which wishes derived from drives find pleasurable fulfillment in images which are at odds with the fabric of reality or fill up gaps in it. R-thinking denotes the "secondary process" in which respect for the undeniable features of reality prevails over the strength of wishes. Since drive constellations and equipment of reality testing are always with us, the battle between the two types of thought leads rarely to a clear-cut victory of one over the other. More often, we find perpetual compromises between the two, with ever-shifting outcomes and greater or lesser degrees of success.

While the broad goal of all thinking may be stated as adaptation, i.e., helping individuals and groups to survive with maximum well-being and satisfaction, the issues in survival are often situational and life is lived in dynamic fields of threats and opportunities, likes and dislikes, stability and change. Thought processes are operative in such dynamic fields and attuned to the nature of the problems that are encountered in these fields. Ideally, there is a type of thought appropriate for each field. The thinking of spouses about each other within a marital relationship has a certain style and a set of rules that are different from those operating in the stock exchange. Thinking about art proceeds differently from thinking about enzymes. Solving crossword puzzles requires a style of thought different from "thinking hard" about one's feelings over the impending death of a loved one. Myth-making is not the same as bridge-building, though both require expert use of thought processes.

This section opened with allusions to imaginative thought processes that resulted in the images of devils and angels, inevitably couched in language forms with evocative power appropriate to those images. But imaginative thought in religion can develop many forms and create many images. If devils and angels seem at this time to have a too large A/R ratio to be respectable, their decline in popularity does not mean the end of A/R thought. And neither does their past or present affirmation detract from the richness of R/A variants that have been produced.

Samuel Butler's wry phrase "An honest God's the noblest work of man"[18] implies that ideas about God are subject to change and that there is considerable latitude in imagining the basic features of one's object of worship. Even the most cursory review of images of the divine shows an astounding range of possibilities. The story has often been told. The Melanesian idea of strange power, mana, which some writers believe is the primordial form of all religions, can adhere to anything that is perceptually remarkable. Anything that stands out in experience: a particularly fierce animal, a very ugly person, an eerie sound, or a strangely shaped rock, may become the carrier of mana, and will subsqeuently become an object of worship. Human beings also partake of mana when their activities are very successful, whether it be hunting, fishing, having many children, or being a good warrior or political leader. In this type of thought, the fantasy starts with attributing mysterious powers to a great variety of things which in turn provide a stimulus for further play of the imagination.

Most of this remains rather diffuse and unwieldy as compared to animism, which attributes human characteristics to animate and inanimate objects. This makes things "see" or "act" or "intend" as human beings do. In order to account for the obvious differences between human beings and all other objects, animism entailed a new image: that of a soul or spirit which is not only "housed" in the human body but which can maneuver (visibly or invisibly) to reside elsewhere through spatial displacement.

This idea is interesting also in that it entails a distinction, including the possibility of a separation, between body and soul.

More focus is achieved by totemism, which selects a species of plant or animal as an object of worship that has both positive and negative social force. It binds the people into a community under a leader who is tribal head, father, and high priest, and it separates certain classes of people from each other by regulating marriage options through strict incest taboos.

Little is known about the historical transitions between these so-called primitive religions and the more highly developed religions which have provided modern man with literary documents, creedal formulations, systematized formulae for worship and evidence of an articulate cult. But in polytheism, whether it is seen as an intermediate stage or as a contemporary form, the process of imagination creates gods which have an increasing likeness to human beings, complete with sexual differentiation, family structures and kinship patterns, and differentiations of labor with specializations of functions akin to the social and individual characters of man. A/R thoughts are here mixed with a good many R/A thoughts for which cues are taken from introspection and social observations. Gods have special interests and concerns: high crop yields, ponds stocked with fish, weather conditions, crafts, arts, commercial transactions, war, love, or laws. Though their potential in everything far exceeds that of man, their features show a strong resemblance to those of man. They are wise or cunning, trustworthy or deceitful, lusty or sober, amiable or forbidding, sweet or sour. Among themselves they love or hate, associate or stay aloof; they are each other's spouses, parents, children, and near or distant cousins. Some are interesting and become very prominent, others are rather boring or supernumerary and recede into the background, not to be heard of any more.

It seems that even the fantasy can become overworked and that life can become unwieldy under its sway. Or the fantasy can become undisciplined, which may result in portraying such a multiplicity of fragments or so much variegation that it no longer takes the unity of experience into account. Economy and unity may then demand novel images: syncretistic fusions between the divine personalia and a selective focusing on the most important personages of the pantheon promote fewer gods, each with greater comprehensiveness. In ancient Hebrew culture, a henotheistic trend appeared which recognized the historical existence of many god-images, if not the metaphysical reality of many gods, but with a concomitant preference for one who was at once more comprehensive, more powerful, and more original and was seen to hold more promise for the concerns of the Hebrew people. At last, this gave way to a monotheistic conception in which all four criteria for his ascendance became more stringent and potent.

"At last," but it was by no means the last image of the divine. With the advent of one god, the imagination, being more disciplined than before, also gained new freedom to create articulate and detailed pictures of who and what this god is, what he does, what his concerns are, and how the transactions among him and nature and man proceed. A whole new series of images arises. He is a maker whose handiwork shows forth through the mere enunciating of words. He no longer works like a potter or a weaver as the old gods did. He speaks. He also listens, so that it makes sense to speak to him. He cares for what he has made in such a broad sense that he also sustains man in thought, word, and deed—not only tribes or nations, but also individuals, even when some of them are at odds with the tribe or the race. He shows preferences, and he shows repulsion. He thinks and acts like a father, not only in the sense of being a procreator but also as head of the household, as educator of the children, and as a good provider. He acts like a wise father, whose intentions cannot always be as direct as his acts. He begins to make distinctions between what a man does and what he intended to do; he has compassion for weaknesses of the mind and body. William Blake called him the Ancient of Days and portrayed him as a white-bearded, stooped, cloud-swept mathematician with compass in hand, "measuring" his creation and his household. Others developed about him an imperial image, the exalted ruler of all men and nations, even the entire world. In this vision, obedience and orderly conduct become critical demands for man. Eighteenth-century deists, themselves competent architects, builders, and technicians, imagined him to be an exalted clockmaker who had invented the perpetuum mobile. Others imagined him as a warm personality in whom one could confide. Poets compared him to a hen protecting her chickens, to military armor, to a tower of strength, and to a kindly shepherd. In all these images, thoughts derived from sensory experience, converted into memories from which common sense or logical extrapolations could be made, and a selective emphasis on the noble intentions of the divine began to change the large A/R heritage to higher R/A loadings.

Excellent examples of a creative play of the religious imagination can be found in the history of the doctrine of the atonement in Christianity.[19] That history shows notable shifts in articulate theological thought, which always aims at logical consistency and scientific respectability, as well as in the concomitant vivacity of images widely held by the mass of believers. In the Ransom theory of the atonement, expounded particularly by the Cappadocian fathers, God is portrayed as creator and rightful owner of man. His creatures have become alienated from him by running over to a false master, Satan. God, concerned to deliver his children out of bondage sends his son Jesus as a ransom price to Satan so as to "buy" back what originally belonged to him. The social image underlying this version is barter on the slave market. A second theory took its cue from the Old Testament institution of sacrifice and the Roman institution of the judicial bench, merged into a fantasy in which God is portrayed as a holy ruler and supreme judge who sternly demands that justice be done to man's transgressions. He does not only demand an eye for an eye and a tooth for a tooth but insists on a fine, because his juristic mind wants restoration for what sin had taken away as well as satisfaction for the offensiveness of sin. In this Satisfaction or Penal theory, a whole set of transactions between God and man is envisaged in which Christ is offered as the sacrificial lamb and at the same time serves as the fine levied against man. Because the fine was too high for any man or all men together to pay, God actually paid it himself through his incarnate son. The judge, exceedingly stern and demanding, is also exceedingly forgiving by paying the fine he himself had levied. A third version, the so-called Governmental theory of the atonement, took its cue from the enlightened sovereigns with which some Western European countries have been blessed since the Renaissance. The good governor applies the law, but as guardian of the social order he knows that love and forgiveness are sometimes higher than law. The statute book can occasionally lead to ethical monstrosities, so that the governor must apply the law with wisdom. He does not punish out of wrath, or for the sake of obtaining satisfaction, but for the common good! He cannot be punitive—he must be an example. God, as the good governor, reinstated the defaced *imago Dei* in man by incarnating himself in his son, who was so noble to offer himself both out of mercy for man and out of the desire to set a lofty example for man's conduct.

The vivid imagery of these speculations has fascinated millions of Christians and has undoubtedly fostered the pursuit of ever-greater detail when individuals tried to appropriate the messages they heard. Each man adds his own associations to the image that is proclaimed to him; each man will try to come to terms with his own idea of a father-slaveholder, a father-judge or a father-governor. Believers of any religion not only hear the myths, parables, and metaphors of their faith which tradition and doctrines have refined and preserved for them, but they also add to these their own active fantasies which keep the myths alive. A very active imagination has been at work on the figure of Jesus, which has created a whole series of distinct images, still more or less alive. Jesus is hailed as the miracle man who heals, sets straight, or repairs by stunning words and acts. Or he is seen as the good shepherd, ever taking care of the flock with a unique tenderness for each individual sheep. More Platonically, or hysterically, he is seen as the lover of the soul with whom one engages in a quasi-marital relation. Some have seen him as a high priest, forever officiating, praying, and mediating. He is also imagined as the lamb, snow-white, meek until the sacrifice which shed his blood. This image led Blake to his intricate poetic mixture of reality perception, corporate mythology, and personal mysticism:

> Little Lamb, who made thee?
> Dost thou know who made thee?
> Gave thee life, and bid thee feed
> By the stream and o'er the mead;
> Gave thee clothing of delight,
> Softest clothing, woolly, bright;
> Gave thee such a tender voice,
> Making all the vales rejoice?
> Little Lamb, who made thee?
> Dost thou know who made thee?
>
> Little Lamb, I'll tell thee,
> Little Lamb, I'll tell thee:
> He is callèd by thy name,
> For He calls Himself a Lamb,
> He is meek, and He is mild;
> He became a little child.
> I a child, and thou a lamb,
> We are callèd by His name.
> Little Lamb, God bless thee!
> Little Lamb, God bless thee![20]

The man who also wrote "Tyger, tyger burning bright, in the forest of the night" used his lively imagination in anything he undertook and could turn the most common things into a surprise. This surprise effect, which makes the image a *fascinans* in its own right, is perhaps the greatest contribution of the creative imagination to established religious ideas. An idea is only an idea; it soon becomes faded and is forgotten. But to turn the idea, even the most common idea or the driest concept, into some lively image that contains treasures of surprising detail, is the art of discovery, inspiration, and pedagogy. Compare the freshness of Blake's little poem with the triteness and stuffiness of the "What would Jesus do?" cult of forty years ago in American Protestantism, and the quick death of that movement causes no wonder.

It is difficult for Westerners to imagine, or even to grasp conceptually, the Buddhist concept of the Empty or the Void. When observation tells them that a life has ended or when logical inference presents them with the idea of nothingness, they will hasten to fill the knowledge gap by an active use of the imagination, which substitutes something for nothing. Rich fantasies have been bestowed on the shape of things to come hereafter: heavens, hells, purgatories, realms of shadows, Hades, Sheol. Despite the heavy weighting of these conceptions with A/R thoughts, it is interesting to note how much extrapolation from R/A thinking has been added to them. They are imagined in space and time, though both these dimensions of terrestrial life had to be stretched "beyond imagination" to accommodate themselves to the tenuous boundaries among reality, myth, and abject fabrication. Not only is there a heavenly city, but it is even named: the heavenly Jerusalem. Its streets have no ordinary bricks or asphalt for pavement; they are lined with gold, interspersed by crystal ponds. I opened this chapter with a quotation from Mark Twain's satire on people's fantasies of heaven and I gladly defer to him for further descriptions. Loftier visions have been offered by Dante. Very turbulent scenic fantasies occur in the New Testament book of Revelation. But the striking fact in all these, from the ridiculous to the sublime, is the contribution of actual perceptions and observations and potent memories to the specific fantasies about the life hereafter. Whether the next realm is one of grace or damnation, its outline is derived from everyday life, with pleasures and pain, bliss and sorrow, rejoicing and sighing. Social roles and prerogatives may be reversed, wrath may be bestowed upon one's enemies, delayed punishments or delayed gratifications may be envisioned, but the take-off point for the fantasy is an aspect of daily experience.

One needs indeed considerable self-discipline to refrain from indulging in fantasies about immortality and the forms of an afterlife. Some people find such a discipline in science with its impeccable ethic of empiricism and reality testing. Others find it in being so busy in the here and now that they have no time or energy left for flimsy speculations. Or it may be a matter of inhibition and timidity: never venture beyond the simple needs of the day! Religion itself can foster or thwart the imagination of things to come. Since the examples of elaborate fantasies of heaven or hell are so ample, one sometimes forgets that many avowedly religious persons and whole peoples do not indulge in such fantasies. The Hebrew people were remarkably restrained in their thoughts about Sheol. They did not aspire to know what went on in that realm. Similarly, Christians have asserted that the *eschaton*—the things to come—is excusively in God's hand and mind and that it is presumptuous to spin fantasies about it. Paul of Tarsus used the image of looking through a glass, darkly, in describing human knowledge; though he hoped to see more clearly some time he was loath to speculate about what he would ultimately encounter.

Religious imagination does not only consider the deities, it also considers man. As late as the eighteenth-century, psychiatric classification systems recognized demonomania as a special form of disease, along with religious melancholia, lycanthropy, and other forms of folly which were earlier seen as evidence of demoniacal possession. An abundance of fairy tales and ages of superstition have documented the belief that people could be transformed into wolves, horses, birds, bats, or dragons by permitting certain demonic manipulations, by seeking traffic with devils or by simply succumbing to the superiority of satanic power. The point is that they acted like animals, emitting grunts, going around on all fours, or flapping their arms in imitation of the motions of birds or bats. Belief in vampires which fed on the souls of the departed and came to disturb the affairs of man has an ancient heritage and is still a potent motif for the makers of horror movies. In the more archaic totemic societies there is as it were a double consciousness in which a man is not only a human being and member of the tribe, but also something else, namely the animal species that has been chosen to be the tribe's totem. He is man and leopard. In ritual dances he may act like a leopard; in the hunt he may imitate the leopard's silent crouching.

A particularly vivid imagination has surrounded the idea of witchcraft. Witchcraft stories were not mere fairy tales or stories with a moral; they were part of the fabric of living. Witches cast spells and demanded counteractivity by individuals or groups of citizens. The village witch was actively held responsible for natural disasters or for odd behavior among the villagers. The belief system from which these practices arose was undergirded by the even more drastic fantasies about incubi and succubi, male and female devils with whom certain persons could have sexual intercourse and bear cursed offspring. Again, these were not only fantastic stories that sane people could tell about others, but they led to active forms of sexual promiscuity among a variety of men and women. Freud wrote a paper on *A Seventeenth-Century Demonological Neurosis,*[21] in which he commented on the morbid imaginations of a depressed man who had sold himself to the devil for a term of nine years, complete with written contracts in blood and ink, and pictures about the negotiations between the devil and the poor patient-artist. Aldous Huxley has described from historical documents the tremendous role that hysterical fantasies have played in nunneries and monasteries; his *The Devils of Loudun*[22] sets forth the cruelties, intrigue, and bloodshed that accompanied the weird fantasies of these disturbed women at every step.

In our own day, the imagination is no less active, albeit that the preoccupation is no longer with incubi and witches. A recent *New Yorker* article[23] documented the very lively fantasies of the Church of God and its bishop, Mr. Tomlinson, whose ambition it is to set up a theocratic world government in Jerusalem. In preparation for this goal, the bishop makes trips to many countries, usually by plane, thus fulfilling the prophecy from Revelation 14:6: "And I saw another angel fly in the midst of heaven having the everlasting gospel to preach unto them that dwell on the earth, and to every nation, and kindred, and tongue, and people." He claims territory by crowning himself king of any country in an unassuming little ceremony on main streets and in market squares. A cheap tin crown, an inflatable world globe, a robe, and an ornamental folding lawnchair are his paraphernalia.

Nearly all sacramental acts call on the powers of the imagination to consider a thing as being itself as well as something else. Holy water is both water and a kind of spiritual liquid. Belief in transubstantiation requires that wine and a wafer be recognized as such, but also as blood and flesh of the body of Christ. To take a sacramental scroll out of an ark, where it is kept with a crown and other regalia of royalty, and to do it reverentially, demands some imagination, even when one knows rationally all the historical reasons for such adornments of a book.

It may be argued that the modern mind, shaped by science and a rational understanding of things that were formerly held to be mysteries, calls for unusually imaginative powers to maintain the idea of God. Long before Nietzsche's profound teaser about the death of God, the development of science and naturalism changed A/R ratios steadily into R/A ratios, in roughly the following progression:

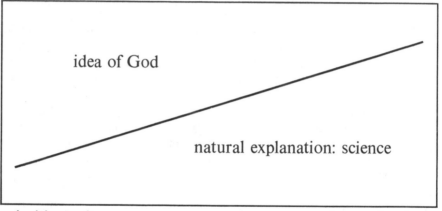

primitive culture
mythological thought

advanced culture
rational thought

As naturalistic explanations of nature increase, the usefulness of the idea of God decreases—that is, as *deus ex machina* for answering questions of the "How does it work?" and "What causes this?" type. Nietzsche's own objections to the idea of God were of a very different order. They took the form: "There is no God, for if God existed, how could I endure not being God?" This keen thought recognizes that God as such has always been a product of the imagination, and that one of his erstwhile functions was to check the boundless strivings toward omnipotence of man. He is a way of keeping men in their place, a ceiling beyond which they should not and indeed could not reach. Nietzsche's further thoughts on this theme changed the image of God into a desirable ideal toward which men could strive in a conscious synergy with nature—if they could only break the shackles of old-time religion and the ethical canons of a bourgeois society. God, a word now meaning "ideal man" in this context, is not yet, but is in the process of becoming. This idea also calls upon the imagination, in order to produce the image of an unfettered, always striving man who is no longer bothered by his own grandiosity, a man who has radically changed his own stature from the rather timid cultural product he has allowed himself to be.

The eclipse or the death of God, which is such a profound preoccupation among modern theological thinkers, presents an enormous challenge to the imagination of both believing and unbelieving people. After the latter ones have pronounced a casual "I told you so," they will have less need to protest. Now that their apologetics have been successful, the constructive part of their system must be shown. The former ones will also have to come up with a constructive thought and they cannot just look quizzically and say: "God is dead—my God!" The death of father gods in favor of a divine son or daughter is nothing new in the history of religion, and that theme has rarely caused a ripple in the flow of human events. All it calls for is what the French monarchists handled so well in their phrase: "Le roi est mort, vive le roi!" The demythologizers seem agreed that the traditional God-language and God-imagery have run their course to where they have become either pure nonsense or grossly misleading. But many of these men quickly substitute modern mythology for the old one, and go on talking as if God has changed his clothes, shaved off his beard, studied at Heidelberg, and started speaking modern German. That series of thoughts too is a product of the imagination, which is all the more remarkable since the imaginative process in this case was checked by a large amount of quite correct R/A thinking that took the seriously declined relevance of the idea of God fully into account. To redefine God as a "God behind the gods" handicaps the imagination a great deal because such a God is so unimaginable. One can hardly sway censers in front of him, and praying becomes a scholarly exercise rather than a heart's outpouring. Benedictions in the name of a Ground of Being can hardly be given with the hands raised up.

An interesting challenge to the religious imagination has come from the side of those who, with Bonhoeffer[24-25] advocate in a sense the abolition of all traditional God-images in favor of a new imaginative approach to problems of social ethics. In this view, "speaking of God" is a metaphor for doing the right thing in society by courageous acts and decisions. Clues to doing the right thing and opposing evil are found in the figure of the God-man Jesus—with the emphasis on his manhood—who was the divine incarnate precisely because of his unusual courage in meeting the challenges of his day, including the traditions of religion itself. The focus is here on Jesus-the-decision-maker, and the accent is on novelty and creativeness of response to the threats and opportunities of life in all its aspects. The imagination must in this context take the form of the creative surprise, which

Koestler[26] has defined as the bringing together of two seemingly incompatible or unrelated views which, at a specific "hookup" point, create an entirely new perspective from which new knowledge or guidelines may be generated. Bonhoeffer's own courageous responses to the proscriptions of the Nazi regime, though they cost him his life, are a case in point. The idea of a peaceful march on the town of Selma in Mississippi and the inventions of sit-ins or kneel-ins are products of a similarly guided imagination which chooses an act rather than a picture.

PRACTICING THE RELIGIOUS IMAGINATION

It has taken modern hospital psychiatry a considerable time to discover, or rediscover, that mental patients who are kept in the monotonous surroundings of bleak state hospital halls, with nothing to do but sit in rocking chairs lined up in a straight row on a brilliantly polished floor, will tend to indulge with increased tenacity in their morbid fantasies. It has long been a practical secret of police science that suspects can be made to lose their composure and even be brought to the madness of false confessions by depriving them for a long time of the intensity and variety of outside stimulation that everyday life provides. Alone in a cell with monotonous walls without view, on a routine diet of scarcity, with nothing to do, and exposed to the perpetual light of an electric bulb which suspends the rhythm of day and night, the prisoner's hold on reality weakens and primitive fantasies are activated. Unless he can keep himself busy with directed thoughts, e.g., posing mathematical puzzles to himself and solving them, trying to reiterate rote memory sequences, or mentally preparing speeches to the judge, he falls victim to the power of his wishes and longings. Repressions become undone and the fantasy surges to satisfy in reveries or daydreams the longings for security at all cost.

The atrocities of the Nazi regime, the practice of thought reform in communist prison camps, the struggles for survival in concentration camps, and the plight of inmates in large and impersonal institutions have been the subject of numerous psychological studies which confirm that the autonomy and intact functioning of the ego are the result of a dialectic of stimulus patterns received from the environment as well as from a person's own drives, in some balanced proportion. Rapaport[27] provided the basic theoretical scheme for the ego's autonomy in the following diagram:

ID in equilibrium with   EGO in equilibrium with   ENVIRONMENT

When the normal input of environmental stimuli is grossly altered or diminished, the system compensates, as it were, by an automatic arousal of id impulses to which the ego "gives ear." Conversely, repression of and control over such impulses result in part from environmental strictures and social support to the extent that these are perceptually or symbolically available to the individual. The psychoanalytic procedure of letting the person lie on a couch promotes free association precisely because the supine position relaxes the ego's watchfulness, diminishes external stimulus input, and thus renders the ego more receptive to the internal stimuli from drives and drive derivatives such as wishes. "Total institutionalization," as Goffman[28] calls the situation of inmates of prisons and patients in large and highly regimented hospitals, deprives the individual of the supports of his identity that used to come from group associations and sexual role opportunities. Prisoners or patients become infantilized by the administrative routines of the institution, which assumes an intangible and oppressive presence like that of the castle and the court in Kafka's symbolic novels.

Religious practices in past and present have included the use of sensory deprivation and environmental manipulation in order to quicken the imagination and guide it into desired channels. "Thought control" is a fighting phrase which one tends to reserve for the practices of one's ideological enemies, but in a neutral sense it describes organized procedures for training people in any ideology. Beginning with the Syrian desert fathers, many Christian believers have sought a solitary existence as hermits or otherwise in a grossly simplified and asocial environment, in order to enliven their imagination toward a more experiential grasp of the truth they pursued. In the course of these pursuits, their imagination has sometimes bordered on hallucinatory and delusional states, which is not at all surprising in view of their self-imposed deprivations.

Loyola's *Spiritual Exercises*[29] are a form of religious thought control which make a very deliberate use of the imagination. In certain phases of the systematic "meditations," as they are called, the retreat master urges the retreatant to imagine as vividly as possible the excruciating sufferings of Jesus at the various stages of the cross, to identify himself with the agonies of his Lord to the point of sweating, sighing, or moaning, and to "live" for a time in these almost hallucinatory stages.[30] In the first prelude of the *compositio* he is exhorted to see with the eye of imagination the length, breadth, and depth of hell; to pray that he may feel deeply the pain suffered by the damned; to see the mass of fire; to hear the crying, shriekings, and weepings of the tortured souls and the curses they hurl at Christ and his angels; to smell the stench of rotting dirt and the smoke of sulfur.

The novitiate in various Catholic orders is so structured as to minimize the individual's sense of identity (former civil identity, that is) in order that his thought and being might be transformed into the ideal of the monastic calling. Though practices vary from one order to another there are some common features. The cell to which the novice is allocated is usually extremely simple, with bare walls, no rugs, no ornaments, and only a bed or cot, a desk, and a chair. It is quiet, and the one who lives in it is supposed to maintain silence. A crucifix or a religious picture may be on the wall—hardly as decoration, however, but as a focus for meditation. In an initiation ceremony he is stripped of civilian clothing, and dressed in the uniform monk's garb. Visits with family are to be very infrequent, as are writing and receiving letters. Hardly any personal property, which is in ordinary life such an important instrument for assuring oneself of his identity, is allowed. There are reduced or simplified sensory stimulation on one hand, and guided meditation of focused thoughts on the other. Safeguards are erected against thought becoming too rational or logical, as there are safeguards against free association. The process is one of disciplined imagination, produced by environmental manipulation and social regimentation. The literature on contemplative mysticism within the Roman Catholic tradition stresses the precarious balance that is to be achieved between looseness of thought and hyperrationality of thinking, between wild fantasy and pure logic, between the pitfalls of hallucination and the dryness of rationalism. If a successful vivacity of imaginative thought is achieved in the contemplative life, the mystic is prone to attribute his insightful state to a special infusion of divine grace.

The postures assumed in prayer and the settings in which prayer is sought may follow the same general features of stimulus simplification in order to enhance an imaginative form of thought. The eyes are kept closed; the hands are folded so as not to engage in any distracting touch stimulus or activity; the posture of kneeling may become an effortless leaning on something, and a few overlearned and perhaps mechanical opening phrases set in motion a train of thought in which wishes, self-accusations, confessions, or promises come easily, with great spontaneity. Speaking softly, or not speaking at all but just "thinking the thoughts" as they come, pry the ideas loose from verbal forms, which further enhances the imaginative process. As a matter of fact, in praying one sometimes "finds oneself talking or thinking" to his own surprise.

But the imagination can also be lit or fired by judiciously offered external stimuli whose purpose it is to stir the mind to a particular stream of thoughts or to a particular image. All forms of art can serve this function, and it is therefore not surprising that houses of worship are often designed or adorned so as to lead the vision or the ear to a particular idea. Altars, backdrops, paintings, and oranaments "draw" the eyes in their direction and stimulate the mind to elaborate a theme or motif. Music can do the same, particularly the thematic or programmatic music of masters such as Bach, whose compositions have an almost pictorial quality, imitative of just those "scenes" that are also important in Loyola's spiritual exercises: sadness, joy, bewilderment, tenderness, compassion, contriteness, as well as the rhythms of processions, whiplashings, mournful sobbing, or ecstatic dancelike jubilations.

An even clearer use of external stimulus arrangement to promote imaginative thought is the religious drama, from grand passion plays by professionals to a humble role-playing by a few children in a church school. I believe that precisely on this point and all the associated processes of stimulus patterning the Puritan forms of Protestantism and the Roman Catholic and Greek Orthodox forms of worship show a sharp cleavage of opinion and method. The whitewashed walls of the Puritan churches, unadorned, with nothing distracting, can be seen as an approach to stimulus minimization through which the individual worshiper might find his feelings and imagination enhanced. Or at least it might help him to become a better receiver of the one stimulus provided: the Word. In the richly adorned buildings of the Catholic traditions, with the abundant visual and auditory stimuli, the process of the imagination is approached from the other side: by maximizing the stimulus input and guiding the fantasy through many motifs at once. In Catholicism, worship is drama; in Puritanism, it is obedient hearing.

In this assessment of intellectual processes in religion we have found that religious persons do not primarily think of special topics, but they think sometimes in special terms about many ordinary things. The critical issue is whether thinking in religious perspective broadens or narrows the scope of a person's thoughts, dulls or sharpens his wits, and arrives at meaningful questions. We saw the powerful role of memory in conserving cherished early impressions of safety and security. We found that the store of religious knowledge is on the one hand influenced by a person's exposure to selected items of historical and doctrinal knowledge, but on the other hand affected by learning blocks which may at times produce a feigned dumbness in matters of religious concern.

In religion as elsewhere, reality-tested thinking and autistic thought occur in various combinations. Active use of the imagination is noteworthy in the images of gods, and in the many changes which occur in these over time; yet, many of these images retain traces of actual perceptions and naturalistic observation. Paradoxically, when god-images are entrenched in the culture, it takes imagination to ponder alternative possibilities, such as a God-is-dead theology or an atheistic conception of the universe.

Among the many intellectual processes which play a role in religious experience, thought merits and allows a special clinical analysis of its organization, which is now to be pursued.

IV

Thought Organization
in Religion

IN THE Thematic Apperception Test, widely used by clinicians for diagnostic studies, a person is presented with a series of pictures most of which depict life situations involving one or more persons. They are somewhat ambiguous so that each picture can be interpreted in many different ways. The assigned task is to narrate a little story for each picture, possibly developing a plot that the picture portrays. One of the pictures is a black surface of about six by six inches, within the left half of which is a sharp cutout in white suggesting a window opening in which a human figure stands leaning with one arm against the window jamb. The entire picture is a silhouette in stark black and white.

From seven clergymen, all with advanced theological training beyond the Bachelor of Divinity level, I obtained the following stories to fit this picture:

A. This is a picture of a small boy in a darkened room, looking out . . . it is night time, but there seems to be a fairly strong moon. He is looking at the stars wondering what makes them tick, and what makes them work, and who put them there . . . and what do they have to do with him. His attitude is one of curiosity and interest, wonderment, even awe. They seem so very far away and yet so very close to him . . . he feels like there must be some connection between them and him, but he is not sure . . . and he is looking for hope of understanding.

B. I was going to say this is perhaps a burglary of some kind. He probably got in through the window.

C. A simple black and white painting about a well-known poem: "Out I have to go, for here it is so narrow and my mind is so restricted. And I wonder what I will see at the other side of the mountains." It is the desire of every man in my country to see the world, as a sailor, or as a student.

D. Jim was the kind of person who was not afraid to be alone. Alone with

74

his own thoughts, alone with his own ideals, alone with his own dreams. One of his favorite diversions was after a day at work, especially in the summer months, simply to return to his home and to sit on the window sill and to look out at the peace, calm, the quiet around him. He found that at these times he could gather his own thoughts, he could make his own plans, he could direct his own life in a calm and quiet and orderly way.

E. Jim Boden was a young man with a great many aspirations. At night, after the others in his home had turned out their lights and gone to bed, he would often stand by the open windows, looking up at the vast distances before him and the beckoning lights across the sky. One night as he stood at the window as usual, he determined he would leave his home and attempt to find a new life for himself in some distant place.

F. This is a young boy looking out the window of his room, looking up at the stars. For the moment he is lost in contemplation of the wonder and beauty of the stars, but he is also dreaming, or soon will be dreaming of his own future. He thinks whether he would like to be a space pilot going out into the great vastness of space, but he dismisses this and thinks more of how he would like to be of some help to people, and this time he feels some sense of the wonder and mystery of God and feels some deep stirrings in himself to want to be in a closer relationship to God, and to want to give himself to some kind of service for God. He has these thoughts, but mainly he enjoys the wonder and beauty of this evening, looking out at the stars, just letting it sink in.

G. This is a young fellow who stood here at this window ten years ago, looking out at the aircraft flying by. It is his home in the city and when he was still in his teens he dreamt of being a great aviator. And today he got into aviation, and he did make a big success of himself: he had a lot of trouble, he was in danger frequently because he did a lot of test flying of new aircraft. However, he still is a young man in his late twenties. He has become the head of the design division of the firm for which he had tested aircraft, or an important engineer, head of the engineering division. Here he is able, though he is so valuable to the company that they will not let him test fly any more. He still stands at the window and admires the craft that are being tested by younger men than himself.

There is an obvious diversity in these seven views of one scene. Some of the stories are rich in detail and imaginative; others are very meager. Some are global and diffuse; others are articulate. Some are poetic or almost mystical; others are pedestrian and commonplace. In some the thought process is highly organized from the start; in others it glides along fairly loosely, *ad hoc,* from thought to thought. Some are quite symbolic; others are factual or operational.

These considerations bring up an important problem which the psychology of religion cannot avoid: the organization of thought in the religious pursuit. In *The Future of an Illusion,*[1] Freud noted sharply what others before him and after him had observed: that the status of religious assertions, creedal formulations, doctrines, and dogmas is cognitively somewhat odd in that they carry an authoritativeness that seems indefensible on the ground of reason. One cannot justify or check the validity of this authority by extraneous criteria. It is an inherent part of the system of thought, and it is taught along with the texts of the formulations. A stock-in-trade example is the various proofs that have been advanced for the existence of God. One can raise all kinds of questions about such proofs. If God's existence is logically proven, does not that turn him into a mere concept? If "proving" is a scientific procedure, is it appropriate to borrow the methods of science for a nonscientific quest? Are not all classical proofs tautologies? Why is it necessary or desirable to prove God's existence at all? And what would be the nature of the "proven" existence anyway—is it a thing, a process, a possibility, a bright idea, or a satisfying notion? Or are we merely talking metaphorically or analogically, in the manner of "x is to the earth as a manufacturer is to his product" or "x is to men as a father is to his children" or "x is to beings what a species is to its members"? And so, since there must be an x, we call it God, as an indication of "there's something there" and it should have a name. Is not religion complete with all its peculiar terminology a language game, just like economics, mathematics, art, or science? Is it a secret or artificial language in which to talk about ordinary things? Is religion entirely a fictional system, like stamp collecting or children's play money?

Before these questions can be answered or even approached, it would behoove us to sketch in broad outlines the major dimensions of thought organization with which clinicians are confronted when they have to make an appraisal of a person's mode or style of thought. I will essay to do this with the help of a model that has given rise to an immensely useful clinical test: the sorting test.[2] The materials of this test consist of about thirty items, all very trite and simple, such as eating utensils, a few household tools such as a screwdriver, a pair of pliers, nails, smoking articles such as a cigarette, cigar, and pipe, a few cardboard forms such as a square, a circle, and a file-card, a lock and key, a rubber sinkstopper, a ball, a bicycle bell, etc. A few of these items are duplicated in toy version such as a tiny fork, knife, and spoon, some toy tools from a toddler's carpentry set, and an imitation cigar and cigarette. The articles are made of various materials: metal, wood, paper, rubber, etc. The articles have different colors and sizes. The task is twofold. First the articles are spread out in random order in front of the subject, who is asked to pick up one article and place it away from the "heap" in a clear section of his table. He is then asked to "put with that everything that belongs with it." When the subject has made his sorting, i.e., when he has established some class or category by practically putting some things together, he is asked why these things belong together. In other words, he must verbalize or give a rationale for the sorting that he has made. In a second part of the test he is presented with some groupings of objects arranged by the examiner, who asks why all these belong together. He is again to verbalize, but this time he must search for a concept which encompasses exactly all the items of the selection in front of him.

Obviously such a test (which can be endlessly varied) allows one to see how a person "chops up" his universe (or at least a sample of it) and by what criteria he establishes groups of belongingness, likeness, relevance, internal consistency, identity, etc. Something about the scope and manner of his thought organization becomes explicit, together with his verbal justification of what he is doing. Moreover, he categorizes actively by "doing" as well as passively by searching for a principle of coherence in selections offered to him.

One of the tested dimensions of a person's thought is the *span* of his groupings. Faced with the random heap of things, which items is he to select and consolidate into a group? Indeed, faced with the chaotic manifold of the world, what is a man to select so as to establish some order in the chaos and "grasp" it? How broad or how narrow shall he be? What can be lumped together? In terms of the test: one can pick out the fork, knife, and spoon and say "eating utensils," but is he to stop there or be liberal enough to include the toy fork, knife, and spoon also? Excluding the latter amounts to a finicky differentiation between "adults' eating utensils" and "children's eating utensils" or between "real eating gear" and "toy (i.e., imitation) eating gear." Could one add the cardboard disk and broaden the idea of eating utensils to include a dish (simulated by the disk)? That would be rather loose, and a little too playful or imaginary. Should one put a cigarette on the dish (i.e., disk) and declare the whole group to be an after-dinner scene? That would be even looser, dangerously loose indeed, for the class concept of "eating utensils" has now moved to the borderlands of fable. And if one would also add the filecard, imagining it as a "menu," conceptual reasoning has given way to fabulation, in which some things are made to be what they manifestly are not. Conversely, one could decide to put only the spoon and fork together, excluding the knife, and end up with a very narrow span. This may be engendered by a fear of knives which puts sharp cutting things in a class by itself on purely emotional grounds and artificially narrows the class of "eating utensils."

Span is an important dimension of religious thinking also. The span of some religious thinkers is enormously broad—it includes everything in the heap from people to stars to iron ore as "creation" or "the world" or "He made it." For others it is narrow, such as church buildings and a handful of worshipers at specified hours of the week, under the heading "piety." For some the span includes only the things that seem orderly or pleasant: lovely woods, vales with sheep grazing, but not storms at sea or a forest fire. Or it includes birth, marriage, childbearing, and death, but not the events between. It may include health and vigor, but not sickness or death. It may reach to embrace all things good: peace, productivity, harmony, loveliness, and clean things; but cataclysms, wars, or sex are the unfortunate mistakes in the perfect order for which the embrace should not reach. The span of "religion" may be worshiping, praying, or going through certain rituals and stop there; or it may spread to include relations between parents and children, basic rules of commerce, and suggestions for "kosher" food as distinct from edibles that should not be used. Some will include politics; others will vigorously exclude it.

It is evident that span goes hand in hand with level of concept. The more inclusive the span, the higher the level of the concept. Narrow spans can do with lower orders of abstraction. "Eating utensils" is of lower order than "after-dinner scene." The whole heap of objects altogether under the heading of "things" is of very high order as compared to the modesty of "paper articles" composed of some cardboard disks, a filecard, and a cigarette. But one could still argue whether the cigarette should be included since it is not only paper, but paper rolled around tobacco.

The idea of conceptual levels, perhaps imagined after the manner of a ladder with rungs, broad at the base and narrower at the top, has its own complexity. If apples, oranges, and bananas, are abstracted into a concept of "fruit," one has moved a few rungs up the abstraction ladder from the perceptual manifold at its base. But the botanist would probably go up a few more rungs for his concept of "fruit," and the grocer would go down several rungs because some of his fruits are vegetables, e.g., squashes and pumpkins and beans, which to him constitute an altogether different class. It all depends on the *realm of discourse* in which one chooses to function, and that may include some very utilitarian considerations. What the proper level of abstraction for any class concept is depends on good taste, usage, consensual validation, and the purposes for which one coins the concept. If one rises very high on the abstraction ladder one makes very broad and inclusive concepts such as "nature" or "objects," "good" or "evil." These are hardly class concepts, for they include so much that the "heap" remains a heap, too chaotic to grasp. At the very top of the ladder one is left with extremely broad dualities such as subject and object, being and nonbeing, mind and matter, God and creation. Above these is unity, the All, God, and the ineffable. It is the ultimate aim of mysticism to overcome the last dualities and to reach unity in merger with the All or God. But it is evident that in such a unity all knowing and speaking would disappear, and it is no surprise therefore that reports about mystical union, being a retroactive account of an ecstatic condition, are always to some degree below the level of unity. Otto once made the shrewd remark that mystics are always wordy, even when they want to convey the sublime silence they claim to have experienced.[3] They have to talk in circles about the ineffable. Talking and knowing can occur only below the level of unity.

In the object-sorting test, things can be brought together in many different ways. Good, consensually validated concepts tend to be of the "eating utensils," "tools," "toys," or "smoking articles" type. But one can cut across such classes by ordering things in terms of their color, grouping a red piece of paper, a toy hammer with a red handle, and a red rubber sinkstopper together, and designating them as "red things." Or one can focus on the material of which things are made, selecting the table silver, the bicycle bell, and some of the tools under the rubric "metal objects." One could group things according to size, length, weight, or glossiness; one could even take softness or hardness of material as a criterion. As long as the verbalization of one's principle is in perfect accordance with one's actual selections, these groupings are defensible and rational. Yet the reader may have noticed that some principles of selection seem to be natural and that others tend to be somewhat spurious, or artificial. The word "natural" in this context is difficult to define. We find it natural that people will use the drawers of their commodes for linens and the open shelves in their studies for books. But one could defend using the open shelves for linens and the drawers for books, no matter how odd this is in the judgment of most citizens. Actually, many young children organize their rooms in just this way, which is taken as a sign that they still must learn "order." And many scientific concepts, even in the natural sciences, are of an artificial rather than a natural order. The word "natural" seems to have here a connotation of artlessness and simplicity of good fit to the world of perception and action; it hints at common sense and unreflected self-evidence. Artificial groupings are less self-evident. They require some distance from naïve perception and some distance from action; they imply a reflective attitude and an analytical set.

In religious thought one can find ample use of both natural and artificial ways of grouping or concept formation. Let me illustrate this by a comparison of a fragment of the commentaries on Paul's letter to the Romans by two German-speaking theologians, Luther and Barth:

Text: Romans 8:24-25. For in this hope we were saved. Now hope that is seen is not hope. For who hopes for what he sees? But if we hope for what we do not see, we wait for it with patience.

LUTHER	*BARTH*
Grammatically, this way of speaking may be figurative, yet, theologically understood, it expresses a most intense feeling in a most direct and telling way. For it is ever so that	Harsh and holy and powerful is the Truth; so also is our salvation; so also is God Himself on our behalf. The victory and fulfillment and presence of the Truth is ours only

LUTHER

when the hope that rises from the longing for a beloved object is delayed, love is made all the greater. And thus what is hoped for and the hoping person become one through tense hoping, or as Blessed Augustine puts it: *"Anima plus est, ubi amat, quam ubi animat."* ("The soul is more where it loves than where it lives.") In the same way, we say in common speech: My flame is here! And the poet says: "You are my flame, Amyntas."[4]

BARTH

by hope. The Truth would not be Truth, if we, as we are, could apprehend it directly. How could the Truth be God, if it were for us but one possibility among others? How could we be saved by it, if it did not with compelling power urge us to hazard the leap into eternity, to dare to think what God thinks, to think freely, to think anew, and to think wholly?[5]

I imply here that Luther's passage uses more natural thought categories than Barth's: it takes hoping in an ordinary sense as longing for something, and describes a common experience that is embedded in proverbs, poetry, and daily language. By comparison, Barth's categories seem at first blush far removed from the hoping of everyday life; he dares to describe salvation as harsh, which is a total reversal of the sweetness which common sense ascribes to it. He makes the word "Truth" something very special, and goes on to place it beyond direct apprehension. From Luther's "flame of hope" to Barth's "leap of hope" a vast transposition of categories and images has taken place, a shift from natural to artificial concepts.

Such differences also occur at lower levels of abstraction and in less articulate formulations. In the Bible Belt, the word "religion" suggests praying and Sunday Schools, perhaps abstinence from alcohol, and certainly the elimination of swearing, foul language, and sexual exhibitionism. In the East Harlem Protestant Parish, however, it may suggest legal aid to evicted tenants, organizing protest marches, mobilizing voters in political campaigns, or discussions with social workers. Religiously, the world can be "chopped up" in many different ways, both at high and at low abstraction levels. In a large sector of American Protestantism, Sallman's picture of a blond, bearded Jesus is the principal criterion for all divisions to be made. In the Pentecostal communities, the gifts of prophecy and speaking in tongues are favored as points of demarcation. In the Reformed tradition, decency, order, decorum, and scholarliness were such basic values that they led to the natural conception of a quasi-royal deity of great dignity and the highly artificial concept of double predestination. The concept of God as Father seems quite natural and of rather low order of abstraction; the concept of God as Lord of Hosts is again rather natural, but at a higher abstraction level; the concept of God as Ground of Being is both artificial and at a very high abstraction level.

Good concept formation, in religion as anywhere else, demands congruence between one's actual sortings and one's verbal statements about these sortings. The sorting is the referent of the verbal formulation. Conversely, the verbal formulation should properly cover the content of the sorting made and leave nothing in the unassorted heap that belongs in the selection made. If a subject groups red things together, but leaves a few more red items in the heap out of sloppiness or concern over the secondary qualities of some red items, he leaves himself open to objections. His groups have unclear or shifting boundaries, and so have his concepts. There is a measure of arbitrariness in his thinking. Many religious questions about morals are engendered by unclear concepts, especially on issues requiring censorship or sanctions. One may define casuistry as the art of settling individual or unique cases of conscience within the larger framework of imprecise conceptual boundaries of right and wrong. When is a movie or a book obscene? Should members of a certain sect attend movies at all? If a qualified positive answer is given, should they only see religious movies? If so, what is a religious movie? Unclear conceptual boundaries are conspicuous in the religious approach to the question of birth control also. At what point can one really speak of killing or thwarting life, anywhere between fertilized ovum and fetus? What are the differences in principle between mechanical or chemical forms of birth control, self-imposed sexual abstinence or use of the rhythm method, and hoping that an abortive accident will happen? Casuistry is itself refined enough to introduce multiple criteria for allocating a case to the "good" or the "bad" group. It can go by positive law, by written statements available in adopted legal codes. But it can also bring in the idea of intention, which assumes a difference between thought and act. It can also bring in the pedagogical criterion: if the case at hand is condoned, the floodgates are opened and "everyone will do it."

A large amount of religious thought and literature is addressed precisely to the questions we are struggling with. How sharp or fluid should the boundaries of religiously relevant concepts be? How incisive are the divisions they make within reality? Should a certain amount of ambiguity be tolerated, perhaps even fostered? Religious persuasions and systems have answered these questions in different ways. To fundamentalists, the Bible is God's word, pure and simple. To quite a few people, sin is cardplaying, drinking, fornicating, lying, stealing, and killing, all in clean-cut situational precision. Law is law, and one can look it up in the Ten Commandments, or in the Deuteronomic scriptures. In Christian Science, the body is metaphysically unreal, and therefore diseases cannot exist. In totemic societies, transgressing on the territory of totems is a grave offense, even when it happens accidentally. In some groups, salvation comes about through a conversion experience that has definite earmarks: falling to the ground with foam on the mouth, speaking in tongues, or reporting a vision. In some faith-healing cults, the idea of demon possession has become so concretely itemized that one counts the number of demons one "has" and gives them a name, and in successful exorcisms they are separately exorcized, one after the other. Sometimes they are being "sent out" to a specific country, far across the border. Heaven holds the saints, and hell the damned, with somebody making a clear choice—there are no gradations or dubious cases. Serving meat from milk dishes or vice versa is a definite transgression of ritual prescriptions, under all circumstances. Eating meat on Friday until recently was just impossible.

All these examples show concepts with definite boundaries which allow a clear application and very little ambiguity. Cognitively, they make sharp distinctions; morally, they foster definite rules. They work, within a given religious system, which is no surprise because they are parts of the whole. But they begin to fail when new viewpoints enter from outside the system. In the writing of Old Testament prophets and again in the religion of Jesus one finds attempts to expose the inadequacies of the system by demonstrating that religious concepts should *not* have the clear and fixed boundaries which people claim for them. Why? Because concepts (and rules derived from them) should serve man. Concepts must be appropriate to man's purposes. The first step in loosening up definite religious concepts is to introduce a distinction between thought and deed, intention and act. The next step is to find borderline situations in which the firm distinctions and rules seem to break down. These are, of course, situations of conflict, crisis, or extraordinary complexity. The third step is an explicit acknowledgment that life is full of contradictions and tensions and that the boundaries of religious concepts (like all other concepts dealing with man-as-he-lives) must have enough flexibility or apposite fuzziness to fit the built-in ambiguities of life itself. Sometimes a fourth step is taken: wallowing in ambiguities, losing all conceptual boundaries and finding hardly any order. But that is a form of cognitive anarchy which is hardly teachable and barely writable, so that it stands little chance of being culturally transmitted.

A classical example of a sophisticated blurring of conceptual boundaries is the book of Jonah. God sent the prophet to announce the destruction of Nineveh and at long last, when Jonah had incorporated the idea of divine wrath and its unerring consequences for the city's inhabitants, God repented and spared the city. "But it displeased Jonah exceedingly, and he was angry." He was suddenly faced with the fact that the dynamics of love may overrule the strictures of morality, and his conceptual world came tumbling down. Many of the sayings of Jesus are of the same order, for instance when he silenced the Pharisees by asking: "Which of you, having an ass or an ox that has fallen into a well, will not immediately pull him out on a Sabbath day?" Such thoughts comprise rules as well as their exceptions under one single heading: concern, care, helpfulness, or love. Luther accentuated the differences between static and dynamic concepts by his dialectic of law and gospel. Calvin did it by a juggler's game of concepts which ended up in the exceedingly tense doctrine of double predestination. Kierkegaard could introduce his version of a dynamic Christianity only by an "Attack upon Christendom." All dialectical thinking is a process of alternately sharpening and loosening the boundaries of concepts. Moral variants of sophisticated blurring of conceptual boundaries can be found in the modern trend toward situational ethics and in Simone de Beauvoir's book *The Ethics of Ambiguity*.[6]

We are now ready to see that religious concept formation allows for a variety of types of thought organization. The categories which it imposes on the chaotic manifold of reality in order to create order can be natural as well as artificial. The concepts which are used can be static, with fixed boundaries and realms, but also dynamic, with the mobile edges and boundaries that one can see in the variable patterns of an electromagnetic field.

DISPARATE CONCEPT FORMATIONS

During the administration of a sorting test it happens occasionally that a person produces a clear and cohesive group of objects, but defines it in ways that are not commensurate with his sorting. The formulation may sound articulate and conceptual enough, but it does not pertain to the actual assortment of objects. For instance, a person may say, "These are all toys" for a sorting consisting of a paper disk, a filecard, and a cardboard cutout. "Toys" is a good concept, and so is "paper articles." But the two do not match; there is a disparity between the actual sorting (i.e., the way in which the person chops up his universe) and his verbal grasp or designation of it.

Such disparate conceptions, in which two realms are brought together, one practically and the other verbally, occur at times in religious thought. A rather trite example of it is the idea of the "Christian gentleman," which suggests a practical sorting (gentleman) that divides the nice, good, or well-behaved people from dishonorable persons and then borrows, from an entirely different realm of discourse, a term (Christian) which makes an essentially different grouping. Christian ideology and literature have much to say about men and women, but are oblivious of the British civil idea of the gentleman. Civil codes and mores may have much to say about polite behavior and desirable manners, but they are oblivious of the ideas of sin and salvation that adhere to the idea of the Christian man. Disparities of this sort between a verbalized thought and a practical referent are seen very frequently in political discourses. They are encountered quite regularly among white American middle-class Protestants who assume that their way of life can be described as the Christian way. Members of such groups will describe their life goals, mores, or preferences with practical references to their friends or business associates, hinting at their playing golf together and voting for the same political party, giving vent to their support of the PTA or their admiration for the FBI, and then formulate all these references as the "Christian way of life," unaware of their having slipped from one category to another.

Once, while I was driving a long stretch through dull country, I heard a radio preacher addressing himself with great vigor to the text of John 14:2: "In my Father's house are many mansions." He was infuriated at the "cheapskates" who wrote the Revised Standard Version of the Bible, in which this text is rendered: "In my Father's house are many rooms." The essence of his sermon was that since he was promised a mansion by the King James Version, he was not inclined to settle for just one room! His concepts were perfectly rational and he described masterfully the differences between mansions and rooms, fully appreciative of the differences in social status and other gratifications that one or the other might confer. But he had no awareness of the essentially different category of thought suggested by the metaphor, which proposes the idea of family-type living arrangements rather than architectural niceties.

The recent debate about the school prayer decision by the Supreme Court gives other examples of false concept formation due to mixing two different realms. The court upheld the differences between Church and State in deciding that no pupil in a public school can be forced to attend prayer. In the babel of tongues following this decision it appeared that many persons and groups became a babel unto themselves, as it were, mixing categories from disparate conceptual systems and different realms of discourse. Public schools are respectable institutions which aim at promoting an intelligent, inquiring, morally sensitive, and loyal citizenry. Praying is a respectable activity which may help some people in becoming morally sensitive and loyal—but not as citizens of a country; the act serves a purpose in the relations between man and his deities. But to some people, praying serves globally the same purposes as the character-building which they expect, rightly or mistakenly, from the public schools, and therefore prayer is both an instrument for and a proof of the morality of public schools. Little do they, who so reason, realize that their formulated concepts, however sharp they may be, do not match their referents. Public morality, however defined, is one thing; praying, however defined, practiced, or advocated, is quite another thing. The two are like different grids pressed into the substance of experience: while each grid has mesh and holes, the patterns which they cut in the mass of reality are different in each case.

Theologians of the Bultmann school, who advocate demythologizing the various messages of the New Testament in order better to serve the task of the churches, have put their finger on the problem we are dealing with. Though they formulate it in terms of mythology (which we will discuss later) and wonder how they might strip their proclamation of the misleading archaisms suggested by New Testament imagery, some of their arguments sound like a protest against the fallacies of disparate concept usage. When biblical cosmology speaks of a celestial domain "above the clouds" and a subterranean domain "down there in the underworld" with the poor earth squeezed between and subject to perpetual intrusions from either side, the problem is not merely that the concepts of "heaven" and "hell" are too archaic and mythical to today's sophisticated minds. They just do not match with heavenly or hellish aspects of the modern world, nor with the kind of extrapolations people tend to make from their experiences of delight or anguish. These are no longer imagined as celestial or volcanic; they are no longer projected into space. Belief in some impending judgment is no longer likely to elicit visions of Jesus Christ sitting on the edge of a mighty cloud formation. It is prone to take the form of some people's making earnest efforts to promote dynamic social changes and ideological innovations, leaving others behind in perplexity or opposition. The children of light will continue to battle with the children of darkness, as before, but the metaphors of light and darkness have worn thin. Enlightenment or obscurantism, progression or stagnation, dynamic or static conceptions, are more likely to be the polarizations of today's world. Old myths will die when new myths are born, and poor myths may be fought with better myths. But such improvements stay within the mythological circle. In comparing mythological cosmologies of old with modern scientific cosmologies, one steps out of the circle into an entirely different conceptual system with essentially different referents in reality. But one cannot use the conceptual language of one system to denote the referents of the other without falling prey to disparate concept formation.

Inadequate matching of conceptual formulations and referent groupings frequently occurs in debates about miracles. To scientists and rationalists, miracles simply do not happen. Stunning things may occur, and intriguing events may be observed, but these are not miracles. The Dutch scientist Simon Stevin (1548–1620) expressed this attitude very well in his phrase: "miracle is no miracle." A miracle that happens is no miracle; it can either be explained by natural laws, or it is a challenging puzzle that awaits such explanation. But for some religious people, belief in miracles is the very fabric of their thoughts. For many others who are neither avowed scientists nor avowed believers in miracles, the miraculous is an occasional odd event that they are willing to attribute to divine intervention while at the same time asserting a naturalistic view of the universe. Such persons are prone to mix categories by trying to advance poorly working, quasi-scientific arguments in support of their belief in miracles. A case in point that has generated much discussion for ages stems from the Christian doctrine of the incarnation. If one is interested in how such a strange event might have occurred or what its mechanism might have been, one places himself automatically out-side the circle which takes the proposition seriously. Inside that circle, however, one can use reasoning in order to elucidate some of its implications, which are then equally doctrinal assertions, or speculations that may become doctrine. For instance, one subsequent step in the doctrinal rationalization process about the incarnation was the assertion of the virgin birth of Jesus, or more properly the assertion of Mary's virginal conception of Jesus. The next step was to speculate, and then to assert, that Mary's own conception must have been an immaculate event, for only a vessel "free from the taint of original sin" could be worthy of receiving the pre-existing Word of God. This form of reasoning is at least loyal to the basic premises of miracle belief and supernatural intervention. However, the doctrinal asser-tions are sometimes defended by plausibility reasoning which borrows from the biological possibility of parthenogenesis known in certain insects. In that case the argument really deadens miracle belief, for it has switched to an entirely different conceptual system. Biology divides reality in its way; theology does it differently, and the myth-forming capacity of man does it still differently. Each discipline has its own practical divisions and coins its own conceptual formulations. The formulae and the referents must be taken from the same system.

System-switching occurs frequently with such prestigious words as *sin* or *sickness, holy* and *whole, healing* and *forgiving,* particularly when the etymology of these words suggests some common root in an ancient tongue. When common archaic roots give rise to diverse terms in subsequent devel-opment it is a sign of conceptual progress. Therefore, arguing back from diverse terms to a common root in the past is often asking for confusion; at best it is pointing to a unity that once existed but for good reasons no longer prevails. If sin and sickness were once one, the unitary x of the past was handled by priest-healers or shamans who knew very little about pharmacology and surgery, sepsis, and modern theology.

In the meantime, with or without awareness of common linguistic ances-try, such a word as "sin" can assume the strangest referents, from traffic violations to telling a lie, and from cocktails to chicken pox. What is entirely lost sight of in such contexts is the metaphorical use of the word at best, and the neglect of the correlative concepts of the word at worst. "Sin" is a theological word that can only be apprehended in the dyad of grace and sin. Traffic violations form a dyad with fines; telling a lie is a part of saving face; cocktails make connections with gustatory pleasures or stomach ulcers, and chicken pox has to do with skin eruptions and contagious disease. "Holy" is an attribute of numinous power that occurs in the context of worshiping, praying, and ritual; "whole" is a structural concept signifying a configuration of parts, which may be wholes to their parts, ad infinitum, upward and downward. "Sickness" is a more fluid concept which requires patienthood as a correlative term, and a patient-doctor relation for context.

After noting these many instances of disparate concept formations the question remains why they occur so frequently in religious thinking. Is religious thought conspicuously sloppy? Does it lack logical discipline? Is it anti-intellectual? Certainly, it sometimes shows all of these. But many of its more articulate spokesmen are highly aware of these dangers and have worked hard on perfecting the instrument of thought through courses in logic and epistemology, much as scientists venerate their courses in method and statistics. The reasons must lie deeper. Two thoughts are suggested. One is that religious conceptions do not stand in cognitive isolation but occur in the fabric of religious activities such as worship, prayer, or mystical experiences. In thinking and talking about one's objects of worship a certain amount of exaltation and a sense of plenitude will rub off on the concepts themselves and give the thoughts a great deal of acuteness and pertinence. Moreover, if religion stems from an awareness of one's contingency upon nature or the universe, any explanation of that contingency will have to deal with the idea of the noncontingent, which, however it be called, is more absolute, more ultimate, and more original. And as soon as one arrives at that point it is easy to slip from a playful assumption or a serious hypothesis into an ontology, in which the object of worship is declared to be the really real, on which all else hinges. In this way, religious conceptions tend to absorb other conceptual domains, and to be impatient with the viability and autonomy of different perspectives. They tend to subdue other points of view or relegate them to a less serious status.

The other thought is Freud's. "The matured stock of religious ideas"[7] which culture transmits (i.e., dogmas) have an aura of authority that transcends the degree of certainty with which one draws inferences from one's own experiences. They claim belief and posit themselves with inherent strength. Where does such extravagant strength come from? The answer is that religious dogmas are illusions, i.e., "fulfillments of the oldest, strongest and most insistent wishes of mankind; the secret of their strength is the strength of these wishes."

FUNCTIONAL DEFINITIONS

When on the sorting test a person selects from the "heap" a pair of pliers, a toy hammer, and a screwdriver and formulates this grouping as "tools," he puts in a generic term the essential common content of these three articles. This is an advanced form of abstraction which requires some perceptual and motor detachment from the objects so that pure cognition may occur which sorts out the essential from the accidental features of the objects and brings their essence under one common denominator. But not all conceptual thinking is so pure and detached. Some thinking is much closer to the motor system, entwined with movements and actions. It is a "thinking with the fingertips," a "thinking while doing" which is characteristic of young children. When it occurs in adults it shows the predominance of impulse over reflection. In our example, the abstract formulation "tools" then gives way to a functional definition such as "you can do carpenter's work with them" or "they are all used in repairing things."

Since life requires much action, functional concepts abound in everyday language, and one may say that a good deal of our daily world is organized along functional lines. Also, it is often much easier to say what something is for, or what its use is, than what it is in essence. This is conspicuously true for tools, gadgets, and practical things; moderately true for things to eat and drink; less so for family rules, and still less for art. Yet children repeatedly ask why they should be home at dark and what such rules "are good for," and artists who aim at pure art are perpetually plagued by people who want to know what paintings and sculptures are for, what use they have, and what one can do with them.

Functional conceptualization is no stranger to religious thought. An abundance of books and tracts beleaguers people in all walks of life with the idea that praying is very useful and always good for something. There is even a book on the power of praying over plants, which sets out to demonstrate that plants grow more vigorously when one prays hard for them. Keyrings and amulets with short prayers can be found in any dime store, for those anxious moments when one will have need of them. Placards on taxis admonish us to go to the church of our choice on Sunday mornings, with the implication that it is good for something. From time to time, juvenile court judges find it useful to sentence a youthful offender to attendance at Sunday School. Biblical movies have proven to be very useful to the film industry. Indeed, one can move mountains if one has only a shred of faith. These examples are trite, but they are a telling demonstration of functional thinking in regard to religion, which permeates the whole culture.

And why not? Gods have always been used. That is their *raison d'être,* from the human point of view. And long before religion became a contemplative exercise, it was a useful activity in the service of man's immediate needs for food, shelter, safety, fertility, and social security. The original stress was on activities-with-accompanying-thoughts such as praying, offering, and warding off danger by dancing and drumbeating rather than on pondering essences in pure thought. The primordial gods themselves, moreover, were far from contemplative. They were always busy doing things, upsetting the order if things became static, and keeping the cycles of the seasons moving. They worked and bred and feasted and traveled; they rarely slept. And if they brooded from time to time, they always came up with something new to demonstrate their activism. Mana is energy and power, and so is the original *numen*. Only gradually does the power become a discerning power and an ethical force.

With such clues from the deities themselves and with so much original emphasis on ritualistic doings, the religious life can hardly ever be divorced from actions and impulses, no matter how quietly sophisticated and pensive it may become in the course of time. And as long as there is functional activity, even conceptual thought in religion is prone to retain a functional orientation. This is not functionalism as a school of thought or a point of view about religion; it is merely that concept formation in religion tends to be of several types, including functional definitions. People use their gods. They use grace and guilt and shame. They use worship and prayer. They use covenants and promises. They use visions of the unseen. They use intimations of the life hereafter. And so their thoughts about all these things will include these uses or focus on them. The energetic Luther put it very well:

> We cannot vex the devil more than by teaching, preaching, singing and talking of Jesus. Therefore I like it well, when with sounding voice we sing in the church: *Et homo factus est; et verbum caro factum est.* The devil cannot endure these words, and flies away, for he well feels what is contained therein.[8]

Teaching, preaching, singing, and talking—not just thinking! The thoughtful Calvin put it this way:

> By the knowledge of God, I understand that by which we not only conceive that there is some God, but also apprehend what it is for our interest, and conducive to his glory, what, in short, it is befitting to know concerning him. For, properly speaking, we cannot say that God is known where there is no religion or piety. . . . But although our mind cannot conceive of God without rendering some worship to him, it will not, however, be sufficient simply to hold that he is the only being whom all ought to worship and adore, unless we are also persuaded that he is the fountain of all goodness, and that we must seek everything in him, and in none but him.[9]

The historical precedence of doing over pure thinking in religion has been well summarized by E. S. Ames, who wrote:

> Communal feasts were celebrated, temples were built, and ceremonials flourished for ages before inquiries were made concerning their efficacy and before the nature of the gods was questioned. Such thoughts as floated through the minds of devotees were of desires to be satisfied and of the prescribed ways by which they could be fulfilled.[10]

This is the issue we are dealing with, though our emphasis is not on the historical development, but on the contemporary occurrence of a kind of thought organization that is determined by what one does. Some conceptualizations in religion are highly functional. It is not uncommon to find in churches and other religious groups persons whose religious devotion is almost exclusively expressed in deeds or in labors of one sort or another. They organize banquets, cook meals, help with the serving, and wash dishes afterward. They participate actively in every social event of their fellowship, writing nametags, serving tea or coffee, introducing strangers to each other, with a real gift for making small talk. They are always on hand for bazaars and potluck suppers. Indeed, they see to it that these are being held periodically. They offer transportation services to shut-ins or elderly people, visit the sick in hospitals, and act as volunteers for various other service functions. It is possible to do any or all of these things on the basis of an articulate set of religious concepts or as a thoughtful expression of reasoned religious principles. But it is also possible to do these things without conceptual grasp of the grounds or reasons for doing them, and without explicit justification. The activities seem their own motive and their own reason, so to speak. As a matter of fact, one finds at times a surprising conceptual vacuousness among these hard workers. Their religion itself is "doing things," and the doings often become ritualistic, self-perpetuating, a doing for doing's sake.

In such cases the thoughts seem to follow in the wake of the activities. Ideas which such persons generate are more a product than a cause of their acts. If one suddenly questions their activities or tries to gain a rational justification of their energetic display, one runs the risk of precipitating a crisis, in which they seem overcome by intellectual perplexity accompanied by a great moral indignation at the questioner. For instance, toward summertime when most people begin to think of vacations and already pleasantly anticipate the relaxation of schedules, there are almost in every congregation a few persons who suddenly see an occasion for stepped-up activity in organizing a vacation Bible school, even in churches that have already an excellent and time-demanding program of instruction. When one dares to question the need for an extra program or simply asks why such a program seems indicated, he is usually met with fury and elicits further intellectual dissolution in the irrational response that "God does not go on vacation!"

Sacramental acts, like all rituals, are particularly prone to entail a short-circuiting of conceptual clarity and to keep thinking at the level of functional definitions. One participates in the act qua act, and feels sometimes pressed into participation before one's thoughts about it are clear. Whether this is a pressure for conformity or for witness is irrelevant here; the point is that members of religious groups often feel obliged to participate in or submit to activities without having had the chance to think through the issues, principles, or implications and before they are conceptually ready for them. A precipitous "doing" may thus come to prevail, and concept formation becomes subordinate to it. One brings his children for baptism, one marries in church, one goes to Mass or attends a communion service because "these are things to be done" and questioning them is held to be presumptuous, inappropriate, or intellectual.

The fact that organized religion is always a mixture of creed, cult, and custom entails a constant pressure against purely abstract conceptual thought. It forces many people, perpetually or only at times, to organize their thinking through what they do, and to engage in a type of concept formation that is based on functional definitions. The triadic relations between creed, cult, and custom both demand and provide opportunities for a flexible use of various types of thought organization. All kinds of patterns may be expected; no type is entirely alien to anyone who reflects about his religious experience.

CONCRETISM

Abstraction is an achievement. What the world presents to the senses may vary from a buzzing, blooming confusion to a patterned scene of sun, sky, green trees, and lakeshore, but what it presents is situationally concrete. It is a specific "this" and "that" of light, colors, forms, tones, hardness, etc. Abstraction rises above the concreteness of situations to the larger units of classes, groups, or families of things; it transforms sense impressions into ideas; it establishes relations of similarity, difference, distance, cause, and effect; it can playfully assume an "as if" attitude. I once knew a patient who, under the impact of an expanding brain tumor, had a disastrous loss of abstraction capacity. Before his illness he was an intelligent man, moderately well-situated, who had been a foreman in a shoe factory. Slowly, as he began to fail, he sank to ever simpler jobs in the plant, till he ended up in the shipping department, where his last job consisted of wrapping several boxes of shoes into large sheets of wrapping paper and tying the package with rope. He had courageously continued working until hospitalization for surgery was inevitable. But great changes had taken place in his mental life. He had gradually lost the capacity to think abstractly; he had even lost the idea of space dimensions, losing his sense for left and right, "in front of" and "behind." He packed his shoeboxes through long-accustomed motor movements of his arms and hands, rather than by "knowing" the relations between the wrapping paper and the boxes.

With this severe disturbance in space relations, he nevertheless left home every morning to walk to work. How did he do it? He followed a written-out list of prescriptions, more or less as follows: "On closing the house door behind me, I look for the gate in the white picket fence and walk to it; at the gate I look in the distance for a telephone pole with a large transformer, and when I have arrived at that point, I cross the street. I look around for a red fire hydrant, where I cross the street again. There I will see one block away the fence of the factory, and I follow it until I reach the entrance gate."

His life had become extremely concretized. Almost everything was a specific "this" or "that." Words such as "if," "supposedly," and "however" made little sense in his speech, though they were still part of his vocabulary.

Concreteness of this extreme degree is an inability to come to grips with mere possibilities, large class concepts, propositions, playful assumptions, or speculations. The world has shrunk to visible and tangible realities, specific memories, movements, one's body, and simple verbal exchanges with a down-to-earth reference. Loss of composure is imminent when wishes are denied, when situations become too complex to handle, or when changes occur that give a baffling strangeness to old and familiar arrangements. Things that are not in their place are seen as a frightening loss of order. Every change in habit or circumstance arouses anxiety, and tears come easily, especially when one is confronted with one's own incapacity to grasp and master a task or situation.

Pathological extremes may be rare, but they can have great teaching value. They can throw a glaring light on common things, hitherto shrugged off as not particularly interesting or meaningful. Enlightened by our sad case of concretization of thought under the impact of brain damage, can we begin to see concretism as a mode of thought in some religious persons or groups? I believe we can, by pointing to all beliefs which insist on a radically literal interpretation of scriptures, which refuse to admit any change whatsoever, or which depict specific and almost tangible Antichrists in popes, taverns, or sex. Such forms of belief arrive at specific dates for world disaster or predict minutely the day and way of Christ's Second Coming. They can lead to concrete repetitions of biblical scenes in the modern world, such as walking seven times around City Hall with a placard spelling doom, in the expectation that the walls will crumble down. They lead to an insistence on ancient and biblically hallowed calendar items, in which Hebraic Saturdays are exchanged for Julian Sundays, at the cost of much embarrassment and sometimes with time lost from work.

In this kind of thought organization, tradition reigns supreme. It extols strange anachronisms, proudly, defiantly, and sometimes stupidly. When buttons on coats were once a luxury and therefore possibly a tempting vanity, there was some sense in anxiously proscribing their use in favor of more humble hooks and eyes, but maintaining this rule in the modern world becomes almost the acme of vanity, since hooks and eyes are now quite a rarity or oddity. Yet, some Amish-Mennonite sectarians insist on such manifestations of piety. Since biblical women do not seem to have shortened their hair (although they did much to ornament their coiffure), some Protestant sectarians feel persuaded that short hairdos on women are sinful. Since Latin was once the common tongue in Rome, and then an international language among the educated clergy through whom it became firmly affixed to the liturgy of the Mass, some modern Americans insist that it is really the only language in which one can worship. Though Gregorian chant stands historically in the monodic plainsong tradition between the fourth and sixth centuries in Europe, it is for certain people *the* music of the church no matter how much it may be at variance with the development of musical styles and tastes. It is, to them, a specific fixture of religious expression and experience that bars experimentation with other forms.

In a broad sense, fundamentalism may be seen as concretism, even when it is defended or advocated by people who are quite capable of making abstractions in their apologetics. It makes the Bible a thing, if not an idol. Biblical phrases become concrete admonitions that require minute adherence. In the Scopes trial, the first chapter of Genesis was taken up as a cudgel against Darwinian propositions, completely misunderstanding the intent, method and nature of scientific formulations. It insists on radical conformity, oblivious of humor and grace.

Concretism is also marked by limited imagination. Its images derive from memories, from homely situations of great familiarity and simplicity, or from over-used story materials. Even when it entertains poetic ambitions, the metaphors it produces are too trite to be seen as imaginative flight. Here is a hymn by William Cowper (1731–1800):

> There Is a Fountain
> There is a fountain filled with blood
> Drawn from Emmanuel's veins;
> And sinners plunged beneath that flood,
> Lose all their guilty stains.
>
> The dying thief rejoiced to see
> That fountain in his day;
> And there may I, as vile as he,
> Wash all my sins away.[11]

In the printing of such hymns, one will often discover another concretism: the insistent capitalization of the first letters of all words that refer to the divine. Personal pronouns, relative pronouns, and all other small words referring to God must bear the royal imprint. Such linguistic concretisms spill over into nominal concretisms: instead of the common word God, concretistic sectarians tend to use archaic appellations such as Jehovah with the conviction that it is his proper name.

Baptismal rituals have been the subject of much bitter contending within Christianity. How complete should the washing be? Total immersion, say some, insisting on a concrete enactment of cleansing procedures. Sprinkling, say others, permitting condensation and abbreviation, and insisting on the symbolic value and intent of the ritual. Shall one "gather at the river" for immersion, or shall one stand erect with babe in arms in a sanctuary with wall-to-wall carpeting for the ceremony? The answer depends on the organization of one's thoughts: abstract, functional, or concrete. The example of baptism highlights a feature of all ritual, namely, that it is always regulated to the finest minutiae, very specific and utterly concrete. It is not free action, but a chained series of motor sequences. But action will demand our attention in a later chapter; the point to be made in this chapter is that *thinking about action* can also become very concretistic, particularly when it is concerned with ritual.

Concretism in religion engenders several more characteristics which are so common that they are of diagnostic significance. One is the fear of novelty. Though the word "system" sounds somewhat high-flown for the organization of concrete thinking, it is nevertheless apparent that concreteness has all the trappings of reasoning within a closed system. Thought cannot or is not allowed to spread its wings; venture requires openness to unheard-of possibilities. Abstraction produces some freedom from bondage to the world of sensory stimuli and motor action. The concretistic thinker, however, is locked in his world of specific situations, literal formulae, and ritualistic activities, and has learned to feel comfortable within it precisely because it provides him with the structure he needs. He is not only suspicious of novelty, but afraid of it, and when conditions may force him to change he responds typicallly with panic and anger.

The other characteristic of concreteness is what Goldstein[12] has called the catastrophic reaction. When a brain-damaged person is confronted with tasks that supersede his slim intellectual resources, and when he becomes aware of impending failure in solving such tasks, he senses an acute loss of mastery. Thus undermined in his control, he may lose his composure and cry. He becomes hyperemotional, and under the impact of strong negative feelings such as fear, anger, shame, or worthlessness he may for a moment resort to irrational thoughts or activities, until he has regained some modicum of self-esteem. So it is with the concretistic thinker in religion. Intellectual challenges beyond his powers can precipitate him into a catastrophic reaction which in due course may produce irrational fantasies of persecution, revenge, and world catastrophe, with the lively images of Antichrists, threatening beasts, or number magic familiar to readers of apocalyptic literature.

SYNCRETISM

Faced with the unassorted heap of objects that comprise the sorting test, a person may make a grouping, usually fairly large, which cuts across the natural categories of tools, eating utensils, paper articles, etc. In straining for a concept that unifies his group he may say: "You can find these around the house," or "They are all man-made objects," or "In some way or other they all come from the ground." These are syncretistic definitions and groupings, which try to bring under one conceptual heading a great variety of things, often unrelated things, which are members of quite distinct or discrepant classes. The subject overlooks or overrules these distinctions in favor of a more embracing idea. Usually this can only be done by moving high on the abstraction ladder, indeed too high above the range in which the more articulate and useful concepts are formed. Syncretism is a fumbling overinclusiveness which combines discordant things under flimsy constructs, with a formula which is usually too trite to be false and too meaningless to be correct.

Syncretism is nothing new in religion. In Ferm's encyclopedia it is defined as:

> the mingling of faiths which come in contact one with another. It may take place consciously as in the case of some modern religions which are products of the deliberate weaving together of various strands of religious thought to form a new religion. More frequently it is a quite unconscious process of give and take such as inevitably occurs where differing faiths meet.[13]

Theologians have used the term for specific eras in the Christian Church in which dilutions of Christianity took place through mixing with Hellenistic and Gnostic ideas. To them syncretism describes the loss of authenticity which occurs when incompatible ideas are allowed to distort original and cohesive conceptions. For instance, the Hebrew unity of body and mind, which is so conspicuous in the Old Testament, gave way to the dualistic language of Hellenism in the New Testament, which in turn became exposed to Gnostic speculations that transposed the Hebrew heritage into an odd spiritualism.

But our concern is not so much with large historical movements as with the way individuals organize their thoughts on religious issues. We have already had occasion to mention the strange mixing of notions about decent citizenship with ideas of piety. Harvey Cox's *The Secular City*[14] addresses itself to the enormous ideological problems that are engendered by this kind of syncretism and exposes the fallacious reasoning underlying it. Cox's efforts at clarification are particularly creative since he not merely wants to disentangle the sticky web of incompatible strands, but wants to arrive at a deeper vision of both political theory and contemporary theology by learning from the inadequacies occasioned when one was thoughtlessly mixed with, or substituted for, the other.

Syncretistic thinking seems to be an ever-present danger for the pious soul who knows by heart all the saintly phrases of his tradition and the seraphic epithets of his God, and applies them wantonly to the economy, the military, mechanics, literature, and the arts in order to explain all that is. "God made it all, and isn't everything wonderful! He wins our battles for us, he endowed Paris with the Eiffel tower, and he foresaw in his wisdom that television would spread the impact of Billy Graham crusades on his behalf. Religion is something beautiful, and art is really so religious!" Syncretism is also prevalent among professional men such as physicians, biologists, psychiatrists, or psychologists who, awestruck by the equally noble goals of their work as well as their religious tradition, make strenuous efforts to amalgamate their scientific concepts with their religious ideas so that "all will be one." An example is the direct comparison and intermingling of guilt (a legal concept), guilt feelings (a psychological concept), and sin (a theological concept) under a nebulous general idea of "wrongdoing." Another example is the life-force concept of a vitalistic biology linked up with the creator-God of Judaism.

Even when one is indulgent toward unhappy metaphors and poetic license, a hard core of syncretism is often present in religious hymns. An example is the well-known hymn, "In the Garden."[15] In the atmosphere it describes, the Jesus of Christianity has been alloyed with the oreads of Greek mythology and a Victorian lover in crinoline or rustling silks. A nebulous idea of romantic pleasantness is used to subordinate such conceptions as lovely roses, the Son of God, a chat with one's lover and the orderliness of a well-kept garden. Syncretisms usually are too trite to be false, too meaningless to be correct. We may now add: so discrepant are these ideas at closer look that the suggested unity is spurious.

From the lines of this popular hymn and its frequent use in funeral services the reader may already have anticipated what is perhaps the most abundant source of syncretism in religion: notions about immortality and their relations to burial practices and funeral rites. The belief in one's personal immortality and the desire to speculate about its forms are so strong that they tend to become juxtaposed with, or even overrule, doctrinal formulations about one's professed religious beliefs. Very often, the speculations about immortality are a far departure from the tenets of corporate faith and contradict them grossly. The result is that two beliefs are held concomitantly, not in creative tension or in paradoxical richness, but abjectly in a loose arrangement. Of an enormous amount of books on this subject, I want to mention only Cullmann's *Immortality of the Soul or Resurrection of the Dead?*[16] as one fairly recent attempt to disentangle biblical thoughts on the issue from the spontaneous beliefs of the mass of believers who claim to uphold Christian tenets but turn out to espouse Gnostic, neo-Platonic, or grossly pagan propositions. It is always a thankless task to confront people with their inconsistencies and the flimsiness of their concepts, and so it is no wonder that Cullmann notes in his preface: "No other publication of mine has provoked such enthusiasm or such violent hostility." According to most Christian creeds and articles of faith, Christians are assured of only one thing at the time of their death, and that is that this extraordinary event too is in the hand of their God, and that his arrangements can be trusted. But the natural proclivity toward denying one's own demise is so strong that even professing Christians invent various *ad hoc* theories in order to reassure themselves of some form of self-perpetuation. Faced with the issue of death, they suddenly use the concept of a detachable soul which is allowed to roam the wide open spaces; they suddenly despise the body as "mere ashes or dust"; they suddenly insist on treating the dead as if they were living and make comfortable arrangements for a quasi-sleep in satin-lined boxes. I have stressed the sudden and *ad hoc* nature of these constructions because they form a jarring note in the symphony of professed corporate beliefs. They cannot be rhymed together with the established framework of thought, and any effort to do so leads to a helpless and hapless straining toward supraordinate concepts at a very high level of abstraction, which are so all-embracing that they become inarticulate or inane.

In syncretistic thought organization, essential differences are glossed over in favor of a loose or highly contrived unity. Thus, there is a range of syncretistic possibilities. Some are due to sloppy thinking. Others derive from suspicion of natural categories or conventional concepts and present an effort at unique assertions of a hyperintellectual sort. I am afraid that most of the syncretisms engendered by immortality fantasies amount to sloppy inconsistencies induced by the strength of irrational wishes. But it is a farfetched and slightly insane syncretism if one argues, as the Gnostic Markos[17] did, that the Holy Spirit which descended in the form of a dove at the baptism of Jesus by John the Baptist must have been the Alpha and Omega alluded to in another scriptural passage, because the number value of the Greek word for dove adds up to 801, the same as the sum of the values for alpha and omega in numerological mysticism. I borrow another passage from a capable thinker, Swedenborg, to demonstrate a fourth type of syncretism produced by such a strong striving for unity in everything that metaphors and similes begin to border on equation:

> It is evident from what has been shown above that from the sun of heaven, which is the first proceeding of Divine Love and Divine Wisdom. . . . light and heat proceed—from its wisdom light, and from its love heat; also that light is the receptacle of wisdom, and heat of love; also that so far as man comes into wisdom he comes into the Divine light, and so far as he comes into love he comes into the Divine heat.[18]

FABULATION

Most readers will know the word "fable" as the name of a literary form and of a story with a moral, in which animals converse with one another. The word "fabulation" in the title of this section is broader:

it denotes a type of concept formation in which objects are being brought together as items in a story or narrative that unfolds. For instance, on the sorting test one might pick up a screwdriver and say: "This is the tool of a carpenter, who is at work on a project (adding a piece of wood); he also smokes (adding a cigarette), and when he hears the whistle blow he will go for lunch (adding a fork and two sugar cubes) and smoke a cigar afterward (adding the cigar)." The resultant grouping is of articles from different classes, which are thought to "belong together" because each of them is related to a central figure (the carpenter), and not because of any inherent common quality. In one sense, such fabulized concept formations are very concretistic in that they represent an extreme case of situationalism; in another sense they are very loose because of their fictitiousness.

I once knew a psychiatric patient whose admission to the hospital was occasioned by the following episode. He was a farmer, and one day, on coming home from the fields, he entered his kitchen and saw on the table three empty Coke bottles. He immediately stepped out into his den, took a gun off the wall, loaded it, and with the exclamation "Father, Son, and Holy Ghost" proceeded to shoot each of the bottles to pieces. In doing this, he used a form of thinking whose rules are: things are not what they seem to be. They may be something else, and it is up to us to let them be what we want them to be.

We have seen in the previous chapter that the imagination can be very rich and daring, and that it plays a large role in religion. In this section our concern is with concept formation and its modalities. Thought organization can take the form of fabulation which creates out of the chaos of things a unique order by permitting them to "act" within the flow of a narrative. Whether the narrative is historical or fictitious, plausible or outlandish, is an important question, but that question is for our purposes here subordinated to the structure of the thought plan, which is that a *plot* can create order and cohesiveness in the "heap" of things and experiences.

In this sense, fabulation plays a very large role in religion. The wish for immortality, which we already encountered, soon leads to the mapping out of plots in which the blessed souls will walk on golden pavements and through pearly gates, assemble in splendid halls, and get ready to join in choruses and orchestras. An October 8, 1966, newspaper release from the Associated Press reports that Bishop Tomlinson of a branch of the Church of God, to whom we referred earlier, has now indeed crowned himself "king of the world" by a plot which required that he first make many airplane trips to the world's major cities proclaiming the kingdom to come, and then a final visit to Jerusalem where his royal gesture places the whole world under God's dominion. In such cases, the order of things is not inherent in what is, but evolves from a fiction, over a stretch of time, and the "things" or "conditions" change their obvious qualities into something else.

Fabulation as a mode of thought is conspicuous in the origin of new religious movements. In 1820 and 1823 Joseph Smith, Jr., claimed that angels had visited him and that they gave him several years later a set of gold plates:

> . . . written by way of commandment, and also by the spirit of prophecy and of revelation. Written, and sealed up, and hid unto the Lord, that they might not be destroyed; to come forth by the gift and power of God unto the interpretation thereof; sealed by the hand of Moroni, and hid up unto the Lord, to come forth in due time by the way of Gentile; the interpretation thereof by the gift of God.[19]

Translated by Smith, these plates constituted the Book of Mormon, which itself is a long narration of the migrations of the so-called lost tribes of Israel till they reached the shores of the New World. The origin of the movement is a story about a story, and the stories link together a great variety of dissimilar things: ethnological puzzles, polygamous desires, traditional Christianity, "a movement nurtured in the revivalist atmosphere of the 'burned-over' district of upstate New York,"[20] the American frontier spirit, and one man's claims of prophecy and angelic assistance.

In order to establish authority for certain beliefs, fabulation is a favorite mode of thought. "Things that are" become "things that have happened" in some sequence. To establish the authority of scriptures, both Judaism and Christianity developed stories about their origins, which advanced propositions that they were written in religious ecstasy, or dictated to the writers by the divine voice, or written by some special inspiration of the Holy Spirit who used the writer as a kind of penman. Historical text research has shown that the actual composition of the four gospel texts from the oral tradition is itself a case of fabulation in that each author created his own narration, for different purposes and perhaps for different audiences, of the alleged facts about the life of Jesus and his reported sayings. Certainly these writers did not purport to copy their predecessors or each other literally; nor do they seem to have been imbued by a spirit of pure research. Each told his story, plausibly, convincingly, or at least persuasively, and with distinct accentuations. Mark has been described as a concise and dramatic storyteller, interested in building up the events culminating in the crucifixion. Matthew's work can be seen as a manual of the life of Christ and of biblical theology, clearly intended for church use. Luke seems to speak to cultivated men, with the intent to defend Jesus' messianic claims against the Jewish opposition. The Johannine narration was called by Clement of Alexandria a "spiritual gospel" and establishes Jesus as the

Logos whose power became manifest in his extraordinary activities, which are "signs" of his supernatural character. Each narration links different selections of things together, by some central thought or purpose which becomes the secret of his plot.

The power of narration to bring discrepant things together is nowhere better illustrated than in the great religious festivals, such as the Jewish Seder celebration or the Christian Christmas observances. The mere thought "Christmas" calls up a great variety of things and events, bound together by strands of meaning which are woven in memory or in anticipation; the fiction (from the Latin, "to form, invent, or feign"—all three) creates order in the following chaotic manifold of things:

> acts of charity: donations, gifts, sacrificing time and effort
> musical pursuits, pageants, singing, bell-ringing
> receiving gratification through gifts
> aiming at parity in the exchange of presents
> snowy landscapes and the pleasures of winter
> profit-making
> display of proud home-ownership through decorations
> coziness near glowing fireplaces
> lectures about Christmas in other countries
> lectures about Christmas 100, 200 or 300 years ago
> stories about "the first Christmas"
> indulgent attitudes towards traffic and parking problems
> special foods
> special moods
> cacophonies in streets and stores
> logistics of mailing cards and parcels
> techniques of wrapping and adorning
> visiting relatives and friends
> keeping secrets
> promises for good behavior
> upsurges of parental goodwill
> learning technical innovations in toys
> festive worship
> displacement of furniture by trees
> changes in lighting

This list is not offered with tongue in cheek, but in an effort to demonstrate the enormous discrepancy of ideas, things, events, motives, and wishes which are organized in one fell swoop by the leading thought of Christmas. Fiction is a powerful ordering principle, and in the case of Christmas there is a veritable historical avalanche of stories about stories in an ever-growing progression of complexity. More and more things become absorbed by it. Without fabulation our list would be no more than a heap of discordant items; with fabulation the heap becomes a cohesive whole.

Fabulation is potentially omnivorous, but its span can be held in check by making distinctions between historical fact, fictitious elaboration, and outright fabrication. Aesthetic and other considerations can be used to bind the formative principle of fabulation into specific literary forms such as parable, allegory, metaphor, drama, myth, legend, saga, fable, commentary, and various poetic styles, each of which has its own rules and patterns.

In distinction to the other forms of thought organization which were presented in the previous sections of this chapter, fabulation imposes order by a process of unfolding. Its "truth" is not in a cross section or a "slice" of reality, but in an arrangement of events in time, related through human or divine actors. Because of religion's preoccupation with the question of origins, with genealogies and with destiny, fabulation in religion tends to be saturated with numinous qualities. It is peculiarly fitted to convey and portray the feeling of createdness, the cosmic *mysterium,* the great acts and passions that rule the events of life, the resolute power of history, and the energies that actuate man, beasts, plants, things, and ideas. In fabulation, what *is* turns into what *happens,* which presents man with the unfathomable mystery of why things happen the way they do or did, rather than otherwise.

Without stories no religion.

SYMBOLISM

The previous section brought us to the brink of another mode of concept formation: the ordering of reality through symbols. Unlike all the previously discussed methods of concept formation, symbolism does not organize the perceptual manifold by intellectual reduction. It retains perceptual impressions in an especially rich and glorious way by letting each thing be itself as well as a hint at something else that transcends perceptual registration.

The sorting test offers interesting opportunties for symbolic groupings. One can place the smoking articles, the eating utensils, and two sugar cubes together and say "carnal desires." One can put the tools together and say "labor." Or one can put together all the white articles, as different as the cigarette, the filecard, and the sugar cubes, while saying "virginity." In such sortings, the articles are not described in their essence, utility, or concrete situational togetherness. Each one is retained as a whole and recognized as perceptually unique, but in addition each article is taken as a pointer to something else: an idea, a cause, or a value.

Similarly, when one walks through a city street and passes by the display window of a perfumery store, the thought "womanhood" may come to mind. If the next store displays baby cribs and the next one flowers, one may well decide that this is a "feminine" section of the avenue. The antique dealer at the corner may have a spinning wheel in the window, or an old

metate on which Indian women used to grind their corn. All these perceptions, widely different as they are, can evoke the idea of femininity and
point far beyond themselves in the direction of something that is held in
esteem, charged with feeling or regarded as an authoritative idea. Each
article by itself, from perfume bottle to *metate,* or all of them together,
can speak that evocative nonverbal language by which it participates in
the power of that to which it points beyond its own essence. With this
Tillichian formulation of the symbol I must warn the reader to assume
an attitude of great sobriety toward the content of this section. It does not
address itself to the theory of symbols. It takes the existence and use of
symbols for granted while recognizing that the origin, life, decline, and
ontological status of symbols can be described or explained in different
ways. Neither are we here interested in the question: What is a religious
symbol? The emphasis will be on the evidence and forms of symbolism
in religious concept formation.

It is tempting to see symbolism as the essential form of all religious
thinking and to single out the idea of God as its most pronounced instance.
As Dionysius the Areopagite put it fifteen hundred years ago:

> And if any one, seeing God, knows what he sees, it is by no means God
> that he so sees, but something created and knowable. For God abides
> above created intellect and existence, and is in such sense unknowable and
> non-existent that He exists above all existence and is known above all
> power of knowledge. Thus the knowledge of Him who is above all that
> can be known is for the most part ignorance.[21]

This sweeping statement about the majesty of the uncreated puts the whole
universe or any part of it at the believer's disposal for use as a symbol of
the divine. As part of creation, anything can point beyond itself to its
originator. The fact is, however, that most religious symbols are far more
specific and lay only a modest claim on representing the *numen* in some
selective aspect. The everyday believer does not harp constantly on the
theme of creation and creator. He lives in the world, and chops it up in
distinct groupings of things and ideas, most of which are banal and commonplace. Only a few have sacral values of the sort that makes them
suitable symbols of the concerns of faith.

Among the most conspicuous religious symbols are institutions such as
churches, monastic orders, synagogues, missions, or store front rescue operations. Whether or not they have a specific location or building, the work and
activities of such institutions are numinous by their goal and arrangement.
An enormous variety of work may go on, from preaching and hymn-
singing to serving food, from studying to entertaining, from setting up
budgets to practicing foreign languages. All these activities can be pulled

together by symbolic phrases such as "the work of the Lord" or "the congregation" or "the sisters of mercy." A large selection of reality, very discrepant in perceptual and conceptual qualities, is thereby brought under a central meaningful heading that justifies the togetherness of the strangest bedfellows.

When specific locations and buildings are added to these activities and human groups, the visibility of the work may be enhanced, and the symbol value of the enterprise may become more pronounced. Their very designations such as St. Benedict's, First Church, the Cathedral, or Beth Sholom become unifying centers of power around which life can become organized from the cradle to the grave. But the higher visibility and the greater specificity in bricks or concrete can also cause the original symbol function to deteriorate into an emblematic decoration or conventional sign which says little more than that at St. Mark's a group of upper-middle-class Episcopalians hold their religious exercises once a week, or that this unassuming office suite is a Christian Science reading room, open on all weekdays.

In a sense, a certain amount of ambiguity between symbol, sign, or emblem is the inescapable fate of most so-called illustrative symbols. The cross can be an evocative symbol of great religious power, but it can quickly become a mere decoration in a design or a rather pedestrian piece of costume jewelry. The eye of God embedded in a triangle could be a symbol of the trinitarian mystery, but it can also be a trite morality piece at the top of a nineteenth-century engraving. The same can be said of statuary, vestments, staffs, chalices, and candelabra.

Scrolls and books have a special place of symbolic significance. As holy scriptures, they have numinous value of the highest order, which is not only evident from the ceremonial ways in which they are handled, bound, stored, and read, but also from the many legends which tell of their divine origins, sudden disappearances, thefts, falsifications, or reappearances. When the ancients said that books have their peculiar fate they meant more than that paper and ink are perishable. They implied that scriptures are often as fickle and flighty as the divine persons themselves, revealing and concealing their messages in the strangest ways. Yet the "things in the book" are enormously varied, comprising history, legend, biographies of kings or high priests or prophets or villains, legal or moral prescriptions, ritualistic specifications, poetry, proverbs, genealogies, cosmological myths, letters, etc. A truly fantastic array of realities, fictions, and experiences is thrown together under the words "biblical" or "talmudic" or "scriptural." They thereby achieve special significance as pointers to the sacred.

More limited and specific are cultic gestures, words, phrases, and dress. All of these symbols can, for a moment, serve as principles of thought organization. A gesture of blessing, or two hands solemnly raised in the sign of benediction, can suddenly alter the contents of thought and the modes of interaction between people: they organize an awareness of creatureliness which cuts through all the divisions of status, wealth, and sex. Such a phrase as "The Lord is in his holy temple" not only evokes an especially numinous feeling, but imposes a hushed silence in which many ordinary distinctions between things and people are temporarily being brought to nought. Encounter a man in long black robes in the street, or one with wide-brimmed black hat and flowing beard, and instantly one's thoughts are channeled to a serious focus and topics of a certain weight, away from trivia.

People can be symbols and thereby become organizing centers of thought. Venerated religious leaders such as Moses, Luther, Augustine, and Wesley gradually assume proportions that seem to lift them out of the human pale to transhistorical significance. They can thereby become potent identity models, and in one's strivings to be like them many other worthwhile distinctions within reality are kept in abeyance. Such symbolic organization of thoughts, stirrings, and longings lies at the heart of the devotion to saints, who are not only seen as moral teachers or wise guides, but who portray a way of life with a powerful sense of the ultimate. Adoration of the Virgin Mary and the imitation of Christ, of which Thomas a Kempis spoke with such complete absorption, can entail such a radical surrender to the symbols "Mary" and "Christ" that many other viable categories of thought recede into the background or play only an ancillary role.

While most symbols have quite marked perceptual qualities which carry the surplus value of the ultimate reality to which they point, we may not overlook the borderline case in which ideas act as symbols, and thereby become centers of thought organization. For instance, the idea of righteousness is, in religious experience, far more than a legal command or ethical demand that could be defined in operational terms. Like the idea of sin, it describes an existential posture vis-à-vis the ultimate and the unconditioned, and is therefore charged with numinous power. Righteousness, sin, grace, holiness, salvation, and other great religious ideas place themselves in an overpowering way beyond the ordinary distinctions of reality. They overrule them, place them in new perspectives, sometimes undermine their validity. An excellent example of this is Kierkegaard's famous proposition of the "teleological suspension of the ethical"[22-23] in which the dynamics of divine love and mercy are held to "suspend" (i.e., defer, adjourn, or waive) the valid distinctions between right and wrong, or even the whole category of moral justice. Divine love, in that context, is a symbolic idea which acts at times as the cardinal principle of human thought organization. Other distinctions vanish; all of reality is now organized under a new, symbolic heading.

AN APPRAISAL

We have seen that religious thought is immensely variegated. It can be organized in many different ways, and in actual practice traces of all types of organization occur in the thought patterns of millions of believers. The thoughtful philosopher and the logician no less than the myth-making poet can find challenges in the stock of ideas that religion has bequeathed to today's man from its long and rich history. Those who love stories and feel edified by them, as well as the utilitarian mind who asks what it is good for, can find examples galore from great minds and small minds who looked for the same and found it. From the highest reaches of the abstraction ladder to the lowest rungs, where the ladder stands on the ground of unreflected perceptions, man has moved up and down, together with the angels which he invented.

Few religious thoughts are original inventions; most of them are taught through a transmission process in which thought, action, story, image, and concept are presented to the learner with various degrees of plausibility and authority. Much of the teaching has always been done by people who themselves have a high degree of authority which in one sense determines their own plausibility and the plausibility of that which they teach. This is true for parents and all metaphorical "heads of household": schoolteachers, church officials, culture bearers, and the representatives of the powers of the state. An ascending series of authorities reaches from fathers and mothers via the ancestors and the cultural institutions to the gods themselves, whose ultimate power and authority are often claimed for the truth of religious propositions. If one *could* escape the rigors of this transmission process and thereby stand outside the religious circle, as it were, both the authority and the modes of religious thinking would present an interesting spectacle. One finds that people assent to strange propositions which they would not endorse in another circle of experience. One finds that they engage in acts and rituals which seem to have no connection with the rest of life. One sees that some thoughts are limping on the crutches of activities and habits. One sees people with low intelligence boldly speculating about great ideas and ultimate realities. One finds highly intelligent people bent forward on a *prie-dieu* mumbling things in an utterly simple vocabulary. Moreover, one finds most of these things in a group setting, as corporate activities.

It is extremely difficult to stand outside the religious circle. In the first place, one needs considerable determination in staying out or getting out of it because such an endeavor is likely to get one embroiled in the ever-present conflict over authority and power. It means, in many cases, flouting one's parents and all those who are made in their image. Hence, most attempts at removing oneself from the religious circle end up in some relocation of oneself within the circle. Religious rebellion tends to remain religious, no matter how rebellious it is.

But there is another and probably weightier reason for the difficulty in stepping out of the religious circle. We have seen the great variety of religious thought organization. Though some patterns are more intelligent than others, more scholarly, more responsible, more vivid, or more edifying, and though some are closer than others to R/A thinking and thus closer to reality as pursued in earning one's living and warding off disaster, the patterns form among themselves a mosaic. It is easy and not improper in religion to move between various types of thought organization, just as in a marital relation one glides from seriousness to humor, from firm reality words to silly terms of endearment, from logical to ridiculous propositions, and from menus to Shakespeare. Indeed, much of the fun lies precisely in the playful elegance of gliding back and forth. These possibilities also say something about the circle itself: the religious circle is perforce very large and extremely accommodating, far more so than the circles which one can imagine for other pursuits in life.

If scientific thought would not aim at being conceptual and functional, if it engaged in fabulations and symbolism, and if it allowed itself to be caught up in utter concreteness, it would simply not be scientific thought. The scientific circle is rather narrow, and deliberately so. Within the scientific circle one stands for rigorous canons of concept formation and methods of verification, and one actively wards off myth and other unwieldy forms of rich imagination. In the economic circle functionalism is a virtue. In art we find much fabulation and symbolism, with an eschewing of conceptual and functional ambitions. In contrast to such other circles, the religious circle covers a very wide territory and tends to encompass all manners of thought which it can hold in juxtaposition or in some kind of integrated superpattern. Its many oddities, seen from outside the circle, may stem from its scope and immense hospitality.

A third reason for the difficulty in eliminating oneself from the religious circle is the nature of the religious object. Whether this is formulated theistically, deistically or atheistically, in any religion one has always to do with vastness or "the embracing," as Jaspers[24] has called the universe, and therefore the religious circle deals with the very idea of plenitude. Obviously, one needs a large circle in which to organize thoughts and actions regarding plenitude. Plenitude and opulence cannot be approached stingily. The proverbial statement that all roads lead to Rome implies a recognition that great cities have many avenues of approach and that it is hard to avoid any one of them if one is in the neighborhood of a metropolis.

When Freud looked at the authority that is attached to religious doctrines, he found its source in the strength of man's enduring wishes which flout so often the canons of reason. Wishes, too, are opulent. They demand much, from security and protection to gratification and pleasure. They are often insatiable. They disregard time, space, and the available resources. Under the sway of the pleasure principle, wishes of this primordial sort constitute the most archaic heritage of man, link us with the stream of nature, and unite us laterally with all our contemporaries. Wishes are thus the most direct experience we have of plenitude.

V

Linguistic Functions

in Religion

IT IS CONSISTENT with the religious world view to assert that the Word was in the beginning. This was not only the conviction of the writer of the fourth gospel, who had absorbed Hellenistic ideas, but it was also the belief of the Hebrew mythmakers who attributed every aspect of the universe to the creative word of God. In the book of Genesis, speaking is *doing* or *making,* on the part of God. Similarly, the first human act described in the Genesis story is *naming* the various units within the universe. One hardly needs more than these few classical hints to realize the numinosity of language. Language is awesome, and religion has always known its power. Magic relies heavily on the magical formula, i.e., special words in one's own or in another language, or even in a fictitious tongue invented for the occasion. Incantations consist of language or language imitations. Praying is, among other things, a language activity. Prophecy is forcefully saying what needs to be said. Congregations gather around the Word. Rabbinic and talmudic scholars spend the larger part of their time on the study of scriptures and the teaching of words. Mystics declare their experiences to be ineffable, which is a much "thicker" and more numinous expression than the mere phrase that it is "impossible to find words for it."

The numinosity of language is also apparent in the devotion that people have toward their mother tongue, and the strenuous search for the origin of language by scholars and would-be investigators of all sorts. Battles have raged over the question of whether Hebrew, Greek, or Latin is the original language of mankind, and human lives have been sacrificed in attempts to settle that question. It is said that Frederick III of Hohenstaufen, the Sicilian despot (1272–1337), at one time ordered a group of newborn babies to be reared by wet nurses from his domain who had specific instructions not to speak, sing, or even hum to these children who would then utter, unaided and uninstructed, mankind's original tongue at the onset of speech. Most of the children died in that experiment, which is not surprising in the light of Spitz's reports[1-2] on twentieth-century illegitimate children whose fate it was, deprived of their mothers, to be reared in orphanages and other impersonal institutions. Frederick III might have read Herodotus, who reported in the second book of his Muses similar experiments on the original language by Psammetichus in Egypt:

> Now the Egyptians, before the reign of their king Psammetichus, believed themselves to be the most ancient of mankind. Since Psammetichus, however, made an attempt to discover who were actually the primitive race, they have been of opinion that while they surpass all other nations, the Phrygians surpass them in antiquity. This king, finding it impossible to make out by dint of inquiry what men were the most ancient, contrived the following method of discovery:—He took two children of the common sort, and gave them over to a herdsman to bring up at his folds, strictly charging him to let no one utter a word in their presence, but to keep them in a sequestered cottage, and from time to time introduce goats to their apartment, see that they got their fill of milk, and in all other respects look after them. His object herein was to know, after the indistinct babblings of infancy were over, what word they would first articulate. It happened as he had anticipated. The herdsman obeyed his orders for two years, and at the end of that time, on his one day opening the door of their room and going in, the children both ran up to him with outstretched arms, and distinctly said "Becos." When this first happened the herdsman took no notice; but afterwards when he observed, on coming often to see after them, that the word was constantly in their mouths, he informed his lord, and by his command brought the children into his presence. Psammetichus then himself heard them say the word, upon which he proceeded to make inquiry what people there was who called anything "becos," and hereupon he learnt that "becos" was the Phrygian name for bread. In consideration of this circumstance the Egyptians yielded their claims, and admitted the greater antiquity of the Phrygians.
>
> That these were the real facts I learnt at Memphis from the priests of Vulcan. The Greeks, among other foolish tales, relate that Psammetichus had the children brought up by women whose tongues he had previously cut out; but the priests said their bringing up was such as I have stated above.[3]

Ebner, in his book *The Word and Spiritual Realities,*[4] goes so far as to say that "the problem of language is not philosophical, nor psychological, nor in any other way scientific, but pneumatological; and as long as one does not approach it in this sense one will never fathom the essence of the word." This is certainly an extreme position, but it shows how numinous and hallowed language is to some of its users.

In the organization of this chapter we will be led by the customary distinction between language and speech. Language is the body of words and phrases in terms of which the members of a community communicate with each other and in terms of which they think. Speech is the system of vocalizations whereby messages are sent back and forth between speakers and hearers. Speech is muscle action by a message sender; it ordinarily results in the sensory process of hearing in a receiver.

FORMS OF RELIGIOUS LANGUAGE

That there is an intimate relation between language and thought is self-evident. Articulate thoughts become formulated in terms of a language structure. Poor or nebulous thoughts tend to be poorly formulated also; clear thoughts are put in concise and unambiguous words. But the nature of the relation between thought and language is a vexing problem that has kept thinkers busy from the dawn of civilization. According to common sense, which is often fallacious, something goes on in the head of a person that is quite private and internal, until it results in that person "having a thought." Subsequently, after the thought has been thought, the person enters the public domain with his thought by "putting it into language," through speech, writing, or gestures. The language thus "expresses" the thought. Similarly, when a person hears or reads such thought expressions of others, something goes on in his head whereby he "translates" the signs of the other man's language into "thoughts of his own," with some degree of correspondence between the private thought of the sender and the private thought of the receiver. In this conception, language plays a secondary role to thinking, by being mainly an expressive function, whereas thinking has almost unlimited freedom and great spontaneity.

Whorf[5] and others have reversed this relationship. They have called attention to certain phenomena that become apparent in the comparative study of languages, particularly those that are not of the same linguistic stock. For instance, Eskimos have several different words for "snow" whereas we have only one. To Eskimos, the snow that comes down from the sky in flakes, the snow that lies on the ground and is good to sled on, and the snow that is packed into the walls of an igloo are three entirely different things, worthy of different nouns. The British word "gentleman" is untranslatable, simply because it is a British concept generated in a British cultural context. From such observations, the hypothesis has been advanced that language precedes thinking, in a sense. Language gives us the forms of our thoughts, by offering us limited selections of nouns, adjectives, adverbs, etc., and by setting, through grammar and syntax, definite rules for combining the words into meaningful sentences. In this conception, each language is like a grid that one presses into reality, and reality becomes "chopped up" according to the mesh of the grid. Each language divides reality in a unique way.

Therefore, the languages that one grows up with or which one acquires are so many ways of dividing reality and so many structures in terms of which one will think. Thinking is thus highly dependent on language. The latter sets the stage for the former.

If language codetermines both what we think and how we think, linguistic behavior should give clues to a person's or a group's religious ideas and practices. At the Council of Nicaea in 325 the Christian Fathers struggled over issues that were in many respects functions of words available to them in Greek or Latin. In trying to formulate the relations between God the Creator or Father and the God-man Jesus Christ to whose teachings they assented, two Greek words channeled their thoughts. Is the Son *homoousios* (of the same essence) with the Father or *homoiousios* (similar in being)? Rarely has one iota made so much difference in an ideological proposition. The Council settled for the first word, and condemned the advocates of the second term as heretics. Its decision was latinized in the definition of the Son's "consubstantiality" with the Father, and that term too represented a culturebound mode of thought, through an available language structure, which imposes quite a strain on modern thinkers. None of these words is natural to modern believers or even to theologians, and the thoughts they suggest are quite elusive because they are not the categories of our time, or of our language.

Compare the following two statements, both dealing with the elusive plenitude of the deity. From an unknown Egyptian scribe we hear:

> He cannot be sculptured in stone. He cannot be seen. Service cannot be rendered to Him. Gifts cannot be presented to Him. He is not to be approached in the sanctuaries. Where He is is not known. He is not to be found in inscribed shrines. No habitation can contain Him.[6]

This is a language of space and space relations, ending in the question of God's locale, as one could expect from pyramid builders. Meister Eckhart put the issue in the language of personhood and possession:

> Thou shalt lose thy *thyness* and dissolve in His *hisness*; thy *thine* shall be His *mine*, so utterly one *mine* that thou in Him shalt know eternalwise His *isness*, free from becoming: His nameless nothingness.[7]

Two cultures, two languages, two men: they think and speak differently about the one they worship. The diversity of language, metaphor, and hence thought about the divine has been splendidly summed up in the following prayer by Finegan:

> O Thou One God, who art spirit Power to the Animist, darkness-conquering Light to the Parsee, Soul of our soul to the Hindu, Peace to the Buddhist, heavenly Order to the Confucianist, universal Way to the Taoist, Ruler of the judgment day to the Moslem, Shepherd of His people to the

Hebrew, and loving Father to the Christian, if it be true that we are ascending the same mountain of truth by different trails, then help us to be kind to our fellow-journeyers upon the ascent, and lead us on toward that single summit, where at last we shall clasp hands with one another in the light of Thy presence.[8]

Let us now consider a clinical example. Two men are looking at the same Rorschach Test card in search of religious symbols. One, a Methodist with a zeal for doing and little patience with theological conceptualizations, says:

This could be a side view of two people. Instead of praying, they are engaged in some kind of dance, maybe a religious dance, or a square dance. They have their hands together: that would symbolize fraternity: the effect of belonging to a religious group rather than a direct worship of God.

The other man, a Mennonite with a penchant for Old Testament themes and preoccupied with the atonement, says about the identical area of the card:

The element of red is very vivid; it reminds me of the slaying of a lamb. The two black sides also have the shape of a lamb, with legs sticking up. It is an animal being burnt as a burnt offering—a ritual sacrifice.

These are not merely the different thoughts of two different individuals. Each individual speaks in words of, and formulates his thoughts in terms of, the religious tradition of which he is a part. Each repeats words and phrases heard a thousand times, which have become second nature to him, as it were. The language favored by his tradition, its cherished metaphors and themes and biblical citations, is a mold for his thoughts.

Two Christians pray. One says "Jesus Christ" and the other makes reference to "Christ Jesus," proudly assuming that his reversal of names is a more glorious appellation or a more pious expression of his sincere devotion. A third one feels that "Christ" is just a little too royal and imperial, and he settles for a simple, straightforward "Jesus." A fourth one, with little concern for the historical figure and much respect for the exalted deity, says "Christ" alone.

If one's family, books, and tradition do not refer to Mary, there is little thought of Mary. But if one hears her spoken of all the time, she becomes a very important personage. If her name is coupled in most instances with the word "virgin" she becomes a very special personage also. If, in addition, she is called "Blessed Virgin" her importance and specialness become exponential to the point of her becoming an object of worship, a deity in her own right. If God's proper name is taboo because of its extreme holiness, as in Judaism, one needs circumlocutions such as "the Lord" or "the Almighty" which set the stage for certain ways of thinking about him. Indeed, the simple word "him" in the last sentence is one of those language structures indicating gender which automatically channels thought about the deity for millions of people toward a masculine identity! If one hears "Our Father" a thousand times one learns to think of him in a personalistic manner, but if one hears a thousand times of a Great Spirit one needs visions of towering mountains and wide open spaces in order to complete the proper thought of him. In Pentecostal groups the Holy Spirit is a very frequent verbal reference, both as a cause and as an effect of his lively presence in emotions and activities.

Aside from the particular appellations of the deities, which are of diagnostic value, there are many religious phrases and citations which give clues to a person's identity and hint at the ways of his thinking. "Sodom and Gomorrah" are on the lips of hortatory and indignant persons who bewail the mores of the times. Prophetic phrases, particularly those implying threats or alluding to coming disasters as revenge, are the favorites of militant groups which are at odds with civilization and band together in tight organizations fostering closed system thinking. "Hallelujah" and "Praise to the Lord" are expletives, explosives, or evocative sayings rarely heard among mainline Protestants or Catholics. They demand an ebullience of experience characteristic of people who seek release of tension states in their forms of worship. "Are you saved?" is considered an uncivil intrusion among middle-class believers, though it is frequently found on billboards along the roads near small villages in the Midwest and in Southern mountain regions. It is the greeting of holiness sects, an expression of solicitous worry and a helping hand. The comparison of life with "the vale of tears" implies a mildness and light humor found among people of moderate means or better who may remember humble origins or the piety of their grandparents.

Not only words and phrases, but whole languages can assume the aura of being religious in a pregnant sense. Latin and Hebrew are a case in point. *Veni Sancte Spiritus* sounds more numinous than *Come, Holy Spirit* to ears which have learned to associate worship with Latin. There is something awesome about a *deus absconditus* which the words *hidden God* can hardly convey. *Satanic* is more threatening and biting than *devilish*. *Shemah Isroel Adonai Elohim, Adonai Echod* has a sovereign appeal which loses something in the English "Hear, oh Israel, the Lord our God, the Lord is one." Whether or not one knows Latin or Hebrew, hearing the hallowed tongue adds substantially to the experience of the holy for those who grew up with its sounds on occasions of worship. Sacred tongues have a religious surplus value of sounds and intimated meanings which, however irrational, cannot easily be replaced by good translations into the modern languages. Shifting from Latin to the *vernacular* (a word which is itself a denigrating latinism for the native language) in the celebration of the Mass entails some re-education of the people to appreciate understandable messages instead of numinous archaic sound sequences.

Hallowed language may even become fixed to a dialect or a historical period in the development of a native tongue. When new Bible translations are offered there are always thousands of believers who feel that only the old or traditional renditions can carry the numinous values of the texts. They see modern translations as dangerous secularization attempts which undermine the status of belief. This feeeling is especially prominent in regard to such favorite scriptural passages as the twenty-third Psalm. Sacred values can even become attached to foreign words such as *Selah* at the end of a poetic stanza. To the ordinary reader who is not trained in Semitic languages these sounds must be nonsense syllables; yet they can quickly acquire a charge of solemnity and can become an expression of piety. To some assiduous Bible readers, the long genealogies that preface some Old Testament books are marvels of sonorous God-sounds, especially when read aloud.

The veneration of religious languages can spread to their scripts and alphabets. The word "hieroglyph" means sacred carving, an indication of the priestly origin of the Egyptian script. The act of writing, once a privilege of a few specially trained tribesmen, has maintained its sacred character as a ritual activity of shamans, priests, and temple scribes. Monuments such as steles, obelisks, the Aztec calendar stone, and large clay tablets; documents such as scrolls and codices, and even the tools used in carving and writing possess a sacred value, which may live on in the collector's value of presidential ballpoint pens used in signing documents of state. Long after Gothic script had been replaced by more legible signs, it was maintained as a special script for numinous purposes, from labels and inscriptions in churches to certificates of birth, baptism, or marriage. It is still used on academic diplomas and certificates to document the quasi-religious rite of passage into the prerogatives of academic status.

In religious experience, names can have special numinous significance. The so-called Christian name is the given name which becomes attached to the person through the ritual of baptism. By this process he is not only the named child of his parents, but he enters into the religious community as a recognizable individual. Between the given name and the family name can be inserted the name of a saint on whose day one is born or who is chosen on other grounds as one's special patron saint, guardian, or identity model. Many common proper names have religious meanings in the linguistic roots from which they are derived: Theophilus, Benedict, Christopher, Jerome, Dorothy, Elizabeth. The Puritans' adoration of the Old Testament resulted in a profusion of biblical names for American citizens: Abraham, Eleazar, Joel, Nathan, Abigail, Deborah, Sarah. The name of God, sometimes declared to be unpronounceable, demands or allows various circumlocutions which in turn become sacred names: Jehovah, Adonai, Yahweh, the Lord, Almighty, Our Father, Blessed Virgin, Redeemer.

The hypothesis of Whorf, that the available language is a powerful determinant of the thoughts of its users, also throws some light on the function of symbols. The reader may have noticed that nearly all the examples of numinous language in the preceding paragraphs are tantamount to descriptions of religious symbols of a verbal kind. Some of them, the scripts and hieroglyphic configurations, are also visual symbols. When one applies Whorf's thesis to the phenomena of sacred language it becomes very clear that the linguistic symbols of religion precede the individual. They are offered to him from birth on, and he finds them continuously available during his years of learning. They not only express and convey his feelings, but they preordain his thoughts from the very beginnings of his feeble cognitive gropings. They pre-exist linguistically, within the community, whose members intone them in worshipful ways which suggest their relation to an ultimate reality. Tillich's idea that symbols participate in the power to which they point[9] thus assumes a new dimension: to the extent that sacred languages, words, and phrases are religious symbols, the religiously reared individual cannot ignore them but is forced to lead his thoughts through their pathways. They divide reality in certain ways, especially by introducing the idea of levels of reality, ordered from ultimacy to various degrees of contingency.

FUNCTIONS OF LANGUAGE IN RELIGION

Every schoolchild knows what *Homo sapiens* is. He proudly acknowledges himself by that term as a rational being. Since Otto, we have learned to speak of *Homo religiosus* in denoting man's relations to religion. Since Huizinga,[10] we have come to speak of *Homo ludens* to describe man at play. Anthropologists have spoken of *Homo faber* to describe man's penchant for making and doing things. Zuurdeeg has fostered the term *Homo loquens* with the declaration: "If it is granted that a man is his convictions, his word, it follows that when we speak of 'language' we mean man himself, man-who-speaks, *homo loquens*."[11]

Language is not only a system or a set of forms which man finds available in his community. It is also an act. Man-who-speaks is trying to accomplish something with and through language. He adapts himself to his world linguistically; he survives through language. In the process of learning and growing up, he acquires certain linguistic styles and mannerisms, adaptively and defensively. His language is *him,* to a significant degree. "My name is Legion," said the man who felt possessed by several demons. "I am that I am" or "I am he who is" proclaims the creator who constitutes being.

Students of religion and linguistic philosophers have introduced distinctions between kinds of language, often in order to evaluate the truth or evidence character of religious propositions. Cassirer[12] and others were concerned with symbolism and the kind of reality it refers to. Feigl[13] recognized a cognitive-informational language, subdivided into purely formal, logico-arithmetical, and factual-empirical statements; and a noncognitive language subdivided into pictorial-imaginative, emotional-affective, and volitional-motivational statements. More recently, Zuurdeeg has spoken of indicative and convictional languages recognizing that religious language is highly convictional, with a "convictor" who has the power to overcome someone else by promises or threats, and a "convictus" who assents to the convictor's propositions, usually in the context of a social system, the "confessional group."

Granted that a large part of religious language is convictional in Zuurdeeg's sense, psychologists are less concerned with the philosophical question of truth. Their concern is with individual differences in language use, the relations among language and thought, emotion, volition, and interpersonal relations. I will therefore endeavor to present through examples a variety of functional language styles, which can be found in religiously "convinced" persons. The categories I will use are themselves not religious categories, but psychologically useful distinctions which can apply to all language behavior. The following list, which lays no claim on exhaustiveness, will guide us:

1. formal
2. logical demonstration
3. empirical demonstration
4. pictorial-imaginative
5. erotic
6. aggressive
7. evocative
8. ecstatic
9. pious and precious
10. hortatory and fanatical

The reader will note that this classification is not focused on problems of reality testing. These have been dealt with as aspects of thought in the previous two chapters. The emphasis is on the qualities of the language act. In the following presentations I will freely use and interweave two series of examples. One series relies on fragments from many different persons writing from different situations and for different purposes. The other series consists of the utterances of one person, Augustine, from whose *Confessions* a great variety of functional language fragments have been culled in order to exemplify intraindividual differences.

1. As an example of *formal-informational language* I cite the following passage from Augustine:

And what did it profit me that, when I was scarcely twenty years old, a book of Aristotle's entitled The Ten Categories fell into my hands? On the very title of this I hung as on something great and divine, since my rhetoric master at Carthage and others who had reputations for learning were always referring to it with such swelling pride. I read it by myself and understood it. And what did it mean that when I discussed it with others they said that even with the assistance of tutors—who not only explained it orally, but drew many diagrams in the sand—they scarcely understood it and could tell me no more about it than I had acquired in the reading of it by myself alone? For the book appeared to me to speak plainly enough about substances, such as a man; and of their qualities, such as the shape of a man, his kind, his stature, how many feet high, and his family relationship, his status, when born, whether he is sitting or standing, is shod or armed, or is doing something or having something done to him—and all the innumerable things that are classified under these nine categories (of which I have given some examples) or under the chief category of substance.[14]

The language of this passage is rather sober. It informs the readers of historical events, cultural facts, and social perceptions. It sums up some aspect of a book's content in a rather dry and expository manner without embellishment. Even the questions "what did it profit me . . ." and "what did it mean . . ." are rather soberly formulated, allowing the reader to find his own answer, or to empathize with the question and address it to himself. Augustine's statement dates from the fifth century; what formal-informational statements can we encounter in our contemporaries? Here is a modern example, taken from Lewis Mumford:

Religion, as I shall here define it, is a body of intuitions and working beliefs that issue out of that part of man's nature and experience which science, deliberately seeking piecemeal knowledge of an immediately verifiable nature, rejects. For the questions that religion asks are not concerned with particulars but with the whole: not specific questions as to What and How? but questions of the widest generality and the most teasing elusiveness: Why? Wherefore? For what purpose? Toward what end? Religion seeks, in other words, not a detailed causal explanation of this or that aspect of life, but a reasonable account of the entire sum of things.[15]

Note again the sobriety of the phraseology, despite the fact that the author is conveying a point of view and an opinion. The statement as quoted here is itself not a religious opinion but a definition of religion in its "otherness" from science. It is worded with precision; it is focused on questions, not answers; it proceeds with reference to the great structural problem of the parts and the whole. It does not attack or slander alternative viewpoints; it deftly places one set of questions alongside another set of questions and puts them into formal categories. The word "whole" is not capitalized, as pious souls might wish. The words "belief," "ultimate," "reality," or "God" do not appear.

2. Logic deals with the formal principles of the reasoning process. Its aim is to bring about sound reasoning, according to certain canons. These canons have shifted over the course of time, from those of Aristotle's *Organum* to the current preference for mathematical demonstration and Boolean algebra. Psychologists are not interested in logic per se, but very much interested in a person's efforts to engage in logical thinking, according to the canons of the time and his powers of reasoning. *Logical demonstration* is a unique language act, and the following excerpt from Augustine shows that thinker's way of coming to grips with it.

> Still, from this time forward, I began to prefer the Catholic doctrine. I felt that it was with moderation and honesty that it commanded things to be believed that were not demonstrated—whether they could be demonstrated, but not to everyone, or whether they could not be demonstrated at all. This was far better than the method of the Manicheans, in which our credulity was mocked by an audacious promise of knowledge and then many fabulous and absurd things were forced upon believers *because* they were incapable of demonstration. After that, O Lord, little by little, with a gentle and most merciful hand, drawing and calming my heart, thou didst persuade me that, if I took into account the multitude of things I had never seen, nor been present when they were enacted—such as many of the events of secular history; and the numerous reports of places and cities which I had not seen; or such as my relations with many friends, or physicians, or with these men and those—that unless we should believe, we should do nothing at all in this life. Finally, I was impressed with what an unalterable assurance I believed which two people were my parents, though this was impossible for me to know otherwise than by hearsay.[16]

Except for using the imaginary interlocutor, God, and attributing to him the insights described in this passage, Augustine is here facing the basic logical concerns of evidence, absurdity, validity of inference, and the difference between sensory data and the constructs of pure thought. He examines premises and conclusions, weighs evidence, and tries to tease out contradictions. He essays to describe the span and the limits of demonstration, and the relations between the assumptions of belief and their consequences. He refrains in this paragraph even from vilifying the Manicheans, as he is wont to do in the rest of his *Confessions,* although there is a definite innuendo of mockery. For a modern example of logical language, I take recourse to the following passage from Lecomte du Noüy:

> Any effort to visualize God reveals a surprising childishness. We can no more conceive Him than we can conceive an electron. We forget that this incapacity is not, in itself, a proof of non-existence. We are in the habit of

juggling nowadays with electrons, protons, neutrons, etc. Individually, they are rigorously inconceivable and physicists, who inspire as much confidence today as did the priests in the past, affirm that without these particles our material objects, the forces we employ—in other words, our whole inorganic universe—become incoherent and unintelligible. (Let us not forget that these particles move in a world where time and space do not have the same value as in ours.) Nobody questions the reality of these now familiar though elusive and strange elements.[17]

Here too is a deft comparison of two kinds of evidence, and an evaluation of the role of "belief" in holding first assumptions.

3. Factual evidence and *empirical demonstration* find their acme in scientific experiment. The language of experiment is curt. The language of facts is confronting: it speaks of events, places, things, and the patterns of observable changes. Augustine writes, and one can hardly find a drier and more fact-minded phraseology:

And I looked around at other things, and I saw that it was to thee that all of them owed their being, and that they were all finite in thee; yet they are in thee not as in a space, but because thou holdest all things in the hand of thy truth, and because all things are true in so far as they are; and because falsehood is nothing except the existence in thought of what does not exist in fact. And I saw that all things harmonize, not only in their places but also in their seasons. And I saw that thou, who alone art eternal, didst not *begin* to work after unnumbered periods of time—because all ages, both those which are past and those which shall pass, neither go nor come except through thy working and abiding.[18]

The language is about "things" and their patterns of relation to each other in space, of patterns of change over time, and finally of the notions of space and time per se. "All things are true in so far as they are"—a more direct reference to sensory evidence could hardly be made. Referring to the same order of evidence—regularity, patterns and order—Einstein said the following:

We have penetrated far less deeply into the regularities obtaining within the realm of living things, but deeply enough nevertheless to sense at least the rule of fixed necessity. One need only think of the systematic order in heredity, and in the effect of poisons, as for instance alcohol, on the behavior of organic beings. What is still lacking here is a grasp of connections of profound generality, but not a knowledge of order in itself.[19]

But Einstein's conclusion is different from Augustine's. He rejects the idea of a personal God interfering with natural events. In this essay he adds: "For a doctrine which is able to maintain itself not in clear light but only in the dark, will of necessity lose its effect on mankind, with incalculable harm to human progress." The "dark" here referred to is the determination of some religionists to maintain the idea of a personal God for all those domains in which scientific knowledge has not yet progressed. Einstein goes on to say:

> But whoever has undergone the intense experience of successful advances made in this domain, is moved by profound reverence for the rationality made manifest in existence.[20]

These two men-who-speak are adapting themselves, through the language of facts and their relations, to the world in which they live which for both of them is characterized by order. Both venerate this order and go on to draw conclusions from it, one ending up with a theistic ontology, the other with a feeling for the nobility of the world and of the mind that can grasp it.

4. There are also *pictorial-imaginative language acts*. Religion has used them profusely, and they are in no way strangers to science. Though Lecomte du Noüy already pointed out that some scientific "things" are only quasi-pictorial and should be understood mathematically, science replicates and produces pictures and has a penchant for pictorial language in microphoto-graphs of cell mitosis, in chromosome maps, in the colorful bands of spectog-raphy, and in the "little animals" of Leeuwenhoek, accompanied by purely descriptive commentary. Here is an example of the pictorial-imaginative flight of Augustine's language:

> And I kept seeking for an answer to the question. Whence is evil? And I sought it in an evil way, and I did not see the evil in my very search. I mar-shaled before the sight of my spirit all creation: all that we see of earth and sea and air and stars and trees and animals; and all that we do not see, the firmament of the sky above and all the angels and all spiritual things, for my imagination arranged these also, as if they were bodies, in this place or that. And I pictured to myself thy creation as one vast mass, composed of various kinds of bodies—some of which were actually bodies, some of those which I imagined spirits were like. I pictured this mass as vast—of course not in its full dimensions, for these I could not know—but as large as I could possibly think, still only finite on every side. But thou, O Lord, I imagined as environing the mass on every side and penetrating it, still infinite in every direction—as if there were a sea everywhere, and every-where through measureless space nothing but an infinite sea; and it con-tained within itself some sort of sponge, huge but still finite, so that the sponge would in all its parts be filled from the immeasurable sea.[21]

Augustine knew that his imagination "arranged these also" and that he "pic-tured to himself" the billion of things and ideas within the plenitude of being. For a modern example of pictorial language I take recourse to Boisen's *Out of the Depths,* an autobiographical account of a life plagued by episodes of severe mental illness:

> I was too much absorbed in my own thoughts, particularly those regarding the approaching end of the world and those responsible for the use of force

and for the charge of homicidal intent. By nightfall my head was all in a whirl. It seemed to be the Day of Judgment and all humanity came streaming in from four different directions as in the accompanying diagram. They all came in to a common center. There they were brought before the judgment seat. But it seemed to be an automatic sort of judgment. Each indi-

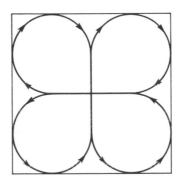

vidual judged himself. There were certain pass-words and they made certain choices. Each person had three chances: a difficult "right the first time affair," a second choice which involved an element of sacrifice and meant that one would become a woman and not a man. The other was only a seeming chance which sent one at once to the lower regions. These lower regions did not seem to be anything very fixed. The whole thing was like a vast circulatory system.[22]

Here the pictorial language even falls back on actual pictograms in order to achieve maximal visualization. Even the prefacing statement "my head was all in a whirl" is a pictorial language act that adds the speaker's own dizzy sense of movement to the grand mass movements he is trying to describe. All people and things in this imagery move, horizontally and vertically, "like a vast circulatory system."

Man-who-speaks pictorially is not necessarily a visionary who only "takes in" and contemplates what he produces before his inner eye. Pictorial language can also be the language of action or preparation for action. The pictorial (and musical) language of the hymn "Onward Christian Soldiers" carries a heavy freight of activism.

5. The language act can be an *erotic act*, both in its imagery and in its rhythmic cadences. A famous instance is the poem by Madame Guyon:

> I love, my God, but with no love of mine,
> For I have none to give;
> I love Thee, Lord, but all that love is Thine,
> For by Thy life I live.
> I am as nothing, and rejoice to be
> Emptied and lost and swallowed up in Thee.[23]

Another example is Emily Dickinson's verse:

> Given in marriage unto thee,
>   Oh, thou celestial host!
> Bride of the Father and the Son,
>   Bride of the Holy Ghost!
>
> Other betrothal shall dissolve,
>   Wedlock of will decay;
> Only the keeper of this seal
>   Conquers mortality.[24]

Biblical literature contains the vast erotic allegory of the Song of Songs which opens with the plaintive, lovelorn exclamation: "O that you would kiss me with the kisses of your mouth!" and then goes on to daringly erotic assertions about two supreme lovers. In Augustine's *Confessions* we find the following passage of a man-who-speaks erotically:

> Since at that time, as thou knowest, O Light of my heart, the words of the apostle were unknown to me, I was delighted with Cicero's exhortation, at least enough so that I was stimulated by it, and enkindled and inflamed to love, to seek, to obtain, to hold, and to embrace, not this or that sect, but wisdom itself, wherever it might be. Only this checked my ardor; that the name of Christ was not in it. For this name, by thy mercy, O Lord, this name of my Saviour thy Son, my tender heart had piously drunk in, deeply treasured even with my mother's milk. And whatsoever was lacking that name, no matter how erudite, polished, and truthful, did not take quite complete hold of me.[25]

This is the typical language of love: to hold, to embrace, to be enkindled and inflamed to love, including the final telling comparison with the earliest love relation in life. With erotic zest, the names of the deity become words of endearment: "O light of my heart." The object of love is also captured in the cherished *name* of Christ, which holds all the sweetness and tenderness that lovers' names have among those who have passion for each other. The passionate feeling spreads even to the aside about the writings of Cicero, by whom Augustine was "delighted" and "stimulated." When man speaks erotically, he bubbles over in friendliness toward the universe and treats serious things, even at times his enemies, with a light touch.

In all strong emotions a regression of language may occur in which sentences are abbreviated to a few exclamatory words or the childish one-word sentence. The fourth gospel account of the meeting between Mary Magdalen and the resurrected Jesus contains such a loving one-word phrase in Mary's exclamation "Rabboni!" followed by Jesus' admonition: "Do not hold me." It is found in the statement "Praise be!" which omits the object. Instead of a prayerful sentence imploring divine assistance, the oppressed soul may say "God," just as the toddler says "Ma" when he means "Please tie my shoelace."

6. If language acts can be erotic, they can also be *aggressive*. The acme of aggressive language in religion is of course swearing and cursing. Most of the time, because of the pressure of vigorous affect, the expletive curse is a regressive one-word sentence. If impotence and embarrassment are added to the anger, the curses tend to take the form "God!" "Jesus!" or "Christ!" If the anger is fiercely object-directed it may take the form "Damn!" or "damn you!" Such expressions as "I'll be damned!" or "for Chrissake . . ." suggest a certain amount of self-directed aggression.

For a full-length flurry of aggressive language I present the following paragraph from Augustine:

> Thus I fell among men, delirious in their pride, carnal and voluble, whose mouths were the snares of the devil—a trap made out of a mixture of the syllables of thy name and the names of our Lord Jesus Christ and of the Paraclete. These names were never out of their mouths, but only as sound and the clatter of tongues, for their heart was empty of truth. Still they cried, "Truth, Truth," and were forever speaking the word to me. But the thing itself was not in them. Indeed, they spoke falsely not only of thee —who truly art the Truth—but also about the basic elements of this world, thy creation.[26]

The original Latin in which this passage was written is even more fulsomely staccato: *Itaque incidi in homines superbe delirantes, carnales nimis et loquaces, in quorum ore laquei diaboli* . . . When one speaks in anger and derision, there is a thunderous roll to the language which almost automatically predisposes one to such phrases as "snares of the devil," "clatter of tongues," "carnal," or Baalzebub, Nineveh, Sodom and Gomorrah, and Armageddon. The latter nouns are the preferred scolding formulas of holiness sects.

Kierkegaard, who was certainly no great stylist, illustrates in his occasional outbursts another feature of angry language: the inability to speak smoothly and connectedly in an even flow. In his exposure of Bishop Mynster we find the following passages:

> If the word "preaching" suggests more particularly what is said, written, printed, the word, the sermon, then the fact that in this respect (to allude to only one thing) Bishop Mynster's preaching soft-pedals, slurs over, suppresses, omits something decisively Christian, something which appears to us men inopportune, which would make our life strenuous, hinder us from enjoying life, that part of Christianity which has to do with dying from the world, by voluntary renunciation, by hating oneself, by suffering for the doctrine, etc.—to see this one does not have to be particularly sharp-sighted, if one puts the New Testament alongside of Mynster's sermons.

A witness to the truth is a man who in poverty witnesses to the truth—in poverty, in lowliness, in abasement, and so is unappreciated, hated, abhorred, and then derided, insulted, mocked—his daily bread perhaps he did not always have, so poor was he, but the daily bread of persecution he was richly provided with every day.[27]

These long sentences contain strings of words without connectives, which come like the explosions of machine-gun fire. The author is driven by a perpetual search for ever-stronger expressions. The language is in written form a replica of the pressure of speech which clinicians observe in exceedingly tense and angry patients.

7. *Evocative language* summons the hidden from its hiding place and conjures the spirits to visibility. In this purpose it resembles incantations. Evocative language is spellbinding also. It fascinates, calls forth, arrests, and appeals even when the object it tries to arrest is the *fascinans* itself in Otto's sense of the *mysterium tremendum et fascinosum*. Regarded as a whole, Augustine's *Confessions* are evocative through and through, because the whole work is in the form of one gigantic prayer. But few of its specific passages are as pointedly evocative as the following:

And what is this God? I asked the earth, and it answered, "I am not he"; and everything in the earth made the same confession. I asked the sea and the deeps and the creeping things, and they replied, "We are not your God; seek above us." I asked the fleeting winds, and the whole air with its inhabitants answered, "Anaximenes was deceived; I am not God." I asked the heavens, the sun, moon, and stars; and they answered: "Neither are we the God whom you seek." And I replied to all these things which stand around the door of my flesh: "You have told me about my God, that you are not he. Tell me something about him." And with a loud voice they all cried out, "He made us."[28]

Less prayerful, but powerfully plaintive and commanding, is the following modern passage from Boisen, who in the depth of despair during an acute period of mental illness wrote to one of his friends:

P.S. One hour later. It comes to me again that the situation is now very, very critical. Everything is hanging in the balance. I need your prayers and your help. You must get me out of here this week, no matter what happens. Oh, it is indeed terrible. Our Christian civilization is doomed and the battle will have to be fought all over again. It must now be fought against evil forces which are greatly augmented.[29]

Perhaps the original model of all evocation is the cry for help, the call "Oh, come!" It desires the absent to be present. Longing and search are inherent in it, and whether the search is direct as in Boisen's case, or indirect as in Augustine's passage, the evoker knows that the trail will lead to the hiding place where power keeps its secrecy. Augustine's passage is a masterful rendition of the hide-and-seek quality which typifies man's calling forth his gods, just as the magical incantations of archaic religions were often acompanied by a ritually slow and halting procession—two steps forward, one step backward—to the divine dwelling place.

8. For the mystic, the road leads from the evocative to the *ecstatic* language act, from "O come!" to *"Tat tvam asi."* If ecstasy is "being beside oneself," there are two obvious reasons for that condition. One is the strong emotion of joy which fills the self to the point of bursting so that it "bubbles over" in motor activities and language acts. The second reason is that in confrontation with the divine "other" one may feel "swallowed up in Thee" as Madame Guyon put it and in that sense be "pulled out of oneself." Since experiences of this sort are very often visionary, one would expect that ecstatic language be filled with visual imagery and visual metaphors, and that many allusions be made to "seeing" or "beholding."

The following example from Augustine shows ecstasy in an intellectual who cannot quite give up the control of reason:

> And when this power of reason within me also found that it was change-able, it raised itself up to its own intellectual principle, and withdrew its thoughts from experience, abstracting itself from the contradictory throng of fantasms in order to seek for that light in which it was bathed. Then, without any doubting, it cried out that the unchangeable was better than the changeable. From this it follows that the mind somehow knew the un-changeable, for, unless it had known it in some fashion, it could have had no sure ground for preferring it to the changeable. And thus with the flash of a trembling glance, it arrived at *that which is*. And I saw thy invisibility understood by means of the things that are made. But I was not able to sustain my gaze. My weakness was dashed back, and I lapsed again into my accustomed ways, carrying along with me nothing but a loving memory of my vision, and an appetite for what I had, as it were, smelled the odor of, but was not yet able to eat.[30]

From its measured pace of philosophical reflection the language suddenly takes wings: "with the flash of a trembling glance." St. Teresa of Avila, beset by hysterical mechanisms, rendered one of her ecstatic episodes in the following form:

> Our Lord was pleased that I should have at times a vision of this kind: I saw an angel close by me on my left side in bodily form. . . . He was not large, but small of stature and most beautiful—his face burning as if he were one of the highest angels who seem to be all on fire. . . . I saw in his hand a long spear of gold and at the iron's point there seemed to be a little fire. He appeared to me to be thrusting it at times into my heart and to pierce my very entrails; when he drew it out he seemed to be drawing them out also and to leave me all on fire with a great love of God. The pain was so great that it made me moan, and yet so surpassing was the sweetness of

this excessive pain that I could not wish to be rid of it. The soul is satisfied now with nothing less than God. The pain is not bodily but spiritual. It is the caressing of a love so sweet which now takes place between the soul and God.[31]

Here we find body language of a highly erotic variety, and the ecstasis is described in terms of a sexual orgasm, which is only very thinly veiled by a transparent symbolism. The woman-who-spoke in this passage is in fact narrating how she spoke with her body during the ecstatic moment, at which time a moan was her only utterance.

The ecstatic experience is not always directly focused upon confrontation with one's God or a striving of union with him. In the following excerpt from Boisen there is an ecstatic appreciation of divine emblems and paraphernalia which suffice for the exalted state:

In Ward 2 I was given first the little room in the southeast corner. I was tremendously excited. In some way, I could not tell how, I felt myself joined onto some superhuman source of strength. The idea came, "Your friends are coming to help you." I seemed to feel new life pulsing all through me. And it seemed that a lot of new worlds were forming. There was music everywhere and rhythm and beauty. But the plans were always thwarted. I heard what seemed to be a choir of angels. I thought it the most beautiful music I had ever heard. Two of the airs I kept repeating over and over until the delirium ended. One of them I can remember imperfectly even now. This choir of angels kept hovering around the hospital and shortly afterward I heard something about a little lamb being born upstairs in the room just above mine. This excited me greatly and next morning I made some inquiries about that little lamb.[32]

In his chapter on mysticism, James made a passing remark about the significance of language in ecstatic conditions. He recognized that words, maxims, and formulas with which one has been long acquainted suddenly reveal their fuller meaning. He paraphrased this idea by saying: "I've heard that said all my life . . . but I never realized its full meaning until now."[33] A new sense of deeper significance gives the words and phrases an experiential "thickness" they never had before. It would seem therefore that the ecstatic, as a man-who-speaks, adds to the common sign-qualities of language an immensely rich symbol dimension, very much like the poet Wordsworth does when he says:

> Visionary power
> Attends the motions of the viewless winds,
> Embodied in the mystery of words.[34]

9. There is one religious attitude which is linguistic to a high degree and significantly alters the utterances of *Homo loquens.* It is piety, expressed in *pious language,* precious phrases and, at times, the exaggerated

and pretentious styles of piosity. Pious language in full dress is exemplified by the following song from a book with the pious title, "Triumphant Service Songs":

> My hope is built on nothing less
> Than Jesus' blood and righteousness;
> I dare not trust the sweetest frame,
> But wholly lean on Jesus' name.

> Refrain: On Christ, the solid Rock, I stand;
>   All other ground is sinking sand.

> When darkness veils His lovely face,
> I rest on His unchanging grace;
> In ev'ry high and stormy gale,
> My anchor holds within the veil.

> His oath, His covenant, His blood
> Support me in the whelming flood;
> When all around my soul gives way,
> He then is all my hope and stay.

> When He shall come with trumpet sound,
> Oh, may I then in Him be found;
> Dressed in His righteousness alone,
> Faultless to stand before the throne.[35]

The song does not merely express pious sentiments or an attitude of devotion; it is full of words, religiously overworked words, that have all the qualities of clichés:

hope	trumpet sound	faultless	throne
Jesus' name	Jesus	blood	solid
sinking sand	Christ	Rock	unchanging
stormy gale	veil	grace	flood
soul	anchor	covenant	righteousness
He shall come			

No less than twenty-one religious clichés occur in this song. In a religious context, these words are all tokens, coins, or little keepsakes of which the devout person has a purseful. He grabs for his purse, as it were, the moment he has to meet a situation which to him is "religious." Pious language is in this sense a habitual language, a special argot or lingo about the divine that one acquires in the course of religious upbringing and group associations.

Piety slips easily into piosity, which is a pretence at virtuousness and an exaggerated show of piousness. Linguistically, such an attitude is characterized by preciousness in the choice of words and phrases. The acme of preciousness is often reached in the forms of address in prayers. Instead of a simple and direct "God" or "Father," the precious soul is wont to say "Oh, Thou Ruler of all, who art . . . ," or "We beseech Thee, Oh, heavenly Father. . . ." The technique is word substitution, whereby the language of today is exchanged for archaic expressions, an antiquated form of the mother tongue, or elaborate circumlocutions, as the following list indicates:

modern direct phrase:	pious or precious phrase:
Israel, Palestine	The Holy Land
book, Bible	scripture, word of God
group activity	fellowship
meeting	gathering
song	hymn
church work	the work of the Lord
Sunday	Sabbath
church	kirk, house of God
Luke 5:4–7	The Gospel is from the gospel of Luke, the fifth chapter, beginning at the fourth verse . . .
Let us pray	Let us approach to the throne of Grace
Jesus	our Saviour
He guides me	He leadeth me
death	valley of death
sin	iniquity
food, bread	manna
eternity	world without end
atonement	precious blood

There is a "holier than thou" quality in pious or precious phraseology. As man-who-speaks, the pious speaker suggests through his choice of words a number of things over and beyond the ideas he refers to. He may wish to show that he has had special training in religious argot and thereby advertise his religious affiliation. He may want to accentuate differences between a secular and a sacred realm, or register his opposition to the world. He may proudly display how well he has learned the court etiquette of a decorous society around his deity, thereby affirming his status or "pulling his rank." Possibly, he finds the mother tongue in its contemporary form unequal to the task of alluding to the divine mysteries. Sometimes, pious language is a way of denigrating other people, particularly when it takes the form: "Brother, I will pray for you!" In that case, piety is only a cloak for hostile relations. In general, however, taking recourse to pious language seems to be a way of hiding the unclarity of one's thinking behind a lofty phrase or a sonorous series of sounds. In the latter sense, one can recognize pious talk in nonreligious circles also. The jargon of science, repeated as clichés, sloppily used to impress others and oneself, serves a similar function.

Augustine talked piously too, at times. Consider the following paragraph:

What, therefore, is my God? What, I ask, but the Lord God? "For who is Lord but the Lord himself, or who is God besides our God?" Most high, most excellent, most potent, most omnipotent; most merciful and most just; most secret and most truly present; most beautiful and most strong; stable, yet not supported; unchangeable, yet changing all things; never new, never old; making all things new, yet bringing old age upon the proud, and they know it not; always working, ever at rest; gathering, yet needing nothing; sustaining, pervading, and protecting; creating, nourishing, and developing; seeking, and yet possessing all things. Thou dost love, but without passion; art jealous, yet free from care; dost repent without remorse; art angry, yet remainest serene.[36]

And consider the following selection from Augustine for an example of preciousness and zealous self-humiliation:

Still, dust and ashes as I am, allow me to speak before thy mercy. Allow me to speak, for, behold, it is to thy mercy that I speak and not to a man who scorns me. Yet perhaps even thou mightest scorn me; but when thou dost turn and attend to me, thou wilt have mercy upon me. For what do I wish to say, O Lord my God, but that I know not whence I came hither into this life-in-death. Or should I call it death-in-life? I do not know.[37]

An interesting paradox shapes up when one compares pious language (today's and yesterday's) with the historical movement of Pietism in the seventeeth century under such leaders as Spener, Francke, Gerhardt, and von Zinzendorf. That movement and those men were opposed to the formalism and intellectualism of their day, and sought the answer in evangelical fervor, with a language of the heart. The pious language described in this section, however, is a formalism of its own and a linguistic ritual. It is neither a language from the heart nor a language of the brain. It is what Shakespeare called "Words, words, words."[38]

10. There is one more significant function of language in religion, describable as *hortatory* or *fanatical*. It is always tainted with anger, at something or somebody, including at times oneself. In excessive enthusiasm for some religious truth, man-who-speaks hortatorily or fanatically loses sight of elegance or propriety, and begins, figuratively, to "thunder." He raises his voice in speaking, he castigates through words, and his zealous intentness gets the better of him. Let us look at a pregnant example of it in Augustine:

But woe unto you, O torrent of human custom! Who shall stay your course? When will you ever run dry? How long will you carry down the sons of

Eve into that vast and hideous ocean, which even those who have the Tree (for an ark) can scarcely pass over? Do I not read in you the stories of Jove the thunderer—and the adulterer? How could he be both? But so it says, and the sham thunder served as a cloak for him to play at real adultery.[39]

This is no "sham thundering" but real exhortation. It uses a typical word for the activities of the accused party: adultery. Even the question marks behind the pseudoquestions are really exclamation points. The real message is "Woe unto you!" and the rest is little more than literary elaboration. This is not surprising, because Augustine was a teacher of rhetoric who knew the tricks of his trade, and he was dealing in this passage with the "falsehoods" of his study books, the works of Homer.

The following selection is an attempt at self-exhortation but no less fanatical:

And I do not blush, O my God, to confess thy mercies to me in thy presence, or to call upon thee—any more than I did not blush when I openly avowed my blasphemies before men, and bayed, houndlike, against thee. What good was it for me that my nimble wit could run through those studies and disentangle all those knotty volumes, without help from a human teacher, since all the while I was erring so hatefully and with such sacrilege as far as the right substance of pious faith was concerned? And what kind of burden was it for thy little ones to have a far slower wit, since they did not use it to depart from thee, and since they remained in the nest of thy Church to become safely fledged and to nourish the wings of love by the food of a sound faith.[40]

This passage also contains some classical features of hortatory and fanatical language, repeated at all times by great accusers. There is the word "blasphemy" which together with "adultery" is the stock in trade of inquisitors. It decries the use of reason and wit and becomes decidedly anti-intellectual, much as Luther became when he vilified reason as "the whore." There is a sudden and unexpected benevolence toward less endowed creatures, here called "thy little ones," who remained in "the nest" of the church. But since the passage is a self-accusation, there is also a sly note of pride in "my nimble wit."

A third selection from Augustine adds several more typical features to our accumulating inventory of hortatory and fanatical phraseology:

Let me now lay bare in the sight of God the twenty-ninth year of my age. There had just come to Carthage a certain bishop of the Manicheans, Faustus by name, a great snare of the devil; and many were entangled by him through the charm of his eloquence. Now, even though I found this eloquence admirable, I was beginning to distinguish the charm of words from the truth of things, which I was eager to learn. Nor did I consider the dish as much as I did the kind of meat that their famous Faustus served up to me in it.[41]

The accused is compared to a "snare of the devil," and he is held responsible for "entangling" innocent people. I do not know whether these phrases and figures of speech existed before Augustine, but religious exhorters have used them profusely ever since his days. When their enemy was formidable, they have also attributed a dangerous "charm" to him, in deference to his capacities, just as Augustine did with his former teacher. Finally, we see how fanaticism divides the world into two camps, of whites and blacks, saints and sinners, "we" and "they," when Augustine takes recourse to the debasing linguistic trick of saying "*their* famous Faustus."

This part of our chapter on language behavior in religion began with a reference to Zuurdeeg's work. It is appropriate to close it with another pertinent quote from Zuurdeeg on fanaticism:

> The fanatical claim is a form of imperialistic language. It is a convictional encroachment upon all other convictions. If the people addressed by the claim do not answer with the right response, they are *ipso facto* condemned, for instance, as enemies of the working class, as enemies of the Aryan race, as traitors, heretics, Communists. Such disqualifications and insinuations are not to be minimized as forms of extreme intolerance. The fanatical claim implies the conviction that something of ultimate importance is at stake, and testifies to the certainty that everyone who does not worship this convictor trespasses upon a cosmic law.[42]

I was tempted to select for this section a passage from Hitler's *Mein Kampf* as an example of modern fanatical language, but after Zuurdeeg's succinct statement this is, thank God, no longer necessary.

SPEECH IN RELIGION

When Luther tried to reform the Roman Mass and replace it with the *Deutsche Messe* he wrote in his commentary that after the Kyrie eleison the priest "reads a collect in monotone on F-faut," the Epistle "in the eighth Tone, in the same key as the Collect," and reads "the Gospel in the fifth Tone."[43] Prior to Luther's reform, the Kyrie used to be repeated nine times: three times Kyrie eleison, three times Christe eleison, and another three times for a concluding Kyrie eleison. Luther allowed only one time for each of the Kyries, thereby reducing the whole from nine to three. He also stated that "the additions of the early fathers, who are said to have prayed one or two psalms *in a subdued voice* before blessing the bread and the wine, were commendable. . . ." He added the following note about the language to be used in the service:

For I would in no wise banish the Latin tongue entirely from the Service, for the youth is my chiefest concern. If I could bring it to pass and Greek and Hebrew were as familiar to us as the Latin, and offered as much good music and song, we would hold mass, sing and read on successive Sundays in all four languages, German, Latin, Greek and Hebrew.[44]

Four hundred years later the same concern about speech in religion continues in unabated vigor. I remember from my Dutch childhood that the word "Christ" allowed for two pronunciations, one in which the first three letters were enunciated as a plosive *kr*, the other as a fricative *ghr*. Each of these pronunciations was specific to a denomination, both within the mainstream of Calvinism. There was a world of differences between these two denominations, less in theology than in style of life and attitudes toward culture. From the sharp *kr* and the soft glottal fricative *ghr* one could fairly well estimate the speaker's value system and the way in which he thought about the relations between the sacred and the secular realms.

These examples are sufficient to indicate both the profound preoccupation with speech in religion, and the attempt to "religionize" speech for sacred purposes. Despite the Psalmist, the adhortation "to make a joyful noise unto the Lord" is not to be taken literally in established religions. The noise is to be regulated in terms of loudness, tone, pitch, timbre, and various other qualities. Gender has long ruled the selection of choir members, and it still rules pulpits and altars. In order to produce certain voices, castration has been applied. The unctuousness of preachers' voices is a standing joke. In certain circumstances the utterance of gibberish or nonsense syllables is hallowed as "speaking in tongues" and a special Person of the Trinity is held responsible for it. Some sacred things have to be said in a whisper; others in a loud voice.

The same impulse to symbolize, which saw the creativity of the word and the possibility of its becoming incarnate, also discovered something special in speech, in the word-as-spoken, and in all noises. Hebrew literature contains the following passage in I Kings 19:11-13:

And he said [to Elijah], "Go forth, and stand upon the mount before the Lord." And behold, the Lord passed by, and a great and strong wind rent the mountains, and broke in pieces the rocks before the Lord, but the Lord was not in the wind; and after the wind an earthquake, but the Lord was not in the earthquake; and after the earthquake a fire, but the Lord was not in the fire; and after the fire a still small voice. And when Elijah heard it, he wrapped his face in his mantle and went out and stood at the entrance of the cave. And behold, there came a voice to him, and said, "What are you doing here, Elijah?"

Prophets have spoken words, but often as "a voice crying in the wilderness." Statesmen have called the voice of the people God's voice, not only because of what they said, but because they "spoke up" at the crucial moment. From all these considerations one is given the impression that in religion, the word-as-spoken is a fetish and the act of speaking is an exceedingly complicated ritual.

The first ritualistic feature of religious speech is *repetition*. "Holy, holy, holy," goes the phrase of the hymn. The sentence of forgiveness at the end of the Kol Nidre prayer is repeated three times. Pater Nosters and Ave Marias are prescribed a number of times as acts of penance. The eighteen blessings in Hebrew worship all end up with the standard phrase "Blessed art Thou, O Lord our God, King of the Universe . . . ," which is repeated eighteen times. While some repetitions can be an expression of increased pathos, in which case the pronunciation becomes increasingly loud or emphatic, in many forms of ritualistic repetition a mechanical quality of the speech act is advocated. Rosaries are in the service of just this mechanical form of repetition. Repetition can also be done through the written medium. In Tibetan prayer wheels, a drum or wheel containing multiple tightly rolled cylindrical scrolls on which prayers are written is turned so that the wheel "scatters" them as it were in all directions. Prayer flags serve the same purpose of letting the prayer, written on the flag, wave in the wind.

Repetition of words and phrases has an ancient heritage. Its justification must be sought in the magical belief that repetition of words makes these words more efficacious; the word serves as token or fetish, and its very utterance makes the speaker participate in the power to which it is addressed. For many of the repeated words and phrases are salutations and invocations, which originally may have had the form of incantations made by priestly specialists and sometimes repeated by the worshipers. Many of the invocations, moreover, are psychologically a form of pleading. Just as children in contemporary families plead with their parents through a relentlessly repeated: "Dad . . ."; "But, Dad . . ."; "Will you, Dad . . ."; "May I, . . . Dad?" so the religious man pleads with his God, endlessly repeating his name in a plaintive voice. And if the gods are many, as in polytheism, there is a whole list of divine names to be repeated. Not to be overlooked also is the penance aspect of repetition, which expects from the worshiper or from the man who prays a certain tedium, so that his praying is a chore to be done. Repetition may also be enhanced by the need to pray for a certain length of time, either to show how serious one is with his supplication or to stress the penitential motive in the praying.

There is also a role aspect in repetition. Ritual was at first the domain of priests and other specialists who knew the secret formulas and possessed skills of voice, words, and body posture. As the congregations changed gradually from the role of mere observers to partial participants in the enacted religious drama, the leaders spoke first, then perhaps their helpers, and then the people as a whole, repeating the same words or sentences ever more massively. In literate societies, worship leaders and congregations may read aloud responsively, the second party either repeating for emphasis what the first party has said, or paraphrasing the original statement, or saying something altogether different.

Formalistic repetition in prayers was what Jesus objected to when he described the hypocrites who "love to stand and pray in the synagogues and at the street corners, that they may be seen by men" (Matt. 6:5), and the Gentiles who "heap up empty phrases" (Matt. 6:7). Despite this and other protests against "vain repetitions," the mechanism of repetition is still an integral part of many highly developed religions. It is manifest in the life of perpetual prayer to which some monastic men and women devote their existence; it recurs in temporary "prayer vigils" for worthy causes in times of oppression or despair. It is kept active in many devotional exercises and in praying prescribed for penance. In moments of anxiety, a person may inwardly repeat some divine appellation, or say the same first line of some childhood prayer over and over again.

A second feature of ritualistic speech is *precision*. Ritualistic speaking is not a matter of building sensible or elegant sentences, but of enunciating certain formulas. The formula has to be "just right" and must be uttered faultlessly. In modern religions this compulsion for exactness and precision is perhaps nowhere better illustrated than in Christianity's preoccupation with the right "words of institution," regarding the sacrament of the Mass or the Lord's Supper. When the communion service stresses the commemorative aspects in repeating the biblical reports about Jesus' Passover celebration with his disciples, the emphasis will be on "What did Jesus say at that time?" If it stresses the sacramental aspects of the ceremony, the words must clearly "set apart" the sacred nature of the ritual in performance and speech. If it stresses also some mysterious transformation of the substances of bread and wine, the words to be spoken must be absolutely correct, for they then constitute a formula of power, which invokes the divine transcendence to become immanent in the elements. In all three cases the issue is weightier than a concern with dignity and decorum. Power and its distribution are at stake.

Closely related to precision in speech is the idea that in religion special pronunciations are called for. There are very special ways of dwelling vocally on the name "Jesus," as a declaration of one's devotion. The very devout may say "Jeé-zos" with a long first vowel, which is stressed, and a slow ebbing of the second syllable. In cursing, or in anger, the word becomes brief, with sharp *s*'s. Most mainline, middle-class Protestants pronounce the word "Amen" as "ah-men" whereas the more jubilant sectarians are prone to exclaim "ay-men," also in more decibels. Congregations accept a slight nasality in their preacher's voice and a measured delivery as signs of devoutness. The formal forms of address of seventeenth-century English, with its "thee" and "thou" and its archaic verb endings in *th* are special church pronunciations which the true believers must learn to master. Other groups, with great evangelistic zeal, prefer the language of the day in preaching, provided it be uttered rapid-fire, with great pressure and agitation, in a hortatory or zealous fashion. When theologians comment that preaching is an *event,* in which the Word of God enters human lives at the *kairos,* i.e., in the fullness of time or at the receptive moment, they imply undoubtedly that preaching is not delivering a lecture or making a speech. It is speaking in a very special way, so that something happens to both the speaker and the hearers. Speaking from a pulpit cannot be casual, or coy, or excessively aesthetic; nor can it be merely dignified and polite. It must be religious, i.e., voice and diction and word choice are to be seen as representational functions through which the preacher participates in the powers inherent in the verbal symbols he uses.

A third aspect of religious speech is *volume.* How shall one pray: silently, in a whisper, *sotto voce,* conversationally, or loudly? May one shout, or wail? Is there a difference between silent prayer when one is surrounded by people, and silent prayer in the empty desert? Is mere thinking praying, or should one at least attempt to verbalize subvocally? It is said that the ancient Romans always prayed aloud, whether corporately or privately, and that they were suspicious of whispered prayers because they attributed these to sorcerers who were bent on casting evil spells. This fear goes back to the earlier times about which Isaiah reported when he alluded to "the mediums and wizards who chirp and mutter" (Isa. 8:19). Casting spells was done softly, in a whispering voice. Elijah was arrested by the "still small voice," not by the storm and the earthquake. To raise one's voice in civil circles is felt as an intrusion upon the rights of authority figures. Somehow, the volume of one's voice is a symbol of "where one stands" in the scheme of things and whether one "knows his place." Religious salutations must be given deferentially, with no more than medium strength of voice. An ejaculative "call" on the deity can be louder, particularly when it is accompanied by praise, or when the inner pressure of one's torment is high. A curse is louder still, usually in a lower pitch. A large amount of subtle self-regulation in the use of volume can be observed among congregations at worship. In responsive readings and various corporate recitations, the group is usually somewhat restrained so as not to sound thunderous or overwhelming. When corporate confessions are read, I have often noted that the speech is more emphatic and the volume louder. When a corporate prayer is said, the volume tends to be low, with many individuals only whispering or mumbling.

When individuals are singled out before the group, as in baptismal rites, in making vows toward assuming a church office, or in making a public confession of faith upon entering into membership, one can observe not only much variation in the loudness of the responsive "I do" but the average listener can perfectly empathize with the struggles the speaker has at such crucial moments. Emphatic declarations always tend to be made loudly, but could in this case easily sound vain or self-assertive, and therefore the speaker will put some constraint on the volume of his voice. But saying these important things softly could be a sign of hesitancy in one's commitment, and therefore the speaker is also bent upon raising his voice, against the concomitant restraint. The tragic result is sometimes a barely audible whisper or a momentary aphonia, all because of one's sincere efforts to use one's voice religiously, with precision and regulated volume.

We have said earlier that words, in religion, can have the properties of a fetish and that speaking can be a sacral activity. We should add to this that from an adaptive point of view all speaking can be seen as a displacement of large muscle activity to the fine musculature of the vocal cords, the tongue, and the palate, for reasons of caution and economy. Saying something is not yet doing the same thing and entails less responsibility. Saying something is also a way of cautiously anticipating the doing of it, allowing for trial and error, without the same degree of accountability. Speaking can be an abbreviated form of doing. And speaking is an excellent way of releasing excessive tensions. The fullness of the heart makes the mouth spill over. When people are tense or oppressed they long to "talk it out" and in the act of repeated talking, which is often a nuisance to other people who have heard the story already several times, the excessive tensions are released so that a tolerable dynamic balance is restored.

Religion uses this mechanism of "talking it out" as a process of unburdening oneself in the confession. In whatever way and in whatever setting this is done, the act of speaking brings at least momentary relief, particularly when there is "so much to be said" or when the "unspeakable" is put into words. The beneficial effect of such talking becomes apparent when one realizes that it involves establishing contact with another person, human or divine, who not only accepts the confessor but recognizes his penitent attitude and his state of turmoil. And whether the confession is used for pastoral-psychological or sacramental goals, the fact is that speech is used in the service of tension discharge, and that further discharges may well be provided by the prescription of ritual prayers in endless repetition, heartfelt if possible, mechanical if need be.

Through the speaking of words, another effect is involved in confession. Roheim[45] has pointed out that the enunciation of the secret or forbidden thought or memory of sin makes the other person cognizant of the secret and makes him share in the burden of guilt feelings. I would add that this is so, because the word externalizes the inner life and "hangs," as it were, as a magical "thing" between the speaker and the hearer. Roheim adds that "a confession of sins is a repetition of them and the person to whom they are confessed is a new partner in committing them."

A further elaboration of the magical "thing" quality of words is given in the Renaissance paintings which depict the Annunciation to the Virgin Mary. A typical setting shows the Virgin kneeling or sitting in one corner of the canvas, being approached by an angel; in the diagonally opposite upper corner from the Virgin is a slight indication of the God-Father (indicated through cupped hands, an eye, a puckered mouth in clouds, or two hands emitting a dove) whose "word" shoots down in a beam of light or as a column of breath which hits the Virgin's ear or other parts of the body. Jones has interpreted such scenes as instances of belief in "impregnation by the ear."[46] It implies that the word is a substance, eroticized as semen or *logos spermatikos* which travels through space to find a hospitable abode. In all these dynamic interpretations of language behavior, the word is concretized as a substance, like a true fetish.

Finally, there is the very special religious speech act of glossolalia or speaking in tongues. Hailed by some as a precious charisma, and as a sign of divine assistance and inspiration, it is scorned by others as a loss of self-control and as a pathological language. It is not confined to religion; spiritistic mediums are reported to engage in it from time to time, and it is a perfectly sane possibility of human playfulness to imitate language sounds without speaking in any definite, known language. But several biblical references to its occurrence in the early Christian church have given the practice a semiofficial status in some branches of Christianity, especially in Pentecostal groups. Glossolalia can be seen as a paraphrase of language and as a pseudolinguistic exercise of the speech musculature, usually done in a trancelike state and in the context of many other automatic or stereotyped body movements. Laffal[47] feels that "in part, speaking in tongues serves to provide verbal form to a conflicted wish while at the same time hiding the wish by stripping the verbalization of communal meaning." Lapsley and Simpson[48-49] see it as motor automatism occurring under the condition of dissociation, in persons who have a strong sense of the demonic as a personal or corporate problem. But they also take note of the regressive quality of speaking in tongues which makes it sound like an "infantile babble." Arising frequently from understandable emotional ejaculations, the ensuing rhythmic gibberish serves on the one hand as an expression of primitive love toward the parents, on the other hand as a projection of hate and fear in the childhood relationship to demonic or satanic powers, which are both "out there" in the universe and "deep down here" within the individual. Practically all those who have commented on glossolalia agree about its momentary cathartic effect, for the practitioners as well as their audiences.

I wish to stress the marked differences in motivation between the practice of glossolalia in groups which have a long tradition of it, in which it is highly ritualized and has become a definite expectation placed upon their members, and its occurrence in persons or groups who belong to mainline traditions which have always put a premium on decency and orderliness of behavior. In the latter case one has to assume that it is in part a manifestation of protest under a pious cloak. It then thrusts through the class and caste divisions that prevail in a pluralistic religious society. The regression is in that case a far more definite break from achieved levels of integration. In 1964 the press reported an outbreak of glossolalia in rather sophisticated urban milieus and among Yale University students. One could have expected that members of such groups, under felt pressures, might have engaged in cabalistic speculations or Gnostic numerology in which they could at least have exercised their intellectual endowments. Or they could have followed the path of Lewis Carroll who let Alice in Wonderland invent a secret language that was only accessible to well-informed initiates. They might even have imitated the Delphic Pythia in composing cleverly ambiguous sentences which present challenging riddles. But all these options were swept aside by the desire to "babble," that is, by the wish or need to regress, to discharge conflicted feelings through the speech muscles, in great solemnity, without humor or playfulness.

From another angle, glossolalia represents the extreme case of ritualization of speech, and in that sense proves the immense power of religious intentions over such integral ego functions as language and speech. In this extreme form, it has all the features of an obsessive-compulsive neurosis: dissociation, doing and undoing, repetition compulsions, preoccupation with anal-sadistic themes, legalism, and a corruptible superego, as Alexander[50] called the conscience of the pseudo-moral individual.

Linguistic philosophers have pointed out that religion owes some of its uniqueness to an odd use of language. The language of religion could be described as convictional, as opposed to indicative. Whatever one makes of such distinctions, the existence of sacred tongues, sacred scripts, and sacred names indicates that numinous qualities may be attached to various aspects of language behavior. Similarly, the function of speech can be ritualized in order to serve religious ends.

In this chapter an attempt was made to introduce clinical distinctions between various forms of the use of language, suggestive of individual differences in religious experience. Such differences give clues on the one hand to the formal aspects of thought organization, on the other hand to the emotional and motivational strata of personality.

VI

Emotional Processes

in Religion

IN THE PRECEDING chapters we have repeatedly asked whether any of the part processes, such as perceiving, thinking, and the language function could ever have a specifically religious quality or connotation. We have found ourselves hedging on the answer. Few thinkers have seriously proposed that religion is perceiving, although the data of perception can be religiously appreciated. Moreover, religions abound in evaluations of perception, which range from praise to disdain. Religion has been far more often defined in terms of thinking, whether by postulating a special kind of thinking such as belief, faith, and mystical reality sense, or by pointing to a special object of thought such as God, the reality of the unseen, the universe, or some other "really real." We also saw that religionists make their own peculiar evaluations of the thought process, which range from affirmation to skepticism. In the last half-century there have been quite a few attempts to define religion seriously in terms of language behavior. This has been done by analyzing existing religious languages, such as the language of the Bible, the language of theology, and the language of faith, or by asking what kind of situations are properly religious, and in what kind of language one could address himself to such situations.

We will try to do the same thing with feeling. And in order to make sure that we approach the emotions with phenomenological directness, the following passage from Jane Hillyer's *Reluctantly Told,* is offered as a starting point:

> Lying there I came as close, I think, as I ever have to a state of emotion unaccompanied by thought. I simply *felt.* Again, I have never learned words to describe sensations so far removed from what is called normal. General misery, physical discomfort, degradation not born of intellectual concept, but a deep, bodily and inner mental state; a feeling of being lost,

lost utterly with no sense of place or time, no idea as to whom voices belonged, no clear realization of my own identity, lost in mind and body and soul, lost to light and form and color; a distinct, acid nausea of self-revulsion—all these were in the feeling that swept over me. But they do not describe it any more than a list of ingredients describes any assembled whole. It was all the more complete in that I was not conscious of intellectual activity of any kind. My whole being was given over to feeling. I had not the slightest defence, either within myself or without. The sensation grew, rolled upon me like a gigantic wave. I gasped, struggled; there was a sickening, acute moment, then a welding. The emotion became *me*.[1]

This is perhaps as close as anyone can come to describing feelings per se, feelings in the raw, feelings *felt* rather than pondered. Miss Hillyer found her experiences abnormal not only because of their tone of intense misery and lostness, but also because they were so purely felt, without thought, without perceived external provocation, without decision-making, without defense. She used the word "feeling" in a very pure and pregnant sense, evocatively; counting on the possibility that the reader may spontaneously reverberate with her experiences, also without defense or intellectualization.

The purity and directness of certain feelings have often been held up as the essence of religion. In 1799 the theologian Friedrich Schleiermacher[2] addressed himself in a famous treatise on religion "to the cultured ones among its despisers" in which he advocated with great learning that religion is neither ethics or morality, nor metaphysics, but a feeling and a "sensitive and appreciative viewing" (*Anschauung*). For Schleiermacher, religion consists of a "sense and taste for the infinite," "a feeling of the eternal," and "a feeling of absolute dependency." Those cultured, nominal Christians and Jews who had learned to despise their religious heritage had done so because of a terrible confusion of religion with philosophy or ethics. Religion is not a rational and systematized world view. Nor is it a well-ordered knowledge about right and wrong eventuating in a system of moral values. Truth, goodness, and beauty may be important human pursuits, and great values in their own right, but they do not constitute the essence of religious experience, much as they may become associated with it. That was a courageous thing for a Plato scholar to say. The heart of religion is the heart, not the mind or the head. Schleiermacher pointed to the following feelings as especially numinous:

longing, yearning	(*Sehnsucht*)
reverence, piety	(*Ehrfurcht*)
humbleness, meekness	(*Demut*)
gratefulness, thankfulness	(*Dankbarkeit*)
compassion, mercy	(*Mitleid*)
contrition, remorse	(*Reue*)
hankering, zeal, aspiration	(*Verlangen*)

He went so far as to say that the strength of these feelings determines the degree of religiosity. The primacy of these feelings makes religion an indispensable aspect of a well-rounded personality, and it makes theology an empirical science instead of an elaborate justification of a system of doctrines.

One may question whether Schleiermacher's so-called feelings are really emotions, or whether they are attitudes. They certainly do not seem as raw and "thoughtless" as Miss Hillyer's unnerving experiences. But Schleiermacher's emphasis on feelings was a potent protest against formalism, ritualism, and rationalism in religion, which summed up for generations before and after him the conviction of all who demand that religious experience touch the heartstrings.

No psychology of religion can silently pass by the work of another great theologian who addressed himself to the role of feelings in religion: Jonathan Edwards' *A Treatise Concerning Religious Affections*.[3] Written in 1746 when Locke's works were widely read, when Berkeley's ideas were debated, and just a few years before Hume's *Enquiry,* Rousseau's *Critique of Culture,* and Voltaire's *Candide* saw publication, Edwards asked how it was possible within the Calvinist tradition to define the earmarks of those who are entitled to God's eternal rewards because they found his favor. The answer was sought in a scrutiny of the religious affections, by a razor-sharp scholar who cannot by any means be called a romanticist. Working with the traditional tripartite division of understanding, affection, and will as the main functions of mind, Edwards saw true religion in the affections of "love and joy in Christ" which render a man "full of glory" in "holy affections." He distinguished between affections and passions, attributing to the former a clarity of understanding and a degree of self-control which the latter missed, since passions entail greater violence of the animal spirits which tend to overpower the mind. This distinction was necessary to criticize both the coldness of rationalism and formalism, and the overheated frenzy of the enthusiasts. Revivalism preached a religion of the heart, but wished to avoid religion of the guts: it preferred liveliness to stiffness, conviction to lukewarmness,

> . . . for who will deny that true religion consists, in a great measure, in vigorous and lively actings of the inclination and will of the soul, or the fervent exercises of the heart.[4]

After having noted the chief affection of love of God, which is the "fountain of all affections," Edwards singled out hope, joy, fear, zeal, and compassion as the main feelings which make up the religious life. Though several of these feelings may occur in the irreligious also, and are in themselves beyond the secular-sacred distinction, in the religious soul they are all subordinate to that chief affection of love of God, which the hard-hearted lack. Edwards divided the affections into a group determined by approval or liking (love, desire, hope, joy, gratitude, complacence), another group based on rejection and disapproval (hatred, fear, anger, grief), and admitted the possibility of mixed forms (pity, zeal). He established a list of scriptural affections documented by chapter-and-verse references:

> fear
> hope
> love
> hatred
> desire, longing
> joy
> sorrow, mourning, and brokenness of heart
> gratitude, thankfulness
> compassion, mercy
> zeal

and considered all affections as "the spring of man's actions," thereby moving from emotion to motivation, much as modern psychologists do.

There is something about emotion that has always had a great appeal to the religionist. Or perhaps we should say, more cautiously, that in many religious commentaries the absence of heartfelt affections is seen as a danger sign for religion. Paul addressed himself to the Christians in Rome by exhorting them: "Be fervent in spirit . . ." (Rom. 12:11, AV). The Deuteronomic rule of the religious life is to "love the Lord thy God with all thy heart, with all thy soul and with all thy might." (Deut. 10:12, AV). And the writer of Revelation lets God say "So, because you are lukewarm, and neither cold nor hot, I will spew you out of my mouth" (Rev. 3:16). Wesley complained of the cold indifference which he saw among the believers in his time; and all revivalism is, in one way or another, an attempt to let religion speak to the heart and the gut, with the conviction that these are the wellsprings of belief, action, and commitment as well as the sources of right thinking about man's relations to the divine.

Religion accepts only in bemused puzzlement such intellectual utterances as Spinoza's *amor dei intellectualis*. It is pleased with the *amor*, it finds *dei* altogether correct, but does not quite know what to do with the adjective *intellectualis*. It sounds too dry, too cerebral, too philosophical. Although Kant has had an enormous influence on Christian theology and morality, his conviction that ethical behavior has no roots whatsoever in passion and inclination stands in direct contrast with the Pauline insistence that "God loves a cheerful giver" (2 Cor. 9:7). Religion demands spontaneity and takes a dim view of anything resembling calculation or mere rational determination. This preference for emotion is all the more remarkable when, as we shall see in the next chapter, we consider religion's equally strong emphasis on ritual, which is the acme of measuredness and calculation. But that seeming contradiction disappears when ritual is seen adaptively as providing a structure for emotional expression or dynamically as a defense against the intensity of any emotion or the unpleasantness of some.

EMOTIONS: HUMAN AND DIVINE

The identification, description, and classification of the emotions is one of the most difficult tasks of psychology. Animals, children, and the mentally ill are sometimes far better than normal adults in spotting the unique quality of an emotion. Poets and artists are better than psychologists in describing or illustrating them. Scientific classifications vary a great deal. Our language has an overabundance of words for emotional reactions that defies even Roget's *Thesaurus*,[5] which deals with them in four large classes, each with several subdivisions. Many of these words describe subtle varieties, complex interactions, or rare combinations of a much smaller number of basic or primary emotions, and there is still no full agreement regarding the number and the choice of such primary, original feelings. But among those that occur most frequently on lists of primary emotions there are two of doubtless religious significance and connotation: *awe* and *bliss*.

Both words have become the keystones to an immensely insightful book on the phenomenology of religion: Otto's *The Idea of the Holy*. Though Otto took issue with Schleiermacher's romanticism and shrank away from its implication that the primacy of religious feelings left only a responsive role to the deity, he also put much faith in feelings as pointers to the ultimate reality with which religion deals. But in making man's own felt contingency on some transcendent power his methodological principle, he was able to describe two different levels of reality, one of the deity and one of religious man, in a parallel series of corresponding aspects. In this theoanthropological parallelism Otto described various aspects of the deity, e.g., constitutive power, mystery, wrath, majesty, energy, admirability, and otherness, each corresponding with evocative human experiences, such as creatureliness, awe, dread, humbleness, commitment to acts, bliss, and nothingness.

In taking up awe and bliss as basic feelings which point to and register the presence of the holy, Otto described two primordial feelings that have a long history of religious specificity. Awe is the *Schauer* of the Germans, the *deima panikon* of the Greeks, the *emat Yahweh* of the Hebrews. It is Kierkegaard's *dread* and the *demonic fear* of primitive societies and fairy tales. It is Schleiermacher's *Angst der Kreatur,* which is too meagerly translated as anxiety or dread. If one wants the word *anxiety* nevertheless, which seems almost unavoidable in our time, it is the special anxiety that overcomes the creature when he stands in the presence of the uncanny. Otto feels that this is different from natural fear and cosmic anxiety, because an essential quality of the numinous is its unnaturalness. The *tremendum* of the holy is that unnatural, uncanny, majestic presence of constitutive power which evokes shuddering (tremor) for awe. As to bliss, its ancestry is found in the Greek *enthusiasmos,* the enraptured state of having God in oneself, in the Dionysian intoxication, in the exaltation of the mystics, and in that hyperacute, uncanny sense of well-being that Prince Myshkin experienced before his *grand mal* seizures in Dostoevski's *The Idiot.* It is the ineffable joy and exultation of which James gave such excellent examples in his *Varieties.*

Awe and bliss, though seemingly opposites, often occur in juxtaposition or alternation, and sometimes are intertwined, as the following quote from Davidson in Landis' collection suggests:

> Few people know what a punishment a short period of real madness is, or even a period of deep depression. We must each one of us, at his or her appointed hour, stand alone, not in the middle of a crowd, before the judgment seat of Christ; and He requires truth in the inward parts. *No saint could wish for greater joy; no sinner could fear a more dread apocalypse.* Even the most blood thirsty conqueror and dissolute pagan would hesitate, if he knew that his latter end meant an ever-lasting headache; and it is worse, far worse, than that[6] [*italics mine*].

In the same collection is a citation from Custance's report of his beatific feeling during a manic episode:

> I can testify from experience that these are the actual sensations accompanying the delusions of power so common in asylums. The sense of being intimately in tune with the ultimate stuff of the universe can become so overwhelming that those affected naturally proclaim themselves to be Jesus Christ, or Almighty God, or whatever deity they have been taught to look on as the source of all power. . . . In that peace I felt utterly and completely forgiven, relieved from all burden of sin. The whole of infinity seemed to open up before me, and during the weeks and months which followed I passed through experiences which are virtually indescribable. The complete transformation of "reality" transported me as it were into the Kingdom of Heaven. The ordinary beauties of nature, particularly, I remember, the skies at sunrise and sunset, took on a transcendental loveliness beyond belief. Every morning, quite contrary to my usual sluggish habits, I jumped up to look at them, and when possible went out to drink in, in a sort of ecstasy, the freshness of the morning air. . . .[7]

An extremely interesting example in Landis' collection of autobiographical reports is the following account of Symonds, an English poet who went through a self-induced episode of chloroform anesthesia. It describes striking alterations of mood, perceptions, and sensations in the midst of which there is a sudden change from ecstatic bliss to abject horror:

> After the choking and stifling of the chloroform had passed away, I seemed at first in a state of utter blankness: then came flashes of intense light, alternating with blackness, and with a keen vision of what was going on in the room around me, but no sensation of touch. I thought that I was near death; when, suddenly, my soul became aware of God, who was manifestly dealing with me, handling me, so to speak, in an intense personal present reality. I felt Him streaming in like light upon me, and heard Him saying in no language, but as hands touch hands and communicate sensation, "I led you. I guided you; you will never sin, and weep, and wail in madness any more; for now, you have seen me." My whole consciousness seemed brought into one point of absolute conviction; the independence of my mind from my body was proved by the phenomena of this acute sensibility to spiritual facts, this utter deadness of the senses; Life and Death seemed mere names, for what was there then but my soul and God, two indestructible existences in close relation. I could reason a little, to this extent that I said: "Some have said they were convinced by miracles and spirit-rapping, but my conviction is a real new sense." I also felt God saying, "I have suffered you to feel sin and madness, to ache and be abandoned, in order that now you might know and gladly greet Me. Did you think the anguish of the last few days and this experience you are undergoing were fortuitous coincidences?" I cannot describe the ecstasy I felt. Then as I gradually awoke from the influence of the anesthetics, the old sense of my relation to the world began to return, the new sense of my relation to God began to fade. I suddenly leapt to my feet on the chair where I was sitting, and shrieked out, "It is too horrible, it is too horrible, it is too horrible," meaning that I could not bear this disillusionment. . . . To have felt for that long dateless ecstasy of vision the very God, in all purity and tenderness, and truth and absolute love, and then to find that I had after all no revelation, but that I had been tricked by the abnormal excitement of my brain [was most distressing].[8]

The selections from Custance and Symonds also demonstrate a point that Otto considers very critical in the experience of awe and bliss: the heightened sense of the presence of the holy and the acute feeling of its unshakable reality. In Symonds' case, as soon as the sense of presence and ultimate reality gives way to the normal contact with the everyday world, bliss turns into horror, which in turn gives way to an angry feeling of being tricked.

In people for whom religion is very much a matter of the heart and who need to feel the fire or glow of the emotions enumerated by Schleiermacher and Edwards, there is probably no more abysmal state than the condition of dryness, lassitude, coldness, or emptiness. In medieval moral theology this was called *acedia* (from the Greek: not caring) and described as indifference to or even revulsion of one's customary religious practices and preoccupations. In modern terms one could call it a religious boredom or spleen. It was especially seen in members of monastic orders, and it followed not seldom in the wake of fervent religious feeling and activity. It has occurred in the lives of great mystics who not only abhorred the experience, but considered it a great sin also, a manifestation of unbelief. The very fact that *acedia* was considered a sin (as a matter of fact, it is a standard item on lists of the seven deadly sins in Patristic and medieval literature and in Chaucer's *Canterbury Tales*) and defined as sloth or spiritual torpor, implies that the deity claims not only intellectual recognition, but heartfelt and feelingful transactions and loyalty. Piety cannot exist without emotion.

But neither can the gods exist without emotion. The Olympic deities roared with laughter, howled for anger, and sobbed in sadness. They harbored resentments toward each other, planned revenge, nurtured their jealousies, and brooded over their anger. They displayed parental or filial feelings. They engaged in erotic embraces. The ancient Hebrew gods are said to have been angry and loving, jealous and patient, threatening and longing for peace. Yahweh's feelings were like those of a father for his sons and a hen for her chicks. Christianity has ascribed all these feelings to its god, but has stressed love, compassion, and tender mercy in a context of justified sternness and wrath. There is always ample room for stressing this or that feeling in the godhead, as long as one first affirms his emotionality per se. When placed in this perspective, Tersteegen's well-known statement that "a god who is understood is no god"[9] makes double sense. It refers in one way to the human situation in which gods should not be solely approached with the head but grasped in a heartfelt emotional response, or else the gods turn into mere concepts, perfectly definable and manageable. It refers in another way to the gods themselves, who are ungraspable and not quite understandable precisely because they are so emotional, i.e., unpredictable, unmanageable, mysterious. What Otto has said about the energetic aspect of the holy, namely that gods are the ultimate sources of energy, has a natural corollary in the idea that gods have vigorous feelings. Feelings, after all, are the felt qualities of energies.

Gods feel and men feel, and their transactions are feelingful acts. They respond to each other emotionally, in solicitation or recoil, in awe or bliss. There is a large range of possible and appropriate feelings, and much is permitted—except cold indifference. Religious literature is full of stories in which gods have endless forbearance with angry men, lustful men, spiteful men—in a word, with sinful creatures in almost any sense of that term. It is also full of stories in which men put up for a lifetime with the vengeance of their gods, with their cruelty and persecution, with their teasing favoritism toward others, with enduring "tests of fire." Job is still quite religious, and emotional, when he says (13:15-16):

> Behold, he will slay me; I have no hope;
> yet I will defend my ways to his face.
> This will be my salvation,
> that a godless man shall not come before him.

or, as the King James Version has it in what has been called a "sublime mistranslation":

> Though he slay me, yet will I trust in him: but I will maintain mine own ways before him. He also shall be my salvation: for an hypocrite shall not come before him.

But the moment anyone would relinquish any feeling toward or about his god, he would stop having that "fear of the Lord" which comprises in one condensed phrase all emotion appropriate to the deity. He would no longer be religious, though he could still be a speculative philosopher concerned with some first principle, some prime mover, or some ultimate reality. Freud too recognized emotion as the essential part-process of religion, when he saw strength of religious conviction, the decisiveness with which religious thoughts (i.e., dogmas and doctrines) are held, as being rooted in the strength of wishes and feelings.

On the other hand, religion does not condone any and all feelings, and it is far from advocating emotion for emotion's sake. Both organized and private religion take a very selective attitude toward emotions. In addition to the primordially religious emotions of awe and bliss, certain other emotions tend to be endowed with a religious halo, for instance those listed as Edwards' holy affections and Schleiermacher's reverential feelings or attitudes. A quasi-religious quality may be ascribed to such feelings as cheer, optimism, solace, regret, care, woe, demureness, or solemnity. In contrast, religion tends to judge certain feelings negatively, condemning them to the demonic. Hatred, lust, gluttony, bitterness, or resentment may become devalued as devilish emotions. Religion may establish a difference between mild feelings and intense affects, or between affections and passions as Edwards did, rejecting the affects and the passions altogether as unbecoming to a religious soul. Such an attitude may be due to a vigorous prescription of temperance as a virtue. Massive suppression of nearly all feeling is the classical earmark of asceticism, and in that attitude even the love of God is not allowed to be a passion or furor, because feelings per se are distrusted.

And then again, almost reversing itself, religion may at times perversely extol certain feelings for which people have a natural aversion, such as pain, grief, or sorrow. Usually, such uncommonly positive evaluations of negative feelings require considerable intellectual elaboration, if not intellectual trapezework in order to make them plausible. Such intellectualizations have beset the never-ending debates about the origin and existence of evil. Some theories are based on the assumption that evil is necessary as a spur to betterment—the instrumental versions. Others hold that evil does not really exist but is only a strange fantasy in some people—the denial theories of Christian Science and various other hyperidealisms. Still others posit that evil is only the absence of the good—the *privatio boni* theory to which Augustine contributed. In the last two theories, issue is taken with pain, suffering, sorrow, etc., as felt, and an attempt is made to reason them out of existence. In the first theory the pain or horror are phenomenologically acknowledged, but subjected to some great or mysterious purpose in whose service they are to be endured. Yet the very existence of all these theories, to the extent that they try to come to grips with the presence of negative feelings, perversely proves the primacy attributed to feelings as a religiously significant, if not indispensable, experience.

Though emotions tend to elude conscious or voluntary control and easily spill over into motor phenomena such as laughing, crying, trembling, and getting red in the face, religions tend to demand from their adherents that some control be exercised over the expression of feelings. This involves some differentiation between the feeling felt, and the feeling communicated through body language, which in the face of the James-Lange theory of emotion seems little more than an abstract nicety. For in that theory feeling and body reaction are one and undivided. "I am sad—therefore I cry" is just as plausible as "Tears fall down my cheeks—therefore I am sad," for emotion and body change are two sides of the same coin. But despite this unity, which is organized by the autonomic nervous system, some central nervous system intervention is possible. Expressions of emotion can be consciously suppressed, and verbalizations of feelings can be entirely withheld. Moreover, one can verbalize the opposite feelings of those that one has, or dissimulate them by neutral phrases or noncommittal activity. All the classical psychoanalytic defense mechanisms and many popular coping devices can be thrown into gear to mask, distort, or minimize the expression of feelings, and to a lesser extent even the subjective registration of the feelings.

THE PURSUIT OF HOLINESS

Which emotional expressions and which feelings do religions suppress? The answers vary with the religious systems, the stages in their development, and the choice of the evaluative frameworks in which the emotions are judged. Some idea of holiness usually serves as a guide. Early aboriginal religions tend to define holiness first in terms of power: holy is he who has mana and therefore can cast spells, manage the black arts, or act as a sorcerer. Thus, since most of these activities involve conjuring up the deities, which are the original sources of all power, the holy men are also the ones selected to lead worship and engage in ritual on behalf of the group. They handle the sacred tools, such as drums, fetishes, and amulets. When ritual grows in importance and complexity, certain rites are developed to augment holiness to group members who eventually form a caste or priesthood, and this leads to various initiation rites. Prohibitory rites are also developed, demanding careful avoidance of the dangerous implications of mana: the taboos. Taboos can be placed on objects, people, words, animals, places, times, and acts; each taboo implies some proscription such as "hands off," "not now," "be careful, or else . . . ," "don't say it," or just "don't." All these variations on the injunction "no!" have first the implication of dangerous power, and only at a later stage do they develop into a system of behavior regulation based on morals, ethics, social propriety, good taste, beauty, or spiritual motifs. Though we shall visit the taboo again in the next chapter, the point here is that directly or indirectly, the taboo is extended to the emotions, through some definition of holiness, sanctity, cleanliness, or purity. Each of these entails some definition of its obverse also, such as profaneness, uncleanliness, or impurity. Eventually, religions deal with emotions through a consideration of virtues and vices, graces and sins.

It is obvious that in each religion or period some parallelism exists between the holiness of the deity and the holiness of man. When power is the central notion, gods and priests are holy because they are powerhouses. When gods become loosened from the matter they created, holy men will similarly have disdain for earth, and for their own bodies. When the concept of god stresses the unitary wholeness of all things, holiness in man is to reflect the wholeness of life in body and mind. When, as in Hebrew religion, man and god engage in covenants, a whole ethics of contracting develops in which man's holiness assumes the character of social justice and concern with the welfare of the people, which is to mirror god's love and righteousness vis-à-vis his chosen people. When gods are perfect, holiness of man is a successful aiming at perfection. When gods are lofty and untainted by the organic changes that occur in their universe, human holiness becomes a striving for purity in sublime detachment from terrestrial preoccupations. When gods are erotic, their worship entails erotic enthusiasm, and holiness may become defined as sexual vigor. Paternal gods are under the same taboo as their human counterparts: they may not sexualize their relations to their human "children," and holiness in men assumes a sacrifice in the form of sexual abstinence. For in one way or another, holiness is always godliness, i.e., a striving for likeness to the god and communion with the god. A mutual assimilation between gods and men is an outstanding goal of all religion, as Plato already saw, both in regard to the selection of virtues and their inherent emotions.

In many religions—Zoroastrian Parsiism, Islam, Greek Orphism, and Christianity—some distinction between feelings and passions is made, and much attention is given to redeeming or disciplining the passions. In such a view, the passions have a vigor, and hence an element of danger, which the milder feelings lack. Not only do they often lead to behaviorial incontinence, but even the sheer inward experiencing of the passions can be so sweeping that religions must watch for its becoming an ungodly preoccupation which absorbs so much energy that too little is left for the more divine things. Nearly all ethical systems have addressed themselves to this point, Aristotle and Kant no less than Calvin, the monastic movements, and the enduring ethos of the so-called peace churches. The question is: which emotions have been singled out as passions that need redemption through self-control, group discipline, and divine assistance?

Classical lists throughout centuries of organized religion and private piety emphasize erotic love, hatred and anger, pride, arrogance and other forms of ardent self-love, anxious clinging to property and possessions, absorbing fear or anxiety, scorn and disgust of fellowman, and the restless search for pleasure at the expense of others or of a well-rounded and sensitive self as the dominant and unholy passions. These are the ones which religion is to curb through various redemptive means. Repression, suppression, re-education, and therapeutic procedures may be used, and at their best the prohibitions are balanced by attractive admonitions which make a "new life" out of the "old life." For who would or could give up passions except that they be overtaken by the glow, at least, of other pleasant feelings or satisfying promises?

Spiritual mentors have often noted that the way of self-renunciation in the control of passions is not without the risk of substituting a new passion for an old one. The besetting risk of continence through fasting and abstaining is the swelling of pride in one's excellent self-control. The ascetic way demands a careful orchestration of all feelings, in the service of which the great monastic leaders, St. Basil and St. Benedict, developed their elaborate rules, which were drawn up not without psychological sensitivity and reality sense. Literary forerunners of these rules can be found in the "Sayings of the Fathers," from which the following terse quotes are pertinent:

> Abba Pambo asked Abba Antony: "What shall I do?" The old man replied: "Trust not in your own righteousness. Be not penitent for a deed that is past and gone. And keep your tongue and your belly under control."

> Abba Evagrius said: "Some of the fathers used to say that a dry and regular diet, combined with charity, will quickly bring the monk to the harbour where the storms of passion do not enter."

> The same said: "A certain monk was told that his father had died. He said to the messenger 'Stop blaspheming. My father cannot die.' "

> Abba Evagrius said that an old man said: "I cut away my fleshly pleasures, to remove the opportunities of anger. For I know that it is because of

pleasure that I have to struggle with anger, and trouble my mind, and throw away my understanding."

When Abba Cyrus of Alexandria was asked about the temptation of lust, he said: "If you are not tempted, you have no hope: if you are not tempted, it is because you are used to sinning. The man who does not fight sin at the stage of temptation, sins in his body. And the man who sins in his body has no trouble from temptation."

Abba Evagrius said that there was a brother who had no possessions but a Gospel, and sold it to feed the poor. And he said a word which is worth remembering: "I have even sold the word which commands me to sell all and give to the poor."

Someone asked an old man to accept money for his future needs. But he refused, because the produce of his labour was enough for him. But when the man persisted, and begged him to take it for the needs of the poor, the old man replied: "My disgrace is twofold. I do not need, yet I accept: and I give to others, and so will suffer from vanity."

Abba Ephraem was passing by when a harlot (she was someone's agent) began to make every effort to attract him to unlawful intercourse: or, if she failed in this, at least to stir him to anger. For no one had ever seen him angry or brawling. He said to her: "Follow me." When they came to a crowded place, he said to her: "Come now, I will lie with you as you wanted." She looked round at the crowd and said: "How can we do it here, with all these people standing round? We should be ashamed." He said: "If you blush before men, should you not blush the more before God, who discloses the hidden things of darkness?" And she went away without her pleasure, confused and nonplussed.

An old man was asked: "What is humility?" He answered: "If you forgive a brother who has wronged you before he is penitent towards you."[10]

Though the modern reader is prone to read these sayings with a smile of bemusement at their quaintness, he should not forget that asceticism is still a lively possibility to which thousands of people take recourse in the control of passions. Contemporary forms of abstinence and asceticism are addressed to the same basic issues which the desert fathers found important. The pleasures of the mouth and belly are curbed by millions who find it virtuous to oppose any use of alcohol, detest smoking and smokers, ban tea and coffee, refrain from sweet desserts, or anxiously watch their weight. The techniques range from strictly enforced group rules to selective and voluntary sacrifice; from totalitarian impositions on virtually everybody to spontaneous ventures by single individuals. So much has been written about the fear of, and disdain for, mature sexual activities even among married partners that this form of asceticism hardly needs to be labored. A posture of retreat from the world's temptations, with an anxious guarding of a closed family unit in the home, is by no means rare. One can find it described in many psychiatric case histories. Though cursing and swearing are not always the most wholesome expressions of feelings, and certainly lack elegance, their all too vigorous suppression can amount to an ascetic elimination of all strong or evocative words from a person's language.

In view of the widespread recognition of historical Christianity's suspicion of sexual feelings, from coarse lust to delicate eroticism, it is clinically important now to appreciate the degree to which anger has been seen as the foe. In regions where pietistic movements have been strong, the suppression and repression of anger are still outstanding features in groups and individuals. It is most pointedly demonstrated at the lowest level of organized church life, in the everyday encounters of people within congregations. No word may be said and no gesture made that could hurt anybody. Expressions of discontent or dissent are taboo. Disapproval is to be couched in soft-spoken admonitions and roundabout language, lest it offend someone. I have witnessed a church-school class in action in which one child, having to read aloud a biblical passage, suddenly stopped in the middle of a phrase and fell into a dread silence under the agonized looks of his peers, because the word "hell" was next in the sentence. On social occasions in the churches there tends to be a forced friendliness and contrived amiability, manifest in stereotyped smiles exchanged across the dinner tables in the "fellowship halls." Tolerance for dull meetings is great, and peaceful nonaction is deemed vastly superior to lively debate or controversial action, all for fear that exposition of ideas and exchange of opinions are tantamount to anger and strife. Such massive repressions and suppressions of anger are a truly ascetic sacrifice of a large part of the emotional life, and often entail a drastic truncation of the group's avowed programs and action radius.

Abstinence can be practiced in many different ways and to different degrees. Professional mental health workers who undertake a personal psychoanalysis for therapeutic or training purposes do not shun it. Practitioners of the ascetic way know that it is not only a means of coming to grips with moral issues, but also a royal road to the emotions. It is, however, not the only way, or the most effective method. Ignatius of Loyola's *Spiritual Exercises* coupled selective asceticism with a zealous and imaginative engagement in special passions, as we saw in a previous chapter. The retreatant is emotionally both "toned down" and "keyed up" by a combination of abstinence and total emotional surrender to the torments and glories of Jesus Christ with whom he is to make a positive identification. In this more complex approach, not all passions are banned. Though the bad life is to be curbed by a control of the bad passions, the good life is to be achieved by a vigorous embrace of the good and godly passions: energetic love, militant compassion, strong hope, active charity, a lively engagement in human affairs, and an ardent faith. Similarly, many mystics of the world's religions combined a "negative way" of selective sensory abstinence with a "positive way" of selective ambitions and passions. We may schematize the options and combinations as follows:

negative approaches (prohibitions)	positive approaches (prescriptions)
mortification	imitation
abstinence	copying
asceticism	identification
withdrawal	incorporation
denial	introjection
repression	devotion
suppression	adoration
isolation and distance	
phobic reaction	

combinations

reaction formation
reversal of affect
counterphobia
identification with the aggressor

All the negative approaches have some prohibition as their core, with the feelings of anxiety, guilt, or shame that are mobilized when transgressions occur in deed or in thought. Mortification, once practiced in the flagrant form of self-inflicted corporal punishments such as fasting, starving, flagellation, or castration, now occurs in more symbolic or attenuated forms. One can seek acts of penance in many ways, for instance, by seeking menial tasks in churches or charitable work, or by volunteering for the chores that religious programs impose. In almost every congregation one sees people who are first in line when hundreds of dishes have to be washed, or when several hundred tiny glasses have to be filled with fruit juice for communion services and then again cleared away from the pews, washed, and stacked. Organizational life entails many tedious tasks, from pasting stamps on envelopes to door-to-door colportage, which provide outlets for symbolic penance whereby the depressive tone of a guilty conscience can be replaced by restored self-respect and good feelings.

Abstinence and asceticism cover an enormous range of concrete acts, but millions of religious people take recourse to their milder forms which do not break too radically into the established rhythms and patterns of the social life and personal habits. Fasting is for most people in the Western Hemisphere little more than forgoing one dish for another, for instance, by shifting once a week from meat to fish. Some groups and individuals keep Lent, only a short period of the year, by making some little sacrifice such as abstaining from alcohol, forgoing desserts, eating egg dishes instead of meat dishes, reducing their smoking pleasures or interrupting their habit of going to movie theaters and other entertainment routines. The highly circumscribed means of birth control allowed within the Roman Catholic Church by the rhythm method demands periods of sexual abstinence, which not a few people undertake though they may be difficult. Ascetic tendencies live on in the ideal of tithing advocated by some religious groups within a society that already levies an abundance of taxes. The slogan "give till it hurts" is not uncommon in religious organizations, and the very choice of words in that expression reveals the dynamics of the intended pedagogical process: one must undergo some pain or distinct unpleasure in order to punish the self for the strength or quality of its desires. And with the "low" desires tamed, new and more noble pleasures may arise from the exercise of self-control and the charitable proclivities. When James suggested that feelings transform the value of things and situations he called attention to the fact that the same landscape looks bright and tender to the person in a loving mood, but gloomy and forbidding to one in a melancholy state.[11] But the process is also reversible: a move from the plains to the mountains can transform moods. This lesson is built into many of the approaches thus far described. Replacing one natural tendency by another one that requires some straining or a battle with oneself entails a change in basic feeling which religion prizes as holiness or sanctification. Gardner, thinking of individual habits and organizational fixations, uses the term "self-renewal,"[12] which entails the zest and liveliness that come with the awareness of greater excellence in one's functioning.

Less dramatic, and perhaps a little more anxious, are the approaches based on withdrawal. The radical forms of withdrawal manifested by the lives of the desert fathers belong mostly to the past, although one should not underestimate the fierceness with which monastics of today, men and women, separate themselves from social and cultural contamination. An ancient keynote in all practices of withdrawal and distance is the idea that the world, or a part of it, is a conflagration of temptations which intrude upon the soul's peace, undermine character, and sap the moral fiber. The tendency to withdraw as a whole requires a pattern of attitudes and judgments. Not only is the world or any of its parts such as cities, entertainment centers, the other sex, commerce, or politics dangerous and potentially overwhelming, but the self is seen as weak in control devices and strong in just those natural urges for which the world offers satisfactions. Furthermore, it is believed that constant exposure to kindred minds in some communal form of living, under some strong guide or superior, will provide the external controls and reinforcement that the individual has come to feel in need of. Such group reinforcement can come from close ties to the family which lives in cultural isolation, from frequent contact with sect or church members that advocate opposition to secularization, from organized group living in special settlements or enclaves in an extended family structure, or from joining a monastic order whose rules and organizational pattern provide the necessary discipline.

In Pope John XXIII's diary[13] one can find very definite rules, self-imposed but group-reinforced, which prescribe withdrawal maneuvers in various situations of temptation. Vile or unworthy companions are to be avoided under all circumstances, as are those who seek the company of the other sex, talk about love-making, engage in drinking, hang around taverns, or are prone to quarrels. To be avoided also are games, places in town where people loiter in front of shops, or circles in which jesting prevails. Special care must be taken not to look at women:

> . . . guard your eyes especially, never fixing your gaze on a woman's face, or on any other source of danger. . . .[14]

In his diary Pope John listed rules for "every day," "every week," "every month," "every year," and "at all times," and many of the entries in his journal over the subsequent sixty-seven years of his life are accounts of his successes and failures in obeying these rules. A very instructive passage about the dynamics of withdrawal is the following:

> I like to enjoy good health, and God sends me sickness. Well, blessed be this sickness! Here starts the practice of that holy indifference that made the saints what they were. Oh if I could only acquire that tranquility of soul, that peace of mind in favourable and unfavourable conditions, which would make my life sweeter and happier, even in the midst of troubles![15]

The words "holy indifference," toward the burdens of life from which withdrawal is impossible, accentuate the basic emotional attitude: eliminate from yourself the stimuli that may arouse unwanted emotions, and for the rest take distance from the feelings themselves. Let nothing stir you, neither the turbulent world without, nor the turbulent world within. Seek distance, first from stimuli, then from feelings.

On the border of withdrawal and denial are the various maneuvers whereby one avoids the dangerous things that really exist, but morally should not be. Censorship is the classical example. It puts all relevant things into two classes which are not only "good" or "bad," but also "permissible" or "not permissible," and finally, in effect, "available" or "not available." For when censorship has power and sanctions, it actually eliminates information or stimuli from the crossroads of culture. If books are withheld from libraries and films from theaters, the option of withdrawal by the individual or his group has given way to the necessity of "doing without," and the opportunity for exposure is simply denied. In the minds of the censors themselves the act of withholding a controversial piece of reality is tantamount to the denial of that reality: the evil thing (which we, the censors, have seen) does no longer exist (for our flock or for our followers).

More flagrant forms of denial in the religious life can be found in attitudes toward the inescapable burdens that life imposes: pain, illness, loss of relatives and friends, death. It is one thing to mortify the body and to suffer its pains with penitential courage; it is quite another thing to deny that pain is painful and that suffering hurts. Institutional and philosophical forms of denial are found in "mind over body" movements which attribute reality only to the mind or spirit, reducing the body and other forms of matter to a mere chimera. But far more common than such movements, which have worked out an explicit thesis about the unreality of bodies and pain and death, is the implicit use of the denial mechanism in funeral practices and bereavement situations. The language about death and dying avoids mentioning these calamities by name; instead, one says that "father has departed" or "our young daughter has passed away." For a last farewell, before the interment, the body is made to look alive, beautiful, and sometimes much younger and more spotless than it was just before death. The corpse, dressed as for a stately occasion, is made to rest in satin-lined, cushioned comfort, in a coffin of choice wood, highly polished, which in turn may be encased in a metal container, then placed in a concrete vault or reinforced grave. Everything is so enacted as to suggest that the dead are really alive, or soon will be alive again. The painful and shocking reality of death is too much to take, even for avowed Christians whose deity is believed to have suffered all of it with abject agony and despair in the crucified Jesus. The denial of the unpleasant reality of death is so strong that it defies the teaching of most mainline churches, Catholic and Protestant, whose orders of service for burial are quite realistic but hardly have a chance to be enacted in the face of the comforting illusions available from the funeral industry and indeed from many fellow Christians.

The docetic heresy in the history of Christianity is a prime example of the denial mechanism. Struggling over the tense theological proposition that Jesus was both God and man, and both fully, the docetists considered him too divine to have really suffered the agony of death and ended up by saying that he only seemed (Greek: *dokeo*) to have suffered. His pain was not real, his death did not actually occur, and hence his resurrection was only a show. This implies an image of Jesus as a kind of jack-in-the-box who goes through the motions of a melodrama, only to tease or to entertain. Although the docetic formula lost its position to the orthodox mainstream which would rather affirm a tense paradox than deny the actuality of a suffering God, the tendency toward denial is so strong that docetism in one form or another recurs ever anew in Christian believers.

In order to contrast denial once more with penitential attitudes, a passage from Pope John's diary is instructive. One entry begins with the note that a violent toothache has prevented the author from writing for two nights and goes on to say, "Although this gave me the chance to suffer something for Jesus, it also took up too much of my thoughts."[16]

The Pope's attitude was realistic vis-à-vis the hurt, the pain, and the use of it as an act of penance; it is psychologically shrewd in recognizing that pain tends to absorb the mind and drain its energies. Denial knows no such realism. In denial one acts as if the hurtful thing, the calamitous happening, or the evil condition does not exist or is simply a gap in the fabric of being. Denial is a very primitive mental mechanism that shows the sway of the pleasure principle in the inability to admit that reality contains a good deal of unpleasure, actual pain, and active evil.

So much has been said in the previous pages about the use of repression and suppression in the pursuit of holiness that new examples are not needed. Suffice it to say that repression acts unconsciously and proceeds almost reflexlike, whereas suppression is a more conscious expulsion of ideas from the stream of thought. In both cases, the unacceptable thought and the forbidden impulse are removed from consciousness and excluded from memory so that hardly a trace of their actuality is left. And with the thought and the impulse, even the feeling of the original desire is eliminated from awareness so that it phenomenologically no longer exists, except in the disguised form of symptoms, errors, slips, dream material, and other oddities of the mental life which the person sees as strange intrusions for which he cannot take responsibility.

The road to holiness demands a heavy toll from man's spontaneous feelings. Some travelers pay by isolating their emotions from the thoughts and ideas to which they naturally adhere. They flee into the cool shade of thoughts, to escape from the heat of affects. They withdraw internally into the realm of words, ideas, and concepts after having severed these from all emotion. The words and thoughts are held to be neutral, cool, objective, and totally unemotional; affects are considered as the peculiarity of wild or romantic souls who "cannot think straight." People who are prone to isolation may appear undisturbed in the greatest misfortune; they show very little emotion or none at all. They are prone to compulsions and rituals such as gnashing their teeth in their sleep, washing their hands frequently, reading scriptural passages in church or home with utmost precision and painstaking exactness. Or, as the captain in *The Caine Mutiny,* they play incessantly with a pair of steel balls from a ball bearing, almost unwittingly, with endless repetition, in moments of stress.

It is especially the tender libidinal feelings and the traces of anger that are liable to isolation. These are the dangerous feelings that an overworked conscience cannot accept, for they are held to be the very works of the devil. But since feelings of love and hate occur often concomitantly toward the same person, who is both "dangerously" loved and "dangerously" hated, isolation can also be a means of dealing with the ambivalence of emotions. The boy who loves his father, but has also much reason to hate him, may isolate his tender longings and project them onto a beneficent, loving God, leaving his mortal father as the object of all his hatred. Or conversely, he may continue to worship his father, despite the man's manifest unlovableness, but project all his hatred onto Satan or some other personified evil who makes life chronically miserable.

Such splitting of ambivalent affects and attributing them to two different objects is particularly marked in cases in which the attitudes toward the two objects are in flagrant contrast. An example is the idealization of the Virgin, indeed her exalted adoration, by men who otherwise despise women and consider them only as seductive stimuli to sexual arousal. One woman stands on a pedestal—all others are trampled underfoot. In previous ages a splitting of affect between God and devil was common, as Luther's periods of anguish so vividly demonstrate. It took Luther considerable time to modify this position of isolation, until he could acknowledge that the devil was "God's devil."

In many of the situations we have just reviewed, a general feeling of anxiety about the world's dangers and temptations, about the strength of one's natural impulses, or of guilt about the vile character of his inclinations pervades the individual. In fight or flight he may seek the path of holiness, changing his feelings in the hope of attaining a better life, or changing his habits and behavior in the hope of experiencing new feelings by which his life may be ennobled. But anxiety has the capacity of following a man like his shadow; as long as he is in the sun it will adhere to him like an irremovable burden. What can one do differently or more than any of the other maneuvers thus far described in order to cope with the unwanted companion?

The phobic reaction gives some solace in that it brings the anxiety to a focus on something specific, thereby turning it into a limited fear. And if the object of the fear is so chosen that it can be avoided or kept at a distance, real relief can be had, until other persons or circumstances force one into meeting the phobic object which then engenders an acute anxiety attack. Religion knows many fears, as Statius recognized when he said that all the gods were created by those fears. But the gods are not only a response to human fears; once arisen they may produce more fears or more specific anxious reactions such as the fear of transgressing a taboo. When articulate theogonies develop and many rituals have become established, there is room for special phobias also. An example is the intense fear of devils and incubi and witches which characterized the late Middle Ages and the Renaissance in Europe, within the context of profound belief in a loving and merciful God. In Huxley's *Devils of Loudun* one can find a vivid portrayal of the infectious outbursts of anxiety and hysterical symptoms that swept over whole populations in monasteries and nunneries; Goethe's *Faust* lets the reader watch a witches' sabbath on a mountaintop, and Hawthorne knew of the profound anxieties that beset New England towns as their populations fought, and created, witches. The point is that in highly elaborated religious systems a large residue of unbound anxiety is turned into a phobia of something specific like devils or witches, which can then be avoided or warded off.

The so-called sin against the Holy Ghost shows phobic features. It is the unpardonable sin, from the effects of which neither men nor God can save a person. The fear of offending the Holy Ghost through blasphemous words or deeds has the intensity of panic which renders a person totally helpless. It is phobic also in the sense that it is so precisely circumscribed that it can be avoided while leaving considerable room for other sins and blasphemies which remain potentially redeemable.

Carrie Nation dared to enter taverns only with a hatchet. But a good many pietists dare not set foot into a tavern at all, become timorous at the sight of a deck of playing cards, or tremble when they meet a prostitute in the streets. What is one to think of such fierce and pointed fears which abound in religious populations? Is their intensity commensurate with the objective dangers of their objects? Not at all. These objects and situations become fearsome only when first there have been implanted a large set of prohibitions which call for the avoidance of temptations, lightheartedness, wit and laughter, frivolous banter, useless chatter, dangerous curiosity, idle gossip, merriment, and other natural proclivities. The prohibitions may extend to the reading of newspapers also, as Pope John reported in his *Journal*.[17] Precisely to the extent that all those prohibitions depict the world as a terribly dangerous place, the level of anxiety is raised and new measures are needed to mitigate its intensity or chronicity. As this point the phobic reaction sets in. It selects certain places and situations as "dens of iniquity" which represent the ultimate in fearsomeness, but which can be more or less successfully avoided, leaving the individual with a modicum of well-being as long as he remains at a safe distance from them.

In the attic of my parents' home was an old nineteenth-century color print depicting the pilgrim's way to the heavenly city, a path steep, narrow, and beset by rocks and thorns; and the pleasant avenue of the children of this world, a road lined with fountains and roses, and having in places a distinct midway atmosphere. The total scene was surveyed by the all-seeing eye of God, encased in a sharp-cornered triangle. The triteness of this moralistic picture was in no small way enhanced by its failure to suggest why anyone would choose the steep path of the pilgrim if given a choice. The heavenly Jerusalem was no more than a miserly speck beyond the last visible hill, far less attractive indeed than the parks and lovers' benches in the foreground on the other road. The picture utterly failed to portray that the larger part of the road to holiness consists in enormous satisfactions, good feelings, and a deep sense of well-being shared with friends, if not with the whole universe.

Here is where the positive approaches come in. Unlike the prohibitive approaches which tend to curb all feelings and capitalize on negative affects, the religious admonitions and prescriptions instill new feelings and try to enhance well-being by promoting acts and attitudes which give rewards. The basic process consists of identification which is rooted in the primordial human desire to be like others, to share good feelings, to idealize the chosen few that one loves, and to find comfort in the successful exercise of one's noblest talents. The toddler wants to be like his parents in every respect, indiscriminately; as the years of discernment arrive he will become more selective in his identifications, picking and choosing attributes from his friends, teachers, literary heroes, religious leaders, and even from divine examples, which he likes to make his own. Whether the process consists of conscious copying and imitation, or a more global and unconscious identification and incorporation, the crucial factor is that all these things are done in order to be more lovable, loving, and love-worthy, in the eyes of others and oneself.

Thus, in church, one's preference turns to the hymns that mother loved to sing. As time goes by, one begins to see intentions of love behind the forbidding gestures of one's parents years ago, sensing a new and more affectionate kinship with them by the time one has children of his own to rear. One remembers good feelings from the past, when one was praised and treated affectionately, and such remembrances of showers of love become spurs to repeating the deeds and attitudes that brought them on. Goodness becomes lovableness, and to be loved means to be good. Ethics and well-being intertwine. To love and be loved is to follow the Buddha, to have the fear of the Lord, to imitate Christ, to be inspired by the saints. The 91st Psalm, that inimitable poetic example of Erikson's idea of basic trust, engages a whole orchestra of instruments in singing of the primordial affection in which lovableness and goodness are one:

. . . who dwells in the shelter of the Most High, who abides in the shadow of the Almighty . . .

. . . he will cover you with his pinions, and under his wings you will find refuge . . .

. . . You will not fear the terror of the night . . .

. . . For he will give his angels charge of you to guard you in all your ways. On their hands they will bear you up, lest you dash your foot against a stone. . . .

. . . When he calls to me, I will answer him; I will be with him in trouble. . . .

Pope John's *Journal* gives ample evidence of the basic trust which fosters, and is at each turn augmented by, the imitations of divine and saintly figures. His notes abound in zeal for saints he admired, and in trying to follow their example he derived obvious satisfactions from being able to count himself, at least by honest intention, as a part of their company. He meditated at one time upon the life of the Virgin "as a baby girl,"[18] and it undoubtedly enhanced his tenderness. He really cared about Jesus, always finding himself falling short of that intense love which to him meant total surrender and full identification, but all the same he was convinced that at least his sincere strivings were already the fruit of his deep trust. Such experiences bring in bold relief the immediate rewards inherent in all positive identifications, no matter how much one may falter in accomplishing the ultimate identity: the very fact that one reaches out toward the beloved model brings new energies and enhances one's self-esteem. For to be loving is in itself an aspect of being lovable, and to be lovable is to receive at least some small amount of recognition and reciprocal attention on which the self will thrive. Each return of attention or praise gives narcissistic gratification, and with each new gratification the defensive stance can be lessened so that energies hitherto used in maintaining one's armor are set free for new investments. Spirals of change in the economics of one's energies are thus set up, for with each slight increase in felt freedom a new opportunity arises to invest more love in others which eventually produces returns for the self, enhancing its zest and buoyancy.

I hope that the reader has not glossed over the sudden frequency of the word "love" in the preceding paragraphs. It is not there from a burst of sentimentality, but as the designation of a primary emotion and a primary drive whose dynamics are of the utmost importance in all of life, including religion. So much has been made of the role of fear in the acquisition of religious ideas that writers and readers have often overlooked the fact that fear is to a large extent a function of love. In Freud's many writings about anxiety, the models for that unpleasant affect became ever more complex, from the toxic theory via the trauma theory to the signal theory, culminating in the recognition that the most elementary form of the affect is a fear of losing the object of one's libidinal strivings. Even the definition of religion in *The Future of an Illusion,* which anchors the religious convictions in the strength of wishes, treats fear as an intervening variable. Behind the fear lies the libidinal wish, the desire for unity with the nurturant mother, the need to fit snugly into a beneficent universe, the urge to find and maintain a vital, homeostatic balance amidst the flux of all environments from subcellular to cosmic levels.

When religions foster love as the criterion affect of the holy or saintly life, their adherents may not always be aware of the awesome complications in the dynamics and economics of this emotion. They have also at times introduced certain moral or cognitive distinctions between one kind of love and another—such as carnal and spiritual love; human and divine love; *eros, filia,* and *agape*—which have had the unfortunate effect of disembodying the feeling until little more than an ethereal glow was left, cold as the stars, and just as remote, with a properly distant Greek name. The beauty and psychological realism of the 91st Psalm lie in its portrayal of the love between God and man as one undivided feeling, which ranges from direct body contact under the pinions of his wings and at the hands of his angels to "being with him in trouble." It does not scorn the expression of *cleaving to* him in love, of which nature offers us a moving model of the infant monkey burying itself in the protective mantle of its mother's breast. The point is that love by any definition and under any name is always expansive: it tends to fill the organism, which embraces its environment for fulfillment.

Mystics have not scorned erotic language in their accounts of proximity to the divine. The Song of Solomon is one long allegory of love which covers almost all the manifestations of this feeling, elegantly preserving its unity under all circumstances. While it is clinically quite justified to say that St. Teresa's ecstatic exaltations had all the earmarks of a hysterical condition, it was also an astutely good judgment of the church that this peculiarity should not stand in the way of her canonization as a saint. For the important point is that it was love and not hatred, envy, or pride that cemented her affectionate bond with her Savior. She made her identifications and held her love object in the best way she could, like all of us, and though we would have liked to see her more healthy, her strange affection towered far above the indifference of cooler souls. Her illness was that she herself fell victim to an overworked distinction between carnal and divine love, which truncated love's expressive range and dissected its unity.

In the long history of moralizations on love, an odd notion has taken hold of the imagination of many religious people. It is the idea of a love that wants no return, of serene selflessness that knows only giving and no receiving. I doubt whether this is humanly possible. What is more, I am sure that such an arrangement says more about the human capacity for high-sounding fictions than it says about the dynamics of love. Most investments of love in others find their return, in the first place because most relations between people are transactional, and in the second place because the act of loving makes one at least lovable in one's own eyes and therefore always gives some narcissistic satisfaction. Moreover, if one loves a God who is defined as love, chances are that one will get ample returns, whether one wants them or not. When Schleiermacher said that religion is neither philosophy nor ethics, he knew that love cannot be moralized beyond recognition.

When Kierkegaard spoke of the "teleological suspension of the ethical," he knew that love, mercy, and forgiveness are at an entirely different plane than even the noblest moral considerations.

To recognize that loving is in itself gratifying does not mean to condone *do ut des* or *quid pro quo* negotiations, or to advocate the idea of barter, as if human-divine interactions were like one gigantic marketplace. Bartering occurs for wares, slaves, articles, and positions—for all kinds of things which, precisely because they are things, are at best only substitutes for the objects of love. What satisfies the libidinal drive is an engagement with other persons, including gods, and in its primary form such an engagement is always reciprocal. It becomes one-sided, exploitative, or parasitic only when trust is absent, i.e, when only one of the two parties seems to benefit from the relation. Seen in this light it is not so strange that one hears from time to time the assertion that gods need men just as much as men need gods. Though such statements seem at first blush somewhat offensive to the divine omnipotence, they are at closer look an effective counterweight to the unbalanced implication that gods are solipsistic spheres in outer space. Angelus Silesius wrote:

> I know that without me God could not live one moment,

and Rilke asked in the same vein:

> What will you do, God, when I die?[19]

Both statements take reciprocity seriously, and although they ring with overtones of inflated self-importance, they are not without insight into the dynamics of satisfaction.

The positive approaches to holiness, embroidering on the material of love, show considerable variety in the patterns and modes of relationship. Most of these variations are due to a consideration of status between the two loving parties; some are bound to levels of development. The term "following" as in the admonition, "Follow me," suggests a master-and-servant or a teacher-and-pupil relation. The word "imitation," celebrated in Thomas a Kempis' famous *Imitatio Christi,* seems to indicate a more distant relation, a following from afar, characteristic of the person who can only falteringly imitate an illustrious example. This distance is artificially accentuated by Thomas' Platonic disdain for the body and the visible world which hold the imitator forever captive, so that he is doomed to remain at a long distance from his example. But on closer study the "imitation" in question has many overtones of an Augustinian sympathy which can be expressed as: "He (Christ) has done so much for me—what can I do for him?" And then there is the mystic, who aims at identity and is making constant efforts to bridge the gap that separates him from his divine object. Though he will never achieve radical sameness, he may sense an ever-greater affinity as he removes, one by one, the obstacles that separate the lover from the beloved. When, in a final regression and only for one ecstatic moment, he feels himself one with the divine, the instant he reflects about this feelingful oneness he is back at a higher level of organization where boundaries, distinction, and separation are inevitable.

It is instructive to see Christianity's perpetual seesawing on the question of the divine immanence or the divine transcendence in this light. Either position taken in the extreme has its dangers. When transcendence is stressed, the distance between God and man can become stretched to the point of loss of contact. When immanence is stressed, the affinity between God and man, suggested in the *imago Dei* theme of creation, can lead to complete identity with its concomitant delusions of grandeur. Theologians who are aware of these dangers have therefore been compelled to hold the two positions in tension by affirming paradoxically that both are equally right, or by using a dialectical pedagogy in defending the viewpoint that seems to be least in vogue at any time. A sole emphasis on "the God within" smacks of incorporation or introjection, and locks the divine object within the realm of kinesthesis and the alimentary tract. But a unilateral emphasis on God's "otherness" puts the divine object out of touch, and even the distant receptors of sight and hearing may not be able to span the vast chasms of separation.

Beyond the intensity of immanence and the starkness of transcendence lies the tenderness of devotion and adoration. These accentuate neither sameness nor separateness, neither incorporation nor intrusion. The master-servant, the teacher-pupil, and the leader-follower models give way to a pattern of mutual enjoyment with great reciprocal spontaneity and an increased sense of freedom. Grown from a basic trust that unifies the Platonic triad of goodness, beauty, and truth, the feeling tones of the devotional relationship are joy and hope.

But some distinctions need to be made. Schachtel[20] has emphasized that affects can have both an integrative and a disturbing function, and has accordingly differentiated between activity affects and embeddedness affects. The activity affects are part of goal-directed action and sustain the optimal tensions which make possible the consummatory activities which satisfy our needs. An example is the vigorous and pleasurable sucking behavior of healthy infants; another is the concentrated curiosity of the schoolchild coming to grips with intellectual propositions. Such affects and activities are not notably the fruits of conflict, and they often remain fairly problem-free. They enhance the inventiveness and success with which one is able to cope with the adaptational tasks in life. The embeddedness affects, however, represent diffuse tension discharge patterns which arise from a feeling of helpless distress. Some infants are rather inept in the nursing situation, sucking listlessly or with frequent distractions, interspersed with periods of random restlessness in which the goal of the act seems missed. The affects of anger, anxiety, impatience, and demandingness which are manifest in this kind of behavior are distress signals whereby the infant cries out for help and insists that the mother, or the environment at large, come to his rescue since he cannot cope adequately with his situation. Hence the word "embeddedness"—it denotes the regressive tendency of refusing to accept the separation and to meet the eventual demand for independence which birth brought on. In the activity affects we see the recognition of that separation by an individual who derives pleasure from his competence in mastering life's tasks. This distinction is not a rigorous classification of all affects into two groups; most situations of affect and action are so complex that they show a mixture of both aspects. Schachtel feels, however, that joy and hope, though not always free from embeddedness features, are excellent examples of activity affect, whereas anxiety is the embeddedness emotion par excellence.

When Edwards extolled joy as a desirable religious affection, he was in a long tradition of writers who saw this emotion as a religious goal. Old Testament literature lets the Jewish believers shout with loud songs of joy; it exhorts people to clap their hands; it lets even the mountains and hills break forth into singing. The desert is said to rejoice. The words "joy" and "rejoicing" have a large number of references in any biblical concordance. Joy, elation, and ecstasy are the emotional goals of mystics. But for complicated reasons, there is often more talk about joy than the experience of it. Within Christianity there is a spotty history of excessive joy manifested in the movements of ecstatics and enthusiasts which seems to have spoiled the joy of the more quiet minds, or at least put them on guard for its dangers. The frenzy of apocalyptic outbursts in the early Christian Church, the social disruptiveness of enthusiasts in Germany and the Netherlands in the sixteenth century, the ecstatic practices of the Russian *khlysti* and *skoptsi* who engaged in flagellation and castration for the glory of God, and the convulsionism that still exists in certain Pentecostal groups are but a few examples of the rapturous intensity of joy for which sedate believers are ill prepared. Moreover, in a religiously pluralistic society such as the United States, intense enthusiasm and the uninhibited expression of joy have come to be associated with the sectarianism of poorly educated, low-income, and socially oppressed groups.

Were it not for some splendid landmarks of church art and the magnificent music of church composers such as Bach, one would be hard pressed to see evidence of experienced joy in the worship activities of mainline churches. Joy is conspicuously absent from communion or Lord's Supper celebrations in which, according to liturgical intentions, it should be visibly present.[21] If one observes carefully the postures and facial expression of participants in such services, one finds, on the whole, considerable evidence of depression as the basic feeling tone. While much of this may be due to the hushed solemnity of liturgical phrases calling to repentance and confession of sin, it is evident that the presentation of the bloody work of the atonement by the suffering Christ leaves a far greater impression than its alleged goal, which is the dispensing of grace and forgiveness. Another reason for the discrepancy between the intended feeling of joy and the prevailing stiffness in the worshipers' behavior may be found in the emphasis on decorum and self-control which is so strong in middle-class religions. But the most potent cause seems to lie in the long heritage of Platonizing efforts which have undercut the ancient Hebrew unity of mind and body, replacing the oneness of feeling and body reaction by a dichotomous system in which spiritualized inwardness has become divorced from a hypercontrolled motor system. The body, in this view, is only a "tomb" for the "soul." In another view, sometimes derived from the Platonic, it is the object of ascetic deprivations and masochistic insults.

As an activity affect, joy sustains the tensions and mobilizes the energies that make goal-directed acts possible. In this sense, joy is the affect whereby believers engage themselves in the things that need to be done in the world, promoting causes, implementing social change, and in various ways "witnessing" to the essence of their faith as change agents. But as embeddedness affect, joy shares in the magical expectation that change will come about only through divine arrangements for which the devout have to wait passively or which they can ritualistically force from the dispenser of all good things by prayer and other mild exercises. Schachtel has pointed to another form of joy as embeddedness affect: the fervent expectation that some radical change will be brought about in a person's character or mood by divine intervention.[22] This dynamism seems inherent in the desire for conversion experiences that will once for all turn depression into elation, or sinfulness into saintliness. Belief in miracles, particularly miraculous cures of ills or deformities, partakes of the same unrealistic fantasy which replaces work, effort, self-discipline, or resignation to unchangeable situations by the wish to be changed magically, by a superhuman feat.

At first blush, magical expectations seem to be particularly prominent in the dynamics of hope. Certainly there is a form of hoping which brushes reality aside in favor of a never-never land whose presence is avowed in the emotional condition of hope. Hope as an embeddedness affect is all too conspicuous in everyday life, where it comes close to, or is identical with, wishing. The farmer hopes for rain; the girl hopes she will find a suitable escort or a marriage partner; the sick person hopes he will find a cure. Believers hope for the kingdom of God on earth, or for Christ's Second Coming. In apocalyptic times the oppressed hope not only to be delivered, but they engage in fantasies anticipating the frightful revenge the deity will make on their oppressors and all unbelievers. One might say, with Marcel,[23] that the more circumscribed or articulate the object of hope is, the more likely it is that wishing, rather than hoping, prevails. In Schachtel's words, this kind of hoping is a form of embeddedness, using magic as a way out of difficulties. It forces reality into the mold of the omnipotence of thought, which is a regressive form of cognition. In a word, this kind of hoping flouts reality.

Hoping as embeddedness affect is closely related to the characteristic optimism that James saw in the once-born person who feels that life is not so bad, that the earth is a pleasant place to be in, and that the universe is of a friendly disposition toward the crown of creation. Clinically, one can see a prevailing optimism in certain pampered individuals whose prominent orality has managed to find satisfactions, perhaps by virtue of that friendly, outgoing, and jocose ebullience which makes them a welcome guest at many a table or the life of many a party. But optimism is not the same as hoping, unless it be of hope as embeddedness and regressive demandingness. Marcel feels that optimism as well as pessimism requires some distance from reality so that obstacles that stand in the way of satisfaction are either unrealistically diminished or loom excessively large. Both positions accentuate the importance of the self and aggressively assert the "I" which holds that its way of seeing things is the ultimate truth. In stating: "If you could only see things as clearly as I do," or "If you would be in my position," the optimist and the pessimist stress their own uniqueness, sometimes quite aggressively in opposition to a more balanced and a more broadly human or communal view. Their positions tend to become argumentative, leading to debate rather than dialogue.

Not so with the person whose hoping is an activity affect. He remains part of the scheme of things and cannot afford to distort reality or deceive himself.[24] When he is visited by a calamity he must fully see how precarious his situation is so that, on the basis of his tragedy, hoping may arise. But how can it arise? Let us consider a classical example of hope in the situation of a person suffering from a serious disease who has been given to understand that his disease is terminal—no one can effect a cure and the downhill course cannot be forestalled by any known means. One reaction of such a patient may be to give up hope and give in to the forces of destruction. Physicians know that such a reaction, which may be described as realistic from one point of view, is likely to hasten the arrival of death, for the organism no longer mobilizes the resources that could prolong life. Another reaction is to accept the gloomy prognosis and to see its implications clearly, and yet to hope. Physicians know that in such cases life may be prolonged, and on occasion life may even prove to be victorious. Which of these two reactions is more realistic and adaptive? Was it the best adaptation of the first patient to give up hope? Was the hoping of the second patient, which seems to be a "hope against hope," an unrealistic maladaptation? One cannot give a trite and simple answer to either question, because hoping is an exceedingly intimate affair, and reality is a great enigma.

The boundaries of reality are fluid and uncertain, despite the clarity of some of its contents. It is precisely because reality as a whole cannot be exhaustively defined that hoping is a most intimate and private prerogative of persons. One cannot convince a hoping person that his hope is poorly based. The fact that he hopes where I may not hope means that his reality is different from mine, but he may still be more realistic than I usually am. Why is this so? Marcel has suggested that arguments against hoping can only draw on past experience. Someone might say: "You better give up hope, because things have never turned out that way." Such objections against someone else's hoping are typically based on experiences from the past, plus the logical extrapolations they contain for the present. To the objector, reality is defined in terms of the past and the present. But to the hoping person, reality takes on the quality of experience-in-formation. The alteration of the time perspective toward the future implies that time is an ongoing process, very much on the move, with the possibility that novelty may occur, precisely because all reality has not yet been exhaustively defined.

Scott[25] has suggested that the dynamics of hoping arise from a sequence in which there is first waiting, then anticipating, then pining, and then hoping. His model is the situation of the infant whose wishes are momentarily unfulfilled and whose predicament is one of dependence upon others for the necessities of his life. Using the classical psychoanalytic theory of thinking, Scott indicates that in the infant whose wishes are frustrated a hallucinatory image appears which portrays the gratifying object. The first step is for the child to wait for these hallucinatory images to be transformed into real sensations. In the stage of anticipating, he waits not only for the gratifying sensations, but also for the feeling of satisfaction to be obtained. In pining, he wishes for change to occur, for sensory satisfaction, and for the object which will give the satisfaction. In hoping, there is the added belief that an object is forthcoming which has itself the desire to satisfy the one who hopes. In other words, in hoping one assumes a complex emotional relation between persons in which mutual desires for satisfaction and tenderness occur. Hope assumes a belief in beneficence and thrives on the conviction that somewhere in the universe an arrangement exists that can create novelty and thereby transcend the knowledge that is distilled from the past and present.

In religious thought, these dynamics of hoping have often taken the special form of belief in two worlds, one in the here and now, and another one in the future or in some distant realm. In this way, the oppressed on earth could hope for better treatment hereafter. Visions of some heaven could thus be engendered in which the fortunes on earth could be reversed, and to make such reversals complete a hell could be added for those who seemed particularly well off while still alive. Such imaginations are an obvious flouting of reality, and are in every sense magical. Moreover, precisely to the extent that the pictures of heaven and hell or any hereafter become articulated in details, such as streets of gold or fires of sulphur, they have all the earmarks of wishing, as defined by Marcel. Wishing has specific objects; hoping has only a global goal such as deliverance, freedom, joy in God. The great difficulty for hoping as an activity affect is to stay with the vision of one world, one reality, one universe, one creation, and one God. But that one world can be seen as an open-ended process of which one has only a limited knowledge, based on past experience. The knowledge of the whole can be left to the gods themselves, and any definite fantasy about things to come could be seen as a meddlesome interference with the divine arrangements. Such an attitude, toward which hoping as an activity affect seems to aim, presupposes of course a profound trust in the existence of beneficence, as Scott's progression from waiting to hoping implies. The theological distinction between apocalypse and eschatology thus seems to hinge precisely on the difference between hoping as embeddedness affect (or as wishing) and as activity affect. The apocalyptic fantasies are too specific, too revengeful, too past-oriented. They assume magical powers whereby drastic changes occur without active human participation. Eschatological thought shuns specific fantasies, affirms one world, leaves the shape of things to come to the deity, and expects from the believer no more than the very difficult posture of trusting that the end of things is just as divinely governed as its beginning, just as mysterious and just as purposive.

We have quoted Emily Dickinson on several occasions. Few people have seen the ambiguities of hope as clearly and have put them as succinctly as this shrewd poetess:

> When I hoped I feared,
> Since I hoped I dared;
> Everywhere alone
> As a church remain;
> Spectre cannot harm,
> Serpent cannot charm;
> He deposes doom,
> Who hath suffered him.[26]

Or, as another of her verses has it:

> Hope is a subtle glutton;
> He feeds upon the fair;
> And yet, inspected closely,
> What abstinence is there!

> His is the halcyon table
> That never seats but one,
> And whatsoever is consumed
> The same amounts remain.[27]

But those whose ambition is the saintly life do not always arrive at the "holy affections" of joy and hope. Neither the negative way of prohibitions nor the positive way of identifications may end in those desirable emotions in which Edwards saw the test of true piety. To use Edwards' own words, one may remain swept by passions, which have that "greater violence of the animal spirits which tend to overpower the mind."[28] The prohibitions may be too weak or poorly enforced. They may be altogether unappealing. Identification models may be scarce. The experience of trust on which a mature emotional life can be built may be entirely absent. God may have been presented as an ogre; the community of faith in which one was reared may have been cold, forbidding, or oppressive. Emotional development and cognitive growth may have been thwarted and stunted in a dozen different ways, resulting in great bitterness, acute or chronic anxiety, hostility and resentment, profound distrust, or the emptiness of *acedia*. The "animal spirits" of fear and anger are then likely to "overpower the mind."

And yet behavior may change significantly, and some degree of saintliness may be obtained, despite the turbulent passions. As a matter of fact, a show of piety may be effectuated because of anxiety or anger. Considerable feats may be accomplished by the mechanisms of reaction formation and reversal of affect, of which the religious life is full of examples. By an odd and poorly understood process an affect may turn into the opposite feeling. Intense fear may turn into great and conspicuous courage, as embattled soldiers know. An original fear of the Lord may turn into an emphatic trust that withstands all argument. Men of property, such as St. Francis of Assisi, may volunteer to be men of poverty. Abject sinners may turn into zealous missionaries and driven witnesses of some faith. An attitude of cold neglect may overnight turn into one of solicitous care. But note the adjectives of intensity which occur in the previous sentences. They all suggest that the turnabout of feeling tones from negative to positive suffers from the same drivenness and impulse strength that constituted the vehemence of the original affect. In reaction formation there is always evidence of overcompensation. Aggressive intentions turn into loving activities of such zeal and vigor that one could almost speak of an "aggressive loving." Swearing may become praising; but the praises are too loud and boisterous. Vows of poverty may become cults of poverty, with aggressive begging that lacks the humility which one would expect from a volunteer for the poor life.

In reaction formation and reversals the original impulse and its emotion are repressed, followed by a conscious elaboration of the opposite intention and affect which is done in part with the energy belonging to the unacceptable impulse. Since the repression has occurred quite automatically, with insufficient insight into its desirability or necessity and with inadequate weighing of alternative courses of action, the results of this mechanism tend to be unstable and the affects may turn out to be labile. Sudden relapses into the original feeling are not uncommon, and even when the results are fairly stable over time, the drivenness with which the positive feeling is asserted lacks the elegance and equilibrium of a more mature integration.

The same is true, by and large, of all those changes in behavior and emotion that are the result of the counterphobic mechanism. As the term indicates, counterphobia is a way of coming to grips with fears in which one actively seeks or exposes himself to the very situations he is afraid of, deliberately and sometimes step by step. The person with a fear of heights may anxiously look down from the window of a skyscraper and gaze into the abyss before him, to prove that he is not falling or jumping down after all, and thus to allay his fear. Eventually he may become a mountain climber. The mechanism often entails an attitude of bravado, whereby one derives some sense of mastery from the good show one puts up in the face of danger. The tendency of young children to "play the doctor" after a painful or disturbing visit to a doctor's office demonstrates another side of counterphobia: the attempt to minister to others and thus to assume the master's role in regard to the very thing one is scared of.

Counterphobic ways of coping with fear are not infrequently used in religion. The movement from a great apprehension of God to a profound trust in him can retain, in the emphasis on trust, the trace of franticness that shows the phobic root. Luther's entry into the monastery where he could struggle with the very God he was so afraid of was probably occasioned in part by such a counterphobic maneuver. His tremendous emphasis on trust in a loving God derived some of its "push" from the feeling of abject terror that characterized his youthful images of the divine.

Within Christianity, the events of the incarnation allow for interesting applications of counterphobic devices. The eye of the believer can shift from a terrifying God-the-Father to a more accessible God-the-Son, and the next step may consist in "doing something for Jesus." Fear thus turns into a process of ministering and with such a role reversal that one's own fears become allayed. The changes in the liturgical year which repeat the cycle of Jesus' life from birth to crucifixion, and from death to resurrection, and on to ascension provide an opportunity, at Christmas, to bring the heart at rest with the infant Jesus. The move from the grave, majestic, and tremendous God to the little divine infant can be the believer's move from being the victim of fear to being its victor, and it may give him enough sense of mastery over his feelings that he can now bestow tenderness upon the very object of which he stood in awe.

Another instance of counterphobia can be found in those public prayers in which the worship leader enumerates at length and with considerable sense of drama all the reasons for his own sure damnation. The long list of his transgressions is not a humble confession at all, but an eloquent assertion of his great sinfulness which becomes in the course of the narration so grand that he derives from it the conviction that he is now in a state of grace. His fear becomes allayed by deliberate and ever-closer moves into the danger zone, and as he perceives at each step that he is not being smitten down, he acquires a feeling of mastery and comfort in his miserable situation.

With this example we have come close to another maneuver frequently found in religious lives: identification with the aggressor. The child who plays the doctor's game is not only deriving a sense of mastery by re-exposing himself playfully to the things he is afraid of, but he assumes momentarily the aggressive or intrusive role of the one who gave him pain. In his game, he becomes the aggressor and symbolically sticks needles into his playmate, drills into his teeth, or forces him to disrobe—the very things to which he was subjected by the physicians who treated him. Identification with the aggressor is clearly visible in the sadistic fantasies that occur in apocalyptic literature. There is not merely a confidence in the eventual divine interventions that will change the cosmic scene: the apocalyptic writers anticipate in terrestrial detail how the enemies will be wiped out, what great suffering and tortures will ensue, and how victorious the loyal believers will turn out to be. The theme of revenge looms large, and although the unleashing of the revenge is left to the divine initiative there can hardly be any doubt that the writers identify themselves in their fantasy with the revenging God and derive some pleasure, if not glee, from the anticipated events.

The celebrated and controversial doctrine of double predestination partakes in one respect of this mechanism of identification with the aggressor. In the Westminster Confession of Faith the doctrine is worded as follows:

> Art. 6 As God hath appointed the elect unto glory, so hath he, by the eternal and the most free purpose of his will, foreordained all the means thereunto. Wherefore they who are elected, being fallen in Adam, are redeemed by Christ; are effectually called unto faith in Christ by his Spirit working in due season; are justified, adopted, sanctified, and kept by his power through faith unto salvation. Neither are any other redeemed by Christ, effectually called, justified, adopted, sanctified, and saved, but the elect only.

This is simple predestination, which assures the elect of the fruits of divine love and grace. It becomes double predestination in the next article:

> Art. 7 The rest of mankind, God was pleased, according to the unsearchable counsel of his own will, whereby he extendeth or withholdeth mercy as he pleaseth, for the glory of his sovereign power over his creatures, to pass by, and to ordain them to dishonor and wrath for their sin, to the praise of his glorious justice.[29]

Now the divine choice goes two ways: one toward salvation, one toward damnation, either way with its own plausibility and reasons. Though the Westminster Confession goes on in the next article to say that "The doctrine of this high mystery of predestination is to be handled with special prudence and care . . . ," those so indoctrinated are being given the opportunity of identifying themselves in certain moods and moments with the divine wrath of which other people might become the victims. The doctrine clearly makes an effort at safeguarding the divine justice, along with which it emphasizes the model of choosing and spontaneity in the making of choices. Since every positive choice entails a rejection of the alternative, double predestination assumes within the divine the possibility of a polarization of feelings between acceptance and rejection, love and hate, grace and wrath, favoring and cold indifference. Such polarizations of feelings are common in human relations, which are wrought with fierce acceptance and rejection patterns. Precisely because of this implied parallelism between human and divine motives or feelings, the believer can identify himself with the rejecting aspect of the divine dynamics and thus become the aggressor toward his fellowman.

We started this section with the thesis that the pursuit of holiness is an endeavor that makes new lives out of old ones by a realignment of emotions. It involves the redeeming of passions. It involves an orchestration of feelings, by selective stimulation and destimulation, by external and internal control, by providing or withholding certain kinds of experience, by channeling, and by exercise. But emotion and action are intimately related, so intimately that it becomes a moot question to ask whether changes of feeling are cause or effect of changes in action and behavior. In this chapter we have taken the view that religion speaks to the emotions, uses them, prizes them selectively, and sees them as instruments for its own attitudinal and behavioral goals. It does all these things also in regard to action, to which we shall turn in the following chapter.

VII

Religion and

the Motor System

PERCEPTIONS, THOUGHTS, and feelings eventually result in acts. Though one may wish to refer to the processes of perceiving, thinking, and feeling as acts in their own right in order to emphasize that they are not passive conditions, there is yet a difference between such acts and the larger, directly observable behavior sequences which involve the motor system. People visibly do things: they walk and talk, laugh and cry, eat and drink, sing and make music, fight or make love, dance or pray—all of which involve the expenditure of energy and the co-ordinated use of muscle groups.

For a glimpse of action and its immense variety, its liveliness, and its impact, one may wish to look at the paintings of Pieter Brueghel the Elder. Almost every canvas of this Flemish painter is densely populated with human figures, and each person is assiduously engaged in some activity. The painting "Children's Games" shows a medieval village abounding with children absorbed in playing; his "Proverbs" shows adult villagers involved in commonplace or weird activities—many of them of symbolic significance—in the street, in attic windows, on rooftops, and in trees. The world is their arena for doing things; they assume postures, engage in body contacts, and are mobile in space. The "Wedding Feast" shows people eating and serving food, with lavish pleasures and nimble movements. Reproductions of "Peasant Dance" are so popular that most readers will have a memory of it. In hanging copies of it upon their walls, they provide their living rooms with animation and introduce into their sedentary lives a forceful reminder that life is motility. Even the quiet postures of Brueghel's people exude activity; the men lying on their backs under the fruit tree in "The Land of Cockaigne," being magically fed by an abundant nature, relax fulsomely and with visible abandon. They are not just lazy. There is a Rabelaisian pleasure in their gorgeous orality.

174

Some of Brueghel's paintings recreate religious themes: "The Fall of the Rebellious Angels," "The Carrying of the Cross," and "Conflict of Carnival and Lent." Like most Flemish and Dutch religious paintings, the biblical story is set in the context of ordinary sixteenth-century village life in the Lowlands. The figures are real everyday people with warts and knuckled hands, who spit with vigor, slander with venom, and fight with utter hostility. It is important to allow oneself to be struck by such updated and lively religious scenes, for one could easily fall prey to the assumption that religion, in the long course of history, has gradually left muscles behind in becoming a matter of heart and mind. One is apt to think that religion now is feeling or disposition, attitude or conviction, but no longer a motoric act. The days of processions, libations, slaughters at altars, dances, and *autos-da-fé* have long since gone; religion has become more and more a sedentary affair.

The truth of this historical observation is only very relative. Visitors to Mexico City can still see penitents hobbling on their knees across the square in front of the shrine of Our Lady of Guadalupe. One can still see processions with flags and banners and statues winding through Mediterranean villages. One can still see kneeling in any Roman Catholic or Episcopal church, in New York, London, and Paris. One can still watch handclapping, shaking, and gesticulating in Holiness sects, and hear the shouting and stamping of feet in churches "on the wrong side of the railroad tracks." One can also see ministers of mainline churches in moral protest marches before capitols. Presbyterians and Methodists can watch themselves standing up and sitting down with organized periodicity during any worship service. Though congregants no longer give the ancient kiss of peace to one another, they do shake hands with their pastor after the service, gather for a cup of coffee, or assemble for a luncheon. They tiptoe through sanctuaries, raise their voices in choral renditions, whisper in responsive readings, or go through the hard work of sitting still for half an hour with utmost self-control. Millions of people stand, bend, stretch, fold their hands, move rosary beads, finger books, suppress coughs and sneezes, look their best, and act most solemnly for at least one hour per week, with the feeling that these are appropriate, necessary, or prescribed activities of religious value and relevance. Religion is unthinkable without action, even when the latter is as inconspicuous as a quiet stroll for meditation or the closing of one's eyes in prayer.

Action is as indispensable to religion as it is to art, craft, making a living, and providing for one's needs. And it is as much regulated by religion in its territory as it is elsewhere by the codes of artists and artisans, the rules of labor and commerce, and the mores of feeding and cleaning oneself. As a matter of fact, religions assume very definite attitudes toward all actions, evaluating them in one way or another, and designating certain actions as specifically religious. For instance, the Judeo-Christian tradition has formulated some special religious thoughts about action, beginning with the creation myth which portrays God as a maker and doer who is the source of all energy. He is the one who takes the initiative and who instigates all the processes of nature. He also maintains what he has made. The acts of nature are responsive activities, just as the acts of primal man are responsive deeds within the limits of the charge given to him. Woman's novel act of giving in to the tempter and man's act of being seduced by his temptress upset the whole order and economy of being, and after the Fall, which was not a passive mishap but a new act, a large group of actions became set apart under a special curse: childbearing, working for one's living, and dying, "for out of it [the ground] you were taken; you are dust, and to dust you shall return" (Gen. 3:19). Working became an obligation and lost the play character it might have had in an earlier mythical age; but it retained its imitative features in letting man do what God did before him: make gardens, name animals, procreate, and increase the order of things.

All acts require energy, power, and authority, and religions have definite opinions about all three. The creator is their fountainhead and has to give his consent to their application. The divine power makes or breaks a man. Insofar as the deity is benevolent, his energy, power, and authority can be used cautiously for the welfare of mankind, but only within specific limits. Access to them can only be had on special occasions, through special persons, and through special activities. The occasions are feasts or days of worship; the persons are the village elders, shamans, or priests; the activities are rituals which need to be followed with great attention and precision. Mortal man cannot brutally appropriate the initiative and power of the gods, but must beg or pray for small portions of them at a time, to aid his own faltering strength and feeble understanding. And he must promise that the additional energies will be used for sanctioned purposes only, such as the increase of herds and crops, the protection of the clan, the killing of the group's enemies, or the defense against evil spirits. If a man could appropriate the divine power, he himself would be like God, and people would take the same precautions with him as they do with the rest of their deities: charm him, put him up in a circumscribed place, and control him through offerings, flattery, or incantations. Or, they may kill him.

A portion of all human activities, then, is set aside as the work to be done for the gods. Worship is work; it is the active side of religion. For the Buddhist, worship is a form of giving. For the ancient Hebrew, as for the modern Jew, it is service. The Greek word *liturgy* means "work of the people." The Germans speak of *Gottesdienst:* rendering service to God. The Latin *cult* means caring, maintaining, exercising, honoring, and serving. The forms of this special work that man does for his gods are in part dictated by his knowledge of the reasons for rendering his services.

One reason for the work of worship is imitation. Man does on a small scale, ritualistically, what the deity does on a large scale, realistically. At Heliopolis in Egypt the officiating Pharaohs and priests enacted a shortened version of the rising and the setting sun. Modern Roman Catholics enact a brief and stylized version of the Christian atonement drama. In fertility cults, human sexual pairings repeat the divine act of creation. Protestant Christians celebrate a symbolic common meal, in imitation of a similar meal taken by their founder with his followers, who were in turn celebrating a much older Passover meal which symbolized the liberation of Israel from Egyptian slavery through a special act of God.

Imitation slips easily into identification based on sympathetic magic. If the land is parched, a priestly sprinkling of waterdrops may compel the rain god to splash more lavishly upon the earth. How many modern home-owners, while sprinkling their lawns, have the fleeting afterthought that this may hasten the coming of rain? To render firstfruits of field or flock on the altar is not only a tribute to the "giver of all goods," but it is felt to help in securing the continued providing of the deity. The offering is a return, as well as an anticipatory gesture. Mexican farmers used to bury small clay fertility figurines in the fields, to enhance crop yields. Lighted candles are not only a symbol of the "light of lights," but they help in compelling the sun to return each morning.

In imitative and magical procedures a high degree of precision and compulsivity tends to be present. Imitative and magical acts are laboriously circumscribed in time, space, and style in order to enhance congruence between the divine activities and the sacred work of man. The performance is tense, following a prescribed course that is worked out into minutiae, and any deviation from the norm is felt to break the spell. A sloppy performance, a halfhearted celebration, or a free rendition of the basic theme are felt to bring the wrath of god upon the actors. In postures, voice, gestures, and the use of tools one must act according to prescriptions which themselves are seen as divinely laid down. They are the contractual terms on which intercourse with the deity is possible.

Another motive in worship, which determines the form of sacred acts, is placation or restitution. When transgressions have occurred, it is appropriate to make sacrifices in which the spilt blood of animals is a symbolic bloodletting of the individual or group which stands in need of punishment. While older patterns of placation prescribe an eye for an eye and a tooth for a tooth, one can shift to a verbal level, at which the group or the individual may make a confession of misdeeds, with solemn voice, in dejected posture, and with a contrite heart. Through object substitution one may restore himself by making gifts of money to his religious group, or by making donations for charity. Or one may use his muscles and mind symbolically, by undertaking a chore or a menial task requiring energetic work or a certain amount of tedium, which are assumed in restitution of guilt.

The work involved in other forms of worship is commemorative. Many religious festivals celebrate an important cosmic event or a historical episode in the life of the people which is in abbreviated form brought to the attention of the worshiping congregation. The Passover, the Feast of Lights, and the Feast of Tabernacles commemorate important elements of Jewish history. The Protestant rejection of the Roman Mass and its replacement by the Lord's Supper or communion service are based on a shift from dramatic re-enactment to commemoration. Whenever this aspect is emphasized one can expect a resistance to liturgical inventions; the commemorative work is a puristic attempt to recapture the original historical situation that is to be celebrated.

But a large part of liturgical work also has the character of a tribute which enhances spontaneity of action and freedom of form. Acts of praise, such as singing, dancing, marching, festooning the place of worship, dressing up, assembling flower bouquets, glossolalia, musicmaking, and spontaneous speechmaking, tend to give a free rein to the imagination and make the resulting action less stilted, although there are still definite limits of propriety and fitness. Compulsivity begins to give way to impulsivity; decorum gives way to warmth and fervor; inhibition gives way to release of energy.

Religion, then, has a definite view of action, and it makes distinctions between acts of god and acts of man. It sanctions or prescribes certain human activities as sacred and holds that the interactions between god and man are subject to rules and regulations. The fundamental distinction between divine and human activity is based on the differences in scale between the creator and the created. The created is contingent—the creator is constitutive, self-active, and self-perpetuating. All human energies, powers, and authorities are derived from a divine source. In a religious world view, the holy poses itself, makes itself felt, and forces man to reckon with it. In regard to the holy, whether it is seen as nature, cosmos, generative principle, father-god, mother-god, deistic order, theistic lawgiver, or divine lover, man's activities are held to be responsive acts. Though they may range from fixed and elaborate rituals to free expressions of good will and spontaneous feelings, their relation to the *mysterium tremendum et fascinosum* demands a certain style, a creaturely feeling, a sense of stewardship, and an awareness of the basic economy of the cosmic order.

A METHODOLOGICAL INTERLUDE

A discussion of the role and function of action in religion brings into sharp relief a basic methodological problem that has been implied, and sometimes alluded to, in the previous chapters. In imposing order on the wealth of observations which can be made about religion, the psychologist can permit himself to be guided by several principles. He can choose theological criteria, accepting a set of basic conceptions that recur in theological thought, such as creation, God, sin, salvation, redemption, grace, incarnation, *Heilsgeschichte,* sacrament, liturgy, etc., and group his own psychological observations under these headings. This does not make him a theologian. But it does mean that he takes theological distinctions as guideposts, which could create disorder in the psychological variables to which he wants to address himself. His psychology, in that case, is a kind of commentary, ideally in the form of an elaborate set of footnotes on theological propositions. The natural cohesiveness and interrelatedness of his psychological concepts tend to get lost.

By a second choice, he could take the phenomena of religion, looking for common themes that recur in everyday speech when people talk about religion. Accordingly, he could group his observations under the headings of worship, prayer, confession, church attendance, sacramental performances, mysticism, conversion, etc., and bring his psychological thoughts to bear upon these subjects. This does not make him a religionist or an adherent of religious beliefs. But in taking religious categories as guideposts, he runs the risk of writing a set of *ad hoc* psychologies in which the view of the whole may easily get lost.

A third choice consists of selecting from the tableau of religious phenomena some presumably essential features, taking from religion the most pregnant, dynamic, or telling instances, and ignoring those that seem less essential. Those who have followed this option have shown preference for conversion, mysticism, ritual, and dogma and have thereby run the risk of identifying religion with just these few manifestations. One can argue whether the four categories thus singled out are indeed the essential features of all religion or the dominant themes of any religion. From the expressed thoughts of religious and secular people one can also argue whether these behaviors, which are held to possess the marked qualities of religion, occur with sufficient frequency to warrant such preferential treatment. The very fact that words like "mystic," "ritualist," and "dogmatist" have a touch of disapprobation suggests that the states they refer to are not the most common features of religion, important as they may be in a study of ideal types.

The approach in this book has followed another option. Its ordering principles are psychological: it has taken standard psychological concepts as guideposts. The chapter headings and the centerheads are psychological variables in terms of which a great variety of religious phenomena are being described, analyzed, and interpreted. The religious phenomena themselves are of several orders: they comprise widespread religious practices and themes, theological propositions, and articulate thoughts about religious life from men and women whose experiences were particularly rich or deep, or whose thoughts were quite keen even about commonplace experiences. Observations made in other perspectives, such as anthropology, history, and comparative religion are not excluded; indeed, they are welcomed when they are felt to enrich the psychological perspective or seem to place the religious phenomena in a clear light. This methodological choice also runs a risk. One could argue whether it does justice to the natural divisions within religion, such as man-and-God, worship, prayer, sin, the holy, saintliness, or the sense of the reality of the unseen. One should ask whether this approach leaves enough room for an appreciation of religious experience as a whole. And some people loath to identify religion with religious experience, might wish to ask whether it contains enough appreciation for and knowledge of religion to provide a firm grasp of its many and complex manifestations.

Every approach has its risk. There is no focus without fuzzy edges. Every choice implies a positive and a negative selection. How should one deal with religious action, when religionists themselves have described worship as "the active side of religion," and when some devout church members define religion as a splendid behavioral quiescence in the storms of life, while their brethren under the same roof define it as prophetic activity in the crossroads of cultural, social, and political realities? What are the significant dimensions of action when, on the whole, the motor system seems now less prominent in religious behavior than it was in more archaic times? Should the social action of churches be included in this chapter?

It is plausible to speak of "types of religious action" that are to be subdivided into ritual, worship, prayer, trance, ecstasy, etc. It is equally plausible to group all religious actions on a continuum ranging from those involving large to those requiring small muscle groups. One could divide them into preparatory and consummatory acts, diffuse and skillful acts, random and purposive acts. It is possible to distinguish between natural and acquired acts and group one's observations accordingly. Some activities are releases of energy, while others are inhibitory. One could sort out "acts of God" and "acts of man." Compulsions and spontaneous acts could form another division. One could differentiate between individual and group activities, solitary acts and interpersonal acts.

Consistent with the methodological choice that has been made, and mindful of the diverse orders of religious phenomena to come under psychological scrutiny, the sections in this chapter will address themselves to action under the following rubrics:

1. energetic aspects
2. economic aspects
3. control aspects
4. developmental aspects

ENERGETIC ASPECTS OF RELIGIOUS ACTION

The door to the meetinghouse of the Society of Friends is open. Men and women quietly walk in, seat themselves on benches arranged in a square around an empty center, and silently assume a pensive posture. Some close their eyes. Twenty minutes or half an hour passes until one of the members rises from his seat, inconspicuously, and makes a brief statement about a theme that concerns him or a truth that was recently driven home to him. He sits down again. A few others may respond, some only briefly, others more elaborately. Perhaps there is a short musical interlude. The group may decide to sing a hymn. There is a moment of silent prayer, and the group disperses.

Elsewhere, on a hard pad a yogi sits, half starved, having practiced for years under the watchful eye of his guru a variety of postures, sensory controls, and digestive privations. His gnarled, bony body shows no animation; his sunken eyes seem turned inward. He meditates, sticks to his vows, and is mindful of the lessons he has received from his masters. Evening is falling, but he forgoes sleep.

In the twelfth century a Christian monk reflected about his religious experience as follows:

> I confess, then, though I say it in my foolishness, that the Word has visited me, and even very often . . . I have felt that He was present. . . . It is not by the eyes that He enters, for He is without colour; nor by the ears, for His coming is without sound; nor by the nostrils, for it is not with the air but with the mind that He is blended; nor again does He enter by the mouth, not being of a nature to be eaten or drunk; nor lastly is He capable of being traced by the touch, for He is intangible. You will ask, then, how, since the ways of His access are thus incapable of being traced, I could know that He was present. But He is living and full of energy, and as soon as He has entered into me He has quickened my sleeping soul, has aroused and softened and goaded my heart, which was in a state of torpor and hard as stone.[1]

The Quaker, the yogi, and Bernard of Clairvaux cherish an experience by which they feel infused with new energies, which they consider to be of divine origin. To the Quaker it comes as Light or enlightenment; to the yogi as harmony with the One; to St. Bernard as a quickening of soul. Whether that energy comes from a Prime Mover, the sun, an embracing and loving father, the ultimate stuff of the universe, a holy ghost, or the depth of a man's own being where it has thus far been locked up or remained dormant, there is little doubt in the devout mind that religious work has the effect of invigorating the basic energies of life and realigning its investments.

Though it may be less conspicuous among the ordinary churchgoer of today, the use of such words as "uplifting," "stirring," "inspiring," and "moving" in describing worship experiences hints at the same phenomenon: that the work involved in acts of worship is at the same time a spending of energy and an experience of replenishment or liberation. The liturgical process which binds energies into specific forms of work can also set a person free for new action, give him new zeal, or arouse his latent powers. From "Prayer can change your life" to "the power within you," and from "renewal" to "satori," some new energy becomes accessible which enables a person to do new things, see things differently than before, or have a fresh appreciation of his belonging to the larger scheme of the universe.

Sometimes, large amounts of energy will first have to be spent in the liturgical work. Ritual can be quite demanding. One may have to beat drums or shake rattles; one may have to "fall on his face," genuflect, or stand for long times in an alert posture, with exerting repetitiousness. One may have to kiss sacred objects or recite prayer formulas. One may have to immerse oneself in water, sing loudly, or convulse. Or one may just have to sit on hard benches, constrained and with great decorum. In all these cases muscle systems are involved, and energies are dissipated in large or small amounts, slowly or abruptly, diffusely or directed to an object. The muscle groups may be large, as in kneeling, or small, as in whispering. The processes may be entirely internal, as in hard thinking or long brooding. Whatever the nature of the work, it brings about changes in energy distribution and in tension level. If the tension level is high as one enters into these activities, there can be the immediate benefit of releasing excessive tension. One can sing his tensions away, fidget with rosary beads, or submit to the rhythmic droning of a corporate prayer. If the original tension level was markedly heightened by conflictual tendencies, the effects of the work of worship can be cathartic. Ritual imposes order and offers in most instances group support, whereby it becomes possible to utter phrases which give praise, confess sins, or express sorrow, even when one would not be ready to do so alone, or without formula. There is a dramatic quality in liturgical work which forces one to "go through the motions" and thereby have the appropriate feelings and emotional realignments, just as a theater audience has in watching a moving tragedy. The unspoken or unspeakable thoughts, stifled in one's breast, become verbalized and released. And if strong inhibitory or defensive maneuvers have contributed to a high tension level, any reduction of the general tension may have the beneficent side-effect of reducing the need for defensive control also. With or without production of insight, the motions involved in the religious act, such as bowing down, folding one's hands, or swallowing some sacred substance, may be just enough to liberate some energies from a defensive to an adaptive use, with the result that one "feels better."

To the extent that in all such liturgical works the mind is directed upon a divine object, be it directly or through some symbolic representation, the actor finds himself engaged in a relationship which he sees as one of give and take. He is, while worshiping, one member in a two-party system of transactions of which the other member is believed to be the constituent source of energy. The Holy, however conceived, is power—and all transactions with it are therefore power transactions. Doing obeisance to power makes one a partaker of power, with the implied consent of the giver of power that its use is proper and good. But to feel entitled to power, as to a gift, is already the beginning of narcissistic gratification, and a proof of one's lovableness. And if, moreover, one is taught to believe that it is good and noble to ask for divine assistance (which is also an act of self-humiliation with its own special reward) the feeble start of "feeling better" may swell to a tide of grace, in which habitual defensive devices may be dropped for a while.

It is, of course, not necessary to assume that such feelings of invigoration which religious exercises tend to produce are the result of extraneous infusions of energy, as if dynamic particles flowing through the air intrude into the person's system and give him a new charge. If one feels aesthetically moved by a great painting and receives an uplift from the artist's capacity to produce beauty, one does not usually make such assumptions either. Supernaturalism explains nothing, and a radical materialism which envisages waves of dynamic particles moving from one body to another calls for a strenuous fantasy. But the fact is that one does feel invigorated through some religious exercises, just as one feels physically more ebullient and buoyant when one falls in love. Something happens to the supplies and distribution of one's energies, which often becomes manifest to others also when the person starts to whistle, moves with zip, and has color on his cheeks and a livelier facial expression than before.

It is difficult, in the face of these observations, not to fall back on interpreting such changes in mind and body by an external cause, and it is therefore not so strange when religious persons attribute their renewed vigor to a divine infusion. This is supernaturalism only when one first affirms the notion of a disembodied, ghostly, immaterial god. It is magical thinking only when one's intention was to extort from one's deity a portion of his power for one's own use. When one wants to convey the feeling of "energy received" or "vigor bestowed," the mechanics of the transportation process may be less important than the affirmation that the renewal happened because of a relationship which took the individual out of his solipsistic confinement.

An alternative interpretation is based on viewing the individual as a closed system, with fixed amounts of energy; this forces one either to declare all such feelings of invigoration as fictions, or to see each change as a new patterning of the internal distributions of energy. A change toward greater buoyancy may then be seen as a change toward greater order, against the leveling processes of entropy which promote disorder and death. Such a model is useful in conceptualizing the forces involved in the internal conflict of drives and defenses, since it affirms the experiential truth that energies absorbed in neurotic defenses may drain the individual of the push he needs to do productive work.

The truth, though poorly understood, is likely to lie between the radicalism of both groups of interpretations. Living organisms are not closed systems, and they are not balloons with a secret opening filled with some spiritual gas. They are open systems in a dynamic equilibrium, in perpetual traffic with their environment from which they take in and to which they give off, with fluctuating levels of energy and with a multitude of regulatory devices which manage to produce some degree of well-being.

When well-being is increased or a sense of freedom enhanced, the metaphors of St. Bernard that "He is living and full of energy" and "He has entered me" can be seen as variations on the perennial theme of love. If the lover cannot actually clasp the loved one in his arms, he can cherish the memory of her last look at him, and it may warm his heart for a long time. With "her" inside him, he may maintain a higher self-regard, feel better, and act livelier. His belief in her disposition toward him need not be fictitious. His feeling of vigor may be quite real. His buoyancy in behavior may be witnessed by others. The behavior change and its internal dynamics should not be explained away as a fiction or as a mere "as if" phenomenon. The basic difference lies between the "loved one seen" and the "living God" of St. Bernard, unseen, but felt.

It is a commonplace observation that fictions can produce behavioral results as much as physical objects do. Hallucinations can give rise to flight behavior. Delusional ideas can force a person into a fight. Illusions may cause misreading of signs and lead a person from his intended path. Hypotheses can lure a person into the exploration of hidden recesses, where he may find novelty. Mere beliefs can be causes of war, rousing whole nations to frenzies of activity and outpourings of energy. Whether St. Bernard's "living God" is fiction or fact, the effect on the believer's behavior and energy dynamics is as observable as the effect of the band's music on a tired group of marching soldiers. In the latter case there are sound waves and symbolism. St. Bernard carefully excluded all light waves, sound waves, and gustatory and touch stimuli. But he kept the "reality of the unseen," and the brain waves of his conviction that "He is living and full of energy." He also kept the symbolism, which is not a second reality, but a special perspective on all reality. Symbolism is a view of the world in terms of power. As we saw in Chapter V, the symbol is not merely a pointer to some specious reality, nor is it only a sensory pattern that participates in the imperceptible reality to which it points. It is a linguistic reality that is learned as part of one's semantic system. Symbols divide reality in certain ways, ordering it in levels of power and energy, from the ultimate to various degrees of contingency.

ECONOMIC ASPECTS

It is a common observation that the ways in which people spend their energies show marked individual differences. Some people prefer large movements which entail lavish energy expenditures. Their whole body moves when they talk. They write with a grand sweep of their pen on the paper. They take two steps at a time when they climb stairs. Others are, by comparison, very frugal with their body movements. They prefer measured, delicate, and small gestures. They can keep their body immobile when they talk—only their lips move, and the manual gestures they make are deliberate and sparing. They do not wear themselves out; as a matter of fact, they may be hard to move into action of the sort which convinces others that they are really doing something. This variable in motor behavior is not a matter of zeal or laziness, but of psychic and muscular economy.

This economic factor is affected by certain psychopathological conditions. In depression the whole pace of life goes slowly: motor movements become fewer; initiative is reduced; thoughts seem to crawl only; speech is at a slow pace. In elation one sees the opposite. There is hypermotility: thoughts rush; speech has pressure; one tends to respond to too many stimuli at once.

Though rituals vary in pace and scope of motor movements, it is an outstanding feature of ritual acts that they are measured, precise, specified in great detail, highly stereotyped, and often very repetitive. Baptismal sprinkling on an infant's forehead cannot take the form of a quick splash. A litany cannot be rattled off. A procession moves in slow and dignified steps; it cannot become a march or a run. Raising the arms in a benediction requires a slow movement, quite unlike the quick flapping of the arm in the Nazi greeting.

The idea of rhythm and number is important in ritual. Joshua had to circle the city of Jericho seven times before the walls would fall down. "Holy, holy, holy," is said three times—one more repetition would break the rhythm and destroy the ritual effect. Luther reduced the Kyrie from nine to three times and thereby managed to keep it a ritual—five or six times would have undone its impact. Long words such as "hallelujah" are themselves ritualistic, and can be uttered twice with good effect. The repetition of sacred acts makes ritual not only time-consuming, thus turning "work" into "much work," but it also provides for a measured, stepwise, and rhythmic discharge process of energy. It is basically an economic proposition from the motoric point of view, which is intertwined with the seasonal rhythms of the divine work in nature from the point of view of meaning.

After winter comes spring, then summer and autumn. After night, daybreak. After seeding, growth and harvest. After storms, calm. The cyclical flux of time gives life meaning and purpose, and these meanings are dramatized in the abbreviated forms of worship rituals. They are also acted out through the motor system, in repetitious movements and gestures and sound complexes.

Spontaneity and efficiency are suspended in rituals. In effect, ritual is antispontaneous; it distrusts impulsivity. It capitalizes on inhibition, delay, and various other control devices. It is in many respects a compulsion which conceals as well as reveals through motor symbols the conglomerate of wishes and counterwishes prevailing in the relations of man to the Holy. Eating the bread and drinking the wine in a communion service have a deeply hidden trace of cannibalism that thrives on flesh and blood, but they also have the manifest features of a dignified acceptance of the divine gift of life through the fruits of the field and the grape. The hand lifted up in benediction is a hand of judgment as well as a hand of blessing. Baptism is both going down and rising up, dying and being reborn, being washed from uncleanliness and being refreshed for the new day. The combination of these motifs into one act is an economy of motion which, because of its short duration, can be often repeated. And because of its compactness it demands periodic repetition so that one can gradually come to appreciate its meanings.

Economic principles can govern religious acts in various ways. Acts of penance, in order to placate for guilt feelings, must have the quality of heavy work requiring exertion, or a degree of tedium requiring a strong effort of the will to continue them. The pilgrimage partakes of both features. The performance of a menial task, with a contrite heart, reaches the same goal symbolically by implying that the person is now doing "slave labor" which he normally delegates to the servants or the lower castes. Saying five or ten Hail Mary's adds the element of multiplication to a simple task, whereby its length or intensity of effort becomes a measure of the severity of the transgression.

Griefwork after the loss of a loved one is an excellent example of the natural economy of drive dynamics. After the immediate shock of the bereavement, in which the person feels empty or dazed, he reviews in his mind the pleasant memories of the deceased, and after that the less pleasant ones until his equilibrium becomes restored. Time is of the essence in such a process, and just as in wound-healing, its optimal duration depends on many dynamic factors. It can hardly be sped up or abbreviated. Time heals precisely because it takes time. It is not surprising, therefore, that religious systems have often prescribed definite intervals for grieving and mourning, in order to make sure that the bereft will do their vital work without undue haste. But the religious specifications of wakes and mourning periods also ritualize the natural economy of griefwork and impose external controls for greater efficacy.

In America, economic distinctions in religious action follow the broad social class divisions and, interacting with these, racial and ethnic differences. The large body reactions, the quick movements, and the lavish expenditures of energy tend to be associated with the worship patterns of the lower class and to a considerable degree with Negro religion. The voices sound louder, and there is, at times, actual shouting in these groups. Gesticulating is more profuse. The sermon rhythms of the preachers are faster, often approaching pressure of speech and flight of ideas. The piano is the preferred musical instrument to accompany singing, and the hymns themselves tend to have faster tempos than the grave songs selected in Protestant mainline churches. In middle-class groups "the minister does not run to his pulpit but goes with a grave pace,"[2] as Van der Leeuw said. For the sake of dignity and decorum the whole pace of the congregation's motoric life is slowed down, from the measured cadences of the sermon delivery to the solemn strides of participants in the procession. Roman Catholic habits seem to stand between these extremes. Since the Roman liturgy is richer and more dramatic, it demands more motor movements from the participants, in kneeling, bowing, standing up, crossing oneself, etc., but most of these movements are ritualized so that they are executed with deftness and self-control.

Though it would be a gross oversimplification to say that the lower-class motor practices in religion are symptomatic of elation, and the middle-class practices are manifestations of depressive tendencies, there can hardly be doubt that less educated sectarian groups have far more tolerance of elated states than their staid middle-class brethren. The popularity of glossolalia, prophecy, and writhing body movements in these groups is unmatched. They simply would not be tolerated in mainline congregations, not only because they would be a break in the carefully maintained decorum, but because they would not fit in the emotional pattern of gravity and solemnity which prevails in the more sedate forms of worship. The snakehandlers about whom La Barre[3] has reported not merely represent a cultic oddity at which one could look in bemusement but manifest an emotional condition to which the members of solemn assemblies would react with panic.

CONTROL ASPECTS

Purposeful acts require control through skill, good timing, and goal direction. Playing football or doing carpentry work requires skills different from those of watch-repairing or surgery. Timing is of a different order in each case, as are the goals. An important aspect of timing is the function of delay. The larger goals must be broken down into a set of smaller sub-goals, which requires postponing the long-range goals for a while until the short-term goals have been reached. Too strong a desire to reach the goal quickly is tantamount to impulsivity, which tends to interfere with the skill-fulness of the movements also. The ability to "hold oneself" and to "wait for the right moment" allows a person to concentrate on the skill needed to do the right thing at the right time.

In regard to religious action, two other sets of requirements are to be considered. Van der Leeuw has pointed out that in historical perspective most religious acts directed toward the Holy have also been aesthetic acts directed toward the beautiful. Holiness and beauty are close together; their relation is acknowledged in the phrase that the Lord is to be praised "in the beauty of holiness." Therefore, sacred, cultic movements also tend to be beautiful movements. Prayer, work, dance, pantomime, and drama are intimately intertwined in the history of religions, and although they have become culturally differentiated into "religion" on the one hand, and "art" on the other hand, each with its devotees and institutionalizations, it is important to be aware of their dynamic unity. This is especially true of the dance, which lives on in attenuated form in processions and religious postures. Van der Leeuw wrote:

> That the dance has religious meaning does not mean that it can express only religious feelings. On the contrary, all feelings, from the most solemn to the most frivolous, find their expression in the dance. The religious is not a particular sensation alongside other sensations, but the summation of them all. Thus the dance can also serve a purpose which we, too, would call religious. An old inhabitant of Halmahera, who did not want simply to give up the feasts for the dead of his people, said, in his defense, to the missionary: "My dancing, drinking, and singing weave me the mat on which my soul will sleep in the world of the spirits." But even when the dance stands in the service of what to our mind is a purely secular matter, it is by its very nature religious, for through it holy power is freed. The primitive man dances for everything, from his wife to eternal life, from a hunting trophy to a profit in trading. The dance not only accompanies all the actions of his life, but also leads it, supports it, and brings it to a good end. To the accompaniment of a dance, one exhibits his wares in New Caledonia; looks for lice in North Queensland; divorces his wife among many Indian tribes, and, in the Cameroons, goes to the gallows.[4]

King David danced before the ark of the covenant. Medieval literature saw God, Christ, and the angels dancing merrily in the dance forms of that period. A compulsive, contagious shaking which affected whole villages was called St. Vitus's dance. The Hindu god Siva is always represented in a dancing posture, as if he were an incarnation of the dance itself.

The point is that through such ancient associations between cultic and aesthetic movements, many sacred motions are guided by aesthetic considerations and controls. Ceremonial processions have a sacred pace which is also a grave rhythm. Pageantry is a feelingful enactment of divine mysteries with dramatic qualities. Prayer litanies underscore in their repetition of phrases not only the weight and importance of the words said, but also the comings and goings between two parties at beautiful rhythmic intervals, as with dance partners. All these things are ordered movements, and as Van der Leeuw suggests, "the power which proceeds from ordered movement extends over the whole congregation and averts evil influences."[5] And the performers of religious motions often require a special dress also, now in the form of liturgical vestments, formerly in the form of masks and animalistic disguises. Van der Leeuw's statement that the dance not only accompanies the actions of the life of primitive man, but also leads it, supports it, and brings it to a good end is of great importance in grasping an essential feature of religious actions of modern man. Religious acts are not merely expressive acts or reactions to sacred stimuli. They are themselves charged with numinous power whose discharge or use must be carefully guided by norms which are attuned to sacred realities. They are held to lead life, support it, and bring it to a good end. They are representations of skill which, as a principle of dynamic order, is just as numinous as the energies which it controls. Liturgical skills are to the energies of the Holy what artistic skills are to the raw materials of nature. They are a principle of form.

In a word, then, religion is not only interested in what one does, but in how one does it. Religion is not only a set of ideas or feelings; it is also a craft. A serious craft, if one insists, but then also not without playful features. In *Homo Ludens*[6] the historian Huizinga has documented his conviction that a large part of our cultural mores and institutions has the character of a play or game. This is not a lighthearted quip, but a serious and penetrating insight. Playing is an activity that can be seen at all levels of civilization and even among animals. It may be a biological necessity, and although there are many theories about play behavior, its essence cannot be entirely reduced to something else like exercise, energy release, sublimation, or pedagogical preparation. It has all these features and many more, but is *sui generis,* in final analysis, irreducible. The opposition between play and seriousness is only partially true, for playing has a seriousness all its own.

Huizinga submits that one plays for fun, not out of duty or by assignment. Playing is a temporary stepping out of the ordinary structures of life, a kind of intermezzo in the flux of things. It has a definite beginning and a definite end which sharply demarcate play from work and the rest of life. Playing requires a circumscribed play space: an arena, a chessboard, a stage, or a temple. Within that play space there are definite rules: the rules of the game. They are invalid outside that space, and they hold only as long as the play or game lasts. Playing creates a new order which is within its space and time absolute: deviations from the rules break the spell and ruin the game. They terminate all play, so much so that dishonest or inept play behavior becomes a topic for discussion in the "serious" world outside the confines of the play space and the play times. Playing binds and loses; it gives release and it gives structure. It imposes rhythms and harmony. Above all, it tends to fixate itself immediately as a cultural form, which can be repeated whenever one wants to "play the game again."

These specifications of play behavior are at several points congruent with definitions of ritual, and they describe with remarkable aptness the form and the spirit of cultic activities. Religious activity too knows the circumscribed space and the delimited time for its unfolding. There are hallowed times—Sabbath, Sunday morning, feast days, vesper—and hallowed spaces—temples, synagogues, clearings in the woods, the "high places" of the Old Testament, chapels, and tabernacles. Religious acts have a beginning and an ending, liturgically marked by introits and benedictions. When one engages in a religious act, one enters into a new order which has rules of its own with prescriptions for postures, gestures, words, and social roles to be assumed. Worshiping places the person temporarily out of the common order of nature and society, subjecting him to a new set of rules which are only valid within the cult. If the rule is that one bows one's head in prayer, it is "foul play" or a break in the game to lift it up. If the rule is to speak Latin, the play is over when one starts speaking English. For the play's the thing, and the players know what's up.

The player has a double awareness: he knows that there is a world "outside" the play circle with whose mores he must be in tune in order to survive, and he knows that there is another world inside the circle to which he must be fair as long as the play lasts. While being seriously and perhaps even strenuously involved in playing the game, giving to it all he has in skill, speed, strength, or cunning, he also knows that "it is only play" and that he can "step out of it." While entering into and getting out of the play are voluntary, being in it is a great compulsion. This double awareness of the player can become so acute that he may find himself playing the game in all seriousness while also knowing that it is not real. I believe that this duplicity of experience is often present during the most solemn and sacred religious activities, particularly when the cultic performance is long and the attention of the participants begins to wax and wane. Though the focal feelings may convince the participant that he is in the presence of the Holy, there may be a dim but persistent feeling in the background of his consciousness that he is involved in an act of "make-believe" and that it is perfectly within his powers to step out of it. This is not a schizoid dissociation or religious lukewarmness; it is an awareness of the play character of ritual and liturgical forms. It enabled the Protestant reformers to take a critical look at the Roman Mass in whose rules they were brought up, and it is a *sine qua non* for any effort at liturgical innovation.

The playfulness of religious action enlightens us also toward a new perspective on the relations between acts and feelings, or acts and thoughts. The repeatability and the playful "as if" character of ritual can enable a person to "go through the motions" with the hope that he will gradually achieve the desired feelings or thoughts which are embedded in the act. Müller-Freienfels made this observation when he said that we pray not only because we are pious, but because while we are praying a feeling of piety is generated or intensified.[7] Religious acts are also a practice, and the more one engages in the practices one has learned, the more likely it is that one will acquire the attitudes, feelings, and thoughts that are germane to them.

Religious behavior is full of playful features. One tiptoes or steps only gently through sanctuaries, but as soon as the threshold to the hallways is crossed, one's gait becomes firmer and more natural. Expert chewers, who firmly sink their teeth into a piece of gum after the service, are at pains to let a small piece of communion bread travel slowly through mouth and throat. One folds his hands, neither too loosely nor too firmly and certainly without a clap, in preparing for prayer. Children know these things and consciously play with them a private game within the game, by trying to squeeze their eyes so closely that the eyelids and sockets become all red, by trying to put the right fingers over the left ones in folding their hands, or by willfully singing just a trifle too loudly, too slowly, or too fast.

The most playful religious acts are those done during festivities. Festivities are combinations of Huizinga's play behavior and Van der Leeuw's beautiful motions. There are the lights, the flowers, the decorations, the more joyful and vivacious music, and such oddities as a smear of ashes on one's forehead on Ash Wednesday, a sprig of holly in one's lapel on Christmas, and flowered hats on Easter. The youth of the congregation is more conspicuous on such days, and many adults rationalize their own activities during the festivals by saying that they do them "for the children." Festivities require extra work and are an impetus toward the creation of beauty, in music, words, diction, gestures, vestments, pictorial designs, and the motions of the whole worshiping group. The festive elements can become so overworked that the awareness of the Holy fades into the background, as in carnivals. The aesthetic element can become so pronounced that one can hardly tell the difference between the divine service and a concert. But these excesses which threaten to estrange the sacred element are only hypertrophies of the sense of play and beauty which normally inheres in all cultic activities.

DEVELOPMENTAL ASPECTS

In an often-quoted experiment by Coghill[8] on the development of action patterns, it was demonstrated that when a newt is stimulated cutaneously a massive body reaction ensues in which a powerful quiver moves through the entire body length from head to tail. In the more fully developed salamander, however, such a stimulation elicits only a reaction in a limited muscle group. For instance, the head is moved to avert the stimulus, while the rest of the body remains in the same position; or a single limb is withdrawn if it is touched. This is a simple demonstration of a general law of the development of muscle action: At the beginning of life the response to stimuli tends to be a massive body reaction, which is replaced during the growth period by a more local reaction of limited muscle groups, whereas in adult organisms there is a more adapted and integrated response of the structured whole, organized with articulateness and flexibility.

Another observation is that young children act their thoughts. Fantasy and memory are close to the muscle system: they easily spill over into pantomime and theatrical portrayal. In an earlier chapter we also saw that in youngsters thought has almost the same power as action: it can magically change things, other people can discover one's thoughts, and one is just as accountable for a bad thought as one is for a bad deed. Furthermore, when a toddler tries to tell a story, his whole body moves along with his speech musculature. It takes considerable maturation to be able to talk without accessory body movements. It also takes a good deal of growth to turn involuntary body movements into articulate gestures which can be used to replace speech or to support it.

It is not surprising that religion, which is normally learned from childhood and, as the saying has it, "drunk in with the mother's milk," has a good deal of tolerance for primitive action patterns, in addition to its highly stylized and very adult motor forms. Under certain circumstances it accepts infantile babbling accompanied by jerking neck and trunk movements in the belief that the spirit is now manifesting itself through "speaking in tongues." The term "glossolalia" is a much too learned and adult name for this activity. Rolling on the floor, shaking, and convulsive movements are primitive reactions of the nervous system which in gross appearance are not very different from childish temper tantrums or diffuse and massive discharges of infantile pleasure. The desire for body contact in Holiness sects is a childlike indulgence in touching, quite unlike verbal greetings or the giving of a formal handshake. Rhythmic rocking of the body and stamping with the feet are closer to childhood than singing to the accompaniment of an organ.

On the whole, a high degree of actionboundness (which is not the same as activism) is the earmark of children, as compared with the adult capacity to wait, deliberate, and meditate. When one tries to take a panoramic view of the various forms of worship now practiced in America, it appears that some forms are far more actionbound than others. In the more liturgical churches there is always something to do; the action never stops. The celebrants and their helpers are busy at the altar, making all kinds of gestures, and congregants in the rest of the building are standing up, kneeling, sitting down, kneeling again, and so on. What a difference with a Quaker meeting! In Reformed Churches and Jewish synagogues the worship is far more verbal than the cult of the liturgists and the Friends, but even in them it is rare to find a quiet moment in which to meditate without undue arousal or stimulus bombardment. The Salvation Army relies on drums and brass instruments, singing, and verbal testimony in quick sequence, and as soon as the instruments have been packed, the hands are busy serving meals, making beds, and giving baths to neglected children, in a very pragmatic combination of activism with actionboundness. In the Army's militant evangelism, worship and ordinary work are almost completely merged, quite different from their sharp separation in most other confessions. Some people flee to their church for an hour's rest in a very busy life; others go to theirs for a charged moment in a dull life. Some go to worship in order to "let themselves go" in a purposeful, temporary regression; others attend with aspirations of the greatest decorum and the most adult wisdom, in utmost self-control which is not easily achieved in their working hours or at home.

Precisely because of the play character of worship described in the previous section, religious action and especially ritual practices tend to entail temporary regressions in the service of the ego which can have a restorative effect. Play, in Huizinga's sense, is not the playing of children as opposed to the working of adults—it is a ceremonial and often quite conscious engagement in new rules which are unlike those that govern the rest of life. The play element of ritual makes possible actions from which one might otherwise shrink away. The gross orality of the cannibalistic feast or totem meal which lives on in attenuated form in modern communion services with their "Take, this is my body . . . ," and "Take, this is my blood . . . ," is possible only when the context of the ritual allows one to regress without loss of self-respect or when there is a promise of benefit in the act. Praying aloud or in an audible whisper with neighbors sitting on all sides doing the same is, in a sense, quite an achievement in disinhibition for respectable adults who have been taught to commune silently and to prize inwardness. Despite their having learned to "put aside childish things" there are ritual moments in which that achievement is suddenly undone. And the rules of the game are such that one may feel good about it.

It is pertinent to religion itself to classify some of its action patterns in terms of the level of libidinal organization needed to enjoy them. To the oral features already mentioned one should add the pronounced emphasis on eating and drinking in the organized life of Protestant congregations. The joint meal in the fellowship hall is a major way in which the members of the congregation are made to feel as if they were "one family." And with the acts there are dozens of words and phrases in the language of religion which show these same oral interests, from "milk and honey" to the story of Jesus' healing the blind man by putting a daub of spittle and dust on his eye (John 9:6). When trust, confidence, and hope are as important in religion as they are proclaimed to be, oral metaphors and acts are the carriers of great psychological values. For the toddler, putting something in the mouth is the most direct and convincing way of knowing that thing, more trustworthy than the knowledge gained by distance receptors. Ezekiel knew this when he wrote:

> And he said to me, "Son of man, eat what is offered to you; eat this scroll, and go, speak to the house of Israel." So I opened my mouth, and he gave me the scroll to eat. And he said to me, "Son of man, eat this scroll that I give you and fill your stomach with it." Then I ate it; and it was in my mouth as sweet as honey (3:1–3).

Seeing is not always believing. Thomas had to touch the resurrected Jesus before he could be convinced (John 20:25). And millions of Christian believers have to put substances into their mouths in order to be convinced of the verbal propositions regarding their salvation. To them communion means eating and drinking, just as loving means kissing.

The other side of orality, its aggressive component, is manifest in spitting and biting, and symbolically in cursing and swearing. Because of religious taboos on aggression and the nature of worship, in which the deity is revered and not slandered, most oral aggression is symbolic and directed to the adversary, such as a devil or evil people. Its high point in contemporary Western religion is reached in the rituals of exorcism in which, with clipped, fierce, and almost spitting voice, the exorcist addresses himself to the devils who are believed to dwell in a poor human subject. In those circumstances, speaking becomes cursing and hissing, and the language becomes interspersed with neologistic inventions full of expletives. But short of such rarities, there is a good deal of hortatory preaching full of biting sarcasm, which is a lively example of oral aggression, to be heard on many American radio programs. As a matter of fact, the phrase "I will spit you out of my mouth" is a cherished metaphor in such rapid-fire, hammer-blowing deliveries.

How different is all this from the preoccupation with cleanliness, washings, purifications, orderliness, and properness that is typical of the next phase of human development. These anal motifs have a long heritage in religion, and much ritual is derived from them. Purification by fire or water, by changing clothes, by wearing white vestments, by anointing with perfumes, or by driving the stench of daily life away with incense is one of the oldest religious activities and it remains alive in symbolic forms. The "Sunday best" is its tritest contemporary example. The clamor for order, neatness, regularity, and precision, and the fierce adherence to rules and regulations in the order of service, are its psychological heirs. The theme: "Is it clean or unclean?" is the anal metaphor for "Is it good or bad?" or "Am I sinful or saintly?" The child who is learning about physical cleanliness develops his sense of order against the natural forces of uncleanliness, dirt, and disorder. The laws of hygiene and the social order are not yet synchronous with the laws of his sphincters. They become so only when he can match his vital clock with the clocks of the family—when he can will what his parents will. Hence the concept of cleanliness and the sense of orderliness are dynamically tied in with the idea of obedience and the subjection of one's will to a larger, more powerful one. And hence, cleanliness is godliness; orderliness is holiness; purity is saintliness. At a higher order of abstraction, Kierkegaard summed all of it up in the title of his book: *Purity of Heart Is to Will One Thing,* with the significant subtitle: *Spiritual Preparation for the Office of Confession.*[9] It calls for repentance, remorse, and the confession of sins.

The repentant person feels dirty, and if he is not visibly dirty he makes himself so by putting on sackcloth and heaping ashes on his head. The modern penitent accepts only a tiny smear of ashes on his forehead at Shrovetide but the meaning is the same: he shows his uncleanliness and will prove in time that he is becoming clean again. Klink[10] reported from his experience as a mental-hospital chaplain the case of a patient, a member of a sect using the sacrament of footwashing, whose turning point toward recovery occurred when some of his brethren were invited to administer to him a footwashing ritual on the ward. In the vivacious services of some Protestant fringe groups one is asked, "Are you washed in the blood of the Lamb?" The Presbyterian says quietly, "Cleanse me, O Lord!" and runs his service "decently, and in order."

The next developmental phase in children is marked by phallic interest, which is a libidinal-aggressive metaphor of self-assertion, daringness, pride, and competition. Hebrew religion under Moses had its fling at it in the episode of the brazen serpent: a masculine fertility symbol on top of a pole, which is itself also such a symbol. In attenuated form, it continues to have its role in standard-bearing in processions. La Barre's description of the snakehandling sects in Southeastern United States clarifies both the daringness of the cult and the bold character of their leaders. To let a rattler crawl over one's neck and shoulder, and to expose oneself to its venomous bite, is more than an innocuous oddity: it is risk-taking of a sort that requires a daredevil who must by an inner compulsion prove his virility in this way. La Barre's psychological sketch amply brings out one leader's phallic features: he likes to bait the police and other authorities, he loves to race on motorcycles, and his playing with the snake in the cult is in itself a defiant act for which he claims authority by a heavenly father who "has told him he can do so with impunity."[11] Aside from these few exceptions, religion, at least in the Christianized West, is not very tolerant of phallic behavior, for it is undoubtedly one of the clearest instances of pride and arrogance. And it was the snake, after all, who incited the first man and woman in the garden of Eden to the flagrant defiance of the divine order, and to the aspiration of being "like God."

If one sees libidinal development culminating in a genital mode of organization with loving transactions between partners, some of the greatest religious themes come to mind. Mysticism abounds in the metaphor of the lover and the beloved; less ecstatic believers abound in phrases and attitudes regarding the father and his children. It would be trite, and not wholly accurate, to single out specific acts such as cultic embracing, marching, singing, dignified handshaking, blessing, and the bringing of gifts as signs of genital maturity. All these acts certainly can express mature attitudes, but the point is that at higher levels of development the relations between the mode of the acts and the nature of the satisfactions to be obained are far more flexible than at previous levels. An infinite variety of acts can be chosen to express genital attitudes precisely because the object is now more clearly recognized and loved as a person in his own right, and the lover, though still having his needs, is no longer fixated on the oral, anal, and phallic rituals in obtaining his satisfactions. One of the signs of maturity is the ability to approach all situations with flexibility and inventiveness.

Genitality does not undo the previous modes, but puts them in a new perspective, in awareness of their limits and with a casual recognition of their historical and dynamic truths. Thus, the cannibalistic ceremony of eating flesh and blood can now turn into a love feast, and the compulsive character of ritual can be dissolved in a more playful attitude. Cleansing can become confessing; the piecemeal forgiving of transgressions on a tit-for-tat basis can give way to an attitude of enduring forgiveness. The terrifying features of the Holy can become softened by its grandeur and beauty. Scrolls no longer have to be eaten, and feet no longer have to be washed concretely with soap and water. Vestments become less important: any dress will do as long as the intentions are noble and the heart is in the right place. The noise of solemn assemblies can be reduced to a pensive silence, which communicates messages in its own way. Gestures can become more spontaneous. Ecstasy no longer requires convulsions but can become intellectual or emotional delight.

The developmental view of religious acts shows on the whole (but with many exceptions and complications) the following long-range trends. Motor activity becomes gradually replaced by verbal and cognitive activity. Concrete cultic "doings" with hands and feet and goods gradually give way to symbolic transactions and exchanges of sympathetic concern. And cultic action tends to become social action. These trends are, however, very global, both in the lifetime of faith groups and in the lives of individuals, and it seems that they are perpetually threatened by the pull of earlier habits. The change from the drama of the Roman Mass to the commemorative and instructional forms of Protestant worship entails a change from actors to proclaimers and lecturers. The beautiful body-language of liturgical postures and gestures is replaced by beautiful rhetoric and elocution, which can stir the emotions just as effectively, much as visual stimulus bombardment does. Or does it? The so-called liturgical movement in Protestant churches seeks renewal of the ways of worship on many grounds, including the recognition that verbalization runs the serious risk of intellectualization with its resulting stodginess and dryness. It also recognizes that much preaching falls on deaf ears, and that words can lead the mind astray just as much as body movements can precipitate it into turmoil. Criticism of too much sacred work at altars and the showiness of religious performances is as old as the Old Testament prophets, and probably much older than they. There have always been warnings by a few that cults are getting out of hand, and that renewal of religious truths is to be found in absence from all ostentation and outwardness, in favor of inwardness and a change of heart. All kinds of prophets and reformers have stood for social action, refusing to accept the radical distinction between the sacred and the secular that underlies the stylized forms of worship.

But these maturational trends are only tenuously held, in an ongoing dialectic with the more traditional and established forms of sacred action. The witnessing in the cultural and political arena, which is such a pronounced aspect of modern religiosity, tends to borrow from the cult certain liturgical forms which it uses outside the traditional sacred places, but they are sacred forms nevertheless. Instead of processions in the church or toward it, there are marches on state houses. After clerical collars have become almost abandoned in houses of worship, they reappear in the streets to identify the agents of social change as men of God. Instead of the ancient hallowed standards and banners, there are placards to be carried around, with the same phallic attitude of protest or assertiveness. Coffeehouses for college youth are places where one can talk about religion and perform guitar-led hymnodies under the avuncular guidance of a young chaplain in ways that resemble the erstwhile Sunday schools. The pull toward ritual is always present, and much of the so-called free and spontaneous acivity becomes quickly stylized into a new liturgy. Sit-ins have some kinship with kneeling. Slogans are chanted, not shouted. Formulas for grievances take on an evocative form and are repeated in the form of litanies. The postures, the gestures, the voices, and at times the clothes worn are liturgical re-creations in which some continuity with ancient forms of worship is affirmed.

This chapter on action cannot be concluded without considering what seems the least active of all activities: sleep. Religion is interested in sleep. It has always been. The Christian hymn says, "Sleepers, awake!" The prophet Elijah on Mount Carmel mocked the Baal priests by hinting that their god might be asleep (I Kings 18:27). Prayers at bedtime, just before going to sleep, are a standard requisite in many religions, as are morning prayers upon awakening.

Sleeping is a numinous activity. There is something sacred about it. Sleep is the great restorer and renewer. It is also something that with great power overcomes a person. Awakening from sleep is like rebirth— falling asleep has been compared to a "little dying." A. de Buck[12] has demonstrated that in ancient Egyptian sun worship the diurnal cycle of sleep and wakefulness had both a cosmic and a personal significance. Just as the sun, on its regular course, enters periodically the realm of *Nu,* i.e., the primeval watery chaos or "underworld," so do the sleepers and the dead. The ancient headrests in the shape of a moonsickle on a short pedestal are identical with the hieroglyph of *Shu,* the god of the air who holds a promise of renewal and refreshment.

Sleepers know no time: a thousand years is to them as one day, just as it is to the deity. Sleepers were often thought to be in a different world in which they encountered different situations recorded in their dreams. Hence, dreams can be regarded as revelations from that other world, which give knowledge of a sort that is ordinarily not accessible. Great dreams are therefore a sign of the divine and may have cosmic significance.

The numinous character of sleep is no longer celebrated with the same thoughtfulness that used to give it status in ancient myths. When the *Iliad* calls Sleep the brother of Death, when Lethe promises forgetfulness, and when the Olympic gods occasionally become somnolent, we are in a mythical world view in which the human soul, when the body is asleep, wanders around in an unseen world, to which it will permanently return in the hour of death. The crucial motifs in this kind of thinking are that there is a spiritual realm which is actually the realm of spirits and gods, and that sleeping is an extraordinary phenomenon which needs an explanation. Modern sleep research espouses the opposite view. It holds that sleep is the primordial condition and that arousal to wakefulness is the enigma that needs an explanation, without the postulate of a more or less detachable soul that can wander hither and yonder. In line with this view, current research on mysticism takes recourse to consciousness-expanding drugs which maximize awareness and make the mystic wide awake to the world outside and the world within, both of which are data of consciousness and therefore in principle external to it.

But there is still something sacred about sleep. When a sleeper is rudely awakened he feels it as a terrible intrusion. But to awaken somebody else is also felt as a more or less sacrilegious act. It is an unpleasant task, indeed an intrusion upon the numinous, to awaken a person from sleep, and it is ordinarily done only for very urgent reasons such as the obligation to shoulder the tasks of daily life, to alert a person to danger, or to help him satisfy his physical needs. And the prayers said at bedtime still go on to compare sleeping with dying, so that the hour of falling asleep is seen as the last chance to set one's affairs straight and be reconciled to the divine intentions:

> Now I lay me down to sleep;
> I pray the Lord my soul to keep.
> If I should die before I wake,
> I pray the Lord my soul to take.

As this old children's prayer indicates, sleeping is also risky. Not only does it overcome a person, but "it" can mean death. The person who needs to stay alert because he finds the world a dangerous place and fears the strength of his own impulses cannot allow himself to fall asleep. For in sleep, his control is undermined and he may be overcome, or give himself away through speaking in his dreams. Hence the great frequency of sleep disturbances at the onset of mental illness or as a sign of chronic disturbance. The depressed person does not feel entitled to the benefits of sleep—he feels unworthy of its blessings and cannot accept it as a grace. The very suspicious person cannot allow himself to be overcome by sleep —it would undo his vigilance and thus expose him to attack. The excited or agitated person cannot fall asleep because his mind is too busy with unresolvable thoughts which bombard his nervous system. The somnambulist has to use the large muscle groups of his body and walks around, while asleep or in a trance state.

On the other hand, sleep has many adaptive and defensive uses. When one is bored or exceedingly comfortable, there is a tendency to fall asleep during the daytime. One can fall asleep in church, during sacred ceremonies. One can withdraw into sleep and daydreaming in order to shut out unwelcome messages and in order to manifest one's hostility to the speaker or the congregation in a quasi-involuntary way, even with a feigned "blessing of the Lord."

It is reported that the disciples of Jesus repeatedly fell asleep during his night of torment, despite his efforts to arouse them (Matt. 26:40–43). This is an understandable reaction and a very human story. The insomniac is absolutely on his own, by himself, in extreme solitariness, just as the dying person. But the sleepers, upon awakening, have their own torment in facing up to their feelings of guilt and shame in having deserted a fellowman. Sleeping, then, has all the awesomeness and grandeur of the Holy. It is a tremendous mystery and perhaps the most basic act of all living beings. Because of its numinous quality it can also have the benevolence and charisma of the Holy: is not the act of two persons, sleeping together, the most moving symbol of basic trust?

To end a chapter on action with a section on sleep may be very disconcerting to those who associate religion with social action and ethical decisionmaking. This chapter, however, was concerned with action in a special sense, which the title described as the action of the "motor system." Social action is, in a sense, more attitudinal and requires ethical convictions. It will be explored obliquely in Chapter VIII and more directly in Chapter IX.

VIII

Relations to Persons

"ALL OF HUMAN life revolves around desire," says Allport[1] in his book on the psychology of religion. And he quotes with obvious approval a statement by Dunlap that "there seem to be no desires that are not, or have not at some time been, items in religions."[2] Both statements imply that one of the functions of religion is to address itself to the desires of man. Religion may aid in the fulfillment of desire. It may modify desire. It may distinguish between desires that should be granted and desires that should be curbed. Religion may also have a wholesale suspicion of desire, and sing instead a tune of duties or obligations. St. Thomas Aquinas, living in a theological rather than a psychological age, asserted that man has three classes of duties: one toward himself, one toward others, and one toward God.

We saw in an earlier chapter that ascetics, notably the desert fathers, have made strong efforts to control or even kill their desires by systematic starvation of their wants. Yoga practices aim at the same state of indifference to the impulses of the body, the needs of organs, and those desires of the mind that might be described as lowly, ignoble, or distracting. But we also saw that despite the gross behavior changes which asceticism can induce, and despite its power over desires, the ascetic way has definite limits. If it could kill all desire, it would by that act kill life itself and thus terminate the virtue—and the satisfactions!—of its own program. Opposition to desire is itself born from desire, and even the categorical imperative "Thou shalt" can be followed only when obedience is felt to be a desirable state which gives unique satisfactions.

Desire promotes practical involvement of the individual in the world, particularly the social world of other human beings and groups. One does not have to be a sociologist or an outright pragmatist to see the truth in the following statement by Ames, for it is self-evident:

Thus the intention of religion is practical, by which is not meant that it is necessarily efficacious, but only that it is felt to be so. The religionist wants something, strives for something. His attitude is that of wishing, expecting, hoping, demanding. The objects of his desires may be little things or great, they may be of time or of eternity, they may be of the body or of the mind, they may be selfish or unselfish. He may seek not the fulfillment of desire but the annihilation of desire. Still, psychologically his attitude is a practical one.[3]

Indeed, religion speaks to desires and regulates them. It judges satisfactions, and it gives them. In providing individuals and groups with the idea that life has a purpose, whatever the formulation of such a purpose may be, it gives at least a satisfying sense of closure to things. In imposing a purposive order on the randomness of "one thing after another," it highlights, and celebrates, the rhythms of life in birth and death, youth and old age, well-being and sickness, marriage and childbirth, joining and departing. Since religion grapples with questions about origin and destiny, it organizes time. The author of Ecclesiastes was well aware of this when he wrote:

> For everything there is a season, and a time for every matter under heaven:
>> a time to be born, and a time to die;
>> a time to plant, and a time to pluck up what is planted;
>> a time to kill, and a time to heal;
>> a time to break down, and a time to build up;
>> a time to weep, and a time to laugh;
>> a time to mourn, and a time to dance;
>> a time to cast away stones, and a time to gather stones together;
>> a time to embrace, and a time to refrain from embracing;
>> a time to seek, and a time to lose;
>> a time to keep, and a time to cast away;
>> a time to rend, and a time to sew;
>> a time to keep silence, and a time to speak;
>> a time to love, and a time to hate;
>> a time for war, and a time for peace.
>> What gain has the worker from his toil?

> I have seen the business that God has given to the sons of men to be busy with. He has made everything beautiful in its time; also he has put eternity into man's mind, yet so that he cannot find out what God has done from the beginning to the end. I know that there is nothing better for them than to be happy and enjoy themselves as long as they live; also that it is God's gift to man that every one should eat and drink and take pleasure in all his toil (3:1–13).

In *Civilization and Its Discontents,*[4] Freud was also concerned with the theme of happiness, and how man tries to maintain a modicum of it in the harsh vicissitudes of life. The program of happiness runs counter to the reality of suffering. Threats of pain come from three sides: our body, the external world, our relations to other people. What can one do to let happiness prevail, i.e., to obtain satisfactions? Freud outlined a number of typical operations, paraphrased as follows:

a. Under the impact of the reality principle, one can moderate one's claims to happiness, for instance by feeling modestly happy over having escaped great suffering, or having borne it rather well.

b. One may throw caution to the winds and aim at unrestricted satisfaction of every need—which only works for a while until reality catches up with the person.

c. One can aim at the happiness of "quietness" by voluntary isolation from people, which spares him the pain of object loss through departures and bereavement.

d. One can join the community which, under scientific guidance, tries to subjugate nature and its capriciousness.

e. One can try to change the sensitivities of the human organism, through intoxication, which at times not only reduces pain but also produces an active feeling of well-being.

f. One can try to kill off the instincts, through asceticism, and reach the happiness of "quietness."

g. Short of killing the instincts one can try to control them by the exercise of higher psychic functions which are loyal to the reality principle, but in that case one is still pursuing pleasures, albeit of a less intense sort.

h. The instinctual aims may be shifted from objects to creative mental activities, through which more enduring satisfactions may be found in the exercise of talents, the sense of belonging to an elite, and the identification with the productive history of culture. But this path is dependent on talents and fortunate circumstances and is thus accessible only to a few people. Moreover, such sublimations are not foolproof against the whims of fate.

i. One may loosen the ties to reality and lean on the powers of fantasy to give satisfactions. The enjoyment of works of art is an example of such an illusory, mildly narcotizing imposition of fantasy upon reality, but it has only transient power. Religions tend to go further than art by recreating the world or doubling it, in a concerted effort at delusion-formation in which the masses of people join.

j. Instead of changing the world or turning away from it, one can take the opposite course of investing oneself deeply in people, making love the central experience and finding one's satisfactions in loving and being loved. But while this seems a very natural course to follow, it has a conspicuous weakness in that "we are never so defenceless against suffering as when we love, never so helplessly unhappy as when we have lost our loved object or its love."

k. The enjoyment of beauty is another path to happiness. Although the aesthetic attitude to the goal of life does not give much protection against pain, it gives compensation for suffering.

Though Freud did not claim that it was complete, this is a long and impressive list of operations. Each of them can be embedded in a *Weltanschauung,* a system of values, a philosophy of life. Each of them implies an image of man, holds out for a goal, and speaks to a sense of purpose, clearly or dimly. Freud prefaced this list by a complex statement: "Once again, only religion can answer the question of the purpose of life. One can hardly be wrong in concluding that the idea of life having a purpose stands and falls with the religious system."[5] If the second sentence is taken as a cue, all maneuvers from *a* to *k* are religious, in the sense that they testify to a purposive stance in life which affirms a certain value. But such an idea would overstretch the definition of religion. One could hold that life has the purpose of promoting beauty, reason, or order, and these goals need not have a religious charge. The first sentence also needs a closer look, for it is ambiguous in conjunction with the phrase that follows. Religion may be more bold or articulate in answering the question of life's purpose, or it may give its answer in a particular form (for instance by referring to a third party who is held to be creator, provider, or ultimate goal), but it is obvious from Freud's list that the alternative pursuits also postulate an answer. The control of nature under scientific guidance implies belief in a rational order which is not so obvious from the direct encounters with nature. Intoxication rests on a belief in psychophysical self-regulation and a trust in chemistry, with the avowal of happiness or equanimity as a goal of life. The object of any desire is a value, and values function as goals for purposive behavior. Thus, the question of life's purpose can be answered, and is in fact being answered in many different ways, and the uniqueness of religion does not consist in its offering to answer it. The practices of life show bold answers everywhere, affirmed with great dedication and profound conviction. It seems rationally more plausible and logically more correct to say that each practical pursuit takes place in a specific perspective, that each perspective is tied to a certain language game, and that each language game is a code which allows certain words and puts a taboo on others. According to prevailing codes, "how" is a scientific question; "why" is a metaphysical or motivational term; "purpose" is religious, ethical, practical, or biological; "origin" is philosophical, archaeological, or linguistic, etc.

The striking feature about religion is that it not only allows, but in certain circumstances actively fosters, any of the maneuvers for happiness which Freud classified so painstakingly. This is not to say that religions are not selective or do not make certain options; in fact, they tend to be highly selective in their favoring some maneuvers and frowning upon others. But in this statement we have moved from the singular *religion* to the plural *religions* and shifted from the general to the specific. And this is the point of my criticism: if "religion" is to be a viable entry on the list of maneuvers, the specific religious systems with their particular doctrines and practices must be listed. One may hold the same for art, which I also find a controversial item as long as it remains boxed under *i*. Distinctions can be made between imitative, representational, or imaginative art, between Fauvism and *trompe l'oeil,* between driftwood and plainsong. Freud's list is an exemplary enumeration of psychological maneuvers or processes, but in *i* (and to some extent in *k*) there is a sudden pairing of process with categories of experience in art and religion, which is unfair to both.

We noted Allport's emphasis on desire, Ames's stress on practicality, and Freud's concern with the pursuit of happiness, under conditions of abundant suffering. It is now time to state that the psychological processes which we have been exploring in the previous chapters have a somewhat different status and quality than those we will explore in this and the next two chapters. The former are "part processes"—the latter are "integrative processes."[6] This distinction is based on the structural model within psychoanalytic theory according to which perceiving, thinking, feeling, acting, speaking, and other distinct processes are functions of the ego whereby the demands from the drives or needs which are derived from a person's basic biological equipment become related to the demands of the outer world, in mutual adaptation. In order that the individual may survive, and thrive, the ego is a specialized "organ system" within the organism which brings about a dynamic equilibrium between the demands from within and those from without. It effectuates a synthesis between the various realities that are relevant to life: the reality of cell and tissue needs; the reality of psychic wishes, feelings, and capacities; the reality of the physical environment; and the reality of social and cultural opportunities and threats. And if one would contemplate apart from these a cosmic reality, the ego would certainly have to take it into account as another party with which transactions have to be made.

It is the nature of drives, needs, and wishes to demand satisfaction. Pleasure is their keynote. And pleasure can never be given up by the individual. But the forces of the physical world, the order of society, and the patterns of culture also make their demands: they demand respect, participation, and often compliance. They also offer opportunities and constitute enticements. Thus, reality (in the sense of the outer world) is an equally powerful keynote for the individual, because he depends on it as much as he does on the pleasure principle of his needs. As a matter of fact, reality offers him the objects (people, ideas, things, norms, etc.) through which his needs can be satisfied. Rapaport's theoretical scheme, which we discussed in Chapter III, can now be reworded as follows: The constant push from within guarantees a measure of autonomy of the ego from the environment—the push from without guarantees a measure of autonomy of the ego from the organism's drives. There is a two-way dependence and independence, in a dynamic balance. Because of this situation, the ego is in a position to be the administrative and tactical agent, as it were, which brings the various parties together for negotiations in which each is heard and gets his due.[7] Another way of saying this is that the ego, originally in the service of the drives, becomes increasingly also a precipitate of experience as development goes on, and thus participates in both worlds. The same is true of the body, which is both private and public, subjective and objective, "in here" and "out there."

In short, the part processes of the ego signal the needs that are felt within, as well as the opportunities and pressures that are present outside. In thought or action the synthesizing capacity of the ego brings person and world together for the satisfaction of the person's needs and in respectful homage to the world, which contains millions of people constituted just like this person, some of whom may look at him as "outside world" and "satisfier" to their own needs. To the individual, reality contains three large groups of parties with which transactions must be made. All three groups are potentially "objects" or "satisfiers" to the individual's needs. More specifically, all three are objects of love and objects of hate, in some proportion. They are: (1) other people; (2) things and ideas; (3) the self. With all three the ego must engage in relations, on the one hand because the drives demand them as satisfiers, on the other hand because these three groups are forcefully demanding recognition in their own right since they form the major aspects of reality. We will devote a chapter to each of these reality aspects because the ego mediates a unique relationship between each of them and the human organism with its motivational sources.

We shall first consider the individual's relations to other people, in which we shall be guided by the following questions:

  a. How does religion structure the relations between the individual and other people?
  b. How does religion affect the depth and constancy of a person's human attachments?
  c. Are interpersonal relations transferable to God-man relations?

RELIGIOUS VIEWS OF INTERPERSONAL RELATIONS

To enumerate what religions have to say about relations among people is tantamount to writing a history about doctrines of man, a history of religious ethics and church history, and a sizable portion of systematic theology. And still the small library which would be the result of such an endeavor would not suffice for our purposes, because there is an obvious difference between written statements about human relations and the actual relations people engage in. This difference holds perhaps even more for religious devotees than for nonbelievers, because the written religious documents tend to set high goals which makes any discrepancy between verbal affirmations and actual behavior all the more glaring. Moreover, there is at times a marked distinction between the sacred scriptures and the historical traditions within a religious group. We can thus do little more than describe a few outstanding features of the way in which religion structures the relations among people.

Theological doctrines about man tend to describe humanity in terms of its origin and its destiny, leaving the specification of the relations among people to a divinely guided system of morality and to a divinely inspired notion of the nature of the church or the community. However origin and destiny are formulated, there is one aspect of practical human life that has a profound bearing on interpersonal relations. It is the idea of life's rhythmicity, and religion has always celebrated it. Two observations may be made right away:

1. the rhythms of life which are of religious interest are almost always festive or crisis situations of a social nature;
2. the root meanings of the word "celebrate" and its cognates are intensely social.

"To celebrate" is "to visit frequently," "to attend in a large group," or "to observe often or with zeal." A "celebrity" is "in the middle of the busy crossroads"; a "celebration" is a "well-attended meeting." The associated meanings of praising and honoring are later derivations.

It is a moot question whether religion has gradually come to recognize and hallow the life crises or whether these crises and their periodicity are one of the original sources of the religious quest. The fact is that crises and religious ideas and practices are thoroughly interwoven. The occurrence of childbirth is a biological fact, a psychological satisfaction to the parents, a social event of some note, and a religious occasion of great symbolic value to the individual, the community, and the cosmos. It is replete with meanings from all possible perspectives, and religion tends to subsume them all in the supersymbolism of "the sacredness of life" and "creation." It may add a special qualification: "made in the image of God." It may become very concrete in its recognition that "Sister Jessica delivered a baby boy, Hallelujah," who will soon be brought into the community for circumcision or baptism. Whatever religion makes of the occasion, it refuses to see childbirth as a mere routine, despite its almost embarrassing frequency. It celebrates birth as a high point in the life of the parents, as the beginning of a journey for the neonate, as proof of divine benevolence to the community or the family, and as an occasion for thankfulness and rejoicing. As a happening, it is set off from the regular flow of things. It is an event, and to the religious mind events are markings in time which make a person ponder the basic arrangements of everything: time, space, cause and effect, man's place in nature, and the relations between man and man.

The arrival of a baby actuates many religious questions. Are the parents married, i.e., do they assume responsibility for the care of their offspring, and have they promised to live faithfully with each other? Was their partnership sanctified by the religious community? Was the child wanted? Should they in the future practice birth control? If this is an acceptable thought at all, what method is allowable? Will the parents pledge themselves to rear their child in the fear of the Lord? If they so pledge, can they really be expected to discharge their promise without the sustained help of the church cr brotherhood? Whose child is this anyway: Roger's and Jessica's, the whole family's, the religious community's, the nation's, mankind's, God's? Who will assume responsibility for his nurture—the state, the church?

Though the answers to these questions may vary widely, the questions themselves are of first-rate importance: they put into words the perennial concerns which attend every crisis or high point in life. To the individual they may come only as fleeting thoughts, inarticulately, in a mixture of glad feelings and anxiety. To the group they may constitute elements in the quest for values, norms, social arrangements, or cultural goals. To the religious community they are the questions that one may not evade, that one is forced to ponder by tradition, if not divine decree. They are all variations on the basic religious theme of the creator and the created, the absolute and the contingent. And sooner or later the religious community will claim a special relation to the newborn child, which is to be sealed in a special ritual, such as circumcision or baptism. The child will thus be symbolically marked as belonging to a special group which claims him and assumes certain responsibilities for him, including the right to confront the child as he grows up with new questions and more pointed awareness of his place in life.

And so there comes a next crisis, when someone will have to decide at what time the child stops being a child and becomes an adult. How is one to approach such a decision—indeed who raises the question and who can answer it? The child himself? The village elders? The parents? The warriors? The priests? The girls who want him for a lover or a husband? Has nature set some rules, or is there some divine command on relinquishing the dependency of childhood? Again, the answers vary from initiation rites set by physical timetables to *bar mitzvah* at the age of thirteen set by psychological fitness to appreciate the divine commandments. Some groups seek an age of discernment; some seek a test of knowledge. Some leave much to the individual, who is to make an intimately personal vow, after much soul-searching, at whatever age. Some leave it to divine intervention, like a call of the Holy Spirit or a demonstrable conversion experience. Whatever one specifically arranges, the point is that the transition from childhood to manhood is celebrated in such a way that the individual and his group are confronted with some large and difficult questions which cause them to pause for a moment, to ponder the cosmic mysteries.

Perhaps we should pause here, too. We have caught a glimpse of a child and his parents. The parents presumably love each other and have established a stable relationship in which many of their basic needs are satisfied. We do not know how they were matched, but it is fair to assume that they find much satisfaction in each other's company. They also have from time to time the primary gratification which sexual intercourse offers; each of them was successful in making a heterosexual object choice, with the sanction of society and perhaps with the sanctification of their church. And now they have a child, a boy. The mother bestows much attention on him, since he is the fulfillment of her life. Perhaps she teaches him to pray. The father felt at first somewhat neglected, but he begins to see a new side to his wife, which has something to do with motherhood, setting up a ménage for three, and expecting the father to provide more liberally than before. Father and mother begin also to realize that they must act as examples, guides, and teachers, and that their new station brings new obligations: their child is to grow up properly, follow the right way, and learn the right things. As he grows up, he must learn to wait, to watch his language, to control his body, to curb his anger, to respect his parents, to fear dangers, to obey those in power, to help those in need, to be amiable to peers, to have reverence for the sacred. He may kiss his mother, but he will soon have to stop kissing his father. He may take pride in himself and his accomplishments, but he should not boast. Nor may he demand too much. He must learn to share. He should treat girls differently from boys. He should not use foul language, and while curiosity is praised in the exploration of nature and school subjects, it is frowned upon when it is geared to someone else's privacy or to sex. He is encouraged to express his feelings, but he must carefully guard the expression of anger. While he is praised when he seems to fend for himself, he is scolded when he pounds his fists too freely or without clear provocation. Once a week or more often he assembles with others in some house of worship where he must accomplish the impossible feat of sitting still and being quiet. With other children of his age he listens to women, and sometimes men, who read stories about someone who is Father of all, who watches all, who cares for all, and who is slow to anger though his wrath is fierce. He is asked to entertain the thought that he is like a little lamb who listens to the beloved voice of his shepherd. He is to have trust in this shepherd, who will lead him to green pastures. He also celebrates, each year, Christmas and Easter, or Hanukkah and a special New Year which does not coincide with the calendar or the dates of the newspapers.

The story is endless, and the variations are many. But enough has been said to suggest a typical complex of growth tasks and problems. How does religion structure the relations between people? So far we have seen an enormous amount of congruence between the biological, psychological, social, and cultural rules which govern the life of this small family. Has religion, i.e., their particular religion, added anything unique? One could point to the fact that this family takes its son to church; that mother prays with him at bedtime, and that father says grace before dinner. Perhaps the boy goes to a denominational school where he learns the same things as at home but with more frequent repetition, greater stringency, and reinforcement by his peers. He has come into contact with things of religious significance: Bibles and other books for instruction, candelabra, chalices, clerical vestments, crucifixes, scrolls, collection plates. He has met certain people: clergymen, acolytes, nuns, boys with skullcaps in Hebrew school.

But above all, he has heard certain words that tend to be uncommon in ordinary conversation but which are frequently uttered in hallowed places and situations. A full list of these words would add up to a religious dictionary. And since all religious people do not use exactly the same selection from such a dictionary but stick to a denominationally determined dialect, one should make allowance for specialization in regard to hallowed words. However this may be, the child has heard and learned words such as: Almighty, heaven, amen, the cross, Virgin Mary, confessing, grace, forgiving, sin, Jesus our Savior, mercy, Holy Spirit, the Law, chosen people. He has also learned short phrases such as: God is love, Our Father who art in heaven, I believe in God the Father almighty . . . , What is the chief end of man? He has observed peculiar acts, such as kneeling, folding one's hands, lighting candles during plain daylight, a priest lifting a chalice upward, a rabbi opening a tabernacle and taking a precious crown off a mighty scroll, a man in black academic gown raising both hands high and uttering a solemn blessing with the phrase "Go in peace." And having heard and seen all these things, our boy may at times have been puzzled, but he has noticed that his parents and all the other people took these things seriously and, while doing so, were somehow different in mood and disposition from other moments in their lives.

It is not easy to say exactly what difference the boy saw on such occasions in his parents and other people. Were they simply so absorbed in their observances that they paid, for a moment, less attention to their son? That could be a blessing. Were they milder than usual? Did they seem very happy? Or was it that they suddenly seemed to humble themselves before a greater authority and thus lost for a moment their aura of omnipotence? Did their friendly disposition linger on after the worship service? All these are real possibilities which are bound to have an impact. But it is likely that other things occurred also. Discussions must have gone on about "the right thing to do" and "what happens when a person dies?" The son will have been curious about where he came from, and his parents may have generalized his question into "where we all came from," and "who made everything." He may have heard that "to hate is unchristian," but he will also have observed that his father chuckled when someone mentioned the words "Baptist preacher" and that mother became tense when a Jehovah's Witness knocked at the door to urge the purchase of religious pamphlets. The words "pope" or "popish" might have been used with great scorn or bitterness in his presence. He will probably have argued with playmates about "his" church and "their" church or temple. He has learned spontaneously what Rokeach has so learnedly documented, that there is a high correlation between denominational affiliation and discrimination in race, creed, color, ethnic origin, or income level.

Depending on his age, intellect, and curiosity he has already drawn some inferences. He realizes that he belongs to a special group, with a special creed and a special ritual. He has learned that regarding religion certain people tend to argue vehemently with each other as if it were a matter of life or death. He has seen others recoil from religion as if it were a poisonous snake. He has noticed that it costs money, and that giving, sharing, and sacrificing are important accompaniments of his parents' convictions. He knows that helping others is not a matter of one's whims, but a serious duty. He has discovered that he must be thankful, cheerful, solemn, reverent, and charitable, just as his parents strive to be, nay, just as everybody should be. He has seen contradictions between what his parents say and what they do, and some of these are striking, painful, and puzzling. But in the meantime, if he is honest to himself, he has noticed such contradictions in himself, too, and he has some inkling of being noble at certain times and vulgar at others. Though he could not state what "awe" means; and though "the idea of the Holy" is probably an empty abstraction for him, he can point in his memory to moments of wonder at a seascape, a mountain scene, a forgiving gesture of his mother when he expected to be rebuked, a death in the family, or a haunting dream. And he may well know from such experiences that there is something ambiguously attractive and repellent in these encounters. Instead of calling these experiences holy or sacred, as intellectually inclined adults would do, he may refer to them as deep, full, trustful, or happy, with the added conviction that "there's something there," something real, albeit mysterious. And in drawing such inferences and sharing them cautiously with playmates, he may have discovered that such mysteries are not so alien after all, for many other children seemed to know what he meant to say, or themselves fumbled for words in sharing their experiences and observations with him. All these very private things apparently can be shared and are thus public in the sense that "the other people have felt them too." And thus they are common human things: feelings, thoughts, fantasies, statements, actions—in a word, beliefs. Hence, having such beliefs creates a common bond among people, in church, in school, on the playground, or in the family. Indeed, it may have dawned on the boy that there is a "family of man" despite all the distinctions among people.

This is only one boy's course. Other children may have had a very different set of experiences. They may have belonged to a small sect, considered odd by the community and scorned by the schoolchildren. In that case, the theme of persecution and the need for aggressive self-assertion or chronic defensiveness may have tainted the belief system. Or they may have belonged to a wealthy, upper-class, exclusive congregation which gave religion the stamp of a noble pastime for the happy few. Suppression of feelings and oppression by strict rules and taboos may have been the earmarks of the upbringing of still other children, associating awe with emotional distance between people and with an abject fear of punishment for forbidden thoughts and deeds. The examples of parents and other parishioners may have taken the exalted form of outbursts of energy and fits of elation with sweat, heat, and irrational behavior. Or there may have been a chronic admonition, and fervent hope, that some day this young life would be completely remade by an act of God in a sudden conversion. Some children may have grown up in families insisting that religion is the ultimate in privacy and self-determination, with disdain for group action, affiliation, scriptures, ritual, Sundays, or clergymen of any kind.

In each case, however, some questions will have been raised, and answered, regarding people: what they are, where they came from, where they are going, and how they should behave. Distinctions will have been taught between believers and unbelievers, clergy and laymen, saints and sinners, orthodox and heretics, good people and bad people, usually in terms of "we" and "they." Distinctions may have been made also between man and nature, the individual and the masses, man and God, "the men of old" and contemporaries. And a large part of the questions will have been stimulated by the uneasy aspects of experience, such as sickness, bereavement, death, pain, injustice, persecution, teasing, madness, war. The problem of evil looms in many forms and gives rise to many situations in which one feels hurt or weak: in one's feelings, in one's grasp or comprehension, in one's powers, or in one's ability to believe in his best and noblest ideas.

However these questions are answered, the fact that they are raised (even if only in the form of a brooding preoccupation) alludes to the help-lessness of the self which Freud singled out as the primary source of all religion. But the helplessness of the self is not only an occasional experience of individuals—those who can admit it are apt to discover that it occurs also in others, indeed even in those who are emulated as bulwarks of strength such as parents, teachers, statesmen, and generals. Whole groups of people admit it, at least from time to time, and have organized them-selves into communions and so-called faith groups in which all thought and action seems to center on this theme of helplessness and how to cope with it. While most of these groups invoke some God to whom they at-tribute exquisite power which eventually can deliver people from en-countering evil, the idea of God is not a necessary assumption of all. The crucial factor is faith that the acute feeling of helplessness is not the last word in human experience. Some are taught to believe in the intellect and its marvelous tenaciousness which, as Freud said, "does not rest until it has gained a hearing."[8] Others are told to believe in a rational order which may now be hard to discover, but which is there for the diligent to find. Any of the maneuvers outlined in Freud's *Civilization and Its Discontents* and many more may be advocated and tried, and if they are pursued with great ardor and devotion they may rise to the highest rank in the scale of one's values. Precisely at the point where a commitment to any of them is reached, with defense against alternatives that are advocated and with practiced rituals (of work, LSD, artistic pursuits, toxic states, or a stoically stiff upper lip) and some sacrifice (in time, money, courage, or popularity), does any maneuver become the "ultimate concern" and the "centered act of the personality" which are the Tillichian earmarks[9] of the religious stance.

But we should return to the young life we are following. We have seen a boy being born, baptized, and entering the community of faith as an adoles-cent or young adult. He has probably seen serious illness in the family, and possibly death. He has raised many questions, and he has been asked many questions. Sooner or later the day will come that he falls in love and dreams of marrying. He will change not only to new social roles, but to a new stage on life's way which places its own perspective on all things. Quite aside from his professed or actual loyalties to some faith group, the step into marriage is likely to confront him again with some question about the corporate if not cosmic significance of the new path he is about to tread and the need to solemnize the decision to marry. Whether the couple will actually go to a clergyman and have a church wedding, or whether they decide in favor of a civil ceremony (or both, as happens in many other countries), the fact is that they are forced to ponder the nature of the ties between individuals, and between themselves and the group, and that their becoming a pair calls for a celebration. Whether religion merely recognizes and sanctifies, or more incisively mediates and regulates, the marital trans-action, it is bound to place the event through a short, dramatic festivity outside the regular flux of time. It introduces the special metaphor of the family with far-reaching meanings on a grand scale: it declares the launch-ing of a new family within the historical family of the faith group; it stages the new family as a fulfillment of the purposes of the old parental families; it puts the new family in the perspective of hope and expectations; it puts a goal before it, and it links the new venture into the chain of being—of all families from the beginning of time to the end of the earth.

And what are the demands or the tasks? Of course there is the celebration of love, and the affirmation that love is a divine gift. It will also be asserted that marriage is a divine institution, and thus holy and sanctified, and that it serves certain cosmic purposes which may include the well-being and happiness of the couple but are in the first place geared to the plenitude of nature and the welfare of the social order. Therefore, the fate of any marriage cannot rest on the whimsical play of erotic attraction alone. It is demanded through a solemn promise (usually in the presence of a congregation and always in the symbolic presence of God) that the partners have loyalty to one another, that they will love each other steadfastly, through thick and thin. They are to reflect on their destiny, which may in-clude the thought that they were, from time eternal, meant for each other in a divine scheme which perpetuates creation through procreation, and providence through providing. They shall not only "cleave to one another" but build up, assist, serve, comfort, and care for each other, under heavenly guidance and protection.

In their way, this language and the celebration of which it is a part prepare the marriage partners for the days ahead which will have their in-evitable share of stress and sorrow. Religious celebration does so in part by looking backward: "Our fathers and mothers since Adam and Eve have had all these experiences, just like your own parents." It also looks laterally: "What you set out to do is shared by millions on earth at this very time." And it adds the cosmic dimension: "It is in the nature of things or in the divine will that man should marry." The forward look thus accentuates repetition, commonality, inevitability. While it does not exclude uniqueness for this particular couple, it gets across the idea that everything, even such a seemingly individual situation as falling in love, is shared and follows certain general human rules. Why? Religion will answer this question by its basic postulate about the maker and the made: The creature is contingent; he is carried by the rhythms of life, and only the Holy is self-constitutive. Thus religion mediates between various perspectives on human affairs; it acknowledges the uniqueness and worth of individuals, it upholds the regularities of nature, it accepts the value of corporate realities from the family to the state and mankind at large. Each perspective creates its own meanings, but the religious perspective aims at encompassing all perspectives and adding a meaning-of-meanings.

Childbirth, coming of age, and marriage are only drastic examples and compact manifestations of the ways in which religion structures human relations. A good deal of that structure rests on a manipulation of time, by dividing time into *chronos* and *kairos* and interpreting the former in the light of the latter category. Chronological time is "one thing after another" in linear progression and with equal weight given to each stretch or unit. *Kairos* is time seen as opportunity, event, fullness, turning point, crisis, or occasion for celebration. If human relations were merely chronologically determined, life would be an unimaginative, dull, undemanding, unexciting, uncreative, serial production, meaningless to the living and the dead, and probably even quite boring to the deities who might have invented it to amuse themselves. This view is so contradictory to experience and so offensive to man's capacities of creative fantasy that the alternative view of time as *kairos* has not only much to recommend itself, but seems closer to life as lived. To Shakespeare's "seven ages" and the series of developmental stages, Erikson[10-11] has added the important idea of personal identities acquired through resolutions of conflicts and crises. These identities are neither a linear progression of phases of growth, nor a doomed waxing and waning which produces the general arc of life. They are individualized solutions to problems which are both common and unique, calling for moments of reflection and decision. They occur in time seen as *kairos*. And each *kairos* is a crisis or an opportunity in which interpersonal relations are assessed and realigned.

Illness, death, and bereavement are the other celebrated moments in the religious view of the rhythms of life. While all three are from one point of view highly personal and individuating, they are exquisitely corporate or transactional from another point of view. Religion celebrates them as multidimensional crises in which questions of ultimate meanings are being raised. Its concern is not only with finding possible answers to the vexing problems of pain and suffering and death, but inculcating a degree of sincerity in living through which meaningful questions about these problems may be raised in the first place.

Smitten by illness, death, or bereavement, the individual is prone to ask first "Why?"—often in the form of an outcry or as a dumbfounded, bungling, defiant groping for some reason. Though some religious persons are prone to answer such a question through an available speculation about the problem of pain, which may sound like a cliché, the religious essence does not lie in the answer but in taking the question seriously and with compassion. All the heroes of faith have asked the same question, have made the same outcry, and have had the same stupefying confrontation with the fact of human contingency. Therefore, in that outcry a human bond is established which is to be celebrated first. The mystical word "presence" applies to the religious apprehension of this situation; it conveys the conviction that suffering is shared not only because it is inevitable, but also because it gets to the roots and ground of existence. Despite the fact that suffering isolates a person, in the "presence" he does not stand alone. But the word "presence" is vague, and one should ask whose presence is meant. The answers will vary with the level of religious grasp, corporate experience, and the kind of religious system. Some people will have a hallucinatory image of Jesus with outstretched arms; others will imagine a line of ancestors, the gas chambers in concentration camps, groups of martyrs or heroes of faith, or all mankind coalesced into one contorted face. Some may have no images at all, but only the shock of loss, or the terror of anxiety. But in each case, the religious conviction is that in the outcry "Why?" there are already at least two forms of presence. One consists in the confrontation with the will of God (or the demonic) which produces the basic dynamic of the encounter with the holy, and leads to awe. The second consists in the sharing of suffering with untold others, now and in the past, which anchors the individual in the matrix of mankind at large.

But the question tends to shift, sooner or later, from "Why?" to a more personal "Why *me*?" and in that moment the dynamics of guilt feelings and anger are actuated.[12] Calamity is now seen as a "visitation" which comes to the individual with a personal aim. It is at this point that the *function* of the religious world view becomes a little clearer; its role is to reconcile the individual to his lot by proclaiming that his situation is not really fate but divine purpose. The myths and theories about evil and the doctrines of sin and salvation have a reconciliatory aim: they apply to the concrete situation in which an individual's contingency has become blatant. Hence the visitation by calamity is religiously counteracted by another visitation which symbolizes divine presence. Job is visited and addressed by his friends, and finally by Yahweh himself; the mourner is visited by his pastor; the sick are visited by friends who bring flowers; the dying Catholic is visited by his priest for the rite of extreme unction.

Life crises of sickness, bereavement, and death are thus seen as occasions for celebration. The celebrants are *all* people: not only the sick, bereaved, and dying, but the whole community of faith. The visits with their symbolic and ritual implications are not only made for the sake of the suffering individual, but they are stylized as a communal duty incumbent upon everybody, so that the community as a whole is attuned to the rhythms of life and death. Time is thereby changed from *chronos* to *kairos*. An attempt is made to see all that comes to pass as purposive and meaningful events, rather than as a dull and fateful grind. The lot of individuals actuates the idea of community, and vice versa. "No man is an island" is one affirmation. The other is exemplified by the old Roman tombstone which carried the inscription *Hodie mihi, cras tibi:* "Today it is me, tomorrow it will be you!"

We have seen, then, that one of the foremost functions of religion is to integrate the individual with the group, whether the latter is large or small, special or generic. Through the idea of life crises religion is able to use its unique process of celebration in order to bring individual and group together. Conversely, the experience of life crises and the sense of *kairos* which are periodically the lot of all men are occasions in which people reach out for religion in order to obtain from it all it has to offer: celebrations, witness to a cosmic presence, a large view of the whence and where of the human race and of man's place in nature, and a cognitive-emotional framework in which man's felt helplessness finds a stylized formulation. In a general sense, the satisfaction of human needs is taken into account in all these religious activities and propositions, and the basic thrust of all of it is to maximize the relationships between man and man. But we must now move to the details of these relationships.

THE INFLUENCE OF RELIGION ON PERSONAL ATTACHMENTS

People need each other. They are the objects of each other's drives and needs. They satisfy each other's wishes. They are each other's goals. We thus find people living, working, and playing in affiliation with others. While some affiliations are no doubt the product of chance encounters, many affiliations are patterned by various social controls, by idiosyncratic needs of individuals, and by social institutions. In such patterns of affiliation, religion enters in a double sense: on the one hand it is itself one of the patterns of affiliation, on the other hand it teaches or prescribes to its affiliated members certain rules about affiliation in general. Many people are born and raised into an affiliation with a specific religious group: they are Mennonites, Jews, or Episcopalians. But being a Mennonite also propels one to live, receive one's schooling, find one's mate, and choose one's occupation within a Mennonite brotherhood, which until recently tended to be a fairly closed agrarian community at considerable emotional distance from the rest of mankind. Being an affiliated Jew means being prone to enter into marriage with a member of the faith, putting emphasis on intelligence, academic learning, and the pursuit of a professional career. Being an Episcopalian entails a certain degree of fence-sitting between the Protestant and Roman Catholic heritage, appreciating a white Anglo-Saxon background, saying "Father" to one's own clergymen, and enjoying a degree of social prestige that may subsequently affect one's marital choice and foster the ambition of becoming a vestryman.

Religion, in a word, regulates the scope of the human objects by whom one is to be gratified and with whom one is to affiliate himself. Theoretically, the scope of human objects is a continuum between few and many people, between "none at all" or "all mankind." As a matter of fact, religion has often addressed itself to either extreme of the continuum, requiring on the one hand a renunciation of normal ties to all mortals, and asking on the other hand that one love all one's fellowmen "as oneself."

In the ascetic tradition, much danger is seen in close affiliation to other human beings because this is felt to detract from the love of God. Hermits have withdrawn themselves from family and friends, even from the organized religious community in which they grew up. Anchorites have made, in addition to withdrawal, very special spatial arrangements: Simeon Stylites sought his abode on top of a column. Hermits still exist on Mount Athos, with acknowledgment of their status and intentions, but aside from these official aspirants to sainthood there are recluses of all kinds, in almost every city or town, whose human contacts have shrunk to almost none. Some of them may be mystics who privately pursue the path to holiness; others are scriptural scholars and contemplatives who have gradually withdrawn themselves from other people in favor of solitary cerebration. Still others have become lonely individuals after having seen their spouses and families die, and instead of reaching out again for human contact, may have felt so wounded by their loss that they have come to prefer the stable company of books, thoughts, or deities.

A step removed from solitariness are the cenobitic arrangements which demand renunciation of family life in favor of affiliation with like-minded, like-dedicated, and like-disciplined peers of the same sex who form a monastic community. Following the rules of St. Basil or St. Benedict these men and women, now called by the generic name "religious," pursue the religious life as a career, in a carefully worked-out pattern of guided solitariness and guided group relations. They contemplate in privacy, but worship in community. Under tutelage of superiors they find their tasks assigned and their social interactions prescribed by general rules or individual pedagogical adaptations of those rules. To those who do not opt for this life it is always puzzling why so many men and women seem to desire it, forgoing the rewards of marital and family relations. Although the words "desire" and "gratification" tend to have a negative value in the parlance of the religious, while positive values seem to be attached to "mortification" and "quietude," one should not overlook the many satisfactions which this life offers, not despite but because of its high degree of regulation.

What Goodenough said about the church at large holds particularly for the members of religious orders:

The Church . . . is to be taken as a corporate body, superior to the individual, itself the medium of revelation, in which the individual can find divine guidance, protection, and the means of grace. It at once minimizes the individual by subordinating him to the larger entity and enlarges him by his sense of membership in it.[13]

Through his twenty-four-hour-a-day, visible, uniformed membership in the monastic group, the individual has a concrete participation in the "body of Christ" or in the "bride" of the divine persons. Enforced distance from the temptations of sex can be a blessing for those who fear its practice or the commitments it is bound to lead to. Obedience, though difficult to accomplish, can be a source of satisfaction and a boost to self-esteem. The natural family is transient, and object loss is the price one pays for deep attachments to spouse and kin; but the love objects offered in the religious community are an enduring hierarchy of God, superiors, and worthy peers, and in some sense the institution remains despite the coming and going of its members. Indeed, the "transference to the institution," which has been described for the mentally ill who are cared for in hospitals, operates distinctly in the cenobitic affiliation patterns in which one "marries" the church, the order, or the brotherhood. The institution's symbol value is such that mere belonging to it can be seen as a "sign of grace."

Though rivalries and other aggressive tendencies are kept suppressed within such a community, the members of the group have much opportunity to direct aggressive feelings outward to worldly powers, the secular society, or any other outgroup. Missionary intervention in the lives of the members of other cultures with different religions is not without aggressive intrusiveness, and some missionary endeavors are quite militant. Indeed, in former eras they used to follow directly in the wake of military conquests. This is abundantly illustrated in the history of Mexico since Cortez. Other aggressions may be directed against members of other faith groups or denominations. It is no accident that the Jesuit Order is organized on the principles of a military organization, even when it "conquers the world for Christ" through educational and pedagogical means—that is, through an army of teachers. Military metaphors abound in the hymns of Protestant churches, from "A Mighty Fortress Is Our God" to "Onward, Christian Soldiers," quite apart from the existence of the Salvation Army which, paradoxically, specializes in acts of mercy. The sharp tongue of Erasmus often singled out these aggressive features of the monastic practices. It described the insistent and hostile begging of mendicant monks; it mocked at the gluttony and other self-indulgent habits of the religious who had made vows of poverty and abstinence.

In the fifteenth century, a different form of religious living was practised by the Brethren of the Communal Life, who formed houses for communal living into which members could enter without lifelong vows and without affiliation with any of the established monastic orders. This is a more open pattern: a close community rather than a closed brotherhood or sisterhood. Such experiments in religious group formation persist in the modern koinonia groups whose members, often married and with families, share income, work, duties, and the care of children in a "model community" which is seen as temporary and with a fairly loose structure.

In all these cases, the attachments between people are in some way regulated and, in practice, restricted, although with varying degrees of strictness. It is too easy to see these phenomena as merely sociological or as characteristics of the institutional side of religion, although these perspectives can hardly be denied. They are also derived from personal dynamics. Group norms and group loyalties, even in popular and well-established mainline churches, foster comfortable feelings in individuals when they find intimacy with members of the faith. Conversely, there are multiple and quite automatic signals of discomfort, if not feelings of impending disaster, when an individual becomes entangled with people who are outside the faith group. Even in a pluralistic society, families may become disrupted through a "mixed marriage" with its attendant problems of separate worship attendance and the choice of the faith into which the children are to be reared. Many a parent heaves a sigh of relief upon discovering that the prospective bride or groom of their grown-up child shares the family's religious affiliation. It greatly simplifies the arrangements for living; it takes away worries and obstacles; it establishes a common language. It automatically creates common friends and common enemies. The specific affiliation establishes an identity for the individual; it affects the superego and the ego-ideal which in turn define for what transgressions one should feel guilty and for what disloyalties one should feel ashamed.

But as Freud warned, making object attachments the central pursuit of life has its inevitable traumas. People die, or are otherwise unfaithful. While group attachments may compensate for the losses of individuals if the group is immensely satisfying or if the object cathexes can be kept flexible, most people are so composed that they can neither renounce spouse and kin for the sake of solitariness or a select brotherhood, nor become so effusive as to attach themselves to mankind at large. There must be something concrete, someone specific to embrace. If solitariness or monastic living demands too much renunciation and too much discipline, loving all mankind as "children of one Father" promises too little satisfaction. The former is too structured; the latter is too loose.

Despite ascetic traditions and mystical penchants, religion cannot make so bold as to assail the basic family structure with its natural psychosexual ties. In fact, religion tends to hallow the family and to extol it as a sacred institution. It prohibits or takes a dim view of divorce. It not only condones the personal satisfactions which its members find in each other, but through the advocacy of monogamy and enduring bonds of loyalty, habituates the members to the unique satisfaction that each one can obtain from the other. Yet, in the religious view, the satisfactions of marriage and parenthood and personal friendships are not the ultimate values. They are demonstrably short-lived and beset with risks. They may detract from the love of God. They may amount to an extended narcissism, a grandiose self-love through spouse and offspring. The family may become an object of idolatry, when it posits itself as a thing to be worshiped, or when it is placed in enmity to fellowmen, to race, or to the species. It is small wonder, therefore, that religion has tended to broaden the scope of human object attachments by insisting on love for all fellowmen, and by demanding man's affiliation with all of creation. But it has also tended to narrow the scope by demanding a love of God so ardent that a man might, at times, renounce his natural ties with others for the sake of this one sublime pursuit. In either case, the old gratifications are replaced by new satisfactions. The love of all fellowmen, though somewhat diffuse and global, has an aura of nobility which may turn the whole universe into a friendly place, after the imagination has effectively denied all enmity. The love of God is an effective safeguard against the trauma of loss, for only he "endureth forever."

Both the scope of, and the selectivity in, object attachments are of religious concern. We already saw the impact of selectivity based on sexual differences, which effectively cuts the relevant human world into half for the monastic. Celibacy in so-called secular priests does not go quite so far, but certainly sets up emotional distance between the man and all women of approximately his own age. We also saw that the scope of intimate human contacts is limited by creedal affiliation. To these should be added the obvious selectivity and subsequent narrowing of scope of relations which are the result of class and caste distinctions which are one of the sources of denominationalism.

Far more subtle is the selectivity in the patterns of human interaction resulting from doctrinal beliefs and moral traits which have the status of family values or family taboos. An anxiously enforced abstinence from drinking alcohol, smoking, gambling, cardplaying, or dancing at one time permeated the Bible Belt, producing children with actual fears of all these things which in turn tended to limit their relations to those with similar morals—and anxieties. When virginity in brides is seen as a radical moral necessity, chances are that marriages will be concluded between parties who solemnly subscribe to this belief. Time and again, psychiatric case studies show that families who are members of pacifist sects tend to engage in massive repression of all aggressive behavior patterns, from verbal family quarrels to the defiance of the adolescent children who want to "break out" of the family constriction but dare not do so. It is more than plausible that adherence to such convictions will restrict the friendships and casual contacts, out of which the enduring affiliations are built, to people with similar beliefs.

Some selectivities, then, are of such stringency that they build a person's identity, not only as a group member, but as an individual. Because of this, a sudden shift from one denomination to another, unless consciously prepared and arranged, e.g., in a marriage contract, has clinical significance as a warning of a personal crisis. Such "church-hopping" is not uncommon as an incipient symptom of mental illness; it can be one of the prodromal disturbances, like sudden spending sprees or drinking bouts. When the changes are downward in the socioeconomic scale from mainline to sectarian churches, they are often accompanied by conversions or shocklike alterations in the belief system. In a last-ditch stand against the forces of dissolution, the individual may line himself up with repressive and suppressive movements which promise corporate reinforcement of self-control through strict and literal interpretation of biblical injunctions. The conscience is strengthened through a confrontation with "no-saying," yet caring, parental figures. In other cases the individual may feel drawn to the greater impulsivity of holiness sects that promise occasional release of tensions under sacred auspices, with frenzy attaining an aura of blessedness. In fact, a good many fundamentalist sects combine the repressive and the abreactive features and therefore have an enduring appeal for the oppressed. Personal crises can also precipitate shifts from the alleged bleakness of Protestant churches to faith groups with a rich liturgy and a presumably motherly warmth. Transfer to Roman Catholicism, moreover, makes it possible to pray to a female divine intermediary.

Such shifts are not unlike the crises which beset adolescents or young adults who, in their strenuous search for independence, sometimes withdraw for a few years from their acustomed church participation or affiliate themselves against parental wishes with a different denomination. Though the latter can be a sincere and positive search for new ties and new love relations, it is often mixed with an aggressive demonstration of one's differences from parents and family style.

MAN-MAN AND MAN-GOD RELATIONS

It is time now to take a closer look at the psychodynamics of object relations in the light of the starting point for this chapter: that all of human life revolves around desire. Objects are not sought for their own sake, but as satisfiers of wishes. The ways in which objects are sought, and the relations which the person maintains with them may differ widely, but the two-party relation between subject and object is cemented by the desires that need fulfillment. This is a point of some importance because people often seek the cause of interpersonal relations in some kind of irresistible appeal located in the object to which they feel drawn, as if they themselves were as passive as a nail that is drawn to a magnet. Such a manner of speaking denies the activity of the subject; it negates the strength of needs, drives, wishes, or longings which propel a person to seek an object. It denies half the story of the dynamics of perception which make one see what he is looking for, and the dynamics of action which make one move even if there is nothing to move toward. Because of a certain manner of speaking about gods, religious people have all too often embraced the parallel idea that only the deities have true "drawing power" which makes people irresistibly move toward them. This too not only denies man's spontaneous activity, but overlooks the role that wishes, needs, and longings play in any man-God relation. Both the subject and the object are dynamic partners in any bond, and the central issues are the acquiring of pleasure and the avoidance of pain, even if the pursuit of pleasure becomes so refined that hedonistic motives are verbally eliminated.

Balint has put the developmental task in object relations quite succinctly: "The more primitive a man is, the more dependent he will be on the particular object."[14] Childish dependency is being stuck to one object who alone can satisfy—maturity means flexibility in object choice, and the building of compromises. Therefore, if a person is to be strengthened in his general stance in life, three approaches are possible. A person must learn to resist the so-called attraction of the objects by discovering the strength of his own contribution to such attractions, i.e., his drives and needs. One could also try to increase his ability to substitute one object for another, thereby alleviating his vulnerability to the loss of a particular object. Finally, it may be possible to learn to substitute one kind of satisfaction for another through sublimation, foresight, or refinement.

Balint goes on to sketch three characteristic positions regarding object relations, which seem to have implications both for man-man and for man-God relations. The anaclitic position goes back to the original bond between mother and child, in which the infant is allowed utter dependency on mother's ministrations. It is blissful to be mothered—it is cold and hateful to be deprived of her care, or to have to wait long stretches of time until she will come. Marked swings between love and hate, or bliss and acute discomfort, are characteristic of such a dependency relation. The pain that accompanies separation always lurks around the corner; in a way it is constantly anticipated and feared. A union is tensely maintained or striven for. Disunion is felt as lifelessness, emptiness, death. In this dynamic situation, longings for mystical union with an ever-present Father or Mother in heaven or with an omnipresent divine Cosmos or Nature are an understandable and expected religious solution to life's problems.

A second position is the idealization of the object. Its faults are denied;

its gratifications are seen as perfect and inexhaustible. Balint feels that an extreme, but transposed, form of this reaction is involved in the cult of the Blessed Virgin. This is indeed an excellent example if one takes into account the history of Mariology, which turned her from a simple "handmaiden of the Lord" to the "Mother of God." That transition from human to divine status also exemplifies the religious style of problem-solving, which places the object of worship outside time and space, thereby guaranteeing its durability and its cosmic omnipresence. With the idealization of the object one is prone to find self-abasement of the subject. It is more important, in this context, to be beloved than to love; the larger share of the initiative has to come from the object. Says Balint: "Man is happy, elevated and strong as long as he feels in grace and beloved; but lost, degraded and in despair if he feels his object has abandoned him."[15]

A third position consists in the humiliation of the object, which usually goes hand in hand with an idealization of the subject. The objects are vilified, squandered, stripped of their power or desirability. The result is an exploitative relation. Balint sees an example of this in prostitution to which I would add that it occurs on both sides of the prostitute-client relation. He adds: "If the objects do not matter very much to us, what will matter is only our own gratification."[16] This points to the ruthlessness of this position. It is, of course, a basic dynamic in all those forms of idolatry in which the idol is a symbolic extension of the self, such as property, collections, cars, clothing, or one's children when these have become of overruling importance in life. And since most people like themselves hardly less than the gods they profess to worship, this position is probably the pivotal point in all idolatry. One could call it *the* idolatry of all times. But humiliation of the object may also assume the form of a militant atheism and, as Ruemke[17] came close to showing without saying it, operate in the psychology of unbelief. It is as humiliating to the object not to believe in grace as it is presumptuous of the subject not to stand in need of it.

One cannot escape the observation that the limited tolerance of dependency in man-man relations is offset by a very wide tolerance of dependency in man-God relations. Theologians will find this entirely proper, for the human dependency on his gods is part of the definition of the divine and the creature. The creature is dependent on his maker, *tout court*. But when one notes the intense resistance against growing up and relinquishing the infantile dependency patterns in man-man relations, it is hard not to see the likelihood that man-God relations are a convenient compensation for the renounced dependencies, since they allow their satisfaction in a new form.*

---

* This is a functional statement which should not be mistaken for an ontological assertion. It describes one way in which people use their gods, but says nothing about how these gods came into being.

Apart from compensation, there are other possibilities. In the first place, while no one would deny the strength of dependency strivings in human beings, it is a patent fact that many people do grow up and do so joyfully, sometimes markedly against environmental pressures that would foster the archaic state. While there are resistances against growth, there are also resistances against the *status quo*. Therefore, not all man-God relations can be seen as compensations of thwarted man-man relations. Instead of compensatory patterns, one may find lines of parallelism between the two sets of relations. Individuals may outgrow a childish interhuman dependency at the same rate as they outgrow a childish man-God dependency. In the second place, the theological assertion that the creature is dependent on his maker is formally different from the psychological assertion that an infant is dependent on his mother. Mothers and infants do not relate themselves to each other as "maker" and "made" but as a symbiotic unit subject to increasing differentiation of labor and specialization of functions. Mothers and infants are only temporarily different in scale and power; they are each at different points on a growth curve—one waxing, the other waning. Creators and creatures are of incomparable dimensions, whether the former are fictitious or not. Their differences are constitutive, not quantitative. To believe that the feeling of dependency is only different in intensity between man-man and man-God relations was precisely the weakness of Schleiermacher's proposition, which Otto tried to correct by focusing on the categorical differences. And with these differences come differences in the satisfactions obtained from the two kinds of relations.

To put it epigrammatically, when human life gives only meager satisfactions, religion may well assume a compensatory function by supplying what human objects do not offer; but when life is already rich in man-supplied satisfactions, religion is more likely to function in parallel fashion with terrestrial object relations. In rich and mature lives, such as those of Bach, Schweitzer, Maimonides, Plato, and Whitehead, to name but a few men of genius, one finds that a great diversity of satisfactions is gained, with physical, rational, aesthetic, and religious exercises in abundance. If richness is gained in one perspective, further richness is found in adding new perspectives to the old ones. This was the explicit ideal of Renaissance man and is a natural outcome of differentiation and growth.

But what are the differences in satisfactions between these two sets of relations? Is it merely that gods are more permanent than men, that their affections are more durable, that they give more liberally in proportion to what they ask? H. G. Wells said:

> Religion is the first thing and the last thing, and until a man has found God, and been found by God, he begins at no beginning, he works to no end. He may have his friendships, his partial loyalties, his scraps of honor, but all these fall into place, and life falls into place, only with God. Only with God, who fights through men against Blind Force and Might and Non-

Existence; who fights with men against the confusion and evil within us and without, and against death in every form; who loves us as a great captain loves his men, and stands ready to use us in his immortal adventure against waste, disorder, cruelty, and vice; who is the end, who is the meaning, who is the only King.[18]

Wells was no sentimentalist and no pietist. The satisfactions he saw in religion have to do with catching a glimpse of the purpose and end of things, with finding a closure or a Gestalt in the chaos of experiences, with finding a meaning of meanings. In this view, religion addresses itself to certain perplexities which may persist in a person's life even when he is well off and well nurtured. St. Augustine's famous phrase, in the sophisticated translation of Outler, puts the emphasis differently:

Still he [man] desires to praise Thee, this man who is only a small part of thy creation. Thou hast prompted him, that he should delight to praise thee, for thou hast made us for thyself and restless is our heart until it comes to rest in thee.[19]

In a special paraphrase elsewhere, Outler renders the last part of this phrase as follows:

You [God] provide man with the stimulus that makes him want to praise you, but you have so fixed the human condition that it is disturbed until it returns to its "right relation" in your presence.[20]

Here the specific religious satisfaction is an existential "righting" and a grasp of the very idea of relatedness—the essence of relationship. The satisfactions which religion offers are, of course, answers to the religious quest. Much of this quest takes the form of an inquiry into the relations between the part and the whole. Mumford put it this way:

The little questions, for which there are definite answers, have an important practical function: yet it is only within the larger frame that they are fully significant. Nothing can be settled until everything is settled. The first step in the re-education of man is for him to come to terms with his ultimate destiny.[21]

And Smuts, the South African general and statesman, and a great theoretician of holism, had this to say:

We thus arrive at the conception of a universe which is not a collection of accidents externally put together like an artificial patchwork, but which is synthetic, structural, active, vital, and creative in increasing measure all through, the progressive development of which is shaped by one unique holistic activity operative from the humblest inorganic beginnings to the most exalted creations of the human and of the universal spirit.[22]

This statement suggests that one of the cardinal features of the religious quest is a synthetic sense of form and style: the desire to participate maximally in the holistic quality of the universe, which is all that prevents reality from being total chaos. Like cognitive grasp, aesthetic finesse, and the sense of meaning and relatedness, the holistic activity of human beings is a primary ego function and not merely a libidinal position. Let us be careful with words. In the previous sentence, "libidinal" refers to an instinctual drive, conceptualized as operating within an organism which is centrally guided by the ego which secures survival and aims at overall well-being. Here the word "libido" is taken in the sense of Freud's *The Ego and the Id*,[23] which introduced the structural model of personality. Some readers, however, may read "libido" between the lines of Smut's paragraph, as a convenient term for just that creative, holistic activity which runs through the universe as a whole. Freud used the term that way, too— but in his metaphysical writings, and in that exalted, speculative conception he attributed to it not only the basic driving power and pulse (as in the human drive) but also the creative synthesis and principle of form (as in the human ego).

The point is that despite the similarities between man-man and man-God relations which psychoanalytic writers have so well documented, there are also striking differences. The differences in object are so obvious that they need no elaboration. The differences in aim are less clear, but the word "union" which has so often been used to describe the aim seems not the best term. Many commentators on the etymology of the term "religion," after transcribing it as "at-one-ment," have too easily slipped from that construct into "union." But at-one-ment is more like *being aligned with, attuned to,* or *in right relation with* than the unity, union, or fusion of the original mother-child relation. The aim in man-man relations has been described as genital or orgastic. The aim in man-God relations is far more cognitive, ethical, and aesthetic, and its accompanying emotions have more to do with awe and wonder than with lust. The differences in satisfaction obtainable from the two patterns of relation are undoubtedly blurred by the metaphoric use of language which describes human objects in terms derived from the divine, and religious objects in terms derived from erotic human experiences. But outside the area of overlap and metaphoric confusion we have noted some real differences in satisfaction: on the one hand the blissful state of being nurtured, cuddled, smiled upon, wanted, and put at ease; on the other hand the tense and daring situation of encountering the novel, the awesome, of having one's powers of comprehension stretched to the limits. The satisfactions of man-god relations are illuminative and discovering to a degree rarely seen in man-man relations, even if one would admit that a part of sexual pleasure also consists in the satisfaction of a certain curiosity. One might add that curiosity about a part requires a very different mental set than curiosity about the whole.

Our search for the relations, if any, between man-man and man-God affiliations has resulted in three possibilities. The first is a compensatory relation: failures in man-man affections may lead to another try for success in man-God relations. The second is a parallel relation: more or less satisfying or successful man-man relations are mirrored, amplified, or repeated in man-God relations. Maturity in one pattern is matched by maturity in the other pattern, by a rule of analogy. A third possibility is evident: man-man relations and man-God relations are totally independent of each other. They are as different as night and day, have no correlation, nothing in common. Their lines do not intersect.

We will have to reckon with all three possibilities. In the first and second pattern there is much room for transference of attitudes, originally pertaining to the human caretakers, onto the image of the divine. But there is need for a qualification: only in the compensatory maneuver can the word "transference" be used in its proper technical sense of displacing frustrated unconscious longings, not satisfied by the original love-object, onto a second object. In the situation which was described as a parallel pattern the so-called transference onto the deity is more like a spread of positive feelings from the original to a second object, not out of scarcity of satisfactions but from an abundance of them.

One of my colleagues, Philip Woollcott, has tried to document some of these relations through structured psychiatric interviews with normal and disturbed persons, all of whom professed to having articulate religious beliefs.[24] Here is a passage from an interview with a young minister who reflects about his relation to his father and God:

> My folks were not practitioners of religion in the home—no grace at meals, etc., but they were religious in their attitude. God and religion were much a part of life without much talk about beliefs. For example, I never recall father swearing, and liquor was never served in the home. My folks were permissive. I seemed self-sufficient, had lots of friends, was active in school, sports, etc. so they let me go on as I pleased. . . . My image of God is powerful, loving, forgiving, full of grace, all-knowing and seeing, non-punitive, not vengeful or wrathful, accessible, personal, concerned in us as individuals, like a father who has high expectations, yet not repulsed because we make mistakes. I can interpret God much as I do my father: he has expectations, yet warm, concerned, forgiving of mistakes, rather than punitive. My own relationship with my father was not the best, however, in that he was a quiet person who never got angry nor upset. He never talked about personal things, yet got the message across through example. I wanted my parents' respect, admiration and approval but the choice was left up to me. Parents would support me in an emergency, but stood back and said "this is part of growing up"—this is my understanding of God, too. He does not impose his will on us.

A good deal of analogy between this man's relations to his father and to God is evident. By and large, the feelings toward both objects are rather positive although there is an intimation that as a boy, this man had expected his father to be more direct and prescriptive than he actually was. A second example from Woollcott's study is the following fragment of an interview with a minister whose father was also a clergyman:

> My earliest religious memories are of attending church—father was a preacher. . . . It appears that early in my life I had a number of little conversion experiences rather than any one particular dramatic experience. . . . The vocational decision for the ministry was not made until my third year of college at age 19. I was struggling with father at the time—father tended to be dominating and I have often thought that the ministry was a way of submitting to father. Yet I went into different aspects of the ministry than father did. This seemed related to my Oedipal difficulties I suppose. It seemed that my whole experience of God early in life fell into a dominance-submission pattern, modeled after my father. I have always been opposed to moralistic pietism as a definition of the religious life; rather, religion is a free experience—one's response to the majesty, wonder and beauty of God in his creation.

This situation is far more complicated. The clergyman-father loomed large like a divine power in the boy's life; God, even in this man's later years as an adult, is described in terms of the father's attributes: majesty, wonder, and beauty. Yet this man's beliefs and his ministry are attuned to something new which the boy-father relation apparently did not provide: a sense of freedom that will avenge the oppressiveness of moralistic pietism. There is much of a compensatory pattern in the relations to the two objects. In this case one may even speak of a split transference. The love for the natural father is transferred to a new God whom the father, as the boy saw it, did not know and could not preach; whereas the hatred for the natural father is transferred to an old God, about to die. The young pastor's ministry (which he claims to be so different from his own father's) proclaims the death of the old and the coming of the new God, all within the framework of one historical religion.

Here is another one of Woollcott's cases, a minister who was born into a family of farmers:

> It was mother's approach that made me first aware of religion: she talked about how God was concerned about us and looking after us. She said at that time prayers with us children. . . . Father was not very talkative about religion: grace at table was said by my mother or older sister or myself. Father did not participate, but he did not object or ridicule it. . . . During those years my attitude towards God was that as long as I did not violate the Ten Commandments, did not swear and that sort of thing, everything would work out all right. . . . At about the age of 15 while working with the crops and with the animals on the farm I became sensitive to the changes in the seasons and the importance of rain and sun, and how much

we depend on God for providing for our natural needs. I began to feel how important it was to feel a part of God's plan, protecting the soil and taking care of it, and I believed that this was God's will. But from age 15 to 17 I began to question a lot of things and the Bible commandments were not a sufficient answer. Father always encouraged our asking questions. . . . During these years in my late teens I felt God led us and guided us, and I had a deep faith that things would work out if we did not exploit people or mistreat them. . . . In the spring of ———— I had my main religious experience. This was following a period of spending a good bit of time with my grandfather and giving much thought to his "reverence for life" concept. For instance, he was against burning the wheatfields. Grandfather used the word "nature" rather than "God."

Here one can see how the same theme and the same relation proceed to spread, like a stone that sets up ripples in ever-widening circles when thrown into a body of water. The father runs the farm according to his plans, but without talking about the undergirding philosophy. The grandfather had undoubtedly done the same for years, but added explicit precepts anchored in a "reverence for life" belief. The son goes a step further, by placing it all into the cosmic frame of God's plan, aided by empirical observations of nature and its seasons. Affection runs through all these relations, and the parallelism is striking. The key theme is participation, from doing farm chores to becoming a minister, from aiding nature to sharing in "God's plan."

We should now pay attention to the third theoretical possibility: that man-man relations have no necessary connection with man-God relations and that the two patterns are entirely independent of each other. Put in a nutshell, this position not only undermines the viability of the psycho-dynamic viewpoint, but also thwarts the aims of religion. If there are no connections at all, the religious thoughts and practices stand apart from the rest of life and are thus spurious exercises. While I do not think that this position actually is what it appears to be, it alerts us to the curious phenomenon that in certain people strenuous efforts are being made to compartmentalize both sets of relations and keep them apart as two distinct worlds. At a very pedestrian level, it may take the form of seesawing between two worlds, the temporal and the so-called spiritual, or between Sunday behavior and weekday behavior. In fact, the individual seems to relate himself to two classes of objects—the deities and the human objects —and strains to keep the two separate. How can this be done?

The classical justification of this position takes recourse to an interesting tour de force in regard to the subject himself: it splits the person into distinct realms, usually in the form of body, soul or mind, and spirit. It also plays a tour de force on the universe, which it splits accordingly into three spheres: nature, mind, and spirituality. Moreover, these triads are typically handled as value hierarchies, with the corporeal at the bottom and the spiritual at the top. There is a large philosophical or theological apparatus available to rationalize these distinctions. Archaic belief systems rooted in spiritism or animism, the more sophisticated dualisms such as Manicheism and distorted Platonism, various forms of metaphysical dualism, and the hypertrophied dualisms of mind and body, or good and evil, can be and have been marshaled in defense of this position.

The neat split of inner and outer reality into distinct orders has of course the grave defect of failing to deal with the unity, such as there is, of reality as a whole and of the experiencing subject. It is unable to envisage adequately the Gestalt laws that govern the parts which have been distinguished within the whole. But these failures are on closer inspection not sins of omission, but sins of commission. For it is evident that this viewpoint too is an adaptive, or more likely a defensive, maneuver, on the part of individuals and groups in coming to grips with the essence of relationships. The divisions are too neat, too strictly maintained, too solemnly proclaimed. They obviously run counter to so much else that religions have taught, namely the continuities within creation, the singleness and indivisibility of personhood, and the relatedness of all things.

What are the satisfactions to be gained from this position? Many of them center on the idea of death. What will happen to the person when he dies? Can some continued, though modified, existence be guaranteed? It is thought that this is possible by some manipulation of the terminal point of life: the soul, the spirit, or the idea of the person, now divorced from his body, will not only continue in a disembodied state, but actually be freer, more essentially as he was meant to be, closer to his origins and nearer to the divine realm out of which he was pushed at the dawn of his conception. This attempt at reconciling oneself with one's own demise implies a negative evaluation of corporal existence, some scorn of the body, and probably considerable fear or disdain of the sexual function with all its sensory appurtenances. With seeming nobility one may proclaim to feel ill at ease in the world; in seeming love for God one may abstain from involvement in the affairs of man; in nostalgic longing for a life hereafter one may refuse to commit himself to the here and now. The narcissistic blow of being "thrown into" the world and having to face one's death is softened by the fantasy of eventually being "lifted out of it," gently, as a lost sheep that is being carried home by its shepherd. To portray life as "a valley of tears" may at once relieve a person from the responsibility of involvement and allow him to engage in it irresponsibly as a temporary pastime in which he practices only his "lower nature" with impunity to his higher and more enduring spirit. Aided by further speculations, such as the conception of devils or demons holding sway in the realm of body and mind, the secondary gains from this position are almost infinite. Luther could advocate the drowning of mentally retarded children[25] precisely because of this remnant of demonology in his mind (and in many of his contemporaries) which made him think of deviants as "vessels of the devil." The same assumption lies behind the organized program of witch hunting and the disastrous success of the Inquisition, complete with its weighty and learned tomes (such as the *Malleus Maleficarum*) which not merely allowed the procedures but systematized them as necessary "for the glory of God."

One can see from these historical excesses that one of the clearest satisfactions in this position is the outlet it provides for aggression. When one denies the biblical affirmation that creation is good, the forces of human destructiveness can be unleashed with great vigor and considerable impunity on the rest of mankind. By the same token attempts have been made to turn evil into good by the rationalization that sending people "into their eternal home" before their time is in its way an act of mercy.

It does not matter too much what this position is called. But it is patently not well described as a form of independence or noncorrelation between man-man and man-God relations. It is, rather, an extreme case of systematic denial and rationalization, with a symptomatic return of the repressed in many forms, which may range from a passive-aggressive noncommitment to the world to the most cruel interventions in its order.

IX

Relations to
Things and Ideas

IN HIS CHAPTER on "Saintliness," James devoted several pages to what he called "the ascetic paradox." It consists of the virtue of poverty "felt at all times and under all creeds as one adornment of a saintly life" running counter to the "instinct of ownership [which] is fundamental in man's nature."[1] But he quickly went on to say that the paradox disappears when one remembers "how easily higher excitements hold lower cupidities in check." There may be some truth in that observation—as far as it goes. All of us who believe in noble causes and donate some of our income to them hoard that much less. But are things and our relations to them really a matter of "cupidity" and a "lower one" at that? I have never felt comfortable about James's statement, for it seems to disdain too easily the point he made so well in his *Principles,* that consciousness of self, or what we would now call identity, rests for a large part on a material self and a social self.[2] He described the former as our body, the clothes we wear, our family, our home, and all kinds of property such as tools, books, art objects, etc.; and the latter as the recognition we receive from others, our honor, fame, the roles we engage in or are forced to assume, and the praise and blame we receive. These are important anchorage points for the consciousness of self, and except for certain fetishists and kleptomaniacs, our relations to things tend to be less cupidious than those we maintain toward people or even to our gods.

It is a psychodynamic truism that in unconscious thought, which does not follow the canons of reason, things and ideas frequently symbolize people. In dreams, people and things can freely change places. Inanimate objects and seemingly impersonal ideas were first conveyed to us by the people we loved, and whom we needed as our primary satisfiers. From birth on, things, thoughts, and persons intermingle in relation to us. One

233

gives the other; one elicits the other; one comes to stand as a token for the other. Milk, blanket, cleanliness, and mother come all at once in early experience. As James noted, things become important tokens of our identity. As everybody knows, things give comfort, power, and some freedom to pursue our desires. Many things have come to us as gifts, and therefore as expressions of love toward us, which in turn become proofs of our lovability. When we want to express our positive feelings toward others we can buy them gifts, say nice words to them, or "give" them our smiles. When we want to express our disregard, we can withhold gifts where giving would have been expected. As Weber noted regarding Protestantism and the rise of capitalism, things can be seen as signs of preferment, of divine grace, of election.[3]

Things and ideas are also the objects of hatred. Hate toward people is frequently displaced to animals, as in the maltreatment of pets, or to lifeless things which get kicked, ripped open, or torn up. Passionate fights are waged against ideas and ideologies, with all the ardor and rancor of blows which belong properly in fistfights. Our attitude toward things is often described in people-language: we are devoted to our books; we care for our gadgets; we cling to our homes; we love our clothes. We also despise the ideas of our enemies, but more neutral persons may give us occasionally "food for thought." Metaphors commingle indeed. Bank accounts are advertised as nest eggs, and psychologists speak freely of investing oneself in another person.

In a word, and using this time a military or electronic metaphor, we cathect ideas and things just as we do people. We love or hate, like or dislike, things. They satisfy or frustrate us. They excite us or bore us. They remind us of people we like or dislike. They may put us into a certain mood; they may elicit fear, or rage, or admiration. We live in a world full of things, people, and ideas, and despite the distinctions we make between nature and culture, animate and inanimate objects, transient and enduring objects, we seem to have a good deal of flexibility in cathecting any of them to suit our needs and our tastes.

It is a religious truism that the man of faith, although he needs things like everybody else, will from time to time assess his relations to the inanimate world from a particular perspective. He is aided in this endeavor by books, clergymen, sermons, and phrases about the providence of God and very likely by the example of his parents who may have forgone some of their wants for the sake of charity or a religiously conceived self-discipline. Or, instead of forgoing their wishes, they may have gladly accepted what came their way, or even indulged in many satisfactions, but with an audible acknowledgment of gratitude toward a heavenly father who gave them these favors. Religions tend to inculcate in their adherents a special attitude toward things, money, food, learning, and ideas which hinges on the words "gratitude" and "stewardship," or whatever cognate term the particular system may use.

We shall explore in this chapter how these religious attitudes toward the inanimate world function in people's cognitive and emotional households. And since we can treat of this gigantic universe in only one short chapter we shall select the following rubrics for the focus of our attention:

1. Possessions
2. Time and space
3. Work and play
4. Authority, power, and responsibility
5. Nature and art

The observant reader will note that there is nothing particularly religious about these rubrics. They are useful in any assessment of people from a conversational sizing-up at a cocktail party to a psychiatric case study. After all, the religious person thinks most of the time about the same things that all mankind is concerned with, but he sometimes places them in a special perspective.

POSSESSIONS

It is an interesting fact that the word "possession," in the religious sense, refers to deities or demons exerting power over human beings and dwelling in them. The history of psychiatry also records that this ancient belief can be extended to animals who may seize hold of persons and dwell in them, turning them, as it were, into members of their own species. Lycanthropy, satyriasis, and tarantism have for years been items in psychiatric classification systems, along with demoniac possession. In the secular sense, possession refers to the power to hold, use, and dispose of things (and human beings, as in slavery). In either case, possession denotes a relation of great intimacy, devotion, and power. It is therefore not so strange that in the mind of religious believers several questions may arise regarding possessions. If a god is lord of creation, how far can the human dominion extend and on what conditions? Cannot a man become too lordly in owning too much? Is not a zealous clinging to goods a serious distraction from the love of God? And how can charity be taken seriously in a system of private ownership?

There are religious adhortations to behold the lilies of the field, not to worry about tomorrow's food and clothing, and not to gather earthly treasures. They have had their echos in socioeconomic theses, such as Proudhon's conviction that property is theft, and in various utopic schemes. They have also led to vows of poverty, communal provisions for individual needs, and the voluntary sharing of goods and gifts. Social history is permeated with attempts to wed possessions to a sense of order and responsibility, and many of these attempts were directly religious or had a religious origin.

In order to know an individual it is important to observe how he deals with possesssions (his own and those of others) and what motivates him in his relations to things. Is he a hoarder who piles up articles and money without giving much thought to their use or the propriety of his ardent collecting? In that case he is likely to have little faith in people, let alone in a divine providence. Moreover, his pattern of relationships bears the traits of stinginess and stubbornness typical of an anal attitude toward all things, animate and inanimate. Others treat possessions with great nonchalance, sloppiness, or even destructiveness, never mending what is broken, and discarding things left and right. Does this give clues about their relations to people also? Indeed, for such an attitude is possible, mostly when there is either plenty of supply and a commandeering demandingness toward rich givers, or a parasitic nagging which brings supplies even from meager resources. Both situations bespeak the narcissism of orality, often mixed with a pervasive optimism which expects the world to stand ready with satisfactions. If things are cherished, prized, and well kept, they are still tokens for people, but it is more likely that their possessor has been able to gain insight into the differences between giving and receiving, so that he cares for the things just as he does for the people with whom they are associated.

A perverse sense of possession is demonstrated in phenomena that range from conspicuous display and snobbery to the potlatch festivals which anthropologists have described among the Kwakiutl of the American Northwest and other peoples.[4] The potlatch is a feast in which two rival aristocrats, who may be tribal chiefs, ceremonially dare each other to destroy choice possessions so that each will try to outdo the other in the amount of goods to be annihilated. The central theme in all these attitudes toward objects is that if one has much, one can afford to be wasteful and somehow flout the needs of others. The same theme is conspicuous in gambling, where is is linked with a counterphobic attitude toward fate. From the accounts of gamblers, for instance Dostoevski's quasi-auto-biographical descriptions,[5] it also becomes plain that the power play between the individual and the game borders on magic: by imploring or teasing the goddess of fortune the player expects to get her on his side. An element of teasing and magical daring seems to be present in all forms of conspicuous consumption or display, and these extreme examples make it quite plain why religions have advocated time and again the idea of stewardship in order to regulate man's attitude toward things, especially possessions. These perversions of property put in bold relief the dangers inherent in all possessions: idolatry and the ultimate enslavement of persons to things. From these may follow other evils that religions have been quick to spot: the exploitation of man by man through economic means, the substitution of man-to-man relations by man-and-thing bonds, and the false likeness unto God that ownership may entail.

At one time, and for many centuries, the Christian Church thought it sinful that money could beget money through interest. But the laws against usury could hardly veil the enormous economic gains that the same church was making through ever-accumulating landholdings by monastic orders and bishoprics. One cannot say that the religious answers to the question of possessions and property have been very consistent or workable. A life of poverty, even if willed by a solemn vow in the pursuit of presumably higher attachments, can hardly be called elegant although it may have an aura of nobility. But it is only fair to remember that the religious injunctions against possessions have at least instilled an attitude of uneasiness toward things which, in broad outlines, is matched by many ethical and political systems. Moreover, this sense of uneasiness squares well, again in broad outlines, with psychiatric advice. A cartoon in the *New Yorker,* of May 13, 1967, showing a psychiatrist's consulting room with a patient on the couch, puts it very succinctly. The psychiatrist says: "I would suggest that you have two means of ridding yourself of that guilt. One, stop watching Channel 13 [which makes frequent requests for money]. Two, send them some money."

If the religious questions about possessions take hold, the individual will put the objects of his attachments in rank order: God and man first, then things. The obvious religious preference is to "love the Lord thy God" and "thy neighbor as thyself." Mystics and ascetics have clearly seen the power of possessions to distract a person from the proper rank order. Saintly abbots refused to give in to their subordinates' requests for psalters, surmising that after having psalters the men would ask for breviaries also and soon end up having whole libraries. Similarly, the Methodist minister who was to be kept ready for itinerant service could not be weighed down by a home and a library, and in the absence of such possessions he could also keep his basic loyalties to God and men straight.

This kind of stewardship, which consists in the attempt to abstain from possessions, has appeal to only those few people who prize contemplation, mystical exercise, or a strained discipline of natural desires. For the masses of believers, stewardship is more like a corrective on ownership or a plea for responsible use of possessions once they have been granted and appreciated. This more typical kind of stewardship demands that the pride of ownership be counteracted by gratitude for what has been received, that ends and means not be confused, and that the creature at no time arrogate himself to the role of the creator. These are theological and ethical considerations of great importance which have undoubtedly also been influenced by the psychological observation that enduring satisfactions are more prone to come from persons, human or divine, than from things. In this sense, stewardship has an erotic base and further concedes the point that things can be worthwhile as aids to, and symbolic extensions of, people. Even more, it accepts the plenitude of creation with gladness, thrills in it, and thrives on it. It is likely to see human culture as continuous with the unfolding of nature, affirming both as good and full of blessings. Nature and culture can be graces; they can support man-man and man-God relations.

On this basis, stewardship is a matter of knowing the vicariousness of all ownership and therefore a matter of practicing charity. And not just as a stern or hard duty, but preferably in a spirit of emulating and imitating a creative and provident Giver-of-all-things. We have already noted the erotic origin of this sense of stewardship, to which we can now add the further observation that its pattern and style is that of the genital personality. Giving and receiving, working and loving, satisfying oneself while one satisfies others—all these processes merge in the creative-erotic act, which is the divine and human act par excellence.

From this lofty vantage point it is easier to see how objectionable it is to destroy things or to use men, things, and beasts for destructive ends! The so-called peace churches whose members refuse to bear arms for their government usually take their stand on the sixth commandment: Thou shalt not kill. But it can hardly be accidental that these churches also have a long tradition of agricultural diligence, soil conservation, thriftiness, and economic caution, all of which bespeak an aversion to sloppiness or destructiveness toward possesssions. They seem to have a general attitude of conserving, preserving, and building up which is paired with a general rejection of hostility and destructiveness. Yet one cannot call this pattern in all respects a successful sublimation, for it is clinically noteworthy that the relations among members of these groups are often quite cold and stiff, and that many individuals among them are prone to mild depression and self-accusations. But the pattern may nevertheless be singled out as an achievement which the larger mainline denominations have failed to reach, despite their verbal denunciations of waste, hostilities, and destructiveness and their emphasis on good stewardship.

Possessive attitudes toward things may extend to corporate property such as church buildings and worship paraphernalia. Utilitarian or aesthetic reasons for building and maintaining church property may become subdued by pride in the investment, pleasure in the social status of a well-chosen location, and the vanity of conspicuous display. Proprietary feelings may even extend to the deities themselves who become "*our* God" or "*my* Savior." Not unlike children who hang onto dolls and stuffed animals, believers may turn their gods into a possession, hanging onto them as if they were precious things. This is facilitated, and perhaps even aimed for, in the talisman or other protective effigy that one can carry as an ornament on one's body. Crucifixes and the divine person they symbolize may undergo the same fate. It is not impossible that an awareness of this danger of turning deities into private property was one of the complex reasons for the Hebrew injunction against portrayals of the divine.

TIME AND SPACE

Pascal admitted that his religious sentiments were in part determined by the fact that the "eternal silence of the fathomless vastness" frightened him. Germans are wont to call the vast space of the universe *unheimlich*, and most of us regard the firmament with awe. Similarly, an acute awareness of the relentless march of time can be overwhelming, and Benjamin Franklin's conviction that time is money is not calculated to put people at ease. Attitudes toward time and space are one important variable in the emotional organization of groups and individuals, and they are being explored here because they are also of note in religious experience.

We already saw in previous chapters that archaic religions have made much of sacred time and sacred space as ways of demarcating the sacred from the secular in general. We also noted two aspects of time as *chronos* and *kairos*. We saw how space is manipulated for emotional ends by desert dwellers, pillar saints, monastics, and hermits, by the ancient view of the three-story universe with its neat divisions, and by the ritual and liturgical movements which turn space into a stage for religious action. All these examples show that time and space are not only philosophical abstractions, but also concrete experiences which entail feelings. In religion, moreover, time and space are also seen as values toward which one may not behave nonchalantly.

Perhaps the most basic psychological question about space and time is whether an individual finds the universe a friendly abode or a horrible, inhospitable expanse. Its dimensions were frightening to Pascal, and they are awesome to almost every person. They are therefore challenges to the sense of security and elicit coping behavior. How can space and time be used and their frightening impact mastered?

The answer has already been given: by manipulations which divide them up, reduce their size, make them reliable, and allow us to feel at home in them. It seems that the human conquest of space has proceeded rather well, but time continues to present serious problems. Vast distances have been bridged; bleak spaces have been turned into livable areas. Global security has become so great that ventures into outer space have become possible. Yet the psychiatric symptoms of claustrophobia and agoraphobia continue to point to a deep uneasiness imposed by space, despite the increased comfort. After nine months of embeddedness in a warm, protective, intra-uterine shell, a person is rudely delivered into an open space and thereafter may continue to long for the snugness of his beginnings. The lifelong result is a clinging to objects which sometimes leads to homes so chock full of furniture and bric-a-brac that one can hardly walk through their rooms. Coziness is equated with spatial narrowness and clutteredness, and spaciousness is felt as cold or forbidding. Architectural plans for new churches tend to elicit fierce reactions from congregants, quite out of proportion to rational or utilitarian issues, so that one wonders whether these deeper and less conscious feelings do not play a large role in the protests which the building committees meet.

The kiva of the Southwest American Indians, an underground ceremonial room into which one descends through a hole by a ladder, is one of the clearest architectural replicas of a womb, hollowed out in "Mother Earth." The hermit in his cave and Diogenes in his casket may not have been aware of the feminine quality of their narrow enclosures, but the fact that they exchanged hearth and family for the solitary grotto is a telltale sign of their deeper longing for a reliable, safe, and private shelter. Simeon Stylites was more defiant in his space arrangements and displayed his independence more aggressively. His behavior was not free from claustrophobic elements. Thus it may be considered a great advance when houses of worship, continuing the feminine principle of all enclosed spaces, were supplied with rising towers and spires which added a masculine note and the fatherly symbol of a "tower of strength."

The appreciation of space can also be tied to movement. Visitors to the Aztec temple ruins at Teotihuacán are impressed by the wide lateral expanses and the dominance of horizontal lines (despite the rising pyramids) in this enormous ceremonial space complex. It suggests that processions, marches, walking, and climbing from terrace to terrace must have been very important aspects of Aztec worship and that much of the believers' zeal was expressed through the motor system. Indeed, the conquest of space requires locomotion and mobility, and the fact that conservatives feel tied to home and a patch of soil while progressives are literally on the march for their principles has a deep symbolic significance as a clue to a whole style of life. If the universe is seen as friendly and potentially good, it is not difficult to move from place to place, and to let the imagination take flight.

Though the archaic idea of the sacred space has become less useful in an age which tries to overcome the all too sharp distinctions between the sacred and the secular, it is still linked with a vital question with which each believing individual has to come to terms on the basis of his own experience: Where is the deity? There are two groups of experiential answers to this question: (1) He is "out there" in outer, upper, or lower space; (2) He is "in here" in the human heart, or where two or three are gathered. In technical language, he is transcendent, or he is immanent. There is a third answer given by classical Judeo-Christian theology which affirms that the Holy is both transcendent and immanent. This is a paradoxical statement as long as one overlooks the pastoral intention of this theology. It is actually a pedagogical device which acknowledges that man can err in two directions, and fail to come to terms with the numinosity of space which impressed Pascal so much.

If the transcendence motif is pushed too far, the gods can become too distant and be kept out of the human domain. As we saw in the chapter on thinking, one can shoot at them from afar to ward them off from one's private territory. Or they may lose their relevance and die. Today's God-is-dead theology is in this sense an understandable response to yesterday's neo-orthodoxy which stressed transcendence almost to the point of no return, literally using the image of a chasm between God and man, and describing him almost exclusively in his "otherness." And when the creators are far away, asleep, or dead, it is a natural tendency of ambitious creatures to take charge and lord it over their fellowmen.

If immanence is taken too strictly, the familiarity between creator and creatures may wash away the distinctions. If the divine is exclusively within man, as a spark of fire or a glimmer of light or some other image, it is easy to assume that all that one thinks, feels, wills, and does has divine sanction. Lack of discernment and pride may go hand in hand. An extreme form of polytheism may be the result, in which each human being has (in a sense *is*) his own god. Moreover, if god is exclusively within the human heart (or breast, head, blood, etc.) or within a small and select group (family, tribe, sect, koinonia group, etc.) subjectivism is greatly fostered and the rest of the world can become ignored.

The inside-outside problem, put in spatial terms, is thus also a problem of the relations between the whole and its parts, of relations between people, of emotions and ambitions, and even of reality-testing. Those who are too prone to subjectivity, who wallow in feelings and cherish too much the light within themselves, will sooner or later have to be confronted with the outside world, with the enormous spaces surrounding them, and with the greatness of their creator whose work they have as yet hardly seen. They must rise to a view of the whole and see its splendor without being so overcome by awe that they shrink away from it. And those who have put their creator far outside his creation must sooner or later be confronted with the richness of their own inner world which is not without evidence of divine splendor. Treatises and studies of prayer have repeatedly emphasized that persons who pray usually feel at a loss to state whether they pray to an indwelling representation or an outer manifestation of the divine. Their predicament is understandable, for an honest, but not so rational, answer is: both. Hence the use of silent language in prayer. On the one hand *silence*, for the words do not have to traverse space in order to reach an outside hearer. On the other hand *language,* for it is to be a communication and not merely a form of musing within oneself, by oneself, and to oneself. But hence also the need for two forms of praying: silently and in privacy, and publicly and aloud. One stresses the immanent pole, the other the transcendent pole of total religious experience.

In the present age of macrophysics and microphysics, classical biology and microbiology, astrophysics and nuclear physics, the human view of space has become doubled. Awesome mysteries and powers have become visible in either perspective, the very small as well as the very large, the inside and the outside dimension of things. The uncanny lies no longer only in the firmament but also in the views seen under electron microscopes. Perhaps the next generation, educated toward this double view, will have less trouble with the age-old controversy over the divine immanence or transcendence, and can approach the processes of praying with greater boldness.

Religious thinking about space has led to the notion of the human body being animated by a soul, which remains detachable from it and proves its detachability by removing itself from the corporal scene at death. There are several variations on this theme, from the Platonic *to soma sema* (the body is for a while the tombstone of the soul) to the more frivolous view that some winged entity, bestowed with grace, will eventually join an angelic host in outer space. Such dualism tends to denigrate terrestrial space as a valley of tears or shadows from which one may escape toward a place of brilliant light or from which one is doomed to descend even further into a lower pit of wailing and gnashing of teeth.

The horizontal and vertical dimensions of space play a large role in religious ideation. Epithets of the godhead allude to his being high or the Most High; designations of demons describe them as base and low. Relations between men and gods tend to be described as transactions along the vertical dimension from heaven to earth. Given this framework, it is almost inevitable that the Incarnation is imagined as a divine descent, which is exactly the way Renaissance painters portrayed the Annunciation scenes. The Christian calendar knows Ascension day, soon followed by Pentecost: as Christ ascends, the Holy Spirit descends. Mountaintops have been traditional places for the gods to dwell, and mystical states are being described as peak experiences. Tillich's proposal that an age which has absorbed the language of existentialism and depth psychology should replace the divine locus from a heavenly height to the ground of being still keeps the man-God relations in the vertical dimension.

In contrast, man-man relations are typically described as lying in the horizontal dimension, or on a plane. The neighbor is literally the one who stands near and next to us, at our side. In the praying posture one bends down or looks up, but in human encounters one faces forward. Hands are raised up in benedictions or stretched down in blessings of food, but human beings shake hands with each other in the horizontal plane. The Christian motif of the cross has been endlessly described as the most fitting intersection or combination of the two basic space dimensions to symbolize the ancient religious concern of loving God as well as the neighbor, and the Incarnation. Words, gestures, and postures throughout the centuries have not only established the religious meanings of these two basic dimensions through use, but the direct and unreflected experience of space could hardly make the outcome otherwise. Even when the idea of the three-story universe has been effectively demythologized, the experience of earth with its horizontal dominance remains a firm datum, and, as we saw earlier, the locus of the divine abode, once loosened from a specific geographical spot, is now more an inside-outside puzzle than a height-or-depth question.

Aside from cosmological speculations, space remains imbued with values and charged with satisfactions for all men. Some see space as something to conquer, venture into, and explore, and they derive great satisfaction from the discoveries which space affords. Children progress naturally from the womb through the arms-and-breast space to the lap, and continue to progress from playpen to the home at large, into an ever-widening world until they reach toward adulthood a feeling of at-homeness in a world of ideas which far transcends their geographical locale. That is, they will gradually break out from the earlier confines only when they have learned to cope with childhood fears and have been encouraged to explore new horizons. They must have the trust that the wide world is basically friendly and hospitable and that, religiously speaking, God is everywhere and not tied to home and hearth.

To illustrate this attitude, here are the responses from two persons to the earlier mentioned card 14 of the Thematic Apperception Test, a silhouette picture of a person looking out a window:

> This is a young man looking out from a darkened room into a moonlit night. He is aware of the vastness of space, particularly as seen from the smallness of his room. He sees the stars and the planets. The open window signifies, however, that he is looking out upon grandeur rather than his own smallness. I would say the outcome of this is that the man becomes a philosopher, in that he tries to work out a philosophy of life which includes the grey dismals of the small.

> The figure in the window is a male with a long haircut who is seeking the perspective of the outdoors. He has felt confined in a small world. His concerns were getting petty. So he shifts to the window—while looking at the stars he is participating in a large world. He experiences a renewal of communication with the real world symbolized by the stars.

Others have learned to regard space as an unfriendly expanse, or as a dangerous vastness, in which one should locate a small spot of one's own, fence it in, defend it against intruders, and then speculate about an evil world outside. This stance is exemplified in another man's story to the same stimulus card, which harps on the theme of intrusion. Its very brevity shows the influence of fear which blocks the stream of thought and makes the narrator tongue-tied:

> I was going to say this is perhaps a burglary of some kind. He probably got in through the window.

Such an attitude of distrust to space also turns the gods into local deities, parochial protectors, or heroes of nation and country; it turns other people into strangers, aliens, or foes.

History has shown intricate combinations of these two basic attitudes in migrations, wanderings, exiles, and the search for a "promised land," all of which have been so important in the founding of new religions. Associated with memories of migrations is the idea of sacred cities to which pilgrimages can be made, such as Jerusalem, Mecca, Rome, and Salt Lake City. Not all of the original wanderings stemmed from wanderlust and a sense of exploration; some of the groups were literally or psychologically pushed out of their original habitat through conflict. The pilgrimage toward the holy city or shrine is a curious religious phenomenon if one considers the enormous sacrifices which millions of people on earth make in money and privations in order to accomplish the long trip. Where are the satisfactions, which must be great enough to balance the sacrifices? A cue can be found in one of the acts which follows upon arrival at the desired spot: kissing or touching the shrine or the sacred stone. As Thomas knew, touching is believing. As every child knows, touching is loving and knowing for sure. And as everyone knows, kissing is being united. A whole complex of psychic functions, from perceptual certainty to cognitive grasp and emotional affirmation, find exercise and satisfaction at the end of the long trip. The trip itself with its deprivations, prescribed or self-imposed, is a catharsis for many tensions and a fitting atonement for feelings of guilt, with the comforting certainty that one is now really "doing something" for one's religion. Further satisfaction stems from knowing that one is setting a good example for others to emulate. If one is also gifted with curiosity, this will provide satisfaction during the journey, which may already mitigate a good deal of the strain on the purse and the motor system. Moreover, one does what one's ancestors did or hoped to do, which may augment one's sense of goodness and conformity to the values of one's love objects.

We should now consider attitudes toward time that are relevant to our exposition. In previous chapters the distinction between *chronos* and *kairos*[6] was described, and we already noted how religion deals with time through the liturgical year, through festivals and the celebration of human life crises. The religious significance of time is perhaps nowhere better illustrated than in the following hymn by Isaac Watts, paraphrasing the contents of the 90th Psalm. As an old favorite throughout Protestantism, it apparently has an enormous appeal to millions of believers, and it behooves us therefore to take a close look at it:

> O God our help *in ages past,*
> Our *hope* for *years to come,*
> Our shelter from the stormy blast,
> And our *eternal home.*

> *Before* the hills in order stood,
> Or earth received her frame,
> *From everlasting* Thou art God,
> *To endless years* the same.

> *A thousand ages* in Thy sight
> Are like *an evening gone;*
> *Short* as the watch that *ends* the night
> *Before* the rising sun.

> *Time,* like an *ever rolling stream,*
> Bears all its sons away;
> They fly *forgotten,* as a dream
> Dies at the *opening day.*

> O God, our help in ages past,
> Our hope for years to come,
> Be Thou our guard *while life shall last,*
> And our eternal home.

Disregarding repetitions, there are no less than seventeen time words or phrases in this poem. They present eternity as an enormous stretching of time backward and forward, and speak of cosmic time through the metaphors of human time experience. They allude to the stream of time which goes relentlessly in one direction only, with its implications for memory and its bearing on hope. They anchor hope in a historically informed time perspective and give it content in terms of an "eternal home." That content specification is vague enough. It leaves the mind free to see the "eternal home" either as point of origin or as future goal; in fact, it leaves room for appreciating both perspectives and may provide application to the present as well.

There is indeed great associative freedom to all the words of this hymn, which is surely one of the reasons for its popularity. But many persons overlook the fact that what appears to be freedom of fantasy was actually a marvelous restraint on the part of the Psalmist and Watts. Both men refused to engage in speculations about the content of the eternity to which they were alluding. Millions of people, however, demand from their religions a much more concrete consolation for the shortness of life, and seek through individual fantasy and collective speculation a detailed picture of survival after death. Despite restraints from responsible theological creeds, religions owe much of their appeal to the chance they give to the masses for manipulating time concepts in such a way as to secure perpetuity for themselves. The realization that one will die is apparently the greatest narcissistic offense. One's own contingency, proven by his being thrown into the world and eventually being pushed out of it without his consent, is the hardest thing to confront. Much effort is spent on denying it, or repressing the thought of it as long as one can afford to do so. And thus the terminus of life is turned into a transformation, a passage or a rebirth, often with very specific fantasies about the form one will assume hereafter and the new space one will occupy in the universe.

And yet this propensity for manipulating the edges of life seems not evenly distributed among all members of the species. True, the wish for immortality has repeatedly been singled out as the greatest source of motivation for religion. And one may infer from what has been said that the word "beyond," so often used to describe the deity or the essence of the religious concern, has an emotional anchorage point in worrying over what lies "beyond the grave." But studies of religious and nonreligious persons show, as Feifel[7] reports, that avowedly religious persons tend to be more afraid of death than persons without religious affiliation. The latter seem to take it more factually and with resignation to the unalterable facts of life, and their fear of dying takes more often the form of a concern for the welfare of the loved ones who will be left behind. Feifel's own preliminary study reinforces a suspicion held by many observers that there is a definite functional relation between the need for religion and the fear of death. Other features of the study also suggest that the religious person's fear stems not merely from uncertainty over whether he will meet his reward or his doom in the hereafter—the concern goes deeper.

Under the influence of existentialism it has become fashionable to take a denigrating attitude toward the human propensity for looking away from death. The trend is to extol a kind of grim heroism that stares death in the face. But while denial of death can undoubtedly be pushed too far at the expense of proper reality-testing, existential heroism can also be pushed too far when it leads to the kind of preoccupation with death that depletes the resources for living. Though opinions abound, there are hardly any systematized empirical data to allow us to say with some certainty how attitudes toward death affect the pattern of one's living; and conversely, how the patterns of life, and its developmental stages, affect attitudes toward death. But there are enough incidental observations to suggest that time perspectives differ markedly within a culture, vary with age, are influenced by physical and mental illness, and tend to accrue religious and ethical values.

We all know from direct experience that time moves slowly when we are bored, and that it goes fast when we are excited. It rushes on at great speed in mystical states according to some reports; the language used to describe mystical states denies the importance of past and future and makes the present "thick" or full. Meister Eckhart says:

> This agent [of the soul] has nothing in common with anything else. It is unconscious of yesterday or the day before, and of tomorrow and the day after, for in eternity there is no yesterday nor any tomorrow, but only Now, as it was a thousand years ago and as it will be a thousand years hence, and is at this moment, and as it will be after death.

> ... the human spirit takes no rest. It presses on further into the vortex, the source in which the spirit originates.

> In this exalted state she [the soul] has lost her proper self and is flowing full-flood into the unity of the divine nature.[8]

These are typical speed-words: "pressing on into the vortex" and "flowing full-flood." James cited a case from Flournoy in which the person actually tried to check how long his ecstatic state might have lasted:

> ... I had wept uninterruptedly for several minutes, my eyes were swollen, and I did not wish my companions to see me. The state of ecstasy may have lasted four or five minutes, although it seemed at the time to last much longer. My comrades waited for me ten minutes at the cross of Barine, but I took about twenty-five or thirty minutes to join them, for as well as I can remember, they said that I had kept them back for about half an hour.[9]

The mystical experience is apparently quite full and its duration is therefore subjectively overestimated, which is another way of saying that time moves fast in these episodes. On the other hand, statements about mystical experience also indicate the irrelevance of chronological time. Aldous Huxley reported on his episode induced by mescalin that there seemed to be "plenty of it" (time) and that his experience was one of "indefinite duration or alternatively of a perpetual present made up of one continually changing apocalypse."[10]

The natural division of time in a past, present, and future perspective can give rise to selective orientations which may become quite characteristic of an individual. There are people who may be described as predominantly past-oriented: they meet present situations with a heavy baggage of memories and look backward very often in order to establish comparisons, find inspiration, or discover norms for right and wrong. The proverbial conservatism of many religions finds ample expression through individuals who cling to the old creedal formulations, the hymns of their grandparents, old Bible translations, and the morality of the good old days when people were allegedly more religious.

Memory becomes a burden in feelings of guilt and remorse; at the same time the flow of days and weeks slows down to a low ebb until expiation is made.

Classical novels about conditions of severe guilt, such as Dostoevski's *Crime and Punishment,* seem, while one is reading, to cover a very long time between crime and confession; but upon analyzing the plot, one finds that the calendar time covered by the story is shorter than one thought. This is consistent with depressions in which the stream of thought is filled with old materials from experience. These are not confined to the actual erstwhile events but comprise a whole complex of facts, repression, rationalizations, promises for betterment, distortions, anticipations of punishment, and all kinds of coping maneuvers. I recall a fifty-eight-year-old patient who had just been admitted to a state hospital after a suicide attempt; his thoughts were filled for weeks with an unethical episode in his early twenties, when he had used his employer's postage stamps to mail three letters of his own. As he told the story later, undoubtedly distorted by his present guilt feelings over different issues, he had restored his debt by sending three stamps in an envelope to his employer. But he could not get the affair off his mind and after a few days sent seven-times-three stamps to the office. Even this failed to expiate him in his own eyes, and he then sent an anonymous letter to his employer explaining why this time again he enclosed seven-times-three stamps. Then the anonymity of the letter kept haunting him, but it led to no further acts, and he was apparently able to suppress his guilt feelings for many years. He was a devout man, a pillar of his church, very strait-laced, and as one will have surmised, given to obsessional thinking. His whole life, seen from within, moved slowly, and he found his outlook on the future almost chronically blocked by thoughts of the past which he could not undo.

This case fragment tells the old story of sin, amply made up for and yet unexpiated, in men of ostensibly good morals who are so perfectionistic that they cannot accept grace. We will discuss it in greater detail in the next chapter, but must emphasize here that the dynamics of such life situations show a remarkable consistency in the person's private time perspectives. Feelings of guilt (of whatever origin) tie the person to his past, and make the past loom larger yet, because the memories are amplified by ruminations to such magnitude that the person can no longer put them behind him. The obsession is a dead-end thought process which depletes energies necessary for adaptation to the present. Therefore, the present becomes too poor in new experiences which could correct the mistakes of the past and help undo the sense of guilt. The path to the future is now blocked by the unfinished tasks of the past, and the person has too little energy and zest to give himself to the venture that every future implies. In fact, he is fearful of the future because he has learned to live without much hope and is wont to mistake forgiveness for punishment. Eventually, one may grow proud of his sinful past, for it may bestow on him the perverse distinction of being a *"great* sinner." Unfortunately, religious language contains phrases and allusions which can be used to beat religion at its own game. The apostle Paul envisaged this possibility in his letter to the Romans (6:1) when he asked, not quite rhetorically, "Are we to continue in sin that grace may abound?" Though he answered with a resounding "By no means!" he apparently knew that some believers could twist reasonable propositions into strange rationalizations, in words with a pious ring.

Emphasis on the present as a basic orientation in time is of crucial religious importance within the Judeo-Christian mainstream. The present is the sphere of action, dedication, and commitment. It is the time in which to make love and brotherhood manifest. It is the time for ethical exercise. Strong positive affects, such as joy and exhilaration, refer to the here and now, unlike anxiety which has an anticipatory aspect and depression which is preoccupied with the past. The Christian advice is not to worry about the future or to feel bound to the past, but to live each day as if it were the "fullness of time." Such a positive and creative approach to the present should be sharply distinguished from the thoughtless addiction to the present produced by infantile pleasure-seeking. The latter lacks foresight and learns little from past experience; the whole emphasis is on the instance of momentary drive gratification regardless of the consequences. Perhaps it is better to see the infantile pleasure-syndrome not as an orientation to the present, but as a deeper disturbance in time perspective caused by fragmentation. In this condition time lacks flow; the inner dynamic of time is broken down into a seriatim arrangement of moments which remain unconnected. Against this condition the religious injunction is to start caring and to take a critical look at one's past in order to perceive its monstrosities, and to hold oneself accountable for them. Responsibility is the keynote to the true orientation to the present; in the fragmented attitude toward the present there is conspicuous irresponsibility and a gross defect in reality-testing.

Just as the past can be repressed or distorted, and the present isolated or wasted, the future can be manipulated in various ways. Though one tends to glorify people who are oriented toward the future, because of their idealism or irresistible cheerfulness, it is important to take a critical look at the specific values with which the future is endowed. Not all looking ahead is constructive.

Looking ahead, throughout life, can be a matter of hankering after wish fulfillment. When life is bitter or bleak it is an expedient antidote to project one's wishes into the future and anticipate their gratification through fantasy. Those who are now oppressed will have their heaven later; and glee over the reverse fate of their oppressors may add substantially to their satisfaction. Though this is a trite and platitudinous theme which critics of religion expose with a certain fondness, one should not err in the other direction by assuming that it is merely a straw man. Unsatisfied desire does create yearning, and frustration is prone to elicit aggressive feelings and revenge fantasies. The strange thing is not that unfulfilled wishes are projected in time, and that millions of people have accepted their troublesome circumstances with patience, having learned to postpone their wants, but that religious leaders have been bold enough to preach it and promise golden mountains. Boisen was struck by the effect of the economic depression in the thirties on otherworldly proclivities and reported, in 1939:

> . . . in the convention of the Church of God in Chattanooga nine of eleven hymns used in their evening service had an otherworldly theme. Among them were the following first lines: "That home of the soul over there," "When we cross the great divide," "Somebody's going to be left behind." At one point, a little girl of seven sang "I'll never feel at home in this world any more." An examination of their hymnbook showed that 75 of their 170 hymns related to the future life.[11]

As we saw in Chapter VI, the more the fantasies are spun out, the more they are sheer wishes; and the more they are extrapolated from current life experiences, the more demanding they are of the deity to deliver the goods wanted. Indeed, in this kind of looking ahead, the future is not open, but already filled with the shapes of things to come.

A second attitude toward the future stems from inhibitions, laziness, or disturbances in volition. The future may become the sphere of procrastination, and its justification. Everything is postponed, put off until tomorrow, pushed forward into a time that does not (yet) demand action. This kind of future orientation stems from a disturbance in the sense of the present, into which one nestles oneself without commitment, without activism, without translating reveries or musings into consummatory acts. From an erotic point of view, one's doings remain in the sphere of foreplay; from an aggressive point of view they bear resemblance to an impotent grudge. Sometimes the reveries may be beautiful enough and the musings quite noble; they may even consist of meditations on the holy name or of verbal devotions! The plans for tomorrow, formulated in thought, may dwell on brotherhood or some other utopic scheme. But not a step is taken toward their actualization. A classical literary example of this state of mind is Goncharov's novel *Oblomov,* whose hero incessantly makes the nicest plans but never realizes them. In his own way, he is an amiable but pitiful character, unless the reader is so imbued with the spirit of the Protestant ethic that he cannot tolerate any idle life.

The inhibitions which can lead to procrastination are sometimes taught through one-sided emphasis on religious prohibitions. When a child is surrounded with too many taboos, when sins lurk around every corner, and when the pedagogical rules are predominantly of the "do not" or "thou shalt not" variety, any activity becomes so danger-laden that one has to minimize action for comfort. Legalistic Sabbath observances and the institution of Blue Laws have not only created much boredom, but have entailed fearfulness leading to general inhibitions. In a more subtle way yesterday's "What-would-Jesus-do?" cult could lead to the stifling of action and commitment by inadvertently overshooting its goal: when one cannot match oneself with the thoughtfulness and nobility of Jesus one may give up trying altogether. The risks of commitment are to be avoided and even one's best intentions remain only projects, to be reconsidered tomorrow, and tomorrow, and tomorrow.

I would describe the third attitude toward the future as one of hope. In contrast to the first orientation, which fills the future with anticipated wishes, the hopeful attitude keeps the future open and its contents undefined. All one accepts on faith is that death, like life, is under divine providence which seems a rather sober assumption if one believes in a creator in the first place. An austere formulation of this conviction will use religious words such as "promise," "renewal," "re-creation," or "rebirth" with some caution so as not to fix their content prematurely. It regards the divine promise of "new life" as a benevolent intention, trusting that things will turn out all right, rather than as a contract to deliver specific goods. For one must reckon with the possibility that the deity, already affirmed as creator, has all the potency for novelty that befits the Holy. Moreover, because the Holy is also affirmed as the ultimate authority and power, it would be rather meddlesome, i.e., sinful, to let the strength of one's wishes prescribe the course of his eventual acts. At any rate to face a future which is open also implies that one meets it with a certain amount of curiosity, trusting that it has novelty which the past and the present have not yet revealed. The satisfactions obtained from this hopeful attitude toward the future are not entirely anticipatory. Since hoping builds on trust in mutual benevolence between two parties, the satisfaction is already present—the same satisfaction which is inherent in a mature genital relation in which both parties enjoy one another through mood, silent communications, and a smile.

Apparently it is more difficult to turn toward the future with hope than with wishes. We met in Chapter IV a radio preacher who refused to put up with *just a room* when the promise made to him by the King James Version was: "In my father's house are many *mansions*." We also saw in Chapter VI that the trust and the tensions required for eschatological thinking are too much even for very faithful believers, so that eschatology is prone to lapse into apocalypse, in which erotic and aggressive wishes take over rather blatantly. Much depends on what is being promised, or in what way a divine promise is being taken. And this in turn may depend on personal experiences with powerful people who made promises to us, or who demanded from us that we make promises to them.

A promise, like hope, is a check drawn on the future. It shares with hoping the delicacy of being an intention or an attitude which must combine sincerity of heart with globality of content. As soon as the content of a promise is spelled out in tangible detail, it becomes poor reality testing, for no one who makes such a promise has that much mastery over future events. Promising is not predicting. A child who promises his mother that he will provide her with a lavish home and a $25,000-a-year income in her old age is likely to have to renege on his promise. But a child who promises that he will do the best he can to give his mother financial support when she will need it is likely to make good on that promise, for it is a statement of a sincere concern, which can be realized in many different ways with many degrees of freedom. So it is with marriage vows; they do not and cannot spell out the number of children one will beget or the life insurance to be taken out, but concentrate on a global "set" of mind and heart, that one will love each other and stay together in fair and stormy weather.

Similarly, religious systems can make their divine personages promise too much, too specifically and too concretely. The globality and vagueness of Paul are admirable when he compares the present and the future by saying: "For now we see in a glass darkly, but then we will see face to face." There is much restraint in this phrase, and the promise implied in it is only an avowal of greater clarity—not a description of the objects that will be illuminated by clarity. It is commensurate with Goethe's last word: "Light!" But when divine promises are made to sound as if heavenly rose gardens and a life of leisure in splendid merriment are in store, one suspects that some human extortionist has applied his art to the gods, and one is back in the sphere of wishing.

WORK AND PLAY

Freud considered loving and working the two most important processes in the maintenance of mental health. Such a positive attitude toward work is not shared by everyone. All too often work is seen as a curse, and in support of that contention both friends and foes of religion are wont to quote Genesis 3:19, AV: "In the sweat of your face you shall eat bread till you return to the ground. . . ." But to quote only this mythical phrase is overlooking the profound ambiguity of work, for in the second chapter of Genesis, Adam had already a definite work assignment even before the Fall, with or without sweat. The point is that within the religious perspective, work has been both blamed and praised. The glorification of work by the Puritan ethic is only one possibility, and it came rather late in the history of civilization. It is also a late interpretation of Christianity, and it should be seen not only as an attempt at positive identification with a creating and providing, i.e., working, God, but also as an attempt to flee from or overcome the devil, whose most tempting opportunities were thought to lie in man's idleness. Idleness is the devil's pillow, says an old proverb.

The Sabbath day is a day of rest, arranged in imitation of the Hebraic creator god. On that day no work is to be done—but liturgy, which is what one does on that day, means literally "work of the people." Ancient texts and hymns exhort *ora et labora,* to pray and to work—but the Messalians, a Syrian cult dating from the fourth century, held work in utter contempt for they felt that praying was the only justifiable human action. The names of Paul, Augustine, Pelagius, and Luther suffice to hint at an even more profound ambiguity of work from the religious viewpoint: one that led to the emotion-laden distinction between *work* in the singular and *works* in the plural. And those *works*, which were despised because of their alleged potency to "buy" one's salvation, were precisely the sacred work of ritual and ceremony!

It seems that play has fared even worse. Zealots of religious education who relentlessly grind out year-round courses of instruction in local churches tend to justify their attitude by saying that "God does not take a vacation." In the first place, how does one know such things about the deity? Second, is not this allegation a complete denigration of playing, which virtually throws recreation out of creation? We noted in Chapter VII that liturgical and ritual acts have themselves a strong play element. And the fact that the word "recreation" is rooted in creation is no accident. Indeed, in the Yahwist creation myth the godhead himself appears far more playful in the act of producing the cosmos than some of his Near Eastern counterparts who laboriously wove the world on a loom or baked it from clay through the potter's craft. What can be more playful than a God who just speaks and things come into being?

Attitudes toward play are influenced by many factors. The equation of playing with idleness makes play insincere and wasteful—or worse, a prank of the devil. The equation of playing with childish activity makes play an immature occupation—or worse, a sign of failing to act like an adult. The equation of playing with amusement makes it in the eyes of some people vulgar or vile. The fact that animals play is taken by some people as evidence of their brutish nature, so much lower than the crown of creation! Playing is sometimes linked with insincerity, in false opposition to the alleged seriousness of work. Play can be linked with fun, which a somber or depressive person may not feel entitled to. "Stop playing and start working" is an adhortation that tends to become part of the superego in the course of growing up. One becomes educated to believe that the right to play (once in a while, as an indulgence to human weakness) is to be earned by earnest, strenuous work (for long stretches of time, until the breaking point is reached).

Cues for these attitudes are taken from what the gods are presumably doing. While the Olympians feasted and made love, the images of the Hebrew-Christian god stress the earnestness of his work, his solemn demeanor, his sincere concern, and his ceaseless productivity: first in the work of creation, then in the work of providence, next in the work of salvation, and finally in the coming renewal of all things which is seen as an unfinished task. These are the things one reads about in religious books, sings about in religious hymns, and hears about in sermons. And grace, which one is bound to hear about too, is solemnized beyond recognition of the spontaneous, playful, good-humored, indeed graceful, element which it is meant to convey. If one would like to make a case for Feuerbach's early projection hypothesis[12] (it anteceded Freud's by almost a hundred years), these similarities between a god who works and his laboring worshipers, both busy as bees and averse to playing, are an excellent demonstration of its pertinence.

The value of this whole chapter, such as it is, rests on the recognition that attitudes toward things and ideas are intertwined with attitudes toward people, and that one wants his things and ideas to be satisfying. Work and play should give pleasure or, if they are imposed by reality demands or conscience, cause as little pain as possible. Hence there are many reasons for work and play: libidinal, aggressive, those that enhance competence and self-respect, those stemming from the ego's own good functioning as an adaptive organ, the adhortations of conscience, and the gratifications inherent in living up to one's own ideals. Many of these reasons are in turn influenced by religious thought and instruction.

For instance, many types of work give erotic satisfactions, either in thinly disguised or in highly sublimated forms. Nursing, feeding, caring, and cleaning can be quite instinctual but are usually so stylized that noble sentiments of benevolence and love of one's fellowman give them more than a modicum of social sanction. They meet with religious approval; indeed, they are the epitome of the classical church office of the deaconate, and quite a few religious orders have adopted these functions for their vocations. The religious approbation of such functions is even more pronounced when the work is shared with others to whom filial relations are maintained, perhaps under the paternal or maternal eye of an overseer. Tilling the soil and cultivating the fruits of the land can be seen as aiding the divine providence and are therefore choice activities of religious settlements, from the early communities of Brethren and Mennonites to the modern Iona community in Scotland; not a small part of the satisfactions obtained in these kinds of life is the brotherly sharing of agricultural work under some paternal leadership pattern. Erikson has pointed out that Luther's penchant for singing, and the great role which singing has since played in the Reformed tradition, could hardly have assumed its prominence in his life if it had not been embedded in his boyhood relations to his mother.[13]

On the other hand, the libidinal element in work may be precisely the basis for religious disapproval of certain jobs. Prostitution, despite its ancient role in sacred rites, is only one glaring example. Of greater practical importance is the religious aversion to taverns, circuses, and large segments of the world of entertainment and the arts, which is based on the conviction that much of this work, and the settings in which it occurs, are frivolous at best and lascivious at worst. To the pietist, such work is charged with conflict, and even work in a hotel (despite the Gideon Bible in every room) is fraught with temptations, as Dreiser has described so well in *An American Tragedy*. And because of the danger of indulgence in erotic temptations, the word "play" is sometimes misused as a denigrating term for all work that involves the art of erotic brinkmanship. "Working" is reserved for the godly, wholesome, earnest, and sometimes dull occupations; "playing" is on the edge of Satan's territory.

The commandment "Thou shalt not kill" is not potent enough to prevent murder and the slaughter of thousands of men on battlefields throughout history. On the other hand, it is a potent enough argument to exclude members of peace churches from military duty. And it can be taken so radically that mosquitoes and other carriers of infection are tolerated to exist in a hospital complex such as Schweitzer's Lambarene. It can also be entirely brushed aside on religious grounds, as in the proclamation of a "holy war." With this much religious (and secular) ambivalence about aggression it is not surprising that the aggressive components of work and play meet with a great variety of religious evaluations and responses, sometimes with very fine shadings. Radical pacifists object to the obviously aggressive intent of all military work and claim not only exemption from combat duty but also refuse to work in the war industry, or to pay that portion of their tax bill which sustains national defense. Others will refuse only to engage in battle, but are willing to serve in the care of the wounded during or after battle, as long as they do not have to carry a gun. Quite a few laboratory physicists have had serious compunctions about the destructive potential of their findings—some have movingly and eloquently questioned whether their basic science pursuits can be ethically separated from the applied science aspects, given the human propensity to aggression.

Something is jarred in the religious conscience when it is confronted with an aggressive or hostile tenor in work and play. Are boxing matches really an acceptable sport? Is the word "sport" at all applicable to bloody fights? Can car-racing, with its enormously self-destructive potential, be fitted into the scheme of doing "all things for the glory of God"? Can a religious man work without inner conflict in a gun factory, as a personal attendant in a prize-fighting ring, or as a circus attendant showing disfigured human bodies as an amusement to the public? Though the answers to such questions are rarely a clean-cut yes or no, religions can consider themselves quite successful if they are able to make people at least uneasy about such aggressive occupations. They will insist that the aggressive means and ends of work or play be considerably neutralized, so that the aggressive energies can be channeled into acceptable, if not constructive, patterns. Missionaries are no longer allowed to denigrate native customs or to ride slipshod over indigenous non-Western religious attitudes. From intrusive converters who followed in the wake of imperial conquests they have become peaceful cultural advisers and pedagogues. Industrial exploitation and oppression need to be thoroughly disguised or alleviated by welfare measures if work in a business firm is to win the religious epithet of an acceptable vocation. On the other hand, most service work and the care-taking professions can count on religious approbation, not only for the "good" which they presumably do, but also for the "evil" which they seek to avoid or mitigate.

And yet there is the embarrassing historical link between the "spirit of Protestantism" and the "rise of capitalism," which, however it be interpreted, shows at least a large tolerance in Protestantism for competition, contest, and conquest in business, law, and politics. Apparently these forms of aggression are part of an acceptable pattern of life about which only a few daring ethical crusaders raise questions from time to time, without power to persuade their denominations into taking a stand. At this time, such religious or ethical compunctions are exemplified in the issue of open housing for racial minority groups. Some leading American denominations would like to take the real estate business to task for the skillful dodging of its responsibility in resolving this deep social conflict, but only a few have dared to make pronouncements or apply pressure toward attitudinal change. Other issues of the day concerning aggression are capital punishment, the possession of firearms by citizens who do not need them, the revenge motif that looms so large in law courts and prisons, parental cruelty to children, and the increased popularity of hunting. Karl Menninger[14] is not amiss when he sees these as evidence that many seemingly peaceful people love aggression and do not shrink away from acts of brutality. Despite many religious codes against killing, hurting, and inflicting suffering, the ambivalence about aggression remains marked, even among the devout.

Religious attitudes toward work and play may be influenced by a third factor: the narcissistic gratifications reaped from competence, success, and self-respect. For a job well done, a difficult task accomplished, how competent should one feel? When does competence become pride, and pride, smugness? Many religious books and pamphlets have argued against the idolatry of success and the worship of steady pay increases which tend to become the corporate symbols of competence in the suburban captivity of millions of "good churchmen."[15] And when does managerial know-how threaten to negate the feeling of creatureliness? In view of such religious questions about narcissistic gratification there is apparently a fine line between pride of one's accomplishments and gratitude for one's competence. The latter attitude takes human energies and skills as grace, and their successful use as a sign of election or special grace. The basic questions are to whom or what one refers the power to work, and whether one's output is accomplished autonomously or in a spirit of stewardship, i.e., vicariously. In a letter to H. G. Wells, William James spoke of "A symptom of the moral flabbiness born of the exclusive worship of the bitch-goddess Success."[16] The religionist, always on his guard against idolatry, is afraid of that symptom of excessive self-respect and fights it with his emphasis on stewardship. Human autonomy is only a relative matter; if it were ever complete it would displace the creator and giver of all good things.

On this point one must make a clinical distinction between the so-called promotion depression and acts of contrition which signal sorrow for the sin of pride. In promotion depression a person becomes acutely depressed when he is promoted to a higher office for which he had had a strong but disguised ambition, envious of his superior who hitherto held the post. The moment his wish is gratified, he becomes depressed, under circumstances in which one would expect him to be pleased and joyous. In the dynamic reconstruction of this symptom one will meet great jealousy and envy of the superior father figure, with intense but repressed hostility to the point of wanting to see him dead; and when the superior retires or becomes ill, the fulfilled wish makes the ambitious person a murderer by his own inner logic. Or, if the envy was not that strong, opening up of the post in fact means the removal of one's object of hatred, with the result that one may have to turn to oneself as the hated object and consider oneself unworthy of food and drink and sleep and all other good things in life. But in contrite awareness of pride one may suddenly wake up to the moral facts of one's life: that one has taken success too much for granted, that one mistook favorable circumstances for one's own competence, that one was well on the way to becoming "like God." Such an awareness may also lead to strange behavior in the form of doling out large sums of money, marrying a poor girl, making confessions of sin to the consternation of friends and acquaintances, withdrawing from one's business, etc. Impulsive though these acts may be, they can be seen as attempts at righting oneself vis-à-vis one's maker, or as acts of penance in order to clear the conscience. David's depressive reaction after Nathan confronted him with his shameful act toward the husband of Bathsheba may be seen in this light.

Working and playing are also of immense importance as ego-preservative and ego-defensive functions. Working forces a person into contact with reality and to that extent curbs his fantasy. Much work is an attempt to change reality and to that extent swings the adaptive balance from mere accommodation to active assimilation. A good deal of work is done in order to improve reality, for oneself or others, and to that extent guarantees greater or more refined satisfactions. But reality also has its immutable features, and therefore much work forces a person to effect compromises. Working, as most people know almost instinctively, wards off regression, which may be one of the reasons why mentally ill persons, despite serious symptoms, tend to keep working as long as they can.[17] Both working and playing are an exercise of human capacities, and all budding capacities seem to strive for pleasurable practice. For this reason, Hendrick[18] has postulated a "work principle" which acts like an independent drive, and several authors have stressed "function pleasure," for instance in the abundant chattering of children at the onset of speech, and the hypermotility of toddlers in the progressive stages of locomotion.

For all these reasons there is a good deal of psychological realism in imposing regular work patterns on the members of religious communities, such as those who follow the rules of St. Benedict. Quite aside from any need to be economically self-supporting, such groups must work, usually with their hands, in order to counteract the dangers of overideationalism, regression, or excessive introversion. A similar recognition of the healthiness of work comes through in the conviction of some theologians that work is a divine gift and a divine command, which are as valid after the Fall as they were in the unspoiled Garden of Eden. Working gives integrity to a person. Conversely, unemployment may ruin him, emotionally and mentally. The psychological need to work may also be one of the reasons why religions have liturgies, i.e., *work* of the people, instead of pious musings. Even worship cannot be an altogether passive, unenergetic affair or it would quickly deteriorate into regressive reverie and intense self-preoccupation. Some contact with reality must go on, perceptually, through the motor system, or in language acts, if necessary in the form of a sacred play.

It is interesting that precisely in this era of psychological-mindedness, clergymen would begin to clamor for some basic rearrangements in the office they are holding. Some priests want to be worker priests, which is not merely a matter of sharing the socioeconomic life of industrial workers for the sake of greater empathy; there is also the recognition that working, as workers do, provides better reality contact than chronic reading and praying do. The new codes for religious professionals stress that they be in the world, right in the middle of the arena where most other people live and work and contend with each other. There is increasing awareness that there is something basically unhealthy and amiss in the classical life arrangements of the clergy, who always seem to be officiating, whether they preach, visit, give public prayers, or do their "shepherding." Huizinga and Van der Leeuw, whose works we cited earlier, have described in detail how playing, sacred or secular, is a means of coming to terms with the basic space and time dimensions of life. Working is also a potent means of structuring space and time relations. It establishes rhythms which reinforce and articulate the circadian cycles of sleep and wakefulness; it also divides the multitude of interpersonal relations in which we are engaged into manageable portions.

I will never forget the following statement made to me by a young priest:

> For other people, the workday begins when they leave their house at eight in the morning, saying goodbye to their wives and children, crossing town to go to the places of their work. Not so for the priest: he lives in a rectory which is part of the building complex of his church, hardly differentiated from it by space. He wears the same clerical garb all day for nearly all occasions. People can call him all times of the day or night: he keeps no office hours, as other workers do. He has nobody to say goodbye to after breakfast when work begins: as a matter of fact, *when* does his work really begin? And when does it end? Does he have a home to go back to at night? He hardly goes back, since he hardly goes out at clearly stated times. Certainly there is no one to greet him very personally when he thinks his day is done. He has no "home" to talk about at work, and no "work" to talk about at home.

In other words, time and space are insufficiently structured in the clerical office: most of the structure has to be imposed by the priest himself through firm self-discipline. And even then, he is likely to feel guilty when souls in need call him for help at odd hours.

And with the last sentence we have come to still another aspect of work which has always been of singular religious significance: the role of superego and ego-ideal. In fact, these two aids to the ego play many roles in work. They determine to some extent the distinctions between working and playing. They help fix the amount of work to be done, prescribe attitudes of seriousness and perfectionism toward work, and make it possible that working can, at times, be seen as a form of placation for transgressions. We will dwell at greater length on the concepts of the superego and ego-ideal and their functions in the next chapter, but from the preceding phrases it is already clear that they are the primary vehicles of religious attitudes toward work.

Working can easily become a compulsion, instigated by a "thou shalt" attitude. It is clinically most prominent in people from devout homes that frowned on idleness as well as playing, the latter being seen either as frivolous or as exposing a person to worldly temptations. Usually the compulsion demands large quantities of output as well as good quality. Whether this attitude is historically rooted in the mercantile Protestant ethic or in the agricultural ethos of pietistic settlements, the fact is that there still are many families today who abide by the rules of long, hard work, even while affluence might allow a good deal of leisure. The stress on working may be religiously buttressed as a means to the end of glorifying God, or it may become an end in itself, quasi-hallowed and sometimes functioning as an idol.

Work has theologically been linked with the idea of "vocation," which is an attempt to give all work, even the lowliest labor, a divine sanction, as well as a way of demanding that all people, even those in the highest places, make their contribution to society and culture by a divine call.[19] In either case, one is in effect told to work because this is a divine command, which in turn reinforces the notion that idleness is sinful. With a slight distortion of the word "idleness," playing may thus also be seen as sinful. Moreover, if one feels that one has to work hard because God, allegedly, also works hard, working is a form of identification with the divine and is proof of the godly life.

We have already alluded to the Reformation dialectic between *work* and *works*. Fletcher has put this matter very neatly in a single sentence:

> Some theologies treat [the faith-works problem] as faith *versus* works, some as faith *or* works, some as faith *and* works, some as faith *is* works (i.e., simply put "faith works").[20]

The plural form has become a technical religious term for the penitential and propitiatory qualities of work. One has to make up for transgressions; this can be done in many different ways, but in people who are already convinced of the need to work diligently it is likely to take the form of doing more work, particularly menial work or the "dirty work" that one normally leaves to others. After a spat with his mother, a young boy will offer to do the dishes or sweep the floor. Active church members who feel guilty for any reason may turn to more church work, particularly the tedious tasks, in order to get straight with their conscience. One speaks of "works of penance." Parents with a work ethos have the habit of prescribing special chores to their children when punishment is needed. In such cases both the ego demands and the superego demands for work are intensified, and work becomes the ideal form of atonement for misdeeds because it at once placates the conscience and strengthens the ego's capacity to cope with negative feelings. Moreover, the extra time taken for the penitential work means some curbing of instinctual wishes which may make a person feel good about his seemingly increased powers of self-control.

To seek lowly work when cerebral work with high social status is available has often been seen as a sign of holiness. Working with one's hands, in the fields, as a cobbler or as a weaver, tends to receive a curious religious praise. There are many literary pieces which stage shoemakers as sages or saints, or describe them as religious mystics. It is not clear why modern worker priests should seek out factory wage earners rather than salaried white-collar office clerks, except that the first choice has an almost automatic religious approbation. But if one recalls our chapter on emotions with its descriptions of the saintly life, things fall into place. Manual labor is extolled because it recalls great religious themes such as "the meek and lowly" and "blessed be the poor in spirit"; and because it is germane to the virtue of humility, which may even assume the form of a vow of poverty. Manual labor is easily linked with obedience, another virtue. And it has, of course, the general quality of menial tasks such as one assigns to servants, which gives it a propitiatory function for all those with greater capabilities who consciously choose to undertake it.

Through a link with orderliness, cleanliness, neatness, and precision the quality of work may achieve that quasi-ethical and quasi-hallowed status which the word "perfectionism" conveys. Perfectionism demands that high standards be met in order to obtain approval. Falling short of these standards elicits criticism, which in the moralistic or religious mind conjures up a list of vices: sloth, sloppiness, disinterest, hurry, irresponsibility, dirtiness. And the typical response to imperfect performance is parental adhortation, coupled with such withholding of gestures of love that the person feels he is unlovable until he can prove his lovability by better performance.

The superego functions of work bring out most clearly the general thesis of this section, that attitudes toward working and playing are, in a sense, attitudes toward values. And attitudes toward values are reflections of the people with whom we maintain relations of love and hate, or ambivalent feelings. We find satisfactions in practicing the values we have learned to cathect, which are dynamically the satisfactions of being found lovable in the eyes of the people on whose love we depend. It is thus no surprise that work, which occupies at least one third of each day of most people, should have the psychological and religious importance which this section ascribed to it. And it is not astonishing either that both psychiatric and religious leaders begin to have grave concern over one of the most impressive feats of the twentieth century: the tremendous increase in the amount of leisure time which has caught the masses of people emotionally, educationally, and spiritually unprepared. This cultural achievement is being praised and blamed in different quarters, but the least one can say about it is that it requires a completely new alignment between work and play.

RELATIONS TO AUTHORITY, POWER, AND RESPONSIBILITY

A few years ago I interviewed a middle-aged psychiatric patient who could well be described as a lone wolf. Since it is almost impossible to lead a completely solitary existence in a modern society, he was in chronic conflict with just about everybody: his employers, the storekeepers from whom he bought his necessities, and later, the personnel in the hospital where he was treated. He had been admitted to the hospital because he had gotten into increasingly serious trouble with his supervisors and co-workers in a succession of jobs, mostly as a janitor or night watchman. In the interview he reflected nostalgically about life thirty years ago, when he was a young man working in a coal mine. He stressed that it was "hard work, but I was completely on my own, with nobody checking on me." His father, a taciturn man, used to do the same work and had actually introduced him to the mines. The patient described with feeling how father and son had worked together, or rather alongside each other, deep underground in half dark, without saying a word. But when the mine had closed, years earlier, the patient had been forced to seek work above ground, in plain daylight (although he still preferred night jobs if he could get them), in perpetual contact with others. The result was that he found himself increasingly at odds with others and himself, until he broke down in his later years, with intense suspicions and anxiety attacks.

The case puts into relief the truism that life is lived in a network of authority relations from which escape is hardly possible, and that some lives are spent fulminating against this elementary social fact. The case was chosen out of many possible ones because of the use of two characteristic phrases: "I was completely on my own" and "nobody checking on me." Every living soul has to come to terms with authority, power, and responsibility. These three categories are charged with affect; they are integral to religion, and conversely, religions have a good deal to say about them. Authority, power, and responsibility are vested in organizations—and among these are religious organizations. They are vested also in thought structures and ideas—and among these are religious creeds, doctrines, and theologies. They are vested in government and positive law—and both individualistic men of faith and organized religions have to come to terms with these two. They are vested in culture—and religions have their hands full steering their members between conformism and protest, the secular city and rustic piety, the responsible self and the authoritarian personality, prejudice and open-mindedness. These issues will be our guide through this section, though they can only be presented in the utmost brevity. Each is worth a whole book. But a psychology of religion cannot omit mentioning them, since they are of singular functional significance.

One of the most striking aspects of organized religious life is that churches and denominations can let authority flow from below upward, or from some top downward. This is what is meant by "low" or "high" church. It is a matter of "who is checking on whom," in the metaphor of our patient. Congregational organization vests authority and power in the lowest possible unit: the local face-to-face group that worships together and appoints a minister. The organization of the Roman Catholic Church is hierarchical and monarchical: authority flows from the top down, via a system of intermediaries, and the highest officer is seen as the direct representative of the divine on earth. Anglican arrangements are aristocratic, with power vested in bishops who form a conference, like a House of Lords. The Presbyterian system is republican with most of the power vested in the presbyteries, which are intermediate between local congregations and national assemblies, and with authority equally divided between clergy and laymen. The point in this enumeration is that organized religions take polity as a very serious matter and charge it with value; in fact, the differences in the distributions of ecclesiastical power seem to outweigh the differences in theological conviction. With it go differences in nomenclature for the clergy: from the venerable *Father* via a respectful *Reverend* to a patronizing *Preacher*. Some congregations feel it is proper to hire and fire their ministers; others feel it more proper to receive them after appointment by a higher body. In the first case the congregations "check on" their own worship leaders; in the second case, the leaders "check on" their charges, to put it somewhat starkly. In most concrete situations, irrespective of polity, there is much give and take between these extremes, and the power used is more one of persuasion than of firing from office or excommunication.

There are several caveats to the stringency of this ecclesiastical typology. Rokeach's[21] studies of the belief-disbelief systems of American church members have shown that members of any denomination have divided feelings toward all other denominations, feeling close to some and distant from, if not antagonistic toward, others. They all rank atheists as extremely distant from their own position. I would like to suggest that there are two more religious persuasions that are rather foreign to most members of organized religious bodies: the individualistic, solitary religionist who seeks no affiliation; and the ecumenist who seeks a unity of spirit which respects the different polities realistically, but with a deep sigh of pity. Both cases impose some strain on the average believer—they are somehow beyond his imagination. A second caveat has to do with discipline. Many churches and denominations have disciplinary rules for the beliefs and behavior of their members, but there seems to be a veritable conspiracy against their use. Only extreme cases which have acquired a certain notoriety or endanger the denomination's public image are adjudged. The third caveat is the widespread ignorance among church members of their own organizational structure and its distribution of authority and responsibility, which seems to imply that those structures are after all not as highly regarded as one would infer from the Rokeach studies. On the one hand there is near idolatry of polity; on the other hand it is taken less than seriously, if not actually thwarted and flouted. The sum of these divergencies is that attitudes toward authority, power, and responsibility are highly ambivalent within the very organizations that claim divine origin or providence for them.

From where does this ambivalence come, and how can it be understood? To the extent that religious activities have a play character, as described in a previous chapter, they entail a double awareness of "this is serious business —as long as I decide to play the game." The power, authority, and responsibility which are harnessed in organized religion function only within the sacred circle, and it is possible to remove oneself from that circle and stop playing the game, just as it is possible to enter into it from the outside and start playing it. This possibility gives not the polity, but the regard for the concepts harnessed in polity, an ambiguous status. A second source of ambivalence is that unresolved conflictual feelings toward the heavenly Father may be matched by similar feelings toward the organization and the polity which are derived from the image one has of him. Opposition and resentment toward this Father, whom one otherwise professes to trust, are then reduplicated toward the institutional framework which symbolizes his authority, and the love toward him may take the form of loyalty to that same institution which one cannot leave despite the negative feelings. But since there are obvious differences between any church and the deity it proclaims, the distinction can provide the member believer an opportunity for splitting his loyalties and dividing his feelings among them: he can trust the former and be suspicious of the latter, and vice versa. A person may feel that he is a dutiful son of his church and a loyal follower of its clergy by making efforts to trust in God, and at the same time know that he really has a less than heartfelt trust in him. Conversely, he may have great faith in a heavenly Provider who deserves all his best feelings, but reserves his gripes for the institution that claims to be founded in his name and for his service. Both positions are manifestations of split transference, which is one way of dealing with ambivalence through division of feelings between several objects.

The achievement of mastery, competence, and authority in certain segments of his life is not conducive to making a person bow to the power of others, whether fellow human beings or divine personages. As some theologians have put it, men (including churchmen) have come of age and claim authority for themselves as well as responsibility. Childish submissiveness can no longer be expected from believers, and the ecclesiastical structure can no longer impose a paternalistic regime. If modern believers feel indeed that they have now come of age, it is entirely proper for them to regard the polities with which they are affiliated with forgiving indulgence at best or with considerable opposition at worst. These reactions are like those of the young adult regarding his family, which he has nearly outgrown. The result is an ambivalent attitude toward the institutional forms and symbols which at one time were taken as representing divine arrangements. In some cases enlightenment and self-scrutiny may change the ambivalence into consciously held mixed feelings.

Closely linked with this position is the awareness of a more basic irrelevance of traditional organized religion by many persons who, without severing their religious affiliations, no longer consider themselves believers in the firm sense of their parents and grandparents. This has been the subject of much social commentary during this century. It leads to a kind of fence-straddling which seems to indicate that belief and affiliation have become separated; they are no longer regarded as two sides of the same coin. Such a separation is bound to enhance the ambivalence toward power, authority, and responsibility vested in religious organizations. In turn, the separation of belief and affiliation can be seen as a contemporary expression of a deeper ambivalence about the idea of church and the idea of God.

Only a small step further lies the possibility of experiencing the death of God. I put this intentionally in terms of experience, because it takes another step to come to the affirmation that God is dead. One may be unable or unwilling to take that second step if one feels too stunned or saddened by the loss, or too timid to articulate its implications. The ambiguity and the ambivalence of this position are quite marked when it is recognized that one needs God-talk, i.e., religious language, in order to describe or proclaim the death of God. Such an event is only relevant within a theological perspective. Moreover, the boldest formulations of this thought (and experience) come from theologians who are, after all, the "basic scientists" of the religious quest; and because they are teachers and researchers of institutional religion their message is likely to be perceived as a jarring note.

One could adduce other and simpler reasons for the existing ambivalence toward power, authority, and responsibility as vested in the specific polities to which believers belong. We should not underrate the importance of anticlericalism in a country that has a profusion of religious leaders, pluralistic to be true, but in very large numbers and with an immense variability of capabilities and professional training. Anticlericalism is manifest enough in civil life, but it has many more subtle forms within the denominations themselves. These range from low salaries for clergymen and patronizing attitudes toward pastors to making them a target of ridicule in cartoons. Not to be overlooked is the intimidation of clergy by members of the business and professional community, many of whom are themselves church-affiliated, when a minister or priest ventures to take an unpopular public stand on social issues. Another obvious reason of ambivalence is that church affiliation in the sense of opting for a specific polity serves as a badge of social identity, much as ethnic background and surnames do. It may lose its intrinsic value and become a historical curiosum of which one is proud for extrinsic reasons, such as prestige status, social fitness, family pride, or convenient identifiability in the marketplace.

Within the Hebrew-Christian tradition, and in some other religions as well, there is a coupling of functions which often gives rise to seesawing movements, ambiguity of authoritative teachings, and ambivalence in the hearts of the denominations' members. These functions are the priestly and the prophetic. They are not necessarily opposed to each other, but they are so different in orientation, style, and consequences that many believers seem unable to reconcile them. Sketchily put, the priestly function of clergy and laymen centers on worship, ritual, prayer, and devotional exercises with such an emphasis on historical precedent and traditional propriety that it is bound to promote a conservative outlook. And with the emphasis on worship and sacraments the priestly function is exercised predominantly within the denominational circle which is seen as bounded off from the secular world. The prophetic role breaks through the distinction between sacred and secular and asks the agonizing questions of the why, where, and how of the traditional forms and attitudes, seeking to deepen the motivation, purify the forms, and renew the relevance of the established religious habits. Although it too draws heavily on the past, the prophetic stance is widely seen as one of precipitous novelty—jarring, upsetting, and provocative. Since the two roles obviously demand different personality traits, they are rarely combined in one person, with the result that there tends to be a polarization in organized religion between priestly and prophetic typologies of men and priestly and prophetic styles of religious life. The two types are found in almost every congregation and much of the problem of power, authority, and responsibility boils down to the question which of the two types shall prevail at a given time. But that is not all: priestly types take a view of polity entirely different from that of prophetic types. To over-state it for clarity's sake: the priestly view of polity is guided by decorum and propriety; the prophetic view is inspired by a search for intellectual honesty and societal relevance. On such a built-in polarity within religious groups its members will tend to take sides, or else bear it with ambivalent feelings. Many denominational leaders try to subdue the conflictual aspects of the polarity for the sake of congregational unity. But since the priestly as well as the prophetic functions claim divine sanctions for their emphasis, open conflict about the two attitudes tends to become an argument about polity, i.e., a challenging of the power, authority, and responsibility which the polity has harnessed. For this reason, church squabbles elicit fierce feelings and are among the least peaceful societal debates.

Closely linked with this polarity is the status attributed to doctrine. Psychologists of religion, with few exceptions, have made short shrift with doctrine, seeing it on the one hand as alien to religious experience, and linking it on the other hand too quickly with the priestly function. Freud was concerned with the peculiar power-status of doctrine which to him went against the canons of reason. Others saw in doctrine merely a "dead letter" which was so much conceptual baggage that feelingful believers, in search of a mystical experience, had—alas—to carry around.[22] Still others have felt that psychologists have to leave theology untouched as an enterprise about which they could not have a professional opinion. But doctrine is, first and foremost, an articulate product of the conceptual process in religion which falls entirely within the purview of the psychology of thought and clinical psychology, as we have tried to demonstrate in Chapters III, IV, and V. The word "doctrine" is, however, a slippery term, and before we consider how it is related to power, authority, and responsibility, we should consider the diverse elements it covers in loose usage.

Basic to many religions is a short creed or "statement of faith." Judaism knows the Shema; Christianity the Apostles' Creed, the Nicene Creed, or the Athanasian Creed. These are not books or even tracts, but short, personal affirmations in the form of a simple testimony on the order of "I believe that. . . ." Though such creeds are bound to a specific time, place, and cultural situation and have traces of controversy in their wording, they are what Zuurdeeg calls "convictional" utterances, which only fanatics would raise to the level of ultimate truth. They are part of the liturgy, and say something about the reason for worshiping.

The more technical Confessions of Faith of specific faith groups and denominations are intellectually far more ambitious. They propound systematized propositions, closely reasoned, usually in the concepts and metaphors of the period in which they were made, which means that they tend to be linked up with a specific philosophical trend. Far more than the creeds, they address themselves to historical conflict situations, mapping out a unique path between affirmations and rejections of certain propositions. Within the denominations, such confessions have a high degree of authority and help to establish the group's identity. For these reasons they are charged with feelings of pride, and are often raised to absolute validity —by legalists, literalists, and fanatics.

A similar fate may befall those various instruction books for children and novices known as Catechisms. Luther said in the preface to his own Catechism:

This sermon is designed and undertaken that it might be an instruction for children and the simple-minded. Hence of old it was called in Greek *Cate-*

chism, i.e. instruction for children, what every Christian must needs know, so that he who does not know this could not be numbered with the Christians nor be admitted to any Sacrament, just as a mechanic who does not understand the rules and customs of his trade is expelled and considered incapable.[23]

There are larger and shorter catechisms, which are an obvious attempt to gear the amount and level of instruction to age groups or comprehension levels. They avoid technical jargon. Some, like the Heidelberg Catechism,[24] are rather evangelical and feelingful; others, like the Westminster Catechism,[25] are decidedly more theological and polemical. They follow the procedures of questions and answers, both short so that they can be memorized. As pedagogical devices they have no inherent authority, but are meant to come to life with a good teacher who can refer to the original sources from which the concise answers are derived.

Holy Writ, Sacred Scriptures, and other sacred *Urtexts* which are interwoven with the history and origins of a religious group, have a quite different status than the previously mentioned documents. From the Torah to the Bible, and from the *Book of Mormon* to *Science and Health with a Key to the Scriptures,* they are claimed as radically authoritative, and they constitute the primary resource and court of appeal for the members of the faith group. Since most of them are very complex, both in ideas and origins, their authority is in a sense ungraspable and depends heavily on the extraneous authority of their interpreters. Pfister said of the Bible:

> The texts of the Bible should not be misused in a fear-neurotic or Pharisaical manner. The Bible itself pronounces sentence of death on the abuse of the letter: "For the letter killeth, but the spirit giveth life" (2 Cor. iii, 6): "Where the spirit of the Lord is, there is liberty" (2 Cor. iii, 17). It is time that men realized there is no such thing as a purely objective and valid interpretation of the Scriptures, completely free from the reader's subjectivity.[26]

Biblical thought and language are a mixture of mythical, historical, documentary, poetic, narrative, legal, epistolary, and mystical styles, heavily edited to fit the changing needs of the religious groups who sought to unite themselves by adopting "the book" (or the oral tradition prior to script), and endorsing it as an infallible rule of faith. Biblical power and authority are therefore both intrinsic and extrinsic: they lie in the persuasion of the texts as well as in the institutional tradition which copied, edited, codified, and disseminated them. When those texts are then described as the "Word of God" it is of some importance to remember that "God" in this connection is a kind of shorthand for "*our* God" or "the God of *our* fathers" —a far cry from the metaphysical absolute or rigid first principle which "God" can become only after an encounter with philosophical systematization. The so-called authority of scriptures is thus open to many different approaches: legalists will interpret it along the lines of an ultimate code; literalists will take the authoritarianism of the letter and forget the persuasive power of the spirit; modernists will look for gems of the spirit and indulgently see all the rest as quaint fictions; demythologizers will distinguish between the medium and the message and seek a new medium in which the message can be conveyed. Others will be so overawed by the mysterious authority of scriptures that they settle for an interpreter's authority, and live by commentaries. Still others will ignore scriptures entirely and engage in their own private musings about some vaguely known Golden Rule taken from proverbial phrases of everyday language. It is not uncommon to develop one's own thoughts independent of any scripture, and then look for scriptural proof texts for added authority. In each case, the attitude taken toward scripture is in effect a way of coping with power and authority.

In theological systematization a rational effort is made to organize the essence of the confessions and creeds (which, as we saw, have a testimonial character) into a closely reasoned cognitive whole. In this effort the theologians draw with more or less freedom on sources of authority which are different from the convictional authority of the creeds, such as the canons of logic and argument, ontological speculations, inductive and deductive reasoning, the prestige of some philosophical system, or a powerful mode of expression germane to an era. People's attitudes toward these mixed authorities of theology differ widely, but the following attitude of scorn and distrust, observed by the pastor-psychoanalyst Pfister, is fairly typical:

> In its frequently savage attachment to an irrational dogma having no connection with love, dogmatics and its history seemed to me to constitute an attempt to evade the central point of Jesus' teaching and claims. I saw men terrified by the letter of the Gospel and the tenets of the Church, any questioning of which was threatened by the stake and hell fire; I compared this with the careless contempt reserved for the love of Christ; and I thought that all this was a straining at gnats and a swallowing of camels.[27]

This is not a description of medieval events but of Pfister's pastoral clientele in the civilized country of Switzerland in the first half of our century! But why blame the authority of cognitive articulation for the evils of religion? And why speak so sweepingly of "irrational dogma" when the function of theology is precisely to give convictional assertions the form of rational propositions? Doctrine, like everything else, can certainly be misused. And dogmatic works do sometimes abound in obsessive-compulsive features, which Reik saw in all dogma.[28] But one should be careful not to consider all theology dogmatic, or to use the words "doctrinal" or "dogmatic" only in a pejorative sense. In doing so one opens himself to the suspicion of defining religion exclusively as feeling, without acknowledging the cognitive process as part of the religious quest. In fact, it would then be presumptuous even to ask about the *right* feeling which was one of the primary interests of Edwards, Schleiermacher, and Otto. It seems that quite a few psychologists of religion, in their denigration or neglect of doctrine and theological thought at large, have unwittingly shown considerable evangelistic, if not pietistic, fervor. Examples are Pratt,[29] Fromm,[30] and Pfister;[31] James shared the tendency to a lesser degree.

If our general thesis for this chapter is correct, namely that ideas are valued as symbolic representations of people, who are the primary love objects, the bane of belief is not dogma but the people who propound it. It has always been very easy for members of any faith group to ignore doctrinal formulations entirely and to be unconcerned with dogma, as long as they consented to follow some ritual obligations that met the public eye. But it has been difficult for many persons to avoid confrontation with zealous teachers and preachers, who indeed may "strain at gnats and swallow camels." There is nothing dogmatic (in the pejorative sense) to doctrinal formulations as such, but there are many dogmatic teachers and learners who attribute power and authority to the letter of any formulation. Few people are threatened by the reading of texts who were not first threatened by loveless attitudes from their early instructors, whether parents, priests, or teachers. Hellfire and brimstone are powerless mythical entities, but hellfire and brimstone preachers (whether parents or religious officials) are realities which can "scare the hell out of" young learners who depend on them for love, approval, and protection.

The case is somewhat different for such works as manuals of moral theology, polemical pamphlets, apologetic documents, books of discipline, encyclicals, and pastoral letters or proclamations, which try to apply the propositions of faith to concrete life situations of the individual in his total world. Their authority is that of the institutional church and its hierarchy; their power is the power of the organization with all its sacred and secular trappings. It may be aided by the power of the state, for instance through the notorious "monkey laws" that forbid the teaching of evolutionary theory in the public schools, or through state abortion laws. Sanctions of various kinds may be attached to the rules, and despite the fact that many people clamor for the guidance through definite "right" and "wrong" rules that many of such writings provide, we already noted that the authority of discipline within religious communities is regarded with marked ambivalence. However, not all codes are to be denigrated as perversions of the original religious intention or as deflections from love. Lewin and his students[32-33] demonstrated years ago that laissez-faire methods of organization can thwart human potentialities nearly as much as authoritarian procedures. Goodenough's discussion of legalism puts it well:

... all advanced societies and most savage societies have developed elaborate rules, taboos, folkways with no approximation to a system, so that many of the rules contradict one another. This conflict lies at the root of much of Greek tragedy. Even if he could understand and reconcile them, the individual, especially a punctilious individual, finds them too diverse. To his utter confusion, he discovers that he is constantly breaking laws unawares or that he is unable to control the id because a confused socialization is a weak one. Or he must make choices and decisions and cannot tell which is the "right" one to make.

Legalism is a type of religion directed primarily to solving this problem. The good man, legalism tells us, can do what is right if he knows what is right, and he will know the right, not by a personal intuition or revelation or by deciding the merits of a situation for himself, but from a code that tells him exactly what to do at every point.[34]

Instead of asking in what way any authority may be related to some absolute, legalism accepts a book or person or organization as absolute authority. The legalist finds some peace and enjoyment in the very structure of his dependent situation. Goodenough also described such codes as "an active and actual curtain from the tremendum."[35] To the legalist, the *tremendum* has the character of chaos, and he must cope with his anxiety about confusion by turning propositions into rules.

Thus, it is clinically important to know whether a person uses codes properly and within their limits, or whether he mistakes convictional assertions, devotional exercises, or discursive gropings for codes. The more items he brings under a code, the more threatened he is by chaos and the more he turns religion into a simple scheme of obedience and disobedience.

A similar view, but with a slight difference in emphasis, applies to what Goodenough has described as the orthodox type of religious experience. Here is his basic description of it:

The great majority of men, we saw, take their patterns of conduct from their society or traditions, get them ready-made as blueprints; most people get their patterns of belief in the same way. How may we know that what we believe is really the truth? "Everybody says so"; or "the priest or church says so"; or "the creed says so"; or "our old men tell us"; or "the best people say so"; or, simply, "my mother or father used to believe"—these are only examples of the usually implicit footnotes to all men's beliefs on most subjects, to most men's beliefs on all subjects. This is by no means the attitude of simple and weak minds alone. Often the human mind fears itself, and we shrink from our own thinking.[36]

This is indeed our thesis, too, but to Goodenough's emphasis on orthodoxy as a way of coping with fear of a bewildering chaos we would like to add the positive satisfaction that is sought in the orthodox (and the legalistic) orientation. It consists in associative bonds between persons loved and respected, and the ideas they stood for when we were deeply under their influence. To be orthodox is to be loved by our important orthodox love objects, to be considered lovable by them, and thus to have self-respect. To be legalistic is to be loved by way of the strict rules of our parents and teachers, to hear once more the inner voice of our conscience repeating their approving "yes" when we stick to the good, and thus be lovable to them and to ourselves.

It is implied in the foregoing that doctrinal and theological thinking can be carried at an entirely different plane with liberating effect and as nutriment for curiosity. Legalistic and orthodox youngsters may become great venturers in the realm of the beyond, where they may discover love and freedom for which their childhood has ill prepared them. Luther's life and theology are one example; Augustine is another one, in which conflict-laden entanglements gradually gave way to cognitive clarity and emotional purification, with an increasingly autonomous use of the power of thought. In both cases there was an intimate pairing of new readings and teachings with new love objects and significant friendships. The tremendous expansion of the consumer's market for theological books in the last two decades does not seem to bolster the legalistic and orthodox positions among the laity; on the contrary, it has features of a liberation from the strait jackets of dogmatism (in the pejorative sense), as gleaned from the titles of such best sellers as *Honest to God, The Secular City, Letters and Papers from Prison,* and *Dynamics of Faith.* It has even become possible to discuss weighty theological problems obliquely and with great humor, as in *How to Become a Bishop Without Being Religious.*

Of all the attitudes toward secular power and cultural authority the problem of prejudice might be singled out as most relevant to both personal religious experience and institutional religion. A concise and enlightening article by Allport, "Prejudice: Is it Societal or Personal?"[37] would in its entirety be a most fitting concluding part of this section. Allport gives an impressive list of arguments for assuming a societal origin of prejudice, which includes the effective reduction of prejudice by political decisions such as the racial integration of the American armed forces during World War II and the Korean conflict, and the Supreme Court school desegregation decision of 1954. But he also lists the evidence in favor of personal origins of prejudice, derived from a great many psychological studies on conformity and the so-called authoritarian personality.

Conformity as a personal disposition is based on a common human preference for the familiar and customary, with a concomitant resistance to change. It has deeper roots, however, in the emotional commitments which people have to a certain way of life as a whole pattern of interrelated values, even when some of these values are, strictly speaking, incompatible. Allport, in the work just cited, says:

Thus a devout Hindu finds it easy to subscribe to the caste system, although his religion, which is his main allegiance, is a much more general value in his life. Similarly, a devotee of "the southern way of life" conforms to *many* constituent practices. He goes to church faithfully, prizes hospitality, honor, and the purity of womanhood; and he favors military virtues, and is partial to fried chicken. He also believes in white supremacy, but only as a part of this preferred way of living. Such anti-Negro prejudice as exists (and, of course, it is never recognized as prejudice) is incident to an habitual and deeply satisfying value-system.

Another source of conformity is status dread of the kind: "What will people say if. . . ." This kind of conformism caters to the idea of a hierarchy of power and authority, and its adherents seek to identify themselves always with the higher rungs on the the status ladder, rejecting those on the lower rungs, whoever or whatever they are.

Various studies have shown that in America, at least, in the 1940's and 1950's, prejudicial attitudes are more abundant in church-affiliated than in secular groups, and Stouffer's[38] work indicates that churchgoers show less tolerance than others do of nonconformist behavior. These findings are not surprising when one recalls the emphasis on decorum and propriety which is characteristic of mainstream middle-class worship and church life. Presbyterians reiterate with fondness the Pauline phrase that everything should be done "decently and in order." Meetings tend to be dominated by *Robert's Rules of Order,* and there is a widespread feeling that dignity is one of the hallmarks of the churchman. A more oblique reason for a conformist trend among church members is that nonconformists are likely to select establishments of religion as a bone of contention, sneaking up and acting out against them in protest. Great intolerance of innovation and change has been shown within the churches in the historical clashes over the right (i.e., customary) way of celebrating the sacraments, including arguments over the amount of water to be used in baptisms, the liquids and solids to be served at communion, and the types of clothes fit for priests during and between moments of celebration. Worse is the history of wars and oppression of civil liberties under the aegis of institutional religion, much of which appears in retrospect as intolerance of deviancy in relatively minor matters of conduct. But even more telling is the fact that innovation and experimentation in religion are often forced to take the form of dissent, with a rupture in the alignment of affiliations. Religious innovators have been precipitated into the establishment of new sects, with different polities from those of their mother churches and frequently with entirely different attitudes toward the power and authority of public government as well. Conformism, then, finds a very fertile soil in the arrangements of organized religion, and the alleged conformism of religious bodies is no myth.

Allport's vignette of the authoritarian personality contains the following descriptions:

> The pattern most certainly involves the status-dread type of conformity we have described—often called "authoritarian submission." With it goes the need for aligning oneself with a strong authority figure, and with a protective in-group. Present too are a strong nationalism, a subservience to existing institutions, conventionalism, rigid moralism, and a need for definiteness. Things are seen as black or white, as right or wrong, as pure or impure, as all good or all bad. There are no shades of gray, no tentativeness, no suspended judgment. The authoritarian seeks well-marked safety-islands where he can resist the confusing cross-currents of life in a democracy. A central theme is power. "We, the good people, must control them, the dangerous people." It is up to us to give to immigrants, to Negroes, what is good for them. And teachers should not worry about what children want, but teach them what is good for their souls—regardless.[39]

We are not citing this passage to intimate that religious people are particularly authoritarian, or that authoritarianism has a particular fondness for religion. Authoritarianism is almost a religion unto itself, and it seems to like God-talk of a conventional, sanctimonious, and rather trite sort. And because of its nationalistic bent, it tends to link phrases about "the God of our fathers" with phrases about "the founding fathers of our nation." It is therefore prone to bigotry toward sources of power, authority, and responsibility, those of religion as well as those of the state.

Allport makes much of the fact that the correlation between church attendance and prejudice is not simple, but curvilinear. In his own words:

> . . . frequent attenders, along with the total non-attenders, are most tolerant. It is *irregular* church attendance that correlates most highly with bigotry. . . . This finding suggests that those who are truly devout, who take their religion as an obligation, and who attend worship every week or oftener have, for the most part, successfully interiorized their faith and live according to their creed. As for the totally unchurched, they seem somehow to have escaped those enticements to bigotry that lie in casual religion. Many secular traps beset casual religion, among them an invitation to clubbishness, to status-seeking through nominal membership, to a utilitarian exploitation of the church for personal ends. All of these inducements to bigotry are pitfalls for irregular attenders.[40]

I am not entirely sure that this is a satisfactory interpretation of the facts underlying the statistical trends, for it is eminently plausible to reverse the argument and speculate that legalism, literalism, orthodoxy, conformism, and authoritarianism are potent factors in leading a person to frequent and notably regular church attendance. Neither am I persuaded by Allport's suggestion in a later article (1966),[41] that the theological doctrines of revelation and election, and the idea of a theocracy, are a special breeding ground for bigotry. Inarticulate theologies are found in some religious groups, such as the Unity movement, Christian Science, and the Oxford group, which are often prejudiced against the mainline churches. Some of the church bodies in the reformed tradition, whose history is most intimately intertwined with the doctrines of revelation and election and who have actually experimented with theocracy in practice, have been noted during the last decades for their vigorous public stand against bigotry, prejudice, and political extremism of all kinds.

There is some clarity now about the dynamics of conformism, prejudice, and authoritarianism, which has resulted from seeing these behaviors as ways of coping with stress. They are attempts to avoid fear: the fear of chaos, of dissolution, of loss of certainty, of parental disapproval, of punishment for wrongdoing and wrong thinking, and many unverbalizable anxieties as well. As all behaviors, they have an adaptive intention. But a fuller understanding of their function and origin must also take into account the drive-dynamic aspects: what are the positive satisfactions sought through all kinds of attitudes toward power, authority, and responsibility anywhere, whether the arenas are called "church," "state," or "culture"? The minimization of pain is one thing; the maximizing of pleasure is another. The need to make tolerable the helplessness of man, which Freud saw as the dynamic root of the idea of God and the motive for religion, leads to a search for a source of power which, like a father, can give protection. The religious person not merely recognizes that fatherly source of power and aligns himself with it, but also elevates it to a model of all power relations, finding satisfaction in being a "son of God" or even "like God." If this feeling is present, there is a direct, positive, narcissistic gratification over and beyond the usefulness of the idea of God as powerful Protector who wards off dangers. Fathers not only protect; they also reward and promote a sense of well-being in their children. Grace is not merely the forgiveness of sins, but active pleasure through beauty, loveliness, splendor, gladness, favor, and other gifts. "I do not condemn you any more" is not the same as "I love you."

What, then, is the *happiness* in prejudice, conformism, authoritarianism, and other forms of aligning oneself with power, whether divine, ecclesiastical, or worldly? There is an obvious pleasure in the enjoyment of privileged status, of belonging to a group, movement, or family that has managed to obtain property and possessions. These need not be solely material possessions such as land and buildings, but comprise books and *objets d'art* and access to recreational opportunities as well. Pleasure can be found in being in a position of competitive advantage for gifts, prizes, honors, public recognition, or rare economic opportunities. Some pleasure may even be found in allowing oneself to grow up slowly, without the external pressures that accelerate the pace of others who are burdened by responsibilities which come too early or in too large amounts. When one considers the undue emphasis which privileged and "settled" people place on verbal education as the exclusive vehicle for social change (a very slow change at best), it is hard to escape the inference that resistance to change (and resistance to growing up at a fair pace) is one of the key motives for those attitudes toward power and authority which maintain the *status quo* of the privileged. A degree of infantile pleasure in the enjoyment of a protected life, without having to face the increasing responsibilities for revision of all aspects of living which normally come with growing up, can be singled out as one facet of the attitudes.

One of the most striking features of prejudice is that it is so refractory to the teaching value of new facts and events which the world presents each day, and which induce many other people to acting as learners who are changing their perspectives and their attitudes, sometimes very fast. The prejudiced person does not allow himself to stand corrected by new facts, or new views of old facts. The rigidity of his attitude points not only to fear, but also to secondary gains from his position. He is fond of the pleasures we just hinted at, and he hangs onto them without realizing that a different order of pleasure may come with the new responsibilities he has thus far refused to shoulder. His secondary gains may also come from the release of aggressive tendencies which are associated with the targets of his prejudice. Crude forms of aggression are actual oppression and exploitation; slightly more subtle forms are denying others their rights and opportunities; popular forms are ridicule and denigrating descriptions of some scapegoat; still more widely used forms are the constant verbal distortions of facts, illogical reasoning, slander, and innuendo. The latter are not merely a lack of straight thinking, but an active, though slight and widespread, thought disorder induced by sadistic propensities.

The search for a source of power with which to align oneself and with which one can identify himself through emulation, if not worship, also involves conscience, and the pleasures that conscience may bestow when one follows its guidelines. Conscience is both positive and negative; it includes "do's and don't's," with rewards and punishments. The primary reward of doing a "do" is the parental smile of love; the primary punishment for doing a "don't" or omitting a "do" is the parental frown or withdrawal of love, perhaps with an aggressive attack as well. Primitive criteria of right and wrong are therefore developmentally tied in with early "do's and don't's" and in turn with bestowals and withdrawals of love. Standing for the good old-fashioned values and attitudes, in which obedience to rules is seen as a high value in its own right, is thus not only an approved and morally proper stance, but one that entails the pleasure of an inner smile from an important love object. To be with the "right people," to have the "right" view of decent government, to be affiliated with the "right" church, to have the "right morality"—all mean dynamically to be "right" with one's conscience or basic ideals, and thus to be loved and lovable. And in order to procure more of this being loved and approved by the inner voice, it is important to guard constantly against doing the "wrong" things and lining up with the "wrong people" and the "bad ideas." The preferred words of prejudiced persons for their victims are: *dirty, dangerous, seductive, subversive, uncivilized, uneducated,* and *"no good,"* all of which allude to just those drive propensities which were conspicuous in the individual's own early years of obedience training. Scapegoating fulfills not only the function of selecting a target for diffuse feelings of hatred, but also helps the individual in staying on the right track with his own conscience. He himself might succumb to temptations and assume attitudes he decries in others, but having defined them as characteristics of his scapegoat he is now constantly warned by the ugly specter "out there" not to imitate what they do. By a trick of projection and displacement he strengthens his ability to obey the "don't's" of his conscience, and in this way he secures for himself internal evidence of lovability.

RELATIONS TO NATURE AND ART

In a whimsical experiment, I once administered to twelve clergymen the Rorschach test, first with standard instructions and then with the suggestion that they might see religious symbols in the ink blots. Caution was taken to leave the idea of a "religious symbol" totally undefined—the respondents had to produce according to their own best light without any guidance whatever. The vast majority of the answers consisted of conventional religious signs rather than symbols: candelabra, votive lights, crucifixes, chalices, church steeples, crosses on hills, doves, temple entrances, totem poles, crowns, scrolls and books, pulpit chairs, seated Buddha figures, etc. The next most frequent group comprised people in religious dress or postures; priests, nuns, medicine men, ritualistic dancers, saints in robes, suppliants, missionaries watching native activities. Third in order of frequency were fanciful entities like scowling devils, demons, angels, abstract forms with arms and hands ascending. There were biblical scenes, Palestine geography, animals being slaughtered for sacrifice. There were some abstractions like good and evil suggested by the left or right side of the cards, and heaven and underworld portrayed by the top or bottom of the blots. Entirely against my expectation, scenes of nature as symbols of religious experience were rather infrequent.

One man said of Card VIII: "It has a certain . . . eh . . . love of nature; a pantheistic appreciation of an animal crossing a rock reflected in the water; a very placid scene." But in the inquiry he deflated the religious relevance by saying that it is "appropriate to romantic ideas of nature." I suspect that this derogation of nature's placidity as "romantic" reflects the temper of his theological training. A second man said of Card IV: "The mottled impression of the gray gives me a feeling of thunder clouds, which may be the mystery of God." But he hastened to add: "But I have to strain to find that." I suspect that the admission of "strain" is an allusion to his theological sophistication. To Card VIII he said: "The feeling here is of a mountaintop; a good, pleasant feeling which I associate with religion: the God-given ability to appreciate beauty, a colorful aesthetic quality." I was struck by this man's need to undo the spontaneity of this percept by rationalizing it as a "God-given ability." Ethics and social justice were this person's leitmotiv.

Only two men gave voice to a directly experienced numinosity of nature itself. One said to Card IX: "Mountains and clouds—there is a sort of awe-inspiring feeling in such natural phenomena." The other saw on Card VI: "An iceberg reflected in the water which to me is religious as a marvel of nature." To Card IX: "The entire figure is symbolic of power and splendor: a mushroom of a hydrogen bomb breaking forth into a fountain of bursting color, and water going up from the center and from the sides." In the inquiry he added: "I think the glory lies in the color—it is related to the burst of power—the beauty of the power." He could see the same card sideways as a sunset above a canyon, to which he added, "It is the beauty of nature, its greatness, strength, and perpetualness." This man could be described from other test materials as a contemplative, meditative nature lover who had a great need to make solitary walks in woodlands and who was fully aware of the religious effect of nature's numinosity on him. He also was fond of music, and saw on the Rorschach test several interesting scenes of musicmaking nymphs to which all nature, including butterflies and crawling insects, chimed in, in great merriment.

Though nature worship is not necessarily the most original form of religion, nature is important enough in the history of religion to require attention as a possible source of numinous experience. Stratton, an almost forgotten psychologist with great interest in religion, wrote:

> Throughout the sacred writings of the Judean faith and the Christian, one is seldom far from nature in its various aspects, homely or sublime—the plowed field, the green pasture, the vineyard; or the wilderness, the desert where the sun smites by day, and men are glad of the shadow of a rock in so weary a land. And in a daring drama never surpassed, the man, Job, is challenged to measure his pride of understanding against that of God who has laid the foundations of the world and sea and holds these in the hollow of his hand; who knows the treasures of the snow, could loose the bands of Orion, and bind the sweet influences of the Pleiades.

and:

... many of the great leaders of religion were immeasurably indebted
to the impression of outer nature upon them, leaving them lonely, or be-
friended; intellectually disquieted, or exalted by mystic intercourse with
the divine.[42]

One does not have to do what the ancients did and turn natural phenomena into objects of worship. Storms, wind, floods, and rain; air, sun, moon,
and stars; thunder and lightning; the rainbow; day and night; rivers and
springs; caves and mines and other "bowels of the earth"; mountains; fire;
plants, trees, and animals—all have been deified and more or less per-
sonalized. Nor does one have to do what philosophers have so often done:
to see nature's order, beauty, power, or glory and draw inferences from
these features about some basic plan, first cause, or other immanent principle. It is not necessary to focus on the seeming exceptions to natural
regularities and use miracles as proof of a transcendent divine power which
uses the cosmos as a plaything. Nor does one have to postulate a supernatural realm to account either for the rules or for the exceptions in nature's processes. It is not even pressing to turn all of nature into the category
of the created and postulate a creator or progenitor who thus demonstrates
his potency and watches over all with fatherly providence. There is something about the very measure of nature, its scope, its vastness, that forces
some people to say, as Margaret Fuller did: "I accept the universe."
Carlyle's quip: "Gad, she'd better!"[43] though in one sense quite apropos,
overlooks the possibility that other people let the cosmos spin without
their assent, or even without their knowledge. The sheer size of nature, if
one is acutely aware of it, gives rise to Jaspers' phrase: "The world is the
encompassing." But whether the encompassing is felt as an embrace or a
tight, oppressive squeeze, and whether one permits himself to be held,
carried, or squashed by it is quite a different matter.

Obviously, the responses to our small and very selective Rorschach
sample show a flight from nature into culture, from nature into some God-
concept, from outer nature into man and man-made things and thoughts.
The frequency distribution of these responses suggests that, at least for
contemporary American clergymen, nature is no longer such a great source
of inspiration and is not the primary symbol of the divine. Perhaps we may
speak of a disenchantment with nature, which could have many different
causes. In an age of science, nature may have lost the original mystery of
which Pope said:

> Nature and nature's laws lay hid in night:
> God said, *Let Newton be!* and all was light.

In an age of existential decision-making, the continuities between man and
nature may no longer be felt, so that the great chain of being stops just
short of where man and reflective consciousness begin. In an age of violence,

one may be more impressed by the chaotic features of nature which Tennyson described as "Nature, red in tooth and claw," without seeing them as expressions of the demonic and without being horrified by that specter of red. In an age of anxiety, one may feel more arrested by the mysteries of one's own inner nature and the fateful vicissitudes of human interaction than by outer nature. Maybe culture has succeeded in defending man against nature, as Freud said it should; and maybe religion is now no longer needed to defend us against the "crushing supremacy of nature," but rather against the inner man and the undesirable artifacts of culture. Perhaps the ethicists are right in pointing to man and human nature and human culture as the outstanding problems, in the face of which the "outer nature" of grasslands and forests, chasms and mountaintops has become irrelevant. Fuller's and Carlyle's universe was rather extraneous to the individual and had at least that illusory order which the transcendentalists derived from their system. Our universe is more intrinsic to ourselves, and we know of its profound irrationality.

In a recent article in *Science,* White comments on some of the sad results of man's "unnatural treatment of nature" and the rising concern over the "ecologic backlash" in the form of smog-covered cities, poisoned rivers, and billboard-cluttered highways. White's point is that man's attitude toward nature has much to do with his religious orientation. In the Judeo-Christian tradition, man is not simply a part of nature but made in God's image. He thus shares God's transcendence of nature and assumes an attitude of dominion over the rest of creation, which entails the conquest of nature, crudely or through his burgeoning scientific competence:

> Our science and technology have grown out of Christian attitudes toward man's relation to nature which are almost universally held not only by Christians and neo-Christians but also by those who fondly regard themselves as post-Christians. Despite Copernicus, all the cosmos rotates around our little globe. Despite Darwin, we are *not,* in our hearts, part of the natural process. We are superior to nature, contemptuous of it, willing to use it for our slightest whim.[44]

This is, thanks to a long historical development in which religious ideology is intertwined with practical activism, the modern predicament in the relations between man and nature. Is there any alternative? In a beautiful disclosure of buried historical wisdom, White (again from the article just cited) points to a slight underground countercurrent within this powerful tradition in the figure of St. Francis of Assisi:

> The key to an understanding of Francis is his belief in the virtue of humility —not merely for the individual but for man as a species. Francis tried to depose man from his monarchy over creation and set up a democracy of all God's creatures. With him the ant is no longer simply a homily for the

lazy, flames a sign of the thrust of the soul toward union with God; now they are Brother Ant and Sister Fire, praising the Creator in their own ways as Brother Man does in his. . . .

I am not suggesting that many contemporary Americans who are concerned about our ecologic crisis will be either able or willing to counsel with wolves or exhort birds. However, the present increasing disruption of the global environment is the product of a dynamic technology and science which were originating in the Western medieval world against which Saint Francis was rebelling in so original a way. Their growth cannot be understood historically apart from distinctive attitudes toward nature which are deeply grounded in Christian dogma.

White's remarks are not a romantic "back to nature" call, nor an exhortation to return to the fiction of a simple rustic life. I take them as a warning to re-examine the very premises, indeed the religious assumptions, underlying the attitudes of man toward nature.

Nature is, of course, an immensely complex whole, and in the practice of life each individual deals only with a small part of it. It is multiform, with great regional and seasonal variations. It is also capricious, but more so in some places than in others. It is in some spots very hospitable to man, but in large regions quite barren. But even dangerous sites like the slopes of active volcanoes have their human lovers, who dwell on them for generations, despite occasional disasters. And even the barren snowlands and scorching deserts have appreciative human inhabitants. While one would expect human attitudes toward nature to vary immensely with climate and region, there are apparently some strange, irrational love relationships.

Nevertheless, there are some attitudes toward nature which, consistent with the thesis of this chapter, are suggestive of basic dispositions toward people and other things as well. A friendly attitude toward nature may not only lead to attempts at conservation and protection, but eventuate in an erotization of the landscape and its contents. Pan and Bacchus, naiads and oreads, are anthropomorphic symbolizations of the sense of "something there" which the view of an opulent but mysterious nature sometimes instills. For "lovers of nature" the word "love" is a serious, well-chosen expression which rolls beauty, goodness, and truth into one deep sentiment. And pantheism will always be a live option for the religious inclination; in fact, it can serve as a good antidote for overabstraction and intellectualizing propensities. In contrast, a hostile and hateful attitude toward nature leads to its wanton destruction and wasteful exploitation, with just those boomerang effects on the destroyers which White described as the "ecologic crisis." Enormous crimes against nature are being perpetrated every day by millions of people, from vandalism in national parks to forest fires caused by careless disposal of matches, and a good part of these crimes are displacements onto nature of spiteful attitudes toward people. The angry boy who cannot hit his father can kick his dog, throw a rock against a tree, pull out plants, or sever a worm. Hunting done as a sport in an affluent society by well-fed people bears no trace of a love of nature, despite the charming lore that surrounds the image of the outdoorsman. It is more likely an imitation, and reduplication, of nature's own red teeth and claws. Bird-watching and wildlife photography are distinctly more peaceful and loving gestures toward the great outdoors.

Schweitzer's radical conservationism has often been criticized as an attitude unbecoming to a healer and a fighter against disease. Why should one spare mosquitoes if they are known to be carriers of infection? The key to Schweitzer's attitude lies, I believe, in the very choice of words in his ideological slogan: *reverence* for life. His posture toward nature was a devotional exercise, a religious loyalty carried out into minutiae. Nature was of immense value to him, and he brought to it the same intensity of devotion which he brought to the historical, not the idealized, Jesus. Lewis Mumford wrote of him:

> This [the study of the historical Jesus] brought him to the conviction that a true believer in Jesus must, in the twentieth century, take up the cross himself and perform some redemptive work of sacrifice. Such a work would not bring fame and honor, but, more probably, neglect, ill-health, possibly death, if not also contumely and oblivion. Plainly many evils need to be abated: many sins Western society has committed cry for atonement.[45]

Though the degree of reverence for life demonstrated by Schweitzer may be rare among Westerners brought up to conquer nature, traces of it are present in many people. Though the killing of bugs is a simple and unemotional act, the man who would kill dozens of them in one swoop is likely to halt if he perceives an insect in the process of turning from a larva into a pupa—arrested by such a wonder he decides to aid nature and give the pupa a lease on life. Hunters follow some code of honor that spares the female animal when young depend on her. This is more than a calculating "conservationism" that thinks ahead to next year's supply; it has some element of reverence in it.

For the pantheist, nature is the *imago Dei*. For the dualist, nature's numinosity has a Janus face: it is divine and demonic. For theists of the middle way, nature's *fascinans* and *tremendum* are only pointers to the more sublime, more orderly, more ethical, and more beautiful power of a transcendant creator and sustainer who is nature's God. In this view the *imago Dei* has shifted its locus from nature to man, and the special bond thus established between the creator and the human creature justifies man in becoming a creator in his own right: he produces art, imposes an aesthetic order, and learns to appreciate all things from the perspective of beauty. In

Pope's enigmatic phrase: "All nature is but art unknown to thee," art is no longer imitation of nature. The higher principle is art, and whether it be divine or human art, the aesthetic order transcends the forms which nature offers.

Freud saw in art an instance of illusion formation. In making or enjoying art, people render themselves slightly independent of the outside world and obtain aesthetic satisfactions which may substitute for those which nature fails to yield, or compensate for the frustrations it inflicts. Art gives pleasure and consoles through a "mild narcosis." In addition, Schachtel has pointed out that the aesthetic approach to reality, mediated as it is by the artistic *image,* can at times stand in the way to a live encounter with the people and things in the world.

Art and religion have often stood in a tense relationship to each other. Goethe felt that the man who has access to science and art has no need for religion; the latter is for those who are deprived of the scientific and the artistic spirit. Kierkegaard developed a sharp dialectical struggle between the aesthetic and the religious stages of life. The widespread fear and contempt toward artists has undoubtedly one root in the conservatism of the mass of church members. Reading the Bible as a book of beauty is to many people contradictory to reading it as a statement of infallible truth. Architects and decorators of new churches seldom have the majority of the congregation warmly on their side. Quakers made their meetinghouses barren of all aesthetic pleasures; Puritans reduced the playful visual ornamentation of church buildings to the stark neutrality of whitewashed walls—though they failed to thwart the increasing magnificence of the more abstract art of music. In fact, the relations between music and Protestantism are a good example of the contrary impulse toward a profound intimacy between religion and art. The ancient Jew praised God "in the beauty of holiness"—seeking a bond between the aesthetic and the numinous, while at the same time banning the "graven image." The Byzantine branch of Christendom first prohibited religious art and then ritualized it by chaining the painters' spontaneity to strict codes of color and form. Organized religion is a great patron of the arts, but also a jealous contender with art, artists, and art lovers.

Could it be that these tense relations between religion and art reflect an intuitive appreciation of Freud's statement about the illusory and narcotic qualities of art? Could it be that the religionist sees in human creativity the danger of the creature aspiring to become the creator? Is it possible that the religious purist has always sensed the danger of the art lover's enslavement to his objects, of the artwork becoming an idol? Or is the basic uneasiness about art in religionists an instance of asceticism which distrusts all sensory impressions as vain, distracting, transient, earthly, and base, if not works of the devil? Is religion's ambivalence toward art perhaps enhanced by an awareness that art, through its choice of subject and medium, can become a frivolous pastime?

Answers to some of these questions are provided by the curious phenomenon of "religious art"—an amalgam of two illusions, a compound of two narcotics, an intersection of two perspectives on reality. Says Tillich:

> The aesthetic realm is used by the church for the sake of the religious arts. In them the church expresses the meaning of its life in artistic symbols. The content of the artistic symbols (poetic, musical, visual) is the religious symbols given by the original revelatory experiences and by the traditions based on them. The fact that artistic symbols try to express in ever changing styles the given religious symbols produces the phenomenon of "double symbolization". . . . The churches knew that aesthetic expressiveness is more than a beautifying addition to devotional life. They knew that expression gives life to what is expressed—it gives power to stabilize and power to transform—and therefore they tried to influence and control those who produced religious art.[46]

The "double symbolization" in religious art is an interesting phenomenon. It can be seen as religion's way of coping with the cultural institution of art, and as art's way of coping with the cultural institution of religion, mediated by individuals and stylized by groups. Two original psychic functions, the religious and the aesthetic, are exercised at once. If they are felt to conflict with each other, for the reasons which we formulated as questions in the preceding paragraph, a compromise may be reached through religious art which actually shrinks the realm and dampens the spirit of each function by tying the Holy to the aesthetic forms of a period, and by limiting the artistic imagination to a sanctified object or style. The result is disastrous for religion as well as art. It gives rise to fashionably bearded, sentimental Jesus pictures, harp-playing angels, and sterile Madonnas in convenient wallet-sized prints; it produces the trite melodies and poor poetry of pietistic hymns; it leads to the use of glossy pictures of the Last Supper and a heroic Jesus as decorative emblems on the walls of church basements. Neither art nor religion come into their own in these compromises. Tillich's double symbolization is reduced to the duplicate use of signs or emblems, which in turn give the user little more than a badge of identity as belonging to a devout crowd.

But if neither of the functions is seriously conflict-laden, their joint operation may enrich either perspective, with more durable or more intense benefits for the individual. Goodenough has recognized this pleasurable situation in his description of the aesthetic type of religious experience. He sees certain people's search for form in the formless running parallel with their search for protection from the *tremendum:*

> Those are poor indeed who have not found the confusion of their lives at least temporarily resolved into form, that is, beauty, as they have listened

to the creations of their companions. Orpheus with his lyre still has the divine power of stilling the savage beasts within us. Those who best know all forms of art will understand my identifying the expression of art, at first or second hand, with religious experience. The experience so warms and beautifies that I wish that I had a less frigid term for it than "the religion of aestheticism."[47]

In this statement, however, we have moved from religious art per se to the wider interactions between the aesthetic and the numinous experience, and what Goodenough says is that the beautiful and the numinous may be one, ultimately, for the person who can freely use both approaches. Music, dance, the visual arts, and eventually sexual intercourse are great condensations of the richness of experience which comes with an erotic commitment to the Holy and the beautiful.

The interactions between the aesthetic and the religious perspectives are enhanced by the play character that both share. We saw in earlier chapters the importance of the play element in ritual, worship, and other religious activities, and the important role which perfectionism plays in the stylization of religious acts. Art too has strong play features. It plays with the ordinary sensory experiences of vision, hearing, and touch by the "make-believe" reality of the object and the medium in their particular, unique combination. In the dance and in sports it yields the motor pleasures of making the perfect movement, performing the precise and meaningful gesture, showing sublime mastery over space and time. These are erotic pleasures of the highest degree for which the word "ecstatic" is a proper expression.

X

Relations to the Self

A YOUNG GIRL of twelve reported to me one day that she had recently had recurrent dreams which provoked some anxiety. All she remembered was that letters occurred in them, scrambled and disorderly, floating in space. When I asked her which letters she remembered seeing, she said *E*'s and *M*'s. With a little further prodding she herself discovered quickly and with much animation that they spelled the word *me,* a topic she was much concerned with during that period. The self is often a puzzle, a source of anxiety, a task, something in transition, and a value. The self can think about itself, and even dream about itself. But the reflexive pronouns in the preceding sentence are awkward and confusing. What or who is the self that does the thinking and the dreaming, and what or who are the "itselfs" thought about and dreamed about? Are they really the same, as the language seems to suggest?

In an era of existentialism, where *being* and *isness* and *I am* are the nuclear terms, it is refreshing to ponder Woodger's remark that it is impossible to know that something exists without knowing more about it. When I say *I am,* I am not merely affirming existence in the subject mode—I am also positing an I that is five feet nine inches tall, fifty-one years old, male, in good health, head of a family, and several hundred more qualifications of which I am focally or dimly aware when I say *I am.* Even the I of pure consciousness, of which the philosophers speak, is in the ultimate reduction when all its possible contents have been objectified, an essence of sorts: an intention, a tension, a life process, a personal consciousness. The I may be experienced as rich or poor, strong or weak, victor or victim, lovable or hateful, free or unfree, happy or sad, in grace or doomed; but in all these experiences it always does something, quietly or overtly, for consciousness is by definition an active process. Even when it takes preconscious or unconscious forms, which momentarily defy verbalization, the I asserts itself always *in a certain way,* for instance in the automatism of an epileptic fit, in the oddities of sleepwalking, or in the strange doings of the amnesic person who goes to the police station to declare that he does not know his name and identity and address anymore.

This chapter will explore the many senses of I and me, the feelings attached to them, the complications arising from the possibility of using *I* reflexively, and some of the implications of religious assertions about *I* and *me*. It will do so in several steps, through the following sections:

1. Consciousness of self
2. The ego and the body
3. The superego and the ego-ideal
4. *Cur Deus Homo*

The last section is an attempt to relate the intrapsychic complexities to some of the most central Christian doctrines in order to explore how certain theological propositions about the deity and his activities are related to the self-experience of human beings.

CONSCIOUSNESS OF SELF

When he was still a psychiatrist, Jaspers described the consciousness of self as a complex of at least four attributes.[1] James, who like Jaspers became a philosopher, addressed himself to the same problem of the self and wrote a magnificent chapter about it in his *Principles*.[2] James's categories of the material self, the social self, the spiritual self, and the pure ego are so well known and have become so completely absorbed into the body of psychology that they need no exposition here. Jaspers' four attributes are of a different order and lend themselves more readily to correlation with religious constructs and experiences.

The first attribute of consciousness of self is its contrast with the *other* and the *beyond*. The self is defined by differentiation from the nonself, which is all other people, all objects, and the whole outer world. Otto's idea of the numinous as the "wholly Other" (*das ganz Andere*) not only stresses the radical otherworldliness of the deity as compared with the created world, but also puts the *Other* over against the *I* of any believer so as to discourage him from assuming any direct affinity between himself and his creator. This is an important theme in Hebrew and Christian religion. God is always the *not-I*, and the self is always the *not-God*. Consequently, the divine impress, if any, on the creature is difficult to conceptualize. Immanence doctrines may not be pushed so far as to lead to fantasies of identity between the creator and the creature; they are to be more than amply counterbalanced by transcendence doctrines which maintain the radical *beyondness* and *otherness* of the deity. The divine impress is cautiously described as the *imago Dei* which, in orthodoxy, may be taken as a seal or stamp. It borders on heresy when it is taken, as in Gnosticism, as a spark of divine light or fire in the human breast. Rivers of ink and mountains of paper have been used in deciphering the meaning of that mysterious code in Genesis: "So God created man in his own image, in the image of God he created him." Gregory of Nyssà[3] interpreted it to mean that human nature is midway between two extremes: between the divine, incorporeal nature and the irrational nature of the brute creation, sharing aspects of both. It is Godlike, but not God. Irenaeus[4] distinguished between the *imago* which refers to the natural features which link the creature inevitably with the author of creation, and *similitudo* which refers to a special divine grace given to Adam whereby he might be loyal to his creator's purposes.[5] The same Irenaeus struggled over the restoration of the *imago* in his account of the Incarnation, which led him to the phrase that Jesus Christ "became what we are to make us what He is." This idea of God becoming man has also entailed rivers of ink and reams of paper for its articulation, and safeguarding it from heretical associations has been one of the major enterprises in the history of Christian dogma.

Apparently, then, the distinctions between the self and the divine Other are a major concern in religion, at least within the Judeo-Christian tradition. Religious slogans such as "in tune with the universe" or "God is all" suggest a different emphasis in which the boundaries between the self and the nonself are far less sharp. In certain forms of Buddhism the problem is handled by declaring the self unreal, and substituting for it the dharmas, which are much like philosophical categories to the Western mind. Whatever the specific formulation may be, the deep concern over this problem gives rise to tense and paradoxical statements, like this one by Meister Eckhart:

> God is in all things. The more he is in things the more he is out of things. The more he is within, the more he is without.[6]

The Meister also called God "the denial of denials,"[7] and like most other great mystics, he spent part of his life trying to experience the relations between himself and the Other on a new plane, by manipulating the usual boundaries of the self. Although mysticism takes many forms, it always plays on the highest rungs of the abstraction ladder: is it possible to experience oneness when consciousness dooms man to a twosome or a plurality? Can the subject-object split in knowing be overcome? And if it is overcome, momentarily, can the experience still be considered a form of knowing? Can it be verbalized?

Mystics divide not only on the path to be taken, but on the outcome of the desired experience. Some will try to *empty* their mind to such an extent that the divine can enter in and fill it with its own plenitude. Others will *open* their mind and its organs, so that they may more clearly see the divine Other as a breath-taking spectacle. Still others will allow their own mind to *stretch* like a balloon and rise to such heights that it loses its boundaries with a burst and is taken up in the atmosphere. And then there are those who are convinced that the deity is already within them, and that it only needs careful nurturing to grow and to fill the self from within with the Other, who finally takes over in his ultimate authority. Romain Rolland spoke of the oceanic feeling of oneness with the universe.[8] Freud interpreted this as a primordial form of experience, dating from before the distinctions between self and others are made; one in which the infant wallows in his own narcissistic feeling of happiness and goodness without recognizing that food and shelter have come to him as a gift from others, who have only to withhold it to precipitate him into terror.

When a few years ago a movie star described God as "a doll," she might not so much have reduced the size of the deity as enlarged her own. Dolls are toy babies, and those that play with them assume themselves to be the producers and generators on whose good will the doll's existence depends. The bloated all-mother bears and, who knows, she may even hatch a god. This is an extreme form of self-inflation which expands the boundaries of the self until they are beyond all horizons.

Consciousness of the self also hinges on the awareness of activity, according to Jaspers. The self is a source of energy, a wellspring of action. The self is an actor, not merely a cog in a machine. In some people, however, this aspect of consciousness is diminished—they do feel just like a cog in a machine that moves without initiative. To be active also means to have a certain degree of autonomy and an area to be active in, perhaps a certain measure of freedom. But how much self-action should the human being be allowed, granted a divine scheme in which he is to function, by appointment? Religion addresses itself to consciousness of the self as action center in very interesting ways. One way is through the idea of possession. The prophet claims that he does not speak his own words but those of another one who sent him. The glossolaliac claims his utterings to be not his own activity, but the outpouring of a spirit within him. Ecstasies overpower a person from without, or by infusion. Even dreams are given or sent to a person, revealing cosmic powers which act on their own, without participation by the dreamer. In all these cases a peculiar disclaimer of self-activity is made in the name of religion and the person feels used, filled, or smitten by energies coming from without.

The case becomes more subtle when self-activity is not wholly denied but reinterpreted in the light of autonomy versus obedience. The book of Jonah shows a prophet struggling not so much over the question of energy and activity as over the ethical question of whose will shall prevail, his or Yahweh's. He does not behave like an automaton; he actively grudges and argues about the sense of the deity's arrangements. He flees from the divine command, he is actively disobedient by pitting his will over against the divine will, and only "when his soul fainted within him" did he "remember the Lord." When he finally decides to obey the command he does his job, only to become spiteful when he sees that Yahweh may have a change of heart and spare the city of Nineveh whose destruction Jonah had announced.

Still more subtle is the case of those who, like Paul, selectively disclaim consciousness of activity as a prop for the self, by holding that any good in them is grace. Paul said: "it is no longer I who live, but Christ who lives in me" (Gal. 2:20). The statement occurs in the context of another assertion which holds that the old Paul had died. All activity from the former self has come to nought; a new self has arisen which is—qua activity—a gift which the new Paul may enjoy and exercise, but not rightfully claim as his own. He identifies himself with both the dead and the risen Jesus, but grants that his own death was self-initiated whereas his new life, after conversion, is really the life of another one within him. In that latter phrase lies a note of caution, and a whole theology which prohibits fusion between the self and the other and prevents the new self from becoming bloated by its remarkable gains. The new self is no less active than the old self, but it now has the insight that much spontaneous self-initiated activity tends in a sinful direction. If grace is bestowed from outside, who sins in sinning? Paul and millions of Christians with him feel that the consciousness of the self as an action center is prone to lead to pride and arrogance, to extreme self-reliance, and eventually to the self-assertion that denies creatureliness—in a word, to sin.

The third aspect of consciousness of self is based on a sense of identity. One knows that he remains the same person through time, despite gross physical and mental changes from infancy to old age. On account of this identity one can make statements like Paul's famous words:

> When I was a child, I spoke like a child, I thought like a child, I reasoned like a child; when I became a man, I gave up childish ways (1 Cor. 13:11).

He was aware of being the same Paul of Tarsus throughout his past and in the present and on to the future until his demise, no matter what drastic changes might occur in his body or mind. Paul's case is interesting also because he had had an incisive conversion experience on account of which he felt a sufficient difference between his old self and his new self to name them distinctly. His original name was Saul; after conversion he changed it to Paul. He also developed a theology in which the mythical Adam is the Old Adam or the Old Man, with Jesus Christ being the New Man, through participation in whom all men can become New Adams.[9] When certain transitions in life are felt to be very radical, people do indeed often take recourse to a change of name. On taking vows toward joining an order, the religious assume a new name, usually taken from some saint who has personal significance for the novice. The Christian name given in baptism was originally meant to set the baptized adult apart, to himself and others, from the natural self he was before his symbolic rebirth. In the practice of infant baptism the Christian name lost its time-marking character and became identical with the given name or first name.

Precisely because the continuity of the self is such an important background feeling that accompanies all our acts, some changes and upheavals attain the value of turning points, dividing life retrospectively into a *before* and *after*. Married people are wont to do this in regard to their wedding date. It occurs with serious illnesses and accidents. We saw that it occurs with conversions. It occurs with all deep, transforming events, even episodes of mental illness. Clifford Beers wrote in *A Mind That Found Itself,* which is an account of his own mental disturbance:

> Since that August 30th, which I regard as my second birthday (my first was on the 30th of another month), my mind has exhibited qualities which, prior to that time, were so latent as to be scarcely distinguishable. As a result, I find myself able to do desirable things I never before dreamed of doing—the writing of this book is one of them. . . . No man can be born again, but I believe I came as near it as ever a man did.[10]

Boisen, whose work we cited earlier, saw a definite link between the dynamics of his mental illness and the religious strivings which characterized all his life. Reflecting upon his recent recovery from one catatonic episode, he stated in a letter to a friend:

> After a short talk Dr. Chambers remarked, "Quite a change, isn't there? It's certainly a good ad for the hospital." Of course, I was glad to hear him say that. I am indeed appreciative of all they have done for me here, but with his conclusion I cannot agree. If I have recovered, as I think I have, I cannot ascribe it to the methods of treatment, but rather to the curative forces of the religion which was largely responsible for the disturbed condition.[11]

Much later he wrote in his autobiography:

> Ideas of self-sacrifice, of death, of world disaster, of mystical identification, of rebirth, of reincarnation, of prophetic mission are to be found not only in my case but in other acutely disturbed schizophrenics also. As I have shown elsewhere, such ideas seem to form a sort of constellation which is distinctive of acute schizophrenia. Where we find one of these ideas we are likely to find the others also. Such ideas do have meaning. Their basis may be found in the structure of the human psyche and in the constructive aspects of the schizophrenic experience.[12]

Other parts of Boisen's autobiography clearly show how much he was preoccupied with renewal and rebirth. He had the strange idea that the race needed to be reorganized on new genetic principles for which he proposed a mythical "family of four." The hydrotherapy tubs in the state hospital where he was treated became part of the scheme. The room contained just four tubs and "the psychopathic ward was the meeting place between this world and the world beyond, and the tubroom was the place for the regeneration of wornout personalities."[13] The meaning of baptism as rebirth could hardly be more positively expressed. Boisen felt reborn, regenerated, and converted by his great psychic upheaval, despite several relapses afterward and despite his candor of accepting for these episodes the classical psychiatric label of "acute schizophrenia, catatonic type." He did not disown his disorganized periods. His sense of identity as continuity through time remained firm, as his autobiography shows, and he did not disclaim his past, nightmarish as it was. But he did celebrate his crisis as a turning point separating the old man from the new man within him.

He could have done something else, for which I need first to formulate Jaspers' fourth aspect of the consciousness of self. It is the consciousness of singularity: the awareness that I am one, and only one at a time. The person is ordinarily a unity which permits no break or fragmentation. If it breaks or falls apart, it may assume the pathological form of multiple personality or split personality, and even then a semblance of unity is striven for by the processes of memory which make Mr. Jekyll amnesic for Mr. Hyde, and vice versa. Boisen could have dissociated himself from his old premorbid self, and he could have repressed the memories of his nightmarish episodes. The fact that he did not is to the credit of his integrative and synthesizing capacities, which in turn may have made him feel all the more strongly that his break with reality was not quite complete but something like the "dark night of the soul" of which St. John of the Cross wrote.

Disunity of the self can have many shadings, from James' descriptions of the divided self[14] to the phenomenon of possession in which a foreign body is felt to exist within the person. The divided self is likely to be an awareness of something dysharmonious, something not right which the person strives in vain to unify. Its most common form tends to be ethical, as in Paul's statement: "For I do not do the good I want, but the evil I do not want is what I do" (Rom. 7:19). Paul followed it by a disclaimer which hints at some dissolution of the feeling of singularity: "Now if I do what I do not want, it is no longer I that do it, but sin which dwells within me" (Rom. 7:20). This diminution of singularity is so common that it has almost become a hallmark of the pious attitude, provided that it be buttressed by repentance which does assume personal responsibility for what was first said to be "no longer I, but sin within me." In possession, by the demonic or the divine, the awareness of singularity is so diminished that the claim of responsibility no longer holds: the "other within" is both felt and reasoned to be utterly alien, projected as something numinous which with its superior power holds the person in its grip.

Somewhere between these two forms of diminished feeling of singularity lie the many phenomena of attempted dissociation of undesirable propensities from the better or higher aspects of the personality. With religious sanction, the whole body may be seen as an inferior, sinful, or unfit piece of baggage that the person has to drag along on his journey to a better land, in the hope of being delivered from it before long. When ascetic neglect of the body becomes a fierce punishment of the body, the mechanism of dissociation is called upon for the good reason that the self-inflicted pain might otherwise thwart the ascetic's noble intentions. Sex may undergo the same fate. When it is held to be a base or evil impulse, a person may make efforts to disown it, only to be severely shaken in his self-image when his attempts fail. He or she then "falls," which is a numinously charged biblical expression alluding to the serpent as an extraneous cause. Clearly, the evildoer is not the person himself, but someone else and the question of responsibility is delicately held in suspense. Aggressive impulses and feelings of intense anger may also give rise to a diminution of the sense of singularity, particularly when the person has been taught that anger is unbecoming to a man who aspires to the saintly life. The expression "in a fit of anger" and the phenomenon of temper tantrums point to what happens in such cases: the anger and the muscle movements are disowned as not quite coming from the person himself. The person "surrenders" to superior powers and claims that he "was not himself" in the fit or the outburst. He was "overcome," momentarily, by alien upsurges; he had an "uncontrollable impulse." The latter phrase even has some legal stature which may turn the person in the law courts from an offender into a patient.

We have seen that the consciousness of self rests on a number of functions which allow some flexibility, but which must operate within narrow limits in order to preserve the person as an integrated whole. We have also seen that religious ideas affect the self in numberless ways, and that religion does not take the natural self for granted. Religion evaluates the self, tests it, attempts to mold it, and prescribes a course for it. But in order to explore in greater detail the ways in which religion does all these things, we must first consider another set of concepts whereby the intrapsychic complexities of the person can become articulated.

THE EGO AND THE BODY

It is quite an achievement to say "I." The toddler says "Johnny" or "Jeanie." Saying "I" presupposes not only the various aspects of consciousness which Jaspers singled out, but also the smooth functioning of an agency that perceives, thinks, feels, speaks, and acts on behalf of the person to whom the little word I refers. Saying "I" requires speaking, the capacity to perceive one's body and to hear one's own voice, the registration of feelings of pride or shyness, the use of the lungs and the larynx for the production of sounds, the innervation of muscles to stand up and direct one's gaze to an audience, and the active guiding of a stream of thought to result in a meaningful set of ideas and a sensible message. Depending on the purposes at hand, saying "I" also implies negative action: not to be so preoccupied with breathing that the voice becomes halting, not to mind a slight bladder pressure at the moment, not to permit memories of a week-old event to enter into consciousness, not to feel again last year's lonesomeness, and not to be so self-conscious that the whole act of saying "I" results in an embarrassing failure.

It is important to make a distinction between the *self* as a name for the total person, and the *ego* as a name for the various executive and administrative functions within the person which the previous paragraph attempted to sketch. The ego is an intrapsychic specialization, undoubtedly a product of evolution, which represents certain governing principles for fostering the survival of the person as a whole.[15] It provides the person with the satisfaction he needs to survive and to grow, and adapts the person to the environment on which he depends for his existence. Besides the ego, the person has other functions which are specialized along different lines or principles. Foremost are the drives and needs which demand gratification, instantly and oblivious of consequences, according to their strength and native make-up and cultural modification. We encountered them already in Chapter VIII as the energies and affects which lead to object relations, and have constantly referred to them throughout this book. They are comprised in the structure of the id, a region of limited access or "off bounds." Another specialized group of functions within the person comprises the functions of conscience and the value system: the superego and the ego-ideal. These are the internal representatives of cultural mores and social structures, with their rewards and sanctions, which aid the ego in its executive functions by automatizing the judgments that have to be made. We will discuss these ancillary psychic structures in detail in the next section.

For the moment, our concern is the ego and the tools it has in order to discharge its role as the administrator and organizer of the person. So far, we have used various metaphors to describe it: executive, administrator, organizer, adapter. We could add: integrator, synthesizer, unifier. From the commercial and political arena we could borrow the roles of bargainer and arbitrator to describe the ego's primary function. Using still another metaphor we could say that, as head of the psychic household, the ego is to effect the best possible give and take between various parties clamoring for recognition and rewards: the physical world with its immutable features; the social world with its opportunities and demands; the inner drives and needs which insist on satisfaction; the internalized value systems whereby a person judges himself, from his overt behavior to his innermost thoughts; and the body with its sensory and motor functions and its fantastic intricacy of co-ordinated organ systems and physiological processes. How can this be done with the least effort for the best possible results and all-round satisfaction of all parties concerned?

With a final set of metaphors, derived from Menninger, Mayman, and Pruyser's *The Vital Balance,* the ego's role could be described as homeostatic and equilibrating. Having access to the sensory and the motor system, and deriving energies from the organism at large, the ego maintains all organismic processes at an optimum level of efficacy, fluctuating only within certain tolerance limits. Like the thermostat of a heating plant, which registers the effect of the system's output on the environment and automatically switches the system on and off between an upper and lower margin, the ego registers the organism's efficiency and accelerates or decelerates certain processes to keep them at optimal levels of comfort and productivity. Like the physiology of internal organs, much of this is automatized and requires no special conscious effort. Breathing, digesting, and many movements and sensory registrations proceed by reflex. Many acquired skills proceed by habit. Some acts, like purposive thinking and problem-solving, require conscious effort and guidance. The total organismic system with its multiple subsystems is kept in a dynamic equilibrium at the lowest possible cost in work and the highest possible gains in satisfaction—not in isolation, but within the ecological supersystem of which the person is a part: the relevant natural and cultural world.[16]

The ego's tools for effectuating such an equilibrium are the psychological processes which form the chapter headings in this book. But these are cast in rather formal psychological language: perception, cognition, emotion, etc. In homelier language, the ego's work of equilibration consists of relatively circumscribed acts such as waking up or falling asleep, touching, eating, boasting, laughing, crying, praying, talking things out, thinking, making muscle movements, engaging in fantasy and dreaming, using symbols, making changes in the environment, smoking, drinking, fidgeting, and feeling little aches and pains in the body. Dozens of these acts can be described, and every person selects from them his own repertoire. They are the coping devices whereby the fluctuations of everyday life are dealt with. Most of them cost little; no more than the average price for living. Most of them are socially approved and widely shared among different people, though with some selectivity in different cultures.

But events may occur, from within or without, which tax or strain the organism to a degree that upsets the accustomed equilibrium and eludes the habitual simple coping devices. The ego then has recourse to emergency measures in order to counteract the upset or to modify the organism's mode of functioning under altered circumstances—but still for the same purposes of a gratifying survival. Emergency coping devices cost more and entail some risks. They are more elaborate than the ordinary ones. They have unwanted side effects. They are often socially irritating. They are personally exhausting. They may become habits whose use is maintained far beyond the moment of emergency. They are, depending on their costliness to the individual or to his fellowmen, symptoms which signal some degree of dysorganization.

One can grade these emergency coping devices according to various criteria. From an economic point of view, their cost to the psychic household is an important dimension. From the psychodynamic point of view, they can be graded according to the degree of satisfaction they secure. From the adaptive point of view, they can be judged according to the degree of reality contact achieved in their use. From the developmental point of view, the degree of growth allowed, stagnation caused, or regression entailed is an important yardstick. From the social point of view, the degree of eccentricity and the nuisance value of the coping devices are critical. Structurally, it is important to assess whether the intrapsychic boundaries between the ego, superego, ego-ideal, and id are intact or dissolved, and whether the distinctions between mind and body are maintained. Using various combinations of these criteria, all psychiatric disturbances from mild neurotic discomforts to severe mental aberrations and eventually to death through exhaustion or suicide, can be seen as points on a continuum of coping devices and emergency reactions.

In the progression from ordinary coping devices to more extreme emergency measures, what starts out as an occasional relaxing drink becomes periodic drunkenness and eventually alcoholism. What starts out as a slight difficulty in falling asleep at night becomes sleeplessness and eventually a chaotic waking and sleeping cycle. What starts out as a slight worry becomes a preoccupation, then obsessional thinking, and finally a severe thought disorganization. An appropriate, *ad hoc* repression of a painful event may become a blanket forgetting, and eventually a severe obnubilation of the contents of consciousness. A slight headache becomes a severe headache, then a splitting headache with gross incapacitation every Sunday. An angry mood turns into swearing (which is still only verbal), but as control weakens it may entail a swing at the furniture, then at a pet, and eventually at a person. It may lose sight of its targets entirely and become a wild furor, or rowdy vandalism. An apprehension enlarges to a fear, which may turn into a phobia. Or it may not focus on anything at all but become general jitteriness, or worse, an anxiety state or a panic. Watchfulness increases to hyperalertness which leaves the person without sleep: in perpetual fear of danger or assault he may start to carry arms, threaten people, and develop delusions of persecution, perhaps organized into a paranoid system of pending world disaster. Neglect of the body may become destruction of its parts, or even of the whole person. Hundreds of acts may thus be described as parts of a series which ranges from innocuous or helpful gambits to very costly, dangerous, and destructive moves, some of which may become hardened into the very character structure of the individual.

People are variously endowed with coping devices and acquire their repertoire through various learning processes. Each person has his own box of tools, so to speak, and the tools he has may be a source of pride or shame. But whether the toolbox is well equipped or of meager content, the successful use of the tools is satisfying. The use of all talents is gratifying; the exercise of all functions is exhilarating. As a consequence, success in coping with the inevitable stresses and strains of life gives a sense of mastery. It gives pleasure over and beyond the gratifications which adequate coping secures for the drives, and the satisfactions it obtains from the environments in the form of praise or encouragement. Good coping means competence, which enhances one's worth and lovableness in one's own eyes. It raises self-esteem, whether other people recognize one's success or not. Competence is indeed such an important motif in life that some psychologists have raised it to the status of a special drive.

We are thus making a distinction between the coping devices as such and the more general act of coping. The reader may already have noticed that some of the most commonly used coping devices are specific religious acts. There is *praying,* a device to which millions of people take recourse routinely to bolster their courage, lift their spirit, and gain confidence for meeting the minor emergencies of each day. If the emergencies become great, one may pray more frequently, more personally, more fervently. It provides an opportunity for talking things out with someone, whether the "someone" is a personal god or a more nebulous idea of power and wisdom. It also provides an opportunity for thinking things over, quietly and in privacy, in the bosom of the family, or in the corporate fellowship of the church. Closely linked with these aspects of praying is *confessing,* which can range from the sharing of a secret with another person, one's god, or even the observing part of one's self, to a ceremonial outpouring of one's shady thoughts and acts to a religious official who hears them sacerdotally, representing the deity and the church in the double attitude of disciplining and forgiving.

Worshiping is another coping device. Whether it be done daily, weekly, or yearly, regularly or irregularly, simply or with pomp and circumstance, worshiping consoles, invigorates, gives tension release, corrects attitudes, and in a dozen other ways boosts the morale of those who need it. The chapters on the part processes of perception, thought, language, emotion, and action have described many of the psychological riches which people find in worship, each in his own way, subjectively. *Singing* and music-making, which are important parts of worship, are excellent means of tension release and have, as all arts, also a synthesizing effect. Participation in *sacramental acts* shades over into the very basic functions of eating and drinking, as in communion celebrations, and washing and cleansing, as in baptismal rites. But in addition to these primitive functions of nature, they are charged with beauty, splendor, and power, and give the corporate support of others who share the act, shoulder to shoulder, in solidarity. Ritual gives structure and support; it heals and gives strength; like the symbol, it reveals and conceals.

One of the most basic forms of coping with stress is *fantasy formation.* If one is angry there can be much release in spinning secret fantasies of revenge. If certain things are missing in life, one can restore some balance by daydreaming about riches. If satisfactions are meager or absent, one can have a pleasant moment through imagined fulfillment. If sources of strength are insufficiently available in the environment, one can playfully or seriously assume that they are yet there, though maybe far away. What is more, when life is bleak, one can engage in the fantasy that somewhere in the universe there is someone who thinks of him with compassion, perhaps with benevolent intentions, and perhaps even with the power of making his deepest wish come true. The imagination becomes religious because religion, as Erikson states, "elaborates on what feels profoundly true even though it is not demonstrable."[17]

Religion may call upon the imagination, just as the imagination may call upon religion. For religion is usually not an entirely private creation, but very much an objective phenomenon. Religion is "around," just like art and science and mechanics are around. It belongs to the oldest cultural and societal givens. Both as ideology and institution, religion is so patently "there" that it is difficult to evade it. Therefore, when anyone's imagination is unleashed in moments of duress, there is a good chance that it will absorb religious ideas. The culture is full of them in its language, representations, acts, and values.

According to the law of effect, when any of the above-mentioned coping devices helps in the re-establishment of psychic equilibrium, when it releases some tension, when it gives some relief, or when it provides some satisfaction, it is likely to be used again in times of need. Objective reinforcement may come to the aid of such subjective strengthening of the habit through social approval, the example of elders and peers, and the shared pragmatism of the culture which condones everything that "works."

But precisely at this point an interesting thing is bound to happen which requires us to shift our focus from the coping devices to the coper, i.e., the ego which copes in order to preserve the integrity of the person. The coper who uses religious coping devices becomes quickly part of a system of like-behaving people who, in sharing their observations and experiences with each other, introduce certain corrections. "So you pray, but do you pray often enough, hard enough, and with tears in your eyes? What do you pray for?" Or: "Are you really contrite when you make your confession?" And so the coper learns from a thousand disputes and exhortations that the pragmatic rule of his success in using religious coping maneuvers is, within the religious system, a very fallible index of his adequacy as a religious man— whatever his successes at coping might be. He is taught to be critical of his own subjective sense of mastery. He is told not to glory in his feeling of competence. He must see these not as an achievement but as a gift bestowed on him through the grace of the giver, or by the sheer plenitude of the source of power which reaches him by its own momentum. So now he must learn to cope with a new problem, and a new stress: the danger of competence becoming pride or arrogance, which is particularly great when the coping devices used are religious activities. For the numinous is the *tremendum* as well as the *fascinans*: it gives and takes away; it makes and breaks; it is both desirable and dangerous.

When numinosity has become part of one's life it is another reality to which the ego must seek adaptation. In looking for a perennial source of strength by projecting an all-father on the mysterious edges of the universe, one soon discovers that he may have projected more than was originally intended. The projection is now a reality in its own right—indeed it is *the* encompassing reality, more powerful, more enduring, and in a sense more enigmatic than the reality of the senses. The transcendent demands from its believers a profound loyalty. It demands not only faith, but evidences of faith, and one of these is that the realities of the physical and social world are no longer the only compass points. Adaptations must thus be made to the reality of the senses and the reality of the unseen. This is no easy matter. Many people ease it off for themselves by imposing upon the conglomerate of realities a distinction between the real (in the sense of demonstrable) and the ideal (in the sense of a far-off demand or an option that could be postponed). Another distinction that is often tried is splitting up all reality into several realities which are more or less separate from each other: the world of the here and now, and the world of eternity; the terrestrial city and the heavenly city; Sunday's world and the workaday world. These distinctions are themselves forms of adaptation to the realities one has contact with. They are coping maneuvers which lessen the stress of keeping things unified.

Other forms of adaptation can be seen in the lives of religious innovators. The creative religionist seems to make a whole new assessment of all the aspects of reality he has experienced. In fact, he espouses a perspectival view which keeps reality unified, but with multiple aspects, each seen *sub specie aeternitatis*. He refuses to seek refuge in the religious establishment with its codes and institutions and common habit patterns. Renewal is sought not only *in* religion, but also *of* religion, and it drives searchers like Kierkegaard to write an *Attack upon Christendom*. It drove the mystic Eckhart to say:

. . . Prate not about God, for prating about him thou dost lie. . . .[18]

It drove seers like Emerson to say:

> In many forms we try
> To utter God's infinity,
> But the boundless has no form,
> And the Universal Friend
> Doth as far transcend
> An angel as a worm.
> The great Idea baffles wit,
> Language falters under it,
> It leaves the learned in the lurch;
> No art, nor power, nor toil can find
> The measure of the eternal Mind,
> Nor hymn, nor prayer, nor church.[19]

In the last sentence of this poem the religious coping devices themselves are taken with a grain of salt. Or perhaps we should say: with a dose of humor, for Emerson knew that their all too serious use could be an obstacle in coming to grips with the Infinite Idea. Religious practices may deteriorate into a juggler's game, and religious thoughts may slide into cheap, spurious fictions. The religious innovator is in some ways like a scientist: he wants to bring his idea to an unsparing test, and he is willing to discard the comforts to be derived from endorsing the established, entrenched thought patterns. In other ways he is like the creative artist who places sensory data in a new perspective, at the risk of being misunderstood or denigrated. In this adaptation to the numinous he is reorienting himself also to the physical and social world, and the latter includes all the religious opinions and practices which have received approbation as useful or true.

The basic psychiatric question about all such adaptations to the numinous is whether the solutions are conflict-ridden or whether they are products of the conflict-free ego sphere. A second question is whether they, however originating, enlarge the conflict-free ego and enhance a sense of freedom coupled with social responsibility. Erikson has demonstrated how Luther's attitudes toward the church of his origins were at first extremely conflict-laden and how it took Luther nearly a lifetime to relinquish the sharp edges of his conflict with paternal, ecclesiastical, and divine authority. In Luther's case, the venom of his pope-baiting was an index of the conflictual charge of his otherwise creative thoughts. Would-be reformers who exhaust themselves in threats of world disaster and who refer too often to Armageddon and Nineveh are too unfree to have time and energy for creative proposals. Geneva's theocratic experiment was not a demonstration of Calvin's sense of freedom, but of his humorless attempt to tie the divine mysteries to the schedules of civic life. The patient who shot three Coke bottles with the words "Father, Son, and Holy Ghost" on his lips was no religious innovator and certainly not a free man. Moreover, he failed to meet another psychiatric criterion: namely, that fantasy is useful only when it functions as a temporary detour to reality-adaptation. A permanent retreat into fantasy, even into the "reality of the unseen," is maladaptive and nonconstructive. One must return to the here and now, and one's capacity to improve the terrestrial condition is the only measure of the adaptive value of fantasy. In this light, Gandhi's introduction of the force of nonviolent resistance and the power of truth into the political and social realities of everyday life was a splendid demonstration of his sense of freedom and was calculated to enhance the conflict-free sphere of his followers. Tillich's capacity to speak theologically to disenchanted intellectuals was a great constructive achievement and a demonstration of his sense of freedom wrested from years of agonizing appraisal of his own intellectual bafflement. Bonhoeffer's hold on the idealistic youth of our time, the stirring thoughts of Buber which rediscover the numinous in I-Thou encounters, and Simone Weil's capacity to "wait for God" with her eyes open are all more impressive because of what they are *for* rather than what they are *against*.

Adaptation to the numinous reality in which one believes can take strange forms. Therese Neustadt identified herself so much with the suffering Jesus that she developed on her hands the stigma of the nails that tied him to the cross. Watchfulness against sin or evil can become a hyper-vigilance so exhausting that the care of the body and the mind falls by the wayside. It has led to witch hunting in which fellow human beings were tortured and sacrificed for the comfort of "regular" believers who were eager to lead their numinous entity to victory over its adversary (which was no less their numinous entity, but repressed). When adaptation to the numinous enlists visions and voices, or when it produces fits and frenzies, there is an obvious implication that the ordinary physical and social world are held in such disdain that they can be set aside temporarily. Such a solution to the problem of adaptation attempts to get the best of two worlds: when the fit or the vision occurs the person feels transported to the transcendent reality of his belief, only to return to the pedestrian world with a claim to numinosity for himself as one who was close to the gods. More than the best of two worlds can be had when the seer, during or after his break with ordinary reality, turns into a vindictive castigator of his fellowmen. Many years before the movement became publicly known, I knew an epileptic patient who was a member of the Black Muslims. He claimed that his seizures were divine visitations. But between seizures he was a most aggressive, nagging man who constantly intruded upon the hospital staff and the other patients with hortatory talk in which he alluded to his divine secrets.

In addition to coping with stress and adapting the person to reality, the ego preserves the person's welfare by regarding the self as a love object. In one's own eyes, the self is not only more or less adequate or competent; it is also more or less lovable. We will deal later with the love that the super-ego and ego-ideal may bestow upon the person. At this time our emphasis is on a more basic and direct love of the self, an affectionate and pleasurable self-esteem, which arises from several sources. One is the function pleasure which Bühler[20] first mentioned, and which Hartmann[21] later described as the pleasure of using the ego apparatus of perception, thought, and motility. The second source for this self-love is joy in the integrated functioning of the personality, which is a direct measure of the ego's synthetic capacity. The third source is more primitive and more stable: it is the narcissistic investment of the erotic drive in the person as a whole. This investment has its developmental root in the early infantile undifferentiated phase, in which subject and object have not yet become separated. In that early phase, the infant is auto-erotic: he is his own love object, providing in part his own stimulus nutriment (e.g., in thumbsucking) and discharging his drive energies on his own body (e.g., falling asleep after vigorous thumbsucking exercises). From this early autoerotic experience, some degree of primary self-love remains throughout life as healthy, vital narcissism which gives the person zest, vigor, and some basic self-esteem, independent of the opinions of others, and independent of love received from outside sources. The major part of the erotic energies turns into object love or becomes sublimated into cultural activities.

The self as love object, within the limits set by the love of outside objects in the course of normal development, has proven to be an enigma for religion. Is one entitled to any self-love if love of God and love of neighbor demand total commitment? Is it proper to adorn the body, that tangible substrate and symbol of the self? Is selfless love possible, or is it only a noble phrase? May a person enjoy himself, delight in his capacities, and be proud of his good functioning? These are not rhetorical questions—I have encountered them time and time again with clergymen enrolled in psychiatric seminars on pastoral care. The religious mind seems jarred by any consideration of the self as a love object. It turns with greater fondness to a figure like Job who, already in abject misery, went so far as to despise himself before his Maker, and repent in dust and ashes. It turns with admiration and approval to the phrase from the fourth Gospel: "Greater love has no man than this, that a man lay down his life for his friends." It is not shocked by Luther's statement:

All natural inclinations are either without God or against him; therefore none are good. I prove it thus: All affections, desires, and inclinations of mankind are evil, wicked, and spoiled, as the Scripture says.[22]

The very idea of self-love seems to go against the pledges toward self-sacrifice made in liturgical phrases such as "we offer ourselves to Thee." The ascetic tradition aims at such a self-offering first by starving or punishing the body, then by stripping the mind of its delights.

This is one side of the religious evaluation of the self as love object. The other side is captured in the idea of the *imago Dei* and the affirmation that creation is good. If these are taken seriously, they should lead to the care of the body and the enjoyment of the mind's capacities. They entail an appropriate pride, an appropriate self-love which the psalmist caught in his verse:

> What is man that thou art mindful of him,
> and the son of man that thou dost care for him?
> Yet thou hast made him little less than God,
> and dost crown him with glory and honor (8:4–5).

So in what way should the self be regarded—as amiable or despicable? The obvious answer is that it is both, depending on the situation. But clinical observation shows that there are marked individual differences in narcissism. In some people this aspect of the libido is so conspicuous that it hampers object love and thwarts human relations. In others the self-despising is so great that one would like them to be more open to their lovable features. In the majority, however, there are alternations between self-renunciation and self-enhancement, with a redress of the balance after excesses in either direction.

The alternating or mixed attitudes toward the self find pointed expression in the religious evaluation of the body. One classical pattern is to make a distinction between body and soul, to despise the one and love the other.

The problem is handled by splitting the person into two entities and dividing love and hate between them. The body is denigrated and, if this were possible, decathected in favor of the soul which receives all the care and love the person can bestow on it. The soul is the jewel, beloved by God; even if it takes much effort and time in the scheme of things to become polished to its ultimate splendor, it is already lovable as a diamond in the rough. If the hymn says: "Jesus, lover of my soul," the person himself, for sure, shares Jesus' admiration for this precious part of himself. The body, which is only a mortal shell, is of no consequence, or actually felt as a hindrance to the jewel's radiance.

Another classical pattern is to keep the person unified and not to allow such a crass soul-body dualism. This is more difficult to do, if one is to remain at once attuned to the reality of the body's decline and loyal to the self as a love object for which the body is such an important source. How can mortality be accepted knowingly? Indeed, how can one know one's own death except by dying which eliminates even *that* knowledge? In this conundrum, which is far more than a logical puzzle, a religious language has arisen which reintroduces the body in a new way. It speaks of the resurrection of the body—one of the most controversial and enigmatic Christian doctrines. It speaks of the body of the church, the church as the mystical body of Christ, the participation in the body and blood of Christ through the communion elements.

Though there are semantic differences in the use of the word "body" in each of these contexts, and though *body* stands at times for *person* (as in the expression "somebody"), there is a dynamic thread which links these products of the imagination into a meaningful sequence. Acceptance of mortality, not as a rational idea but as preparedness for dying, requires coping with the narcissistic wound of the body's decline and demise. The physical body as a source of pride and self-love must be given up, if this were possible. One way to approximate this condition is by an actual diminution of body cathexis for which illness sometimes prepares people by making the body painful, frail, or deformed. Though it is true that illness at first produces increased secondary narcissism in the form of concern with the self by partial withdrawal of object love (analogous to wound-healing), the course of the illness often changes this condition to a steadily diminishing investment in the self. The dynamics of hoping in patients with terminal illness sometimes show a liberating unconcern with the body as death approaches. Such a process is likely to be enhanced by offering the patient a means of turning narcissistic libido into object love, by providing him with perennial, enduring objects: the church, the person of Jesus as lover, the idea of a caring and nurturing God. But belief in Jesus entails affirmation of his resurrection, which is in turn the cornerstone for further belief in the efficacy of the church and her sacraments to produce in the individual the same kind of resurrection or renewal of life manifested in her founder. At this point, religious body-language gives further aid. Instead of having one's own body to love, the person is given the body of his church, the body of the faithful, the body of Christ, and the body and blood of the sacramental elements to cathect. They are all nurturing "bodies"; they feed and give warmth with a tenderness that cannot fail to remind the individual of his first love relation. Church, Christ, and sacraments can also be eroticized, as the mystical literature with its words "bride" and "groom" amply shows.

Instead of demanding narcissistic love to become straight object love, the body language of religion enables the person to recathect his body symbolically and in an expanded sense. He does not have to give up entirely the notion of having a body; the divine example of a resurrection and the participation in a corporate body of greater endurance allow him to continue to believe in his personhood, even when his physical body will give out. If then the imagery is further elaborated into a final rising from the grave on a far-off day of judgment, there is also an anticipatory investment in the new body, free from decay or limitations, something to be truly proud of and to be cherished.

THE SUPEREGO AND EGO-IDEAL

In reviewing how consciousness of the self comes about and is maintained, we saw that it rests on an awareness of difference between the self and others, awareness of activity, awareness of identity, and awareness of singularity. We then considered the ego as a specialization within the self, and saw it fostering the well-being of the person as a whole through the process of coping, adapting, and regarding the self (notably the body) as a love object. But the self has still another quality: it is almost constantly involved in an ethical evaluation process the outcome of which profoundly affects the person's feelings and actions. Evaluation requires criteria, and in this case these criteria are generally known as *values*.

The intimacy between values and religion hardly needs elaboration. Goodenough put it succinctly:

> . . . man's conduct and the legal structure of his society, man's sense of right and wrong, play as deep a part in man's religious structure as his cosmogonic myths and ritual requirements for worship. Men cannot live without some sense of right, and every society must have a sense of the rightness of its own customs. An individual may break off, call himself amoral, or feel himself as completely independent of ordinary social rules as did the Greek tyrants whom the Sophists defended—or as did Hitler. But people can do this only when they can convince themselves that popular notions of right are really wrong, at least for the more energetic and capable spirits, and that they do a higher right in flouting them.[23]

On this sense of right and wrong, religionists and psychologists have held very different opinions. Though the phrase "sense of right and wrong" is cautious enough, the religious tendency is to assume that the sense is divinely implanted in a man's bones, as it were, with a knowledge of the rights and wrongs to boot. It was therefore somewhat of a scandal when early psychoanalytic work suggested that evidences of a conscience guiding the person inwardly arrive relatively late in development, say at the beginning of school age, and that the preceding years are quite amoral, except for the child's succumbing to social pressures on account of his obvious weakness and dependency. This seems, at first blush, a very un-Kantian position if one remembers the famous statement about the categorical imperative as "the law which man as thing-as-such prescribes to man-as-appearance." Moreover, Kant's awe for "the starry heavens above me and the moral laws within me" suggests a solidity of conscience which in the minds of many requires it to be ready to function at birth.

Freud saw conscience arise as the Oedipal phase waned. Values are internalized by the process of identification with the father, after the boy has discovered the dangers inherent in his erotic desire for the mother and the terrible entanglements it produces with the mother's husband. The boy represses his desire by dint of recognizing that the odds are against him because of his weakness and immaturity. Father has the power of retaliation, and mother will eventually side with father anyway. But father is also loved and admired; therefore, becoming like him—even if this means waiting— is probably the best long-range policy. And so the son imitates father: he curbs his wishes under threat of physical harm (castration) and with the aid of adulation. He exerts self-control, he learns to postpone his wishes, he incorporates the parents' own norms and ideals, and he develops an internal value system that guides his behavior even when external control is absent. His ego, which governs his adaptive moves, is now aided by an ally, the superego, which channels the choices and automatizes the action to produce some degree of social reliability. While external reinforcement of the superego is still necessary by continued admonitions and prohibitions and by "good" and "bad" examples, there is now a controlling power within the person which provides guidance and judgment even when one is unobserved, and even within the privacy of one's thoughts and dreams.

As more refined observations of children were made, and as more young children were seen in psychiatric evaluation, new ideas about value behavior were added. Particularly the anal phase of development yielded interesting data. Though toilet training seems rather remote from ethics, it entails nevertheless some very basic moral issues. Who should obey whom—even in such matters as finding the right time, place, and ritual for eliminating the body's waste products? What is clean and what is dirty? Which time clock is to prevail: the child's biological rhythm or the time schedules of social living? Which of the two is more powerful: biological need or social custom? Whose will shall prevail: the parents' or the child's? Does society have the right and the power to regulate the individual's sphincters? We have only to cite the trite saying "cleanliness is next to Godliness" to demonstrate the common religious overtones in these questions. Many religious rituals are elaborations of the acts of cleaning and of giving up something of oneself. Obedience is one of religion's central ideas, as is the will. Purity is not only a good habit, but a virtue. Parents are wont to speak of the anal phase as the time in which "to make or break" the child's little will. The word "housebroken," used for pets, goes beyond excretory deftness and moves over into politeness, knowing one's place, and general manageability, all of which imply some reverence for the power inherent in social customs.

As the spotlight turned on still younger children, infants were seen to approach and withdraw from their mothers, to smile and cry, to drink and spit out, to be peaceful and frustrated. From these observations of the oral phase came the idea that the infant makes a differentiation between the "good mother" and the "bad mother." The one gives pleasure and the other withholds or frustrates it. The infant loves the one and hates the other— yet she is the same mother and neither biologically nor psychologically quite so separate from the infant that there is a clear subject-object distinction. For the infant, "good" is what tastes good and feels warm, what gives pleasure and comfort, what fosters a rapid and triumphant growth. "Bad" is what tastes bad and feels cold, what gives pain and discomfort, what stagnates development. Even when one admits that these differentiations are not stable conceptual distinctions but at best preconcepts and proto-affective reactions, the striking feature is that some kind of evaluation is going on, a first primitive manifestation of a vague good-bad scheme which is exercised with heart and soul within the mother-child relation.

It is now almost a semantic choice whether one will continue to distinguish sharply between the superego and its forerunners, or speak of super-ego development broadly for the whole process whereby values become internalized and the intrapsychic structure of the superego becomes articulated. Soon after birth there is evidence of "a sense of right and wrong," put first in terms of an affective "good" and "bad"—not unlike the biblical "O taste and see that the Lord is good," the promised land of "milk and honey," and the "pure spiritual milk" that prepares a man for salvation.

Each of the critical stages of superego development can be charged with numinous associations, on the teacher's as well as on the learner's side. Goodness in the sense of caring and nurturing, goodness in the sense of cleanliness and orderliness, and goodness in the sense of impulse control and sublimated eroticism—they have all been used as metaphors for the divine and as metaphors for the man of faith. What is more, in religious families the basic values and the protoconcepts of morality are taught verbally and behaviorally, in a context of religious practices. They are often enforced by religious sanctions.

It is of note that in the early years of value learning the child's physical and mental weakness prepares him for a full-scale and rather indiscriminate identification with the parents on whom he depends. He identifies himself with the parents massively, wanting to be totally like father or mother. Much of the early identity formation proceeds by primitive psychosomatic modes: introjection, incorporation, and other predominantly unconscious ways of making external things one's own. Similarly, a major part of the teaching procedures is unconcious and nonverbal: it consists of frowns and smiles, and expressions of delight or nausea. An encouraging "that's good" or a discouraging "that's bad" adds verbal labels to some very complex and diffuse behavior bits. The moral admonitions and prohibitions are sometimes little more than an authoritarian yes or no; very often they consist in spontaneous expressions of feelings which are more telling than the verbalizations which follow. Even the wisest parent who has read Gesell and Spock gives himself away affectively in facial expressions of disgust or anger upon discovering a fault in his children, no matter how patient and understanding he may try to be a few minutes later. In fact, many of the parental reactions to children's behavior are manifestations of the parents' own superego activity over which they have at the time insufficient ego control. Their censor works, reflexlike, before their ego can institute a more informed and balanced approach.

As the superego develops, fear of external authority becomes a special anxiety of the internal pacesetter and taskmaster.[24] This anxiety has a unique emotional tone: it is a feeling of guilt. It contains a unique threat or sting: "I will be punished, for I am no good." Even the threat of punishment is fairly specific, since it derives from the Oedipal fear of bodily harm or castration. Guilt feelings pertain not only to overt misdeeds but also to private thoughts. This peculiar power of the superego derives from the child's view of parental or divine omniscience. The all-seeing eye of the outside source of power becomes an all-seeing inner eye which spares neither furtive thought nor inhibited motive.

Since guilt feelings are painful to bear, the person will seek to rid himself of them, usually through an act of expiation. Normally, the modes of expiation are taught along with the value system that is enforced. Some children must first make a full oral confession and then make a solemn promise for betterment. Others must allow themselves to be exposed in their "badness" and castigated by various parties. Some must accept physical punishment; others must accept deprivation or forgo some pleasure. Some must do work, hard or menial, in order to win back parental favor. Some must concentrate on doing an especially nice deed in retribution for their misdeed. One can seek restoration by buying a gift, by being conspicuously friendly or charming, by working for a good cause, or by donating to charity. In an atmosphere of carefree love and basic trust, an inventive mind can find dozens of ways in order to placate for guilt feelings. But some are bound to a specific tit-for-tat rule: "an eye for an eye and a tooth for a tooth."

Many expiatory maneuvers are themselves established religious practices. Prayer is one example, particularly when its emphasis is on confessing one's sins, errors, or misdeeds. Both sins of commission and sins of omission may lead to confessional prayer. Every weekend, millions of people the world over engage in such corporate statements aloud as the following:

Minister:

> If we say we have no sin, we deceive ourselves, and the truth is not in us. If we confess our sins, he is faithful and just, and will forgive our sins and cleanse us from all unrighteousness.

People:

> Almighty and most merciful Father: we have erred and strayed from thy ways like lost sheep. We have followed too much the devices and desires of our own hearts. We have offended against thy holy laws. We have left undone those things which we ought to have done; and we have done those things which we ought not to have done; and there is no health in us. But thou, O Lord, have mercy upon us, miserable offenders. Spare thou those, O God, who confess their faults. Restore thou those who are penitent, according to thy promises declared unto mankind in Christ Jesus our Lord. And grant, O most merciful Father, for his sake, that we may hereafter live a godly, righteous, and sober life; to the glory of thy holy name. Amen.

Minister:

> The mercy of the Lord is from everlasting to everlasting. I declare unto you, in the name of Jesus Christ, we are forgiven. Amen.

In this case the confessing itself is the expiatory act, followed by a declaration of prompt forgiveness because recourse is had to the vicarious atonement of Jesus. The penitence to which the confessional prayer alludes is mostly a matter of attitude, rather than a contract to undertake specific acts of penance such as giving alms, burning candles, saying multiple ritual prayers, putting on sackcloth and ashes, or making a pilgrimage. There is not even a promise for betterment, as many parents demand from their children. Instead, there is reliance on a divine promise and a request that God may give more strength to the penitent.

All rituals associated with cleansing and purifying can be used as expiatory maneuvers to reduce guilt feelings. All offerings and sacrifices can serve the same purpose. Ancient religious body language which led to cutting out tongues, plucking out eyes, and castration can still be used to justify mutilating one's body as an act of expiation. As we saw before, religious number magic can induce a person to make up sevenfold for a misdeed, as it can induce the offended party to forgive seven or seventy-times-seven times.

But before we go deeper into the religious complications and meanings of the internal value system, we should consider another aspect of the self-as-valuer, structurally known as the ego-ideal. Moral development does not stop at the end of the Oedipal phase. Indeed, as school life begins and mobility increases, the child is exposed to a great number of new models: teachers, peers, merchants, police officers, club leaders, physicians, and what not. These people too issue their yeses and nos, their smiles and frowns, their lectures on "good" and "bad." They give rewards and punishments. All of these give form and content to the sense of right and wrong. Even fictitious or dead persons serve as models: the heroes of novels, important figures from history books, characters seen on the film screen and television. All kinds of identifications are made with these people. They are idols or villains, i.e., positive or negative identity models. In comparison with the process of superego development, the ego-ideal depends far more on selective identifications: an interesting trait, manner of speech, artistic taste, or cultural pursuit is seized upon as an item to copy, for a while, until other models come along. Thus the eight-year-old suddenly begins to imitate the speech habits of his homeroom teacher; the twelve-year-old suddenly changes his handwriting, experimenting with strokes and slants and angles; the avid reader is fascinated by certain characters in the novels he reads late at night. These are only partial identifications, and the person is often quite conscious of making them. They can be openly discussed, and the pros and cons can be debated. A world of human ideals is thus built up from many fragments, which can be consciously copied and imitated, talked about, and exchanged for new ideas derived from a never-ending series of models as one gets older.

The ego-ideal also, like the superego, helps the ego in making choices and decisions of an ethical sort. It provides guidance by setting standards worth aiming for; it sets a level of aspiration and specifies what the aspirations are. It sets values of an enticing kind, which should be approximated or realized. If the person falls notably short of these values the ego-ideal produces a specific anxiety with a unique emotional tone: a feeling of shame. Its intrapsychic message is: "You are unworthy!" It describes a unique situation: "I have not reached the goal—I have forsaken my own heroes—I have failed." The sting in feelings of shame is a fear of contempt, a threat of exposure, and eventual abandonment. Hence the language of shame: "I could sink through the ground for shame." And hence the body language of shame: one covers instinctively the expressive parts of the body—face, chest, and sexual areas. One could indeed "die for shame."

Dying for shame is not an impossibility. First missionaries, then anthropologists, and finally the physiologist Cannon[25] have described cases of sudden death entailed by the ritual practice of "boning" among Australian aborigines. In a great ceremony the priest picks up a charred bone from a heap of carcasses which has been turned into a bonfire. He points the bone toward a member of the tribe, thereby ritually "marking" him as the "one who must die" and within twenty-four hours the person dies indeed without anyone's laying hands on him. The story of Ananias and Sapphira in the biblical book of Acts allows a similar interpretation. Ananias and his wife had made pledges and promises and failed to live up to them. In an encounter with Peter the apostle, they were confronted with their moral failure and died on the spot.

It is sure that the dynamics of guilt feelings and shame have more continuity than our sketch suggests. Many theorists link the superego and the ego-ideal as merely two aspects of one intrapsychic structure, one referring to the early and more unconscious roots, the other to the later and more conscious origins. But there are interesting phenomenological differences between the two, as indicated in the previous paragraphs. There is also the question of how one restores one's feeling of worth and one's acceptability to others after an episode of shame. Does one atone for shame, or make expiation? Is penance possible? How does one "make up"? By and large, all one can do under the pain of exposure and the threat of abandonment is try to prove oneself by acting better next time. Shame thus turns into a spur toward improvement. One has to prove that one will be loyal to the company of one's own idols, to their values and standards that one has striven to make one's own.

Anthropologists have distinguished between shame cultures and guilt cultures. One could similarly distinguish between the shame and guilt aspects of religious systems, particularly in the enforcement of "the Christian life," "the Jewish life," or "the Moslem life." As we shall see in the next section, doctrinal formulations are sometimes couched expressly in the language of guilt or the language of shame. But in the meantime we have gained the perspective that the relations to the self are importantly influenced by the inner voice of the superego and ego-ideal which constantly evaluate our acts, intentions, and thoughts in terms of ethical propositions. Depending on these internal and automatic evaluations, the self is enhanced by a feeling of self-worth, self-esteem, and "being in tune with all things good and noble," or the self is shaken and deflated by feelings of guilt and shame, unworthiness, lowness, or sinfulness.

From an adaptive point of view, the ego's task of mastery and coping demands that it be attuned to outside reality as well as inside reality, including the drives and instinctual needs, and the demands of the superego and ego-ideal. Coping with the superego and ego-ideal is therefore always a matter of relative strength between the ego and these other parties. No party can be ignored; each must have its due, in perpetual give-and-take or synthesis. Ideally, superego and ego-ideal function as the ego's aids, repeating as it were the do's and don't's and the smiles and frowns of all the important love objects one has admired, loved, or accepted as authorities on whom one depended. But in some persons one can find evidence of hyperactivity of superego or ego-ideal in the form of chronic feelings of unworthiness or low self-esteem, depression, and self-dejection. It occurs in perfectionists who, in their own eyes, never measure up to standards. This does not necessarily imply that the standards are too high. More often, the high standards were inculcated under threat of blame, rather than with the enticement of praise. And very often, a portion of the person's own aggression has become attached to the superego and increased its severity. Hyperactivity also occurs in scrupulous people who carry such burdens of guilt feelings that they have to invent spurious occasions of failure or sin in order to account for their sense of insufficiency. Strange things and paradoxical situations follow from the function of the internal taskmasters. On the one hand one can find upright people, pillars of society and church—whom others would regard as impeccable characters —haunted by feelings of guilt and contemplating suicide. On the other hand, one can find villains who are morally and legally very guilty without *feeling* guilty at all. Some people feel so guilty (without overt trespass) that they look for punishment and finally commit some misdeed in order to be apprehended by the police. In that case the guilt feelings precede the guilty act rather than follow it.

At the risk of anthropomorphizing a psychological construct it should be pointed out that some superegos seem more often to say no than yes. Their function is largely negative and prohibitive, with the result that the person rarely feels good when he does well. More often he feels bad when he hears the frequent no. He only gets internal blame and no praise. Some superegos frequently say no and leave the person feeling guilty without pointing the way toward betterment. They impose restrictions without mapping out strategies for atonement. The person does not know what to do with his guilt feelings since he knows no mode of placation and has not learned to trust in forgiveness. In other persons the superego imposes its sanctions strictly on a fixed tit-for-tat basis with absolute rules for retributive justice. Some superegos "love" abundantly[26] without insisting on justice, which is not always the best aid to the ego in its task of adapting the person to all his external and internal environments. There are also superegos which are both strict and forgiving and make distinctions between thought or intention and acts. And although I spoke at the beginning of this paragraph of the "risk of anthropomorphizing" the superego, that risk now appears not so great any more, for it must have become clear that the superego's functions reflect the life situations with real people who taught us both the standards and the ways to uphold them. While self-hatred and sadistic propensities may substantially add to the cruelties of the superego, so that one cannot directly infer from a given superego what the parental demands and sanctions were, the superego is derived from processes of nurture and discipline and has always an external referent. It is a product of object relations, socialization, and acculturation, steeped in experiences of love and hate.

Among the multitude of admonitions and prohibitions which become internalized there are many unquestionably religious items. The admonitions insist on loving God and following his commandments, and loving the neighbor ("as oneself"). They tend to specify some of the work that is to be done to establish the kingdom of heaven on earth: in the first place worshiping and praying, then supporting the activities and programs of the faith group and being loyal to denominational traditions, and perhaps engaging in social activities that improve the lot of mankind. This sequence is only very tentative. Depending on the denomination and the individual family, more emphasis may be placed on social action and less on formal worship participation. More vague admonitions center on associating with "good people" and living by "the golden rule." In some families there is strong insistence that the young be confirmed into the faith group at the earliest possible age; in others the admonition is to do this knowledgeably and with conviction at an unspecified adult age. There may be pressure on the children in certain families to aspire to a religious vocation. The admonitions may center in the practice of virtues and the learning of lists of virtues. They may be phrased in situational terms such as "What would Jesus do?" Specific texts or prayers may serve as themes around which the educational process revolves: "As you wish that men would do to you, do so to them"; "Judge not, that you will not be judged."

But all these admonitions would remain only an assortment of fragments if there were not some key idea or leitmotiv to give them a hierarchical structure. Life is so complex that the choices between one good thing and another need to be guided by some ranking procedure. If there is a divine rule against work on the Sabbath, may one attend to a sick cow, or pluck an apple from the tree when one is hungry? Granted that all rules are absolute and demand a total commitment, are there some rules that are higher than others, so that difficult choice situations can be settled with some degree of comfort? Here is where a typology of religious experience gives some answers by describing empirical patterns of value organization. Goodenough's[27] descriptions encompass legalism, supralegalism, orthodoxy, supraorthodoxy, aestheticism, and symbolism-sacramentalism, which in effect are not only forms of religious experience, but also value hierarchies. They are principles whereby the superego and ego-ideal are acquired.

The *legalist* puts a premium on rules, taboos, folkways, or anything else that helps individuals and groups to "do the right thing." Legalistic codes are not only guides for conduct, but they serve as meaningful curtains whereby one can shield oneself from the terrors of the *tremendum. Supralegalism* is also concerned with right conduct, but approaches the established codes with creativity and originality, sometimes even to the point of abolishing the old codes in the name of a newer or greater ideal. Luther's dialectic between law and gospel is one example; Kierkegaard's teleological suspension of the ethical is another. Statements like "Perfect love casts out fear" are of this order. *Orthodoxy* is concerned with having the truth, and "right knowing" or "proper thinking": in this way it shields the individual from the *tremendum* while allowing him at the same time to participate in its power. The emphasis is here on having the right beliefs, which in turn depends on being aligned with the proper sources of authority for those beliefs: creeds, priests, "father always said . . . ," or tradition. *Supraorthodoxy* depends on new integrations of old meanings and a creative critique of established doctrines. The right belief is no longer what "everybody thinks" but what an individual has discovered by himself through an enlightening experience in which he gained a new perspective. In *aestheticism* the "right thing" means perfect form and formal practice. The value of beauty is of the highest order, and full appreciation of it sometimes entails a disdain for the other precepts that find their way into the superego and ego-ideal. In *symbolism* and *sacramentalism* the value of participating in sacred rites which link the individual with a divine source of power is so high that other values rank lower in the scale, or tend to fall by the wayside when choices have to be made. For instance, sacramentalists may remain oblivious of charity or social action, because their sense of right and wrong puts a premium on the individual's own salvation through direct contact with sacred objects and ceremonies.

So far, we have dwelt on the positive admonitions which may be incorporated into the intrapsychic censor. This was done at some length because the word "censor," often used as a shorthand expression for the superego and ego-ideal, suggests only negative action. This is far from the facts. The superego and ego-ideal are not only taskmasters but aids to the ego, and often bestow love on the person over and beyond the gratificacations derived from social approval and object relations. At times the love given by an approving superego is enough to keep a person going in adversity, when outsiders take issue with him or cast him out. Luther's "Here I stand" is one dramatic example.

But it is nevertheless true that the prohibitions of the superego tend to be more conspicuous, in strength or number. Countless nos and don't's find their way into the forbidding aspect of conscience, and among these are many with an explicitly religious character. Many of the celebrated Ten Commandments are couched in "thou-shalt-not" language. Lists of virtues are counterbalanced by lists of vices. Taboos and bans are specific prohibitions which, if ignored, entail a direct confrontation with divine powers and the derived power for sanctions by the religious group. Sin is pluralized into sins, with categorical subdivisions between mortal and venial sins. The prohibitions comprise both specific behaviors and attitudinal propensities. They may be directed against such acts as stealing, blaspheming, or killing, as well as against dispositions such as striving for pleasure, thinking highly of oneself, or exposing oneself to temptations. They may be directed to feelings, such as anger and hatred, declaring these wrong to have. They may be focused on biological activities such as sex or eating, requiring that these be curbed by abstinence or fasting. All the don't's which one encounters may be stylized into wrongs and incorporated as infallible negative rules, with sanctions attached for trespasses. These wrongs, by the hundreds, may round off into a mood of severity which blankets many of life's opportunities. They may create an attitude of hypervigilance and suspicion of all natural proclivities, which makes Thomas a Kempis' version of the *Imitatio Christi* such an arduous and dreadful task.

But the picture is not all gloomy, even if the don't's are many and the sanctions strong. For the superego normally also prescribes means of expiation whereby guilt feelings can be reduced and self-esteem raised. And again, many of the means of expiation are themselves religious practices. Auricular confession, confessional prayer, and corporate confessions are among the most widely used. They can be augmented by doing special acts of penance, upon prescription by a religious official. Sacrifices and offerings are among the oldest forms of expiation; they tended to have the earmarks of specific fines, graded according to the seriousness of the offense. But the principle of making sacrifices for atonement of guilt feelings can be used more diffusely; much can be left to the individual's inventiveness in seeking ways to forgo a pleasure, making a gift, or doing something that goes against the grain of his natural inclinations. Religious institutions have so many tasks to do and are engaged in so many campaigns requiring work, goods, or funds that an individual has a multitude of opportunities for sacrificial acts by merely involving himself in the programs of the institution. He can make promises or pledges, for work or money. He can sit through many tedious meetings, sacrificing time in which more exciting things could have been done, with the feeling that he has donated something in retribution for his moral inadequacies. He can undertake a menial task, like cleaning up the premises or preparing bulk mail, which make him feel "in grace" again. In fact, although the expression "means of grace" refers technically to sacraments, any form of atonement which has the psychological significance of reducing guilt feelings is to the individual a means of grace. In the past, some religious leaders extolled crying as "the gift of tears," but the old-fashioned ring of this expression should not lead one to underestimate the enormous role of crying and "humbling oneself" in the release of guilt feelings. Millions of people take recourse to it, if not publicly, then privately; and if tears are hard in coming, a "lump in the throat" serves the same purpose.

Self-imposed punishments and deprivations are widely used, in the form of fasting and abstinences from pleasure. Sleep deprivations are typical, and natural, when a mind is tortured by its own sinfulness; and if much sleep has thus been lost the individual may look back at his sleepless nights as the price he had to pay for his moral offense. In clinical depressions, when guilt feelings are pronounced, sleeplessness and loss of appetite are almost standard symptoms. They are not only expressive of the person's conviction that he is unworthy of sleep and food, but also to some extent the means whereby he imposes expiation upon himself. Though public torture and burning at the stake are no longer everyday occurrences, self-torture is still a viable item on any list of expiation maneuvers. It occurs in the endless, circular, unresolved thinking of obsessional episodes to the point of producing headaches. It occurs in handwashing rituals endlessly repeated until the skin of the hands is raw. It occurs in bearing aches and pains unnecessarily, when a simple medication could end them promptly. Even using the lash on oneself is not entirely a thing of the past.

While forbearance is a virtuous attitude, when it is assumed far beyond the call of duty or nobility it may have the quality of being practiced as expiation for one's own moral miseries. To forgive seven times is already beyond the tolerance of most people, but to aim at forgiving seventy-times-seven times requires more than heroism. It may require a very scrupulous conscience that finds some internal purpose in "letting people walk over" one. Exposure to ridicule, and being the victim of the malicious delights of others in one's misfortune, are aspects of shame, which is in turn a temporary shouldering of psychic pain with expiatory benefits.

We see then that the ability to love oneself, or, as the case may be, the need to despise oneself, is to a large extent dependent upon the functions of the superego and ego-ideal. Though these two structures are by no means the only forms in which the numinous is presented to the individual, they tend to embody particularly those religious ideas which carry the weight of tradition. The values acquired in the early years of superego development are almost inextricably intertwined with the emotional displays of approval and disapproval which stem from parental superego activity, i.e., *their* guilt feelings and sense of shame, *their* fear of temptations or weaknesses of the flesh. These are too often expressed more emphatically than wisely, for their core is also largely unconscious and the parent figures also obtained their basic value system largely in preverbal modes. And so we have the phenomenon to which Freud pointed, that the basic moral and religious values are passed on from one generation to the next with much less rapid change than all those cultural pursuits to which the ego has direct access, such as the arts, the sciences, and technology.

This finding not only describes the conservatism of religious individuals but also throws some light on the alleged conservatism of religion per se. A good deal of it may be ascribed to the peculiarities of that part of the transmission process of religious ideas which is mediated by the superego. These ideas consist in the first place of the various admonitions and prohibitions which become the positive and negative values of conscience. But they also comprise the sanctions, which directly or symbolically are ways of bestowing love or hate; and the restorative means of expiation which are ways of obtaining love and avoiding hate. In the meantime, these sanctions *of* love and hate hinge on some larger vision of the power *to* love and hate. If parental figures dispense love and hate at will, combined with the rules they set forth and enforce, are they themselves numinous beings? Are they gods? Or are they in turn the objects on which love and hate were bestowed by their elders and their gods? These questions can be repeated ad infinitum until they resolve in the last analysis to the most basic question about the relations between power and love or hate: Is power benevolent or wrathful? To this question the next section will be addressed.

CUR DEUS HOMO

We said earlier in this chapter that when numinosity has become part of one's life, it is another reality to which the ego must seek adaptation. The projected all-father is seen and felt not only as a helpful source of power, but also as a demanding figure who insists on loyalty, righteousness, and the best use of human potentialities. He has the power to demand faith, and also to give faith. There remains an ambiguity about him which Paul captured in his statement: "O the depth of the riches and wisdom and knowledge of God! How unsearchable are his judgments and how inscrutable his ways!" (Rom. 11:33). Thus, the result of identifying the numinous as Father, whose works are to be discovered in nature and history, and whose word is to be heard in recorded human events, is not altogether happy. While his gifts may be great, so are his demands; and while his love may be felt as everlasting, so is his wrath. For the man of faith who feels caught between the *fascinans* and the *tremendum,* can the scales be tipped in favor of security and happiness? Can the *tremendum,* which is now a paternal *tremendum,* be covered by a new protective blanket, to use Goodenough's image? At this point, Christianity asserts the incarnation and the atonement of Jesus Christ as a crucial solution to the continued bleakness of man's situation in the universe. And we must now look at some of the psychological implications of this solution, taking the atonement as our point of entry.

Nearly every comprehensive theological handbook makes it plain that speculations about the atonement have produced several alternative models or theories, each with its own metaphors, analogies, historical accidents, and cultural images. [28-29] They are roughly classifiable into three main groupings which have shown many permutations in the course of time: the Ransom theory, the Satisfaction theory, and the Moral Influence theory. To the psychologist of religion, these three main theories of atonement constitute three types of thematic material, three thought structures of men pondering the divine intentions toward mankind, three fragments of religious ideation, three symbol systems. About these, he can ask what he asks about any psychological datum: what is its structure, function, and purpose? How is it motivated? What economic role does it play in the psychic household? What conflicts or problems does it solve, if any? How did the theme or the symbol originate? What are its vicissitudes during the life of the individual or of the religious system?

Let us begin our search for answers by trying to describe concisely each major theme. In the thinking of the Greek fathers the image of the "powers of darkness" plays a large role. Whether personified into Satan, Devil, or Adversary, or described as Death, Realm of Darkness, or the idea of mortality, one main trend in Greek-Christian thought is a duality between powers, one of which is thought of as genuine and true being, while the other is not. Man is alienated from the true ground of being, and has fallen into the captivity of a faked owner who has power over him. He is in bondage to a foreign master from whom he cannot liberate himself. In this cosmic setting, the atonement became dramatized as a set of power transactions between the righteous and the unrighteous owner of men in which Christ, with varying emphases on his birth, life, suffering, and death, but with equal emphasis on the dual nature of his God-man-hood was seen as a ransom. In the works of Origen, to whom we owe a succinct description of this cosmic power struggle, the death of Christ is the ransom price which God pays to Satan in order to reclaim the creature estranged from him by original sin. Man's bondage to the foreign potentate is now abolished; his alienation from God gives way to realignment with the ground of being. But the power of darkness was fooled in the barter, since Christ, the perfect God-man, triumphed over Satan's temptations during his life as well as in his resurrection and thus abolished in principle the ultimacy of death.

While much of this imagery recalls the deals in which buyers engaged on the slave market, the elaborations introduced by the Cappadocian fathers, especially Gregory of Nyssa, added an element of clever deceit on the part of God. Since God did not want to use force in reclaiming his rightful ownership over captivated man, he used, as it were, the lure of a more perfect, more desirable, more tempting possession in barter, and Satan fell for it without foreseeing what he was in for. Indeed, Gregory freely used the image of the fishhook in order to describe Christ's dual nature: Satan, lured by the bait of his humanity, sank his teeth in the hook of his divinity and found it too much to swallow.

The point to make is that this group of theories of atonement assumes a dualism and for this reason runs counter to the dominant monotheistic position. It is also frankly demonological, assuming as it does the existence of a powerful, pseudodivine adversary in heaven, on earth, or in man himself whose essential goal is destruction, i.e., death. But perhaps most noteworthy of all is the image of God in this context: he is seen as creator and rightful owner of man, who pities his creature's predicament of alienation, estrangement, slavery to a foreign master, captivity, or bondage. His love for man outweighs his anger over their corruption. He works for their delivery by identifying himself with their plight through his divine son who became man. His work of deliverance starts at the incarnation and ends in the resurrection with promise of the *parousia,* at which time man will be completely renewed by a final re-creation. In this scheme, the major points of emphasis on incarnation and resurrection of the God-man parallel the two choice points by which man discovers his own contingency: birth and death. In Heidegger's[30] ontology, man's *Geworfenheit,* whereby he feels thrown into existence and out of it without any power of decision of his own, is experienced as anxiety. In Tillich's terms, anxiety is the awareness of our alienation from the ground of being.

The ransom theory seems to address itself to the anxiety aroused when man feels himself in the dominion of foreign powers, which eventually produce death. These powers can be seen as cosmic, in the form of Satan and the tortures which he inflicts, or as the internal powers of all that is ego-alien in man, especially his unconscious antisocial instinctual impulses which are bent on destruction. In either case, the emphasis on the demonic nature of these powers is to be seen in the context of ancient cosmological myths which hold that the powers of darkness are real since they derive from the misappropriated power of God.

But human relations are not confined to the slave market, and human experiences are not confined to anxiety. Another choice of metaphor in describing redemption and deliverance from evil is possible. From a cultural point of view it is small wonder that the Latin church fathers began to take hold of another image of great antiquity, derived on the one hand from the institution of sacrifice elaborated in the Old Testament, on the other hand from the Roman institution of the judicial process. These two trends are merged into the one idea of satisfaction. They derive from the image of God as just and holy, sovereign ruler, supreme judge and lawgiver, whose domain in priestly terms is the altar of sacrifice and in civil terms the law court. While the theme of satisfaction is as old as Christianity and can be found, together with the ransom idea, in the Pauline epistles, its clearest and most elaborate form was reached much later in the work of Anselm,[31] whose Cur Deus Homo I take as paradigmatic.

The satisfaction theory portrays, in essence, a God who is both just and forgiving, angry and merciful, offended and long-suffering, whose wrath demands reparation, satisfaction, penalty, or repentance from offenders and transgressors of his holiness and his law. It portrays man as an offender of law, blasphemer of the holy, rebel against sovereign, disobedient and obstreperous child, violator of rules who stands in need of punishment and correction. Sin, according to this theme, is basically transgression of rules and boundaries, with a great deal of rebellious arrogance. In a Barthian phrase, it is refusal to let God be God, i.e., sovereign being. The result of original sin, thus interpreted, is life under the curse of work and pain, and death as inescapable punishment.

Crucial to Anselm's reasoning are his adhortations to his interlocutor: "You have not yet considered what a heavy weight sin is," and his emphasis on the centrality of willing both for the sinning of man and the saving done by the God-man. With hairsplitting logic the necessity for the death of Christ is proven, and yet it is said that he died freely, of his own will, in order to render for man the sacrifice exacted by an offended God. But most important to the satisfaction theory is the idea of punishment and penalty: sinning is likened to thievery, but merely to give back to God what was stolen from him may provide restoration, but not satisfaction. Since God's dignity and honor are at stake, more than restitution must occur. His justice is necessary and his mercy optional.

Subsequent variations on the satisfaction theme have placed greater emphasis on the penal element and upon the Son as the propitiatory victim, whereas in other versions the ancient theme of sacrifice was re-enlivened. Both had the effect of keeping the satisfaction theory associated with blood and suffering. This elicited an understandable reaction in thinkers such as Socinus who found the tension between God's mercy and justice in these portrayals so intolerable that he denied the possibility of their combination.

Throughout the satisfaction and penal theories the model for sin is disobedience, arrogant rebellion, transgression, and violation of God's laws, with a parallel emphasis on Christ as a model of obedience who renders himself a sacrifice, fine, penalty, Paschal lamb, or vicarious criminal for man, depending upon the particular version. Through this process of atonement God's honor is restored and death is abolished because the punitive reason for man's perdition has been taken away by the divine pardon. Man is now justified, and a life of rectitude is made possible in principle.

What is the experiential matrix, the basic feeling tone out of which this theme might have emerged? There can hardly be any doubt that guilt feelings were preponderant, with a sense of transgression and disobedience as the essence of human misery. Whereas the ransom theory is based on anxiety over the uncanny phenomenon of death, the satisfaction theory is based on guilt feelings over incorrect conduct. The redemptive side of the ransom theory turns anxiety into joy over adoption and deliverance; in the satisfaction theory it relieves guilt feelings through justification and expiation. To the extent that man's own felt intrapsychic conflicts have served as model for these themes, the ransom theory is a typical expression of conflict between the ego and the id, whereas the satisfaction theories are typically modeled after conflicts between the ego and the superego.

There is a third group of atonement doctrines, essentially as old as the others and also to be found embryonically in the Pauline writings, but which took a longer time to become clearly formulated. Its central theme is taken from another sacrosanct social institution: government with public justice and positive law, projected onto God who is now seen as governor and guardian of the social order. With antecedents in another Cappadocian father, Gregory of Nazianzus, and in scholasticism through Abelard, it found a competent systematizer in Grotius who was also the founder of international law. It also had one root in Athanasius' conviction that the consequence, if not the purpose, of the atonement was to restore the defaced *imago Dei* in man so that moral and social betterment might ensue. Two notions are crucial to the theory: it ranks God's goodness as his highest attribute, making his mercy necessary and his justice optional (the opposite is true of the satisfaction theories). God punishes not out of wrath but for the common good, for except from this end, said Grotius, punishment has not the character of being desirable. In the second place, it sets up Christ as an example to be followed rather than as an expiatory sacrifice, though elements of the latter are not missing.

The influence of the governmental theory extended even to such a staunch Calvinist and penalist as Jonathan Edwards, who let God be a ruler who maintains order and decorum in his kingdom and Christ a benevolent mediator who seeks man's welfare by offering to pay his penalty for him. Christ identifies himself with man out of sympathy and mercy, whatever his function toward God might be, and this has the moral effect of making man desire to identify himself with Christ, his life, his teachings, and his perfection. In these and other versions of the moral influence and governmental theories rings the echo of Augustine's compassionate idea: "Christ did so much for us—what can we do for him?"

Most of the governmental and moral influence doctrines maintain in some way the major tenets of the satisfaction theories, but they add something essentially new, namely that among God's attributes mercy and goodness prevail, and although he also is just, he is not absolutely tied to his own laws since the wise governor dispenses justice with the common good in mind. It avoids the classical pitfall of *summum ius summa iniuria,* whether or not it betrays a Socinian streak.

Although these theories involve an element of fear of punishment for sin and an awareness of guilt feelings (to the extent that they are intermixed with satisfaction theories of one sort or another), the new stratum of human experience they tap is selective identification with Christ as a model to be followed, the desire of belonging to him and the new life, and feelings of shame. In psychological terms, the underlying conflict situation is one between the ego and the ego-ideal with shame as the essential affect.

This exposition of theological constructs must suffice to undergird the thesis that each of the three described groups of theories of atonement is a close parallel to each of the major types of intrapsychic conflict situations characteristic of human life. The ransom theories of atonement are germane to the psychological situation of anxiety produced by ego-id conflicts, in which the ego feels in captivity by strange symptoms and has lost access to the motivating grounds of personality. The healing of such a conflict situation and the reduction of this anxiety proceed in principle by the therapeutic demonstration that the feared impulses are not really as dangerous as they seemed, and that greater awareness of them rather than shutting them out of awareness is a better mode of control over them. Instead of bondage to autonomous impulses there can now be mastery over them, with much greater all-around satisfaction. On this basis, new love relations become possible with more lasting gratifications which in turn mitigate fears, both realistic and irrational ones. Significantly, the ransom theories portray the old life as estrangement, and the new life in terms of *deliverance* and *adoption,* by a God whose attitude toward men is one of *pity, compassion,* and *concerned sympathy.*

The satisfaction and penal theories show a definite parallel with the conflicts engendered by a strict and forbidding superego. Their major emphasis is on guilt feelings and the horror of transgressions, whether in thought, word, or deed. The ego feels haunted by the internal taskmaster, is forced to damn itself and to live in a world of doom, and is preoccupied with real or imagined corruption, violation of rules or orders, transgression of laws, and other heinous crimes or vices. To the relentless demands of the superego, sacrifices must be made, purifications tried, fines and penalties paid, in the hope that these will serve to alleviate the nagging guilt feelings. Some suffering must be shouldered to effect a tolerable correctness of the person.

The healing of this type of conflict usually proceeds by bringing ego and superego closer together, which in principle can be done by clarifying, softening, or refining the demands of the one as well as by heightening the capacities, effectiveness, and versatility of the other. The *differentiation of justice from love* is an important therapeutic goal in this situation, and the *reality of forgiveness* must be learned to counteract the perpetual fear of punishment. Sometimes these goals are not reached, and all that can be done therapeutically is to offer possibilities for innocuous symbolic atonement for persistent guilt feelings.

The clinician who knows the symptoms and mechanisms of depression and compulsivity is in an entirely familiar sphere of thought when he reads the classical satisfaction and penal theories of atonement. They portray a God of wrath, whose love is deeply hidden behind insistence on his sovereignty, honor, holiness, and outraged sense of justice; who insists on sacrifice and penalty and to whom blood must be shed in order to restore acceptable relations. Typically the goal of salvation in this framework is stated as *justification,* and were it not for his vicarious self-sacrifice, the love of this God could not easily be seen behind his face of wrath.

And what about feelings of shame? They play a large part in the moral influence and governmental theories in which the emphasis is on the sanctification of behavior. God, having the common good in mind and acting as a benevolent governor, exacts satisfaction from one who is to serve as a model and example for the many. He makes the perhaps all too optimistic assumption that people are educable. Whereas the satisfaction theories seem to assume that man is trainable through fear, the moral influence theories stipulate in addition (or instead) that men can be led positively to a sanctified life by being given the opportunity *to identify themselves with an enlightening example* to whose circle they are moved to belong out of love.

To fall short of one's ideal and to let the example down henceforth produce shame, an unearthing experience indeed if one recalls how close to total abandonment one can feel in that predicament. But shame has the seeds of betterment in it, and it may spur one on to love the example all the more and demonstrate one's intentions in changed behavior. It is future-directed and lives from hope.

It will by now have become obvious, however, that these categorizations of conflict are somewhat artificial and academic. One may object that intrapsychic conflict is rarely confined to discord between just two internal psychic structures. More often it is the whole personality which is in discord with itself, with an involvement of all its structures in a complex set of interactions. The point is granted. Typology cannot be pushed too far, or one ends up with static entities which have nothing to do with life. But while it is true that most psychic conflict is complex, it is also a clinical fact that in each case some lines of conflict are more focal or conspicuous than others.

Thus far we have pointed out a close parallelism between three typical intrapsychic conflict situations and three typical formulations of the atonement. It is chiefly one of symbol structure, prevailing metaphor, predominant affect, and role behavior. The basic roles considered are those of lord and servant, judge and accused, governor and citizen. The psychologist need not thereby take the position of those who assume an *analogia entis* between the structure of man, the nature of God, and the person of Christ. But I wish to remind the reader that in some philosophical contexts, such as extreme personalism, scholasticism, and some forms of Gnosticism which stress structural identities between microcosm and macrocosm, the *analogia entis* idea can be applied in order to make assertions about God's nature in terms of man's self-experience. One example of its use by a psychologist is Jung's[32] speculation about God gradually resolving his own intrapsychic conflicts by an increasing awareness of some of his unconscious strivings.

The observation of so close a parallelism between experienced human motives and the supposed motives, feelings, and aims of the divine could be used to confirm Freud's suspicion that much religious thought and imagery is a projection of man's own inner experience onto some external object, real or imagined. Especially since all three atonement models arose during the long era of frankly supernaturalistic thinking in Christianity (shared alike by "popular religion" and theologians) which reinforced the "old man in the sky" notion of God, the projection hypothesis is a potent explanation of how the idea of God arises in the first place, and then becomes doctrinally articulated in modes of theological thought which retain a mythological, if not autistic, premise. The other side of this hypothesis is that all such thoughts are illusory in the special technical sense which Freud gave this word: "fulfillments of the oldest, strongest and most insistent wishes of mankind; the secret of their strength is the strength of these wishes."

Assuming that some sort of supernaturalism continues to permeate the thought of many ordinary believers and that Freud's psychological interpretation of it is at least in part valid, one is tempted to ask about the relevance of the dissemination of certain atonement doctrines for mental health. At first sight it would seem appropriate to say that since each atonement symbol represents only one aspect of experience, instruction might aim at appropriate richness by fairly representing all three models and their possible combinations. Favoring one while rejecting the others might not only lead to truncated religious development and closed-system thinking, but also to overstimulation of certain affects, eventually leading to preoccupations and perhaps even obsessions with at worst quite morbid consequences. For instance, one can think of irresolvable guilt feelings leading to flagellation, self-castration, and suicide or martyrdom; one can find in some persons or groups chronic feelings of shame and insufficiency; or paranoid delusions of evil invasions, persecutions, or demon possession leading to the mass madness of witch hunting or the cruelties of the Inquisition. Indeed, anyone who is informed about historical psychopathology and the peculiar geographical and cultural distributions of contemporary religious psychopathology knows that this is exactly what has happened, at least occasionally.

But what is perhaps more important than the viability of atonement theories as such is to recognize the impact of each symbol system, even when not verbally taught, on related religious doctrines, practices, and experiences which the faithful learn, as it were, by osmosis. For along with each special view of the atonement goes a practical selective emphasis on some special aspect of the life of Christ such as his birth, teachings, miracles, sayings, suffering, death, resurrection, ascension, or *parousia*. In the wake of this there is a further selective stress on certain fragments of the liturgical year, and even a special interpretation of the sacraments, especially the communion elements. With which of all these should a particular believer be most identified? Should he rejoice at Christmas, or rather at Easter? Can he rejoice at all on Good Friday? Indeed, is there any ground for joy at all? Can he afford to neglect Pentecost, or can he allow himself to overemphasize it? Is there any special feeling to be emphasized about Advent? What do or should the communion elements mean to the contemporary believer? Is the wine a symbol of spilled blood, messy suffering, and brutal aggression, or of new life, gentle nurturance, and rich vitality, or is it perhaps the seal of a promising new pact or covenant? The various doctrinal answers to such questions correlate far less with one's logical acumen or grasp of truth than with the whole cluster of interacting psychological, sociological, economic, theological, denominational, and ideological factors which determine one's concrete religious identity. The power of this correlation resides in the fact that each believer is immersed, as it were, in a vast symbol system around a given atonement motif.

In our focusing on the atonement we have thus far left out of view the more basic idea of the incarnation. *Cur Deus Homo*—why would God become man? Or: Why a God-man? We have seen that themes of the atonement are symbol systems through which people attest to their own identity by the detour of reflections about a divine-human figure. Does the atonement motif lead to the further assumption of the incarnation; or is the incarnation an independent idea, needed for its own sake, which in one particular life led to unforeseen consequences?

Comparative religion scholars are wont to point out that the case of Jesus of Nazareth is not the only example of incarnation in the history of religions. The idea that gods walk on earth unrecognized in their numinosity and in the form of human beings is ancient. The mythological imagination is capable of almost anything if the wish is strong enough. It can freely change men into gods and gods into men. This *metamorphosis* is the great subject of the Latin poet Ovid. Any unusual person can be seen as a specific vessel of the numinous: kings and prophets, even the mentally ill and epileptics. Whole tribes can be seen as having descended from the deity. Soederblom[33] sees the Christian idea of incarnation as unique only insofar as it confines itself to "one solitary incarnation of the deity." One might add: within the monotheistic conception of one solitary deity.

Our interest here is not in the ancillary doctrines which specify the mechanics of the incarnation process, such as the angelic annunciation and the virgin birth of Jesus. We are concerned only with the question in what way the Christian idea of the incarnation is a metaphor of people's feelings and thoughts about themselves and about their relation to the God they worship. And even for this narrow focus one has to keep in mind differences between the origination of the idea in the immediate followers of Jesus and its later use by those newer generations who were instructed in the symbol after it had become crystallized, dogmatized, and institutionalized. This is similar to the differences between the creative artist and the art lover.

Granted a God who is already worshiped as the creator of all, revered as the numinous partner in a covenant with a chosen nation, and venerated for his fatherly concern with people and sparrows, why would anything else be needed to give greater security, more protection from the power of nature, or more knowledge of the numinous mystery? His status is secured by his own positing himself in his primordial *is*ness—"I am that I am." His word is already known from the law and the prophets. His relation to man is already so intimate that he knows the innermost parts of any person, including the mind, the heart, and the bowels. His will and concern are already disclosed in the events of a people's history. His service is already established: religious life is organized, priests and preachers are about their tasks, and there is a magnificent literature in which he is extolled.

One can only make informed guesses at reasons for wanting anything more or different. If the divine transcendence is stressed to the point of psychological distance, one may begin to long for greater closeness. If the divine self-disclosure is still felt as unclear or enigmatic, one may long for increased clarity. If the divine word seems too rational, or even stilted, one may long for greater affective display. If it is too abstract, or if the ethical aim seems too high, one may long for a concrete example. If his words sound too forbidding and strict, one may long for evidence of graciousness. If the emphasis is too much on his role as a father, one may wonder whether man's sonship is adequately taken into account. If the human sons quarrel among themselves, some may begin to ask who is the "real" son. If the divine fatherhood becomes stilted in a managerial role, one may ask for proof of a more vital fatherhood in new progeny. If the human sons feel that their voice no longer carries with their father, they may seek a special man, as delegate, to mediate with him on their behalf; with the corollary idea of his being a herald to man on God's behalf.

One can also start with a cognitive question: What is truth? Behind this question may lie much disenchantment with classical answers such as: truth is in concepts; truth is knowing rules; truth is engraved on marble plates or written in laws and commentaries; truth is knowing the divine will; or truth is in oracles. For those who are disenchanted with rationalism and logical finesse, but keep searching for truth, there may come the insight that truth is a man! Truth is an existential posture, a life lived, acts committed. The corollary of this position is that truth-language cannot be merely indicative and analytical, but must be convictional. Convictional words have life and are creative. In fact, the Hebrew creation myth had portrayed a creator who called things into being by just such words, convictional words which also affirmed that all things were good. And in the dramatic unfolding of the incarnate's short life span there could have been hardly a more fitting byplay than Pilate's question near the end, which echoes the quest of any devout searcher.

And then there is the question of power. If great power per se is numinous, as it seems to be in all religions; and if it has been displaced from nature to a personal god, as it was in Judaism, one may begin to wonder whether there is any power germane to human beings. Not those special human beings who are kings, priests, or prophets, but the common man who has nothing to distinguish himself. Even if he is told that he is a son of the heavenly father, does he not feel like a second-rate son at best when the mighty of this world have usurped the divine power for themselves? Has not "sonship" become a hollow phrase? Will anyone take up the cudgel for the low man on the totem pole? Or, if it is not a matter of battle, is he entitled to any good feeling about himself? If so, should it be based exclusively on subservience to his superego—on strict obedience to all the rules and values he has been taught? Could he have zest, buoyancy, pride, and pleasure in feeling that he is somebody with an identity, with an ego that functions with some degree of autonomy?

It is plausible that any and all of these motifs may have played a role in producing a longing for a God-man and may continue to uphold the idea of a divine incarnation once the thought had been completed and was transmitted as historical fact. It was fairly easy to arrive at the thought two millennia ago, when all kinds of vital analogues and predecessors existed in the Mediterranean and Eastern civilizations. It would be much more difficult to generate the thought now and find sympathetic hearers for it. On the other hand, it is easier for contemporary persons to consider the incarnation idea an existing and traditional symbol, and ponder its possible meanings.

But whether we think of two thousand years ago or the current situation, what seems evident is that in the symbol of the incarnation man projects his own role as a son onto the screen that already contains the image of the Father. This modifies the original Father image into a "begetting Father" who demonstrates his procreativity, and his ability to produce novelty. It also modifies the Father's language to man: he speaks now in the form of a concrete man. Word is man and man is word. This man, moreover, speaks consistently of the Father as *his* Father, whose son he is; but since the Son is also divine, the language is that of the Father speaking and the Father spoken about, as well as the Son speaking and the Son spoken about. The Son also insists that power has already been redistributed: "The kingdom of heaven is within you." He insists that power is benevolent, since it renews and re-creates all things in a way that the mighty of this world would never have dreamed of. The old *imago Dei,* blurred and frayed at the edges, is being restored not by the imposition of more rules for the superego to absorb, but as an ego identity, as a badge of approval and appreciation. This is what Irenaeus meant when he wrote:

. . . our Lord Jesus Christ who did through His transcendent love become what we are, that He might bring us to be even what He is Himself.[34]

Irenaeus wrote these words to the heretics of his time, who in his opinion obscured simple things by their philosophical and moralistic hedgings. He felt they thereby missed the point of the incarnation as being, through love, a view of the self in transformation, the self renewed.

We have thus far sought to distinguish between the idea of divine atonement and the idea of divine incarnation, trying to find autonomous psychological justification for each of the two. But that separation is somewhat artificial, historically as well as psychologically. In the case of Christianity, atonement and incarnation go hand in hand, and one is seen as the proof of the other. But the efficacy of the atonement rests on the viability of the incarnation and the radical realism with which the two-nature paradox is asserted: a God-man, or both wholly God and wholly man. The interdependence of the two doctrines, yet with the edge given to the incarnation, is analogous to the intrapsychic situation with its complex internal relations. We have direct access only to the ego. The path to the superego, the ego-ideal, and the id requires a detour via the ego's perceptions, feelings, and acts. In the last analysis this means that the ego's zest and effective functioning are the yardstick of health and wholeness. When there is positive self-esteem without undue narcissism, and when the scope of the person's freedom has been enlarged through autonomous ego functioning, some gain has been made and some maturity has been reached. All three of the atonement models which we reviewed address themselves, each in a different style, to the three intrapsychic structures with which the ego has to deal: the superego, the ego-ideal, and the id. They deal with guilt feelings, shame, and anxiety. The incarnation model works directly on the ego, in the most crucial dimension of its activity: the roles in which fathers and sons may enjoy each other.

XI

Some Perennial Problems

DIFFICULTIES IN DEFINING RELIGION

THROUGHOUT this book we have been making use of the word "religion" without defining it. Such a carefree attitude may be a sign of the times, for half a century ago, when some of the great psychologies of religion were written, much effort was made to come to a satisfactory definition of religion in the belief that anyone who endeavors a psychology of something must be able to define his field of investigation sharply. In that vein, Leuba[1] in 1912 discussed no less than forty-eight different definitions of religion and added several more of his own. James, on the other hand, was quite sober in his emphasis on "the belief that there is an unseen order,"[2] the reactions to which he set forth in his brilliant *Varieties*.

Even Ferm's short and unpretentious *Encyclopedia of Religion*[3] contains a whole list of classes of definitions, together with a critique of each, prefaced by the telling sentence: "The term religion belongs to that large class of popular words which seems acceptable as common coin of communicative exchange but which on closer examination fails to carry the imprint of exact meaning." The same can be said about art. Theories of aesthetics and definitions of the beautiful abound, but they are of little avail to students who want to set up clear boundaries to "art" as a field of investigation. Indeed, the use of spatial terms such as "field" and "boundaries" is inadequate, for neither art nor religion is a territorial affair. The photographic term "focus" is better in that it leaves room for sharp centering as well as blurred edges and thus keeps a necessary amount of unclarity "in the picture."

Our approach has been perspectival, not only for the psychology we practice, but also for the subject matter we have dealt with in this book: religion. We regard religion as a perspective on things, a certain way of looking at the world and all reality, including ourselves. And again, we look at the phenomena which arise in the religious perspective (including the religious way of seeing things) from a psychological perspective. We are thus dealing with a perspective *of* a perspective. In addition, we psychologists sometimes look at the same things religionists look at, since common phenomena exist in both perspectives. What counts in this endeavor is the ability to identify oneself on the one hand with the religious perspective in order to "see things as the religionist sees them," and on the other hand to make no assertions of religious belief which are germane only to the religious, but not to the psychological perspective. Empathy, sympathy, or antipathy do not imply a wholesale taking over of the other man's point of view or situation—they rest only on a partial, temporary and, as it were, playful identification.

The word "playful," just used, is a crucial term. It lies at the heart of our endeavor, and has some interesting implications. The most obvious one is that I regard scientific thought as a fascinating combination of discipline and tinkering, in which one can play many "as if" games. A psychology or a sociology of religion can play with religion, tinker with it, look at it curiously, not only from the outside but also from the inside, for the psychologist or sociologist can for a while "play along" with the religious attitudes that he studies. He can step in and out of the game at will, as long as he knows that he thereby submits himself each time to different rules.

A second implication is that such exercises of curiosity are fun, that they give a certain satisfaction, and that they are pleasurable in their own right, which is in no small measure engendered by their open-endedness. Scientific endeavors do not have to be completed. To go one small step forward is enough, and even about that small step one should entertain some doubts—playful doubts. For science has much to do with humor and lightheartedness. In fact, if it becomes too serious it runs the risk of being ponderous, ritualistic, priestly. In a word, it then becomes a religion. And this leads to the third implication of the world "playful."

One of the outstanding features of religion is its seriousness. Whether religion be defined as belief, behavior, feeling, or attitude—religious belief is a serious belief, religious behavior is serious behavior, religious feeling is serious feeling, and religious attitudes are serious attitudes. They deal with serious matters, such as the nature of reality and how it might have come into being. They deal with serious questions such as the meaning of life or death, why there is evil, pain, and suffering, and how one might find some relief from these. They deal with serious issues such as how life should be lived, which responsibilities should be shouldered, and how much and what kind of pleasure one may feel entitled to. Religion's seriousness is not necessarily heavy, sad, or somber, although it often takes on these shadings of feeling. Rather it is a seriousness which implies a grave concern, a commitment, an attitude of caring, or as Tillich said, "centered acts of the personality." Even if gladness or joy and hope are emphasized, these are considered in their seriousness, to be differentiated from levity or lightheartedness. If humor, which is certainly not the most conspicuous feature of religion, is incorporated at all into the religious framework, it quickly turns into a divine humor of a god who may at times smile gravely or benevolently, but not laugh heartily. He may be amused, or ironic; but he may not joke.

I have always felt partial to the following passage from Freud's *The Future of an Illusion*:

> Critics persist in calling "deeply religious" a person who confesses to a sense of man's insignificance and impotence in face of the universe, although it is not this feeling that constitutes the essence of religious emotion, but rather the next step, the reaction to it, which seeks a remedy against this feeling. He who goes no further, he who humbly acquiesces in the insignificant part man plays in the universe, is, on the contrary, irreligious in the truest sense of the word.[4]

There it is: Religion does not merely assess man's place in nature, but it seeks a remedy. It is concerned with diagnosis for the sake of instituting a change, hopefully a cure. Diagnosis alone remains merely a *gnosis* for which indicative language suffices. But seeking a remedy requires urgent searching, and instituting change requires a serious commitment; both entail an imperative or subjunctive mood. They entail phrases like: "Now you must . . . ," "I wish that . . . ," "It would be nice if . . . ," "Let there be . . . ." The feeling of insignificance and impotence in face of the universe is one that requires drastic action for its elimination. It requires a remedy, or an *Abhilfe* (a word that presupposes someone's calling "help!"), as Freud's original German text has it. To acquiesce in the situation is to use the indicative mood: "That's the way things are." But to call for help or assistance means that the situation is felt as a predicament: "It should not be this way" or "Help me to find a way out." Rescue work is serious work, both for the helper and the person to be helped.

There are those who would disagree with Freud's distinction and insist that "humbly acquiescing" is also a religious attitude. In fact, Freud's choice of the German word *demütig* (which turns out a little too flat in the English "humbly") is not free from pietistic overtones. It also has close kinship with the gist of Stoic philosophy, and stoicism happens to be just the perfect borderline case about which one could endlessly argue whether it should be classified as religion, philosophy, or ethics. The obvious fact is that Freud himself did not see it as a religion, and in thus extricating himself from any religious pretensions his judgment about the distinctions between religion and philosophy was quite in line with that of many experts.

We have been at pains, in the foregoing chapters, not to identify religion with just any one of its many aspects. Our approach to religion has been rather broad in the sense that it did not give undue emphasis to mysticism, conversion, ritual, prayer, or the idea of God, all of which tend to be book titles or standard chapter headings in works on the psychology of religion. Indeed, some readers may have felt that these topics were slighted, since each is the center of an extensive body of literature which could have been cited or quoted from. Each of these could have been treated in greater depth and more detail, and should have been presented if the aim had been to produce an authoritative textbook which synthesizes the whole body of knowledge known as the psychology of religion. Nor did we identify religion with any particular psychological process which plays a role in it, such as thinking, feeling, willing, believing, or valuing. On this point too there may be readers who wished that we had treated religion in much greater detail as belief, as practice, or as a world view. They too could have pointed to specialized bodies of literature on each of these topics and demand that we take them into account.

There are several reasons for choosing a different course. I must first quote from James's *Varieties* the following sentence:

> Although some persons aim most at intellectual purity and simplification, for others richness is the supreme imaginative requirement.[5]

I leave it to the reader to decide whether I belong to the first or the second of James's cognitive types, but what I have consciously aimed for is richness rather than purity. This has an implication for the working definition of religion which is written between the lines of this treatise: it has been broad and quite accommodating, too much so for purists. This is a matter of taste, native or acquired, which may, moreover, change with the stage of life one is in and the subject matter one is interested in. Second, I have used as a leitmotiv the following passage from Goodenough on the difficulties of defining religion:

> Those who think they know most clearly, for disapproval or approval, what religion "is" seem to recognize least what amazingly different aspects of human life the term has legitimately indicated. We can, therefore, best approach religion by getting in mind the various experiences that men have called religion, rather than what we think should ideally be given the name.[6]

This statement relies on a common, and almost colloquial, use of the word "religion" to designate a multitude of phenomena in which we are interested. It does so not from naïveté or irresponsibility, but from a base of considerable knowledge and scholarly finesse. It is one thing to use the word "religion" as a concept with sharply defined contours. It is quite another thing to be sensitive to the subjective claims whereby people assert that this or that experience is for them a religious experience. The first attitude runs the risk of being doctrinaire, the second of being loose. The first attitude is less empirical than the second but undoubtedly more neat. More-over, in practice, the first tends to be exclusive, the latter inclusive. These are choices which one has to make, on a reasoned basis, commensurate with one's goals.

Third, one must also take into account historical shifts in nomenclature, whether this means technical vocabulary or popular word usage. Yester-day's magic became today's religion. Today's religion may become tomor-row's idolatry. Yesterday's heresy may be today's orthodoxy. "Primitive religion" in the sense of prehistory requires a different interpretation of primitivity than "primitive sects" in contemporary America. One conse-quence of these considerations is that the term "religion" would have to be defined in age-specific and culture-specific terms if one wanted to be precise and pure. But that would, in turn, work havoc with the develop-mental point of view which is such an important consideration in the life of religion.

My fourth guide has been the recognition that religion is both private and public, individual and institutional, subjective and objective. Religion is not merely an intimate and deeply personal feeling, or a highly idiosyn-cratic belief. It has a visible apparatus in buildings, books, schools, organ-izations, holidays, instruments, art products, and programs in the mass media. It has departments in universities, academic degrees, and a vast body of scholarly studies. It has orthodox and liberal wings. It has enormous libraries. All these features must be taken into account in a useful defini-tion of religion. However, the distinctions between the private and public aspects of religion do not coincide with the division between the psycho-logical and sociological disciplines. Therefore, the psychology of religion cannot confine itself to the private side of religious experience such as solitary prayer or mystical episodes, but must also come to grips with such public phenomena as theological treatises and liturgical processes. All the phenomena of religion which are so patently, visibly, almost tangibly, present can be placed in psychological perspective. Hence I have deliberately avoided placing too much stress on religious *experience,* since that term suggests a preoccupation with the private at the expense of the corporate aspects of religion. The term has been used defensively in the past to indicate that psychology's only legitimate access to religion was through uniquely private experiences, as distinct from such objective and corporate phenomena as Holy Scriptures and church life. The term has also been used preferentially throughout the nineteenth and the beginning of the twentieth centuries as a description of the essence of religion. This was a part of Schleiermacher's heritage, and it formed the thrust of the romantic schools. Many things have changed since those days within the self-defini-tion of religion, notably in Protestant Christianity, not the least of which is an increased appreciation of the corporate conception of the religious life.

Fifth, despair at finding a concise verbal definition of religion does not mean surrender to chaos. One can work within a tradition which has its own implied or explicit formulations about religion, or its own selective focus. There are schools of thought in which global ideas gradually become articulated. While I do not claim membership in any school, I know that I have in the course of years aligned myself with certain viewpoints and convictions, and have become loyal to a few leading ideas. These I must now set forth in order to show from whence my own thoughts came and where they might be going.

A HERITAGE OF GREAT IDEAS

At the conclusion of his *Varieties,* James once more considered the theme which he had worked out so well in his text, namely that life is lived by millions of people as if there were for them "something more"[7] than the ordinary sense data. This "more," believed to exist objectively, and the possibility of union with it, was his great theme. He asked whether it could be particularized and perhaps identified with a deity, say, Jehovah. But he thought it wiser to remain more global and avoid the over-beliefs of special faith groups. He discerned in the "more" a *farther* side and a *hither* side and then proposed that "the 'more' with which in religious experience we feel ourselves connected is on its hither side the subconscious continuation of our conscious life." He saw in the "subconscious self" a bridge concept between theology and science. For James as a scientist, the subconscious was an established fact amenable to further scientific investigation; for theologians, he argued, this fact would satisfy their contention that the religious person is moved by an external power. For the subconscious does produce objective appearances, many of which James had been at pains to describe in his book. Would it be possible to step through the doorway of the transmarginal consciousness on to the farther side of the "more"? James suggested that such a step is precisely what is taken in over-belief: those who have had conversion experiences and mystical states report on what the "more" is on its farther side, and the transient bond which their finite selves had with the infinite. James was candid enough to state his own over-belief and added, tongue in cheek, that it might appear "a sorry under-belief" to some of his religious audience.

James's insistence on global notions such as a "more" with a hither and a farther side, and his use of the subconscious mind as something which the conscious mind, though continuous with it, senses as "objective" (ego-alien or externalized, we would now say), were a stroke of genius. Apart from his immense charm as a writer and his felicitous use of case studies, he found a bridge concept which allows further ventures into the reality of the unseen. The doorway is a beautiful and useful image, since it combines continuity with discontinuity. It can be open or shut, wide open or ajar, tightly closed with locks and bolts or easily moved by a slight push. Many years after James, Huxley spoke of the "Doors of Perception," and drug addicts speak, quite appropriately, of "trips," good or bad, on which they are shown the farther side of reality's face, in an interesting combination of things sensed as internal as well as external.

But "more" is a scarcity word; it suggests not only that there might be more, but that people want more. Is there plenitude on one side of the door and starvation on the other? Can the goods be redistributed? What are the economic patterns? Does plenitude spill over from its own abode into the area of scarcity by a principle of entropy, or are the underprivileged doomed to long in vain and see the rich become richer? And in what direction does the door open? How is it hinged and locked? On the hither side or on the farther side?

Schleiermacher had so strongly emphasized people's need for a god, born from their primordial feeling of dependency, that it seemed to some that the divine reality was at best a secondary reality, even a pseudo-reality, invented as a response to the intensity of human feeling. And Feuerbach had gone a step further by stating that God is made in man's image. In response to these questions and ideas, Otto's work stands as a great monument. *The Idea of the Holy,* to which we have frequently referred in our text, is a methodological model. If the Holy is an original, irreducible category of experience, and if it is an attribute of just that aspect of reality which James called the "something more," it should be possible through a detailed phenomenological study to arrive at two parallel series of data. One series would describe all the fine qualities of which the idea of the Holy is a composite, as specific disclosures in which the Holy manifests itself. The other series would describe the fine details of the composite attitude of reverence toward the Holy which are disclosed by religious feelings, language, and practices. The "moments" of the Holy and their corresponding human experiences are interdependent and presuppose one another. Schleiermacher's "feeling of nothingness" is not an isolated feeling of nothingness, but of nothingness *in relation* to the "something more" that is sensed at the same time. The mysteries of experience which become numinous are not logical puzzles or scientific problems, which will disappear with the use of already available keys to their solution, but they are inherently experienced as objective and self-constitutive, and the correlated feelings which they invoke are inherently experienced as responsive. Otto was careful with his further epistemological and ontological assumptions. Convinced as he was that the idea of the Holy and the sentiment of reverence are an original human capacity, he could grant that much of it is stimulated or activated by experience, like any *Anlage* for any function within an organism.

Otto did something else, of crucial importance, something that makes him a *modern,* psychologically sensitive thinker of our century. He rescued the numinous from being invested only by pleasant, positive affect. The numinous mystery is, qua mystery, both a *tremendum* and a *fascinans.* It always invokes both shuddering and admiration. It attracts and repels at once. It elicits devotion and fear. It instills dread and trust. It is dangerous and comforting. It inspires awe and bliss. Moreover, Otto inferred that the aspect of the *tremendum* is more conspicuous at the beginning of religion, and that the scales are only gradually being tipped in favor of the *fascinans.* It is quite a step from awe to trust, or from a God of wrath to a God of love. The dynamic core of awe persists, no matter what else is added in later refinements. As long as the Holy remains a mystery, it is a *tremendum.* The moment it loses its mysterious features it ceases to be holy; it is then a concept or a rational insight. Power is always of its essence, for the Holy is not a concept but a symbol, charged with energy.

In Otto's work, the door seems so hinged as to swing open from the farther into the hither side. For on the farther side are the great sources of energy and power, which display themselves at will. But it can be pulled open from the hither side, for in the original feeling of reverence man has a key to open the door, if ever so slightly. Man has, as Otto says, a *talent* for relating himself to the numinous,[8] and although he does this only as a creature, with minor force and in dependency, he is not altogether passive in the process. In fact, that talent has in some people at times the strength and intensity of a drive! Man, however, engages frequently in another activity at the door: he is perhaps more concerned with its being closed than open. For the *tremendum* is so potent that it is felt as overpowering and intrusive. In self-protection, the door must be kept shut, tightly locked if possible, from the hither side.

Otto used the word "covering" (*Bedeckung*) to indicate that one cannot confront the Holy without protection, or without armor. The profane cannot meet the sacred without further ado. We already met in the previous chapter the gesture of covering oneself as an expression of shame or fear of exposure. Before the Holy, one covers the face. Rites of consecration and the use of "means of grace" are symbolic ways of such covering, with the added conviction that they have been instituted by the Holy itself.

The idea of the cover may be a happier metaphor than the image of the door. It has been used by another writer to whom we have frequently referred in our text, Goodenough. Informed by Otto's work, Goodenough took over the idea of the protective cover. Informed by Freud's psychology, he used it to added advantage in the following manner:

> Man throws curtains between himself and the tremendum, and on them he projects accounts of how the world came into existence, pictures of divine

or superhuman forces or beings that control the universe and us, as well as codes of ethics, behavior, and ritual which will bring him favor instead of catastrophe. So has man everywhere protected himself by religion.[9]

I think this is an extremely felicitous image. The cover serves two purposes: one as a protective blanket, the other as a projection screen. It is a modification of a more ancient image which has played a large role in Eastern religion: the idea of the veil which shields the divine mystery in the sense that it cannot or will not yet reveal itself fully. The veil is a divine piece of clothing to preserve secrecy; the curtain, a human instrument of protection. The veil indicates hiddenness; the curtain, safety. But in addition to its role as a safety device, the curtain is also a wonderful background on which one can paint pictures which suggest in some kind of ideogram what may lie hidden behind it.

Goodenough was informed by Freud on another point: he recognized that the *tremendum* is not just an external or all-encompassing reality. There is also a *tremendum* within man, namely the dynamic unconscious which contains some very important forces of nature which must be controlled. The *tremendum* consists of "all the sources of terror," all the threats which exist or are sensed. From this inner *tremendum* too we shield ourselves by throwing a curtain before it, a curtain of repression on which appear ideograms of our sense of guilt, our transference propensities, our censored motives. Although Goodenough does not mention it specifically, his text suggests that he did not think of two screens to cover two distinct *tremendums;* like James, he seems to have been open to the thought that the unconscious is in some way linked with the "something more" on its hither side.

A third theme stems from Goodenough's knowledge of both comparative religion and psychoanalytic metapsychology. It is that in some of the great Eastern religions the *tremendum* is not warded off, but welcomed. The devout Hindu and Buddhist hope to be engulfed by the *tremendum* and to have their individuality eventually extinguished. Mystics of all hemispheres have the same attitude. Goodenough saw in this tendency, which may appear only in attenuated form in the masses of adherents of those religions, a manifestation of the death instinct. He pointed out in passing how typically Western, in his opinion, the resistance to the concept of a death instinct is.

At any rate, projected or painted on the curtains are such things as creation stories and conceptions of an afterlife, ethical rules, gods, rituals of expiation, ideas of the sacrosanctness of the state and social arrangements, and various formulations of truth, which help us to adjust ourselves to the *tremendum.* The curtains and what is on them are clearly adaptive devices in the broadest sense, whether they are very much conflict-laden or relatively conflict-free. But then, after having used the image of the painted curtains to advantage, Goodenough made toward the end of his book an interesting transposition:

> At last it has emerged that the metaphor of the curtains with their patterns is only a colorful way of talking about symbols. We do not think *things* . . . but symbols—words or forms which call to mind the material object. In physics and religion, it is as in language: we can think of reality, think at all, not by the things themselves, but by symbols for them. . . . As the *Homo religiosus,* man may and must still live by the symbols which seem to him to give meaning to the tremendum and, in giving it meaning, take away its terror. This is not a new phenomenon. The Catholic has no use for an image of Shiva; the Hindu, none for a sophar. All of us, especially in the West, reject other people's symbols. Modern man is not irreligious because he has no use for traditional symbols; he is still religious because he still envisages and utilizes the tremendum through symbols and quiets the terror which the tremendum would arouse in him if he had no symbol-painted curtains.[10]

Now, after having used the image of doors that open and close, of covers which shield, of veils which hide secrets, and of curtains which protect and act as projection screens, we are asked to be less perceptual and more cognitive or abstract in recognizing the role of symbols in life. The symbol is also two-sided: it conceals and it reveals. It combines the hidden and the manifest; it combines the light of knowledge with clouds of unknowing. What comes to mind spontaneously at this point is Tillich's openness to the symbolic and his idea of the God-behind-the-gods. James saw the unconscious stretched toward the hither side of the "more" and occasionally getting a glimpse from its yonder dimension. Otto saw the Holy confronting a man under covers and eliciting his talents for numinous thoughts and acts. Goodenough saw fearful man throwing curtains between himself and the awesome unknown, convinced with James that the "something there" behind the curtain is full and not empty. Tillich[11] also sees a fearful and curious man projecting ideas on a screen, which to him, looking at its hither side, are gods. But Tillich sees the screen itself as the outer lining, as it were, of the ultimate reality which is God. This God is self-constituted and no human projection. On the contrary, God's own revealing and concealing activities make the human projections of gods possible. For symbols (here gods) participate in the reality to which they point.

At the end of this account of intellectual debts I feel moved to offer a slightly altered version of the imagery (or symbolism if one wills) we have been reviewing. I lay no claim to knowing what ultimate reality is. I am far from sure how access to it can be gained. But I see myself, and others, working with curtains and screens in order to seek protection from the "something more" which we fear and affirm. Even if the "more" were none but our own fear, our abject feeling of helplessness, it would have a psychological thickness which we could experience as a numinous reality. Whatever the *tremendum* is and wherever it may be, our very act of erecting doors, covers, curtains, or screen helps make it an "it." What "it" is must be searched by any feasible method. If scientific hypotheses and tests can clarify it, so much the better. If ethical thought and action bring us closer to its character, we all stand to benefit. If art can hint at its form or capture its message, we will have some enjoyment. If mythological or poetic thought can help us fathom its depth, we learn at least to appreciate its grandeur. If religious thought can make its peculiar truth more articulate or meaningful, we may gain wisdom and understanding. I see no reason why man at large could not use all these approaches at once. Indeed, I see no reason against any one person using them all at once.

For the moment, I have only an image to offer. Suppose that we reduce the functions of doors, covers, veils, curtains, and the outer lining of the ultimate to the basic role of a screen. Projections could be made on this screen from both sides. Men will continue to cast on its one side, with what light they have, all the pictures which Goodenough and Freud described. And those pictures need not be simple still slides, they can be movie pictures complete with sound and color. I can imagine a second show to go on at the other side of the screen. James's "more," Otto's *numen,* Tillich's ultimate, Schopenhauer's Will, Allah, Jehovah, the Trinity, and "it" are all busy revealing (and concealing) themselves by projecting pictures on the other side of the screen. It does not matter who erected the screen; for each party it has a hither and a yonder side. It does not matter in what plane the screen stands: the horizontal is just as effective as the vertical. Any angle will do. But what does matter, ontologically and epistemologically, psychologically, and theologically, is the *goodness of fit*[12] between the two projected images. Are the two shows different or the same? Paul could not answer the question of goodness of fit. Though he was concerned and curious, he kept it open. Living in an era before photography, he could only use the primitive optics of mirrors: "For now we see in a glass, darkly, but then we will see face to face."

Notes

I: ORIENTATION

1 M. Casaubon, "A Treatise Concerning Enthusiasme; as It is an Effect of Nature: But is Mistaken by Many for Either Divine Inspiration, or Diabolical Possession," in R. Hunter and I. Macalpine, *Three Hundred Years of Psychiatry, 1535–1860* (London: Oxford University Press, 1963), pp. 145-146.

2 O. Strunk, Jr. (ed.), *Readings in the Psychology of Religion* (New York: Abingdon Press, 1959).

3 Much of the following material is taken with permission of the publishers from: P. W. Pruyser, "Some Trends in the Psychology of Religion," *Journal of Religion,* XL (April, 1960), 113-129.

4 W. James, *The Varieties of Religious Experience* (London: Longmans, Green & Co., 1945).

5 H. N. Wieman and R. W. Wieman, *Normative Psychology of Religion* (New York: Thomas Y. Crowell Co., 1935).

6 G. A. Coe, *The Psychology of Religion* (Chicago: University of Chicago Press, 1916).

7 J. H. Leuba, *The Psychological Study of Religion: Its Origin, Its Function, Its Future* (New York: Macmillan, 1912).

8 R. Müller-Freienfels, *Psychologie der Religion,* 2 vols. (Berlin: Sammlung Goeschen, 1920).

9 S. Freud, "From the History of an Infantile Neurosis," in J. Strachey (ed.), *The Standard Edition of the Complete Psychological Works of Sigmund Freud,* Vol. XVII (London: Hogarth Press, 1955).

10 S. Freud, "Totem and Taboo," in J. Strachey (ed.), *The Standard Edition of the Complete Psychological Works of Sigmund Freud,* Vol. XIII (London: Hogarth Press, 1955).

11 S. Freud, "The Future of an Illusion," in J. Strachey (ed.), *The Standard Edition of the Complete Psychological Works of Sigmund Freud,* Vol. XXI (London: Hogarth Press, 1961).

12 O. Pfister, *Christianity and Fear* (London: George Allen & Unwin, 1948).

13 O. Pfister, *Some Applications of Psychoanalysis* (London: George Allen & Unwin, 1923).

14   E. Jones, "The Psychology of Religion," in *Essays in Applied Psycho-analysis,* Vol. II (London: Hogarth Press, 1951).

15   E. Jones, "A Psychoanalytic Study of the Holy Ghost Concept," *ibid.*

16   E. Jones, "Psychoanalysis and the Christian Religion," *ibid.*

17   T. Reik, *Ritual* (New York: W. W. Norton & Co., 1931).

18   S. Freud, "The Future of an Illusion," *op. cit.,* p. 30.

19   P. Tillich, *Dynamics of Faith* (New York: Harper & Brothers, 1957).

20   E. Jones, "Psychoanalysis and the Christian Religion," *op. cit.,* p. 203.

21   G. M. Stratton, *The Psychology of the Religious Life* (London: George Allen & Co., 1911).

22   E. J. Shoben, "Toward a Concept of the Normal Personality," *American Psychologist,* XII (April, 1957), 183-189.

23   C. G. Jung, *Modern Man in Search of a Soul* (New York: Harcourt, Brace & Co., 1933).

24   C. G. Jung, *Psychology and Religion* (New Haven: Yale University Press, 1938).

25   C. G. Jung, *Answer to Job,* trans. R. F. C. Hull (London: Routledge & Kegan Paul, 1954).

26   C. G. Jung, *Symbols of Transformation,* trans. R. F. C. Hull (Bollingen Series XX, Vol. V [New York: Pantheon Books, 1956]).

27   C. G. Jung, *Aion: Researches into the Phenomenology of the Self,* trans. R. F. C. Hull (Bollingen Series XX, Vol. IX, II [New York: Pantheon Books, 1959]).

28   A. T. Boisen, *The Exploration of the Inner World* (New York: Harper & Brothers, 1936).

29   A. T. Boisen, *Religion in Crisis and Custom: a Sociological and Psychological Study* (New York: Harper & Brothers, 1955).

30   A. T. Boisen, *Out of the Depths* (New York: Harper & Brothers, 1960).

31   L. Feuerbach, *The Essence of Christianity,* trans. G. Eliot (New York: Harper & Brothers, 1957).

32   K. A. Menninger, M. Mayman, and P. W. Pruyser, *A Manual for Psychiatric Case Study* (New York: Grune & Stratton, 1962).

33   P. E. Johnson, *Psychology of Religion* (New York: Abingdon Press, 1959).

34   P. E. Johnson, *Personality and Religion* (New York: Abingdon Press, 1957).

35   E. H. Erikson, *Young Man Luther, a Study in Psychoanalysis and History* (New York: W. W. Norton & Co., 1958).

36   E. la B. Cherbonnier, *Hardness of Heart* (Garden City, N.Y.: Doubleday & Co., 1955).

37   W. H. Clark, *The Psychology of Religion* (New York: Macmillan, 1958), p. 308.

38   F. Heiler, *Prayer* (New York: Oxford University Press, 1932).

39   S. Hiltner, *Preface to Pastoral Theology* (New York: Abingdon Press, 1958).

40   F. E. D. Schleiermacher, *The Christian Faith,* trans. and ed. H. R. Mackintosh and J. S. Stewart (Edinburgh: T. T. Clark & Co., 1928).

41 R. Otto, *The Idea of the Holy,* trans. J. W. Harvey (London: Oxford University Press, 1928).

42 R. Otto, *Mysticism East and West,* trans. B. L. Bracey and R. C. Payne (New York: Meridian, 1957).

43 G. W. Allport, *The Individual and His Religion* (New York: Macmillan, 1951), p. vi.

44 A. N. Whitehead, *Science and the Modern World* (New York: Macmillan, 1925).

45 J. H. Woodger, *Physics, Psychology and Medicine* (Cambridge: Cambridge University Press, 1956).

46 A. N. Whitehead, *Process and Reality—an Essay in Cosmology* (New York: Harper & Brothers, 1960).

47 Woodger, *op cit.,* p. 62.

48 P. Tillich, *The Courage To Be* (New Haven: Yale University Press, 1952).

49 Tillich, *Dynamics of Faith, op. cit.*

50 K. Menninger, M. Mayman, and P. W. Pruyser, *The Vital Balance* (New York: Viking Press, 1963).

II: PERCEPTUAL PROCESSES IN RELIGION

1 A. L. Huxley, *The Doors of Perception* (New York: Harper & Brothers, 1954).

2 R. M. Rilke, "Verkündigung," in *Ausgewählte Gedichte* (Leipzig: Insel Verlag, n.d.).

3 *Selected Poems of Emily Dickinson* (New York: Modern Library, n.d.), p. 72.

4 L. Lévy-Brühl, *Le surnaturel et la nature dans la mentalité primitive* (Paris: F. Alcan, 1931).

5 *Augustine: Confessions and Enchiridion,* trans. and ed. A. C. Outler (Philadelphia: Westminster Press, 1955), ix, 7, 15, p. 187.

6 W. La Barre, *They Shall Take Up Serpents, Psychology of the Southern Snake-handling Cult* (Minneapolis: University of Minnesota Press, 1962).

7 M. Eliade, *Shamanism, Archaic Techniques of Ecstasy,* trans. W. R. Trask (Bollingen Series LXXVI [New York: Pantheon Books, 1964]).

8 J. M. Guyon as quoted in F. Heiler, *Prayer,* trans. and ed. S. McComb (New York: Oxford University Press, 1958), p. 195.

9 F. Schelling as quoted in S. Freud, "The Uncanny," in J. Strachey (ed.), *The Standard Edition of the Complete Psychological Works of Sigmund Freud,* XVIII (London: Hogarth Press, 1955), 224.

III: INTELLECTUAL PROCESSES IN RELIGION

1 M. Twain, *Letters from the Earth,* ed. B. De Voto (New York: Harper & Row, 1962), Letter II.

2 J. R. Fry, *A Hard Look at Adult Christian Education* (Philadelphia: Westminster Press, 1961), p. 104.

3   W. James, *The Varieties of Religious Experience* (London: Longmans, Green & Co., 1945), pp. 53-54.

4   D. Bakan, *The Duality of Human Existence* (Chicago: Rand McNally Co., 1966), pp. 217-218, sees in this injunction also a shift from visual to auditory modes of worship.

5   "The Ballad of Reading Gaol," in *The Works of Oscar Wilde* (London: Collins, n.d.).

6   P. Woollcott, "The Patient's Religion as an Object of Psychiatric Study" (Graduation paper, Menninger School of Psychiatry, 1960); an abbreviated version later published as "The Psychiatric Patient's Religion," *Journal of Religion and Health,* I (1962), 337-349.

7   *Augustine: Confessions and Enchiridion,* trans. and ed. A. C. Outler (Philadelphia: Westminster Press, 1955), I, 1, 1, p. 31.

8   J. W. von Goethe, "Die Natur," as quoted in I. Ramzy, "Freud's Understanding of Anxiety," in S. Hiltner and K. Menninger (eds.), *Constructive Aspects of Anxiety* (Nashville: Abingdon Press, 1963), p. 15.

9   J. A. T. Robinson, *Honest to God* (Philadelphia: Westminster Press, 1963).

10   D. L. Edwards (ed.), *The Honest to God Debate* (Philadelphia: Westminster Press, 1963).

11   *Selected Poems of Emily Dickinson* (New York: Modern Library, n.d.), p. 36.

12   A. M. Greeley and P. H. Rossi, *The Education of Catholic Americans* (Chicago: Aldine, 1966).

13   R. L. Johnstone, *The Effectiveness of Lutheran Elementary and Secondary Schools as Agencies of Christian Education* (St. Louis: Concordia Seminary, 1966).

14   *Malleus Maleficarum,* trans. M. Summers (London: Pushkin Press, 1951).

15   L. Cristiani, *Evidence of Satan in the Modern World,* trans. C. Rowland (New York: Macmillan, 1962).

16   E. Swedenborg, *Angelic Wisdom Concerning the Divine Love and the Divine Wisdom* (New York: American Swedenborg Printing & Publishing Society, 1885), I, 10, p. 5.

17   P. McKellar, *Imagination and Thinking; a Psychological Analysis* (New York: Basic Books, 1957).

18   S. Butler as quoted in *The Concise Oxford Dictionary of Quotations* (London: Oxford University Press, 1964), p. 50.

19   P. W. Pruyser, "Anxiety, Guilt and Shame in the Atonement," *Theology Today,* XXI (1964), 15-33.

20   *Selected Poetry and Prose of William Blake,* ed. N. Frye (New York: Modern Library, 1953).

21   S. Freud, "A Seventeenth-Century Demonological Neurosis," in J. Strachey (ed.), *The Standard Edition of the Complete Psychological Works of Sigmund Freud,* Vol. XIX (London: Hogarth Press, 1961).

22   A. L. Huxley, *The Devils of Loudun* (New York: Harper & Brothers, 1952).

23   W. Whitworth, "Profiles: Bishop Homer A. Tomlinson," *New Yorker,* XLII (September, 1966), 67-108.

24   D. Bonhoeffer, *Prisoner for God* (New York: Macmillan, 1959).

25   D. Bonhoeffer, *Ethics* (New York: Macmillan, 1955).

26   A. Koestler, *The Act of Creation* (New York: Macmillan, 1964).

27   D. Rapaport, "The Theory of Ego-Autonomy: A Generalization," *Bulletin of the Menninger Clinic,* XXII (1958), 13-35.

28   E. Goffman, *Asylums* (Garden City, N.Y.: Doubleday & Co., 1961).

29   *Obras Completas de San Ignacio de Loyola,* trans. de I. Iparraguirre, S.J., and C. de Dalenases, S.J., (Madrid: Biblioteca de Autores Cristianos, 1963).

30   B. Hegardt, *Religie en Geestelijke Oefening: een Studie van de Exercitia Spiritualia der Jezuieten* (Rotterdam: W. L. & J. Brusse, 1939).

IV: THOUGHT ORGANIZATION IN RELIGION

1   S. Freud, "The Future of an Illusion," in J. Strachey (ed.), *The Standard Edition of the Complete Psychological Works of Sigmund Freud,* Vol. XXI (London: Hogarth Press, 1961), p. 26.

2   D. Rapaport, M. Gill, and R. Schafer, *Diagnostic Psychological Testing,* 2 vols. (Chicago: Year Book Publishers, 1945).

3   R. Otto, *The Idea of the Holy,* trans. J. W. Harvey (London: Oxford University Press, 1928), p. 2.

4   M. Luther, *Lectures on Romans,* trans. and ed. W. Pauck (Philadelphia: Westminster Press, 1961), p. 239.

5   K. Barth, *The Epistle to the Romans,* trans. E. C. Hoskyns (London: Oxford University Press, 1933), pp. 313-314.

6   S. de Beauvoir, *The Ethics of Ambiguity,* trans. B. Frechtman (New York: Philosophical Library, 1948).

7   S. Freud, *The Future of an Illusion,* trans. W. D. Robson-Scott (Garden City, N. Y.: Doubleday & Co., n.d.), p. 40.

8   *The Table Talk of Martin Luther,* ed. T. S. Kepler (New York: World Publishing Co., 1952), p. 106.

9   J. Calvin, *Institutes of the Christian Religion,* trans. H. Beveridge (London: James Clarke & Co., 1953), I, 2, 1, p. 40.

10   E. S. Ames, *Religion* (Chicago: John O. Pyle, 1949), p. 18.

11   W. Cowper, "There Is a Fountain," in *The Hymnal,* published by authority of the General Assembly of the Presbyterian Church in the United States of America (Philadelphia, Presbyterian Board of Christian Education, 1936), No. 241.

12   K. Goldstein, *Human Nature in the Light of Psychopathology* (Cambridge: Harvard University Press, 1947).

13   *An Encyclopedia of Religion,* ed. V. Ferm (New York: Philosophical Library, 1945), p. 756.

14   H. Cox, *The Secular City* (New York: Macmillan, 1965).

15   C. A. Miles, "In the Garden," in *Triumphant Service Songs* (Winona Lake, Ind.: The Rodeheaver Hall-Mack Co., 1934), p. 168.

16   O. Cullmann, *Immortality of the Soul or Resurrection of the Dead?* (New York: Macmillan, 1964), p. 5.

17   H. Leisegang, *Die Gnosis* (Stuttgart: A. Kroener Verlag, 1955), pp. 326 ff.

18   E. Swedenborg, *Angelic Wisdom Concerning the Divine Love and the Divine Wisdom* (New York: American Swedenborg Printing & Publishing Society, 1885), III, 242, p. 97.

19   *The Book of Mormon,* trans. J. Smith, Jr. (Independence, Mo.: Board of Publication of the Reorganized Church of Jesus Christ of Latter Day Saints, 1953), p. iii.

20   W. Walker, *A History of the Christian Church,* rev. C. C. Richardson, W. Pauck, and R. T. Handy (New York: Charles Scribner's Sons, 1959), p. 516.

21   "Dionysius the Areopagite," in *The Universal God,* ed. C. H. Voss (Cleveland: World Publishing Co., 1953), pp. 106-107.

22   S. Kierkegaard, *Fear and Trembling,* trans. W. Lowrie (Garden City, N. Y.: Doubleday & Co., 1955), pp. 80 ff.

23   S. Kierkegaard, *Concluding Unscientific Postscript,* trans. D. F. Swenson (Princeton: Princeton University Press, 1941).

24   K. Jaspers, *Existenzphilosophie* (Berlin/Leipzig: W. de Gruyter & Co., 1938).

V: LINGUISTIC FUNCTIONS IN RELIGION

1   R. A. Spitz, "Hospitalism, an Inquiry into the Genesis of Psychiatric Conditions in Early Childhood," in *Psychoanalytic Study of the Child* (New York: International University Press, 1945), Vol. I, pp. 53-74.

2   R. A. Spitz, "Hospitalism: a Follow-up Report," in *Psychoanalytic Study of the Child* (New York: International University Press, 1946), Vol. II, pp. 113-117.

3   Herodotus, "The History," trans. G. Rawlinson in R. M. Hutchins (ed.), *Great Books of the Western World,* Vol. VI (Chicago: Encyclopaedia Britannica, 1952), p. 49.

4   F. Ebner, *Das Wort und die Geistigen Realitäten* (Vienna: Verlag Herder, 1952), p. 71.

5   B. L. Whorf, *Collected Papers on Metalinguistics* (Washington, D.C.: Department of State, Foreign Service Institute, 1952).

6   *The Universal God,* ed. C. H. Voss (Cleveland: World Publishing Co., 1953), p. 60.

7   F. Pfeiffer, *Meister Eckhart,* trans. C. de B. Evans (London: John M. Watkins, 1924), p. 246.

8   J. Finegan as quoted in *The Universal God,* ed. C. H. Voss (Cleveland: World Publishing Co., 1953), p. 121.

9   P. Tillich, *Systematic Theology* (Chicago: University of Chicago Press, 1951), Vol. I, p. 239.

10   J. Huizinga, *Homo Ludens* (Boston: Beacon Press, 1955).

11 W. F. Zuurdeeg, *An Analytical Philosophy of Religion* (Nashville: Abingdon Press, 1958), p. 59.

12 E. Cassirer, *An Essay on Man* (Garden City, N. Y.: Doubleday & Co., 1956).

13 H. Feigl, "Logical Empiricism," in H. Feigl and W. Sellars (eds.), *Readings in Philosophical Analysis* (New York: Appleton-Century-Crofts, 1949).

14 *Augustine: Confessions and Enchiridion,* trans. and ed. A. C. Outler (Philadelphia: Westminster Press, 1955), IV, 15, 28, p. 92.

15 L. Mumford, *The Conduct of Life* (New York: Harcourt, Brace & Co., 1951), p. 59.

16 *Augustine, op. cit.,* VI, 5, 7, p. 118.

17 P. L. du Noüy, *Human Destiny* (New York: Longmans, Green & Co., 1947), p. 188.

18 *Augustine, op. cit.,* VII, 15, 21, p. 150.

19 A. Einstein, *Out of My Later Years* (New York: Philosophical Library, 1950), p. 28.

20 *Ibid.,* p. 29.

21 *Augustine, op. cit.,* VII, 5, 7, p. 138.

22 A. T. Boisen, *Out of the Depths* (New York: Harper & Brothers, 1960), pp. 88, 89.

23 J. M. Guyon, "Adoration," in C. M. Hill (ed.), *The World's Great Religious Poetry* (New York: Macmillan, 1945), p. 512.

24 *Selected Poems of Emily Dickinson* (New York: Modern Library, n.d.), pp. 207-208.

25 *Augustine, op. cit.,* III, 4, 8, p. 65.

26 *Ibid.,* III, 6, 10, p. 66.

27 S. Kierkegaard, *Attack Upon Christendom,* trans. W. Lowrie (Boston: Beacon Press, 1956), pp. 5, 7.

28 *Augustine, op. cit.,* X, 6, 9, p. 206.

29 Boisen, *op. cit.,* p. 117.

30 *Augustine, op. cit.,* VII, 17, 23, p. 151.

31 *St. Teresa of Jesus,* ed. J. J. Burke (New York: Columbia Press, 1911), p. 266.

32 Boisen, *op. cit.,* pp. 89-90.

33 W. James, *The Varieties of Religious Experience* (London: Longmans, Green & Co., 1945), p. 373.

34 W. Wordsworth, "The Prelude," in *The Oxford Dictionary of Quotations* (London: Oxford University Press, 1955), p. 579.

35 E. Mote, "My Hope Is Built," in *Triumphant Service Songs* (Winona Lake, Ind.: The Rodeheaver Hall-Mack Co., 1934), p. 26

36 *Augustine, op. cit.,* I, 4, 4, p. 33.

37 *Ibid.,* I, 6, 7, p. 34.

38 *Hamlet,* Act II, sc. 2.

39 *Augustine, op. cit.,* I, 16, 25, p. 45.

40 *Ibid.,* IV, 15, 31, p. 93.

41 *Ibid.,* V, 3, 3, p. 96.

42   W. F. Zuurdeeg, *An Analytical Philosophy of Religion* (Nashville: Abingdon Press, 1958), p. 79.

43   M. Luther, "Liturgy and Hymns," in U. S. Leupold (ed.) *Luther's Works*, LIII (Philadelphia: Fortress Press, 1965), pp. 72, 74.

44   M. Luther, "The German Mass and Order of Service, 1526," in B. Thompson (ed.) *Liturgies of the Western Church* (Cleveland: World Publishing Co., 1961), pp. 124-125.

45   G. Roheim, *Animism, Magic and the Divine King* (London: Kegan Paul, Trench, Trubner & Co., 1930), p. 364.

46   E. Jones, "A Psycho-analytic Study of the Holy Ghost Concept," in *Essays in Applied Psychoanalysis* (London: Hogarth Press, 1951), Vol. II.

47   J. Laffal, *Pathological and Normal Language* (New York: Atherton Press, 1965), pp. 87-88.

48   J. N. Lapsley and J. H. Simpson, "Speaking in Tongues: Token of Group Acceptance and Divine Approval," in *Pastoral Psychology*, XV (May, 1964), 48-55.

49   J. N. Lapsley and J. H. Simpson, "Speaking in Tongues: Infantile Babble or Song of the Self?" in *Pastoral Psychology*, XV (September, 1964), 16-24.

50   F. Alexander, *Psychoanalysis of the Total Personality* (New York: Nervous and Mental Disease Publishing Co., 1930).

VI: EMOTIONAL PROCESSES IN RELIGION

1   J. Hillyer, *Reluctantly Told* (New York: Macmillan, 1931), pp. 71-72.

2   F. E. D. Schleiermacher, *On Religion*, trans. J. Oman (New York: Frederick Ungar Publishing Co., 1955).

3   J. Edwards, "A Treatise Concerning Religious Affections," in P. Miller (ed.), *The Works of Jonathan Edwards*, Vol. II (New Haven: Yale University Press, 1959).

4   *Ibid.*, p. 99.

5   P. M. Roget, *Thesaurus of Words and Phrases* (New York: Grosset & Dunlap, 1947).

6   C. Landis, *Varieties of Psychopathological Experience*, ed. F. A. Mettler (New York: Holt, Rinehart & Winston, 1964), p. 273.

7   *Ibid.*, p. 287.

8   *Ibid.*, pp. 33-34.

9   G. Tersteegen as quoted in R. Otto, *The Idea of the Holy*, trans. J. W. Harvey (London: Oxford University Press, 1928), p. 188.

10   "The Sayings of the Fathers," in *Western Asceticism*, trans. O. Chadwick (Philadelphia: Westminster Press, 1958), pp. 37-189.

11   W. James, *The Varieties of Religious Experience* (London: Longmans, Green & Co., 1945), pp. 147-148, 192 ff., 256 ff.

12   J. W. Gardner, *Self-Renewal: The Individual and the Innovative Society* (New York: Harper & Row, 1963).

13   Pope John XXIII, *Journal of a Soul*, trans. D. White (New York: New American Library, 1966).

14 *Ibid.*, p. 71.

15 *Ibid.*, p. 149.

16 *Ibid.*, p. 97.

17 *Ibid.*, p. 107.

18 *Ibid.*, p. 105.

19 W. Köhler, *Angelus Silesius* (Munich: Georg Müller, 1929), p. 27. Köhler pairs the lines from Silesius with those of Rilke.

20 E. G. Schachtel, *Metamorphosis* (New York: Basic Books, 1959).

21 P. W. Pruyser, "Joy," *Journal of Pastoral Care*, XX (June, 1966), 90-94.

22 Schachtel, *op. cit.*, p. 37.

23 G. Marcel, *Homo Viator, Prolégomènes à une metaphysique de l'espérance* (Aubier: Editions Montaigne, 1944).

24 P. W. Pruyser, "Phenomenology and Dynamics of Hoping," *Journal for the Scientific Study of Religion*, III (Fall, 1963) 86-96.

25 W. C. M. Scott, "Depression, Confusion and Multivalence" (Paper read at International Psychoanalytic Congress, Copenhagen, 1959).

26 *Selected Poems of Emily Dickinson* (New York: Modern Library, n.d.), p. 35.

27 *Ibid.*, pp. 45-46.

28 Edwards, *op. cit.*, p. 98.

29 "The Westminster Confession of Faith," in *The Constitution of the United Presbyterian Church in the United States of America* (Philadelphia: Office of the General Assembly of the United Presbyterian Church in the United States of America, 1961).

VII: RELIGION AND THE MOTOR SYSTEM

1 St. Bernard of Clairvaux, as quoted in *The Universal God*, ed. C. H. Voss (Cleveland: World Publishing Co., 1953), pp. 259-260.

2 G. van der Leeuw, *Sacred and Profane Beauty: The Holy in Art*, trans. D. E. Green (New York: Holt, Rinehart & Winston, 1963), p. 37.

3 W. La Barre, *They Shall Take Up Serpents, Psychology of the Southern Snake-handling Cult* (Minneapolis: University of Minnesota Press, 1962).

4 Van der Leeuw, *op. cit.*, p. 17.

5 *Ibid.*, p. 41.

6 J. Huizinga, *Homo Ludens* (Boston: Beacon Press, 1955).

7 R. Müller-Freienfels, *Psychologie der Religion* (Berlin: Sammlung Goeschen, 1920), Vol. I, p. 69.

8 G. E. Coghill, "The Early Development of Behavior in the Amblystoma and in Man," *Archives of Neurology and Psychiatry*, XXI (1929), 989-1009.

9 S. Kierkegaard, *Purity of Heart Is To Will One Thing, Spiritual Preparation for the Office of Confession* (New York: Harper & Brothers, 1956).

10 T. W. Klink, unpublished case study, Topeka State Hospital.

11 W. La Barre, *op. cit.*, p. 134.

12 A. de Buck, *De Godsdienstige Opvatting van den Slaap, inzonderheid in het oude Egypte* (Leiden: E. J. Brill, 1939).

VIII: RELATIONS TO PERSONS

1   G. W. Allport, *The Individual and His Religion* (New York: Macmillan, 1951), p. 9.

2   K. Dunlap, *Religion: Its Function in Human Life* (New York: McGraw-Hill Book Co., 1946), p. 126.

3   E. S. Ames, *Religion* (Chicago: John O. Pyle, 1949), p. 37.

4   S. Freud, "Civilization and Its Discontents," in J. Strachey (ed.), *The Standard Edition of the Complete Psychological Works of Sigmund Freud,* Vol. XXI (London: Hogarth Press, 1961), pp. 74-85.

5   Freud, *op. cit.,* p. 76.

6   K. A. Menninger, M. Mayman, and P. W. Pruyser, *A Manual for Psychiatric Case Study* (New York: Grune & Stratton, 1962), pp. 68-76.

7   K. Menninger, M. Mayman, and P. W. Pruyser, *The Vital Balance* (New York: Viking Press, 1963), pp. 76-152.

8   S. Freud, "The Future of an Illusion," in J. Strachey (ed.), *The Standard Edition of the Complete Psychological Works of Sigmund Freud,* Vol. XXI, (London: Hogarth Press, 1961), p. 53.

9   P. Tillich, *Dynamics of Faith* (New York: Harper & Brothers, 1957).

10   E. H. Erikson, *Identity and the Life Cycle* (New York: International University Press, 1959).

11   E. H. Erikson, *Childhood and Society* (New York: W. W. Norton & Co., 1963).

12   P. W. Pruyser, "The Challenge of Mental Retardation for the Church," *McCormick Quarterly Special Supplement,* XIX (March, 1966), 10-25, contains a sketch of typical questions raised by persons in moments of suffering.

13   E. R. Goodenough, *The Psychology of Religious Experiences* (New York: Basic Books, 1965), p. 147.

14   M. Balint, *Problems of Human Pleasure and Behaviour* (New York: Liveright Publishing Corp., 1957), p. 23.

15   *Ibid.,* p. 31.

16   *Ibid.,* p. 32.

17   H. C. Ruemke, *The Psychology of Unbelief* (New York: Sheed & Ward, 1962).

18   H. G. Wells, "Mr. Britling Sees It Through," in *The Universal God,* ed. C. H. Voss (Cleveland: World Publishing Co., 1953), pp. 285-286.

19   *Augustine: Confessions and Enchiridion,* trans. and ed. A. C. Outler (Philadelphia: Westminster Press, 1955), I, 1, 1, p. 31.

20   A. C. Outler, "Anxiety and Grace: an Augustinian Perspective," in S. Hiltner and K. Menninger (eds.) *Constructive Aspects of Anxiety* (Nashville: Abingdon Press, 1963), pp. 92-93.

21   L. Mumford as quoted in *The Universal God,* ed. C. H. Voss (Cleveland: World Publishing Co., 1953), p. 51.

22   J. C. Smuts, "Holism and Evolution," in *The Universal God,* ed. C. H. Voss (Cleveland: World Publishing Co., 1953), p. 223. Also: J. C. Smuts, *Holism and Evolution* (New York: Macmillan, 1926), pp. 107, 299.

23   S. Freud, "The Ego and the Id," in J. Strachey (ed.), *The Standard Edition of the Complete Psychological Works of Sigmund Freud*, Vol. XIX, (London: Hogarth Press, 1961), pp. 19-27.

24   P. Woollcott, unpublished data, The Menninger Foundation, Interviews with pastors.

25   L. Kanner, *A History of the Care and Study of the Mentally Retarded* (Springfield, Ill.: C. C. Thomas, 1964), pp. 7-8. The author mentions Luther's advocating the drowning of mentally retarded children, referring to: *Colloquia Mensalia* (London: William Du-Gard, 1652), p. 387, and *Sämtliche Schriften* (Ausgabe von K. E. Foerstermann, Band XXII, pp. 56 f., 69 f., 70 f.

IX: RELATIONS TO THINGS AND IDEAS

1   W. James, *The Varieties of Religious Experience* (London: Longmans, Green & Co., 1945), p. 309.

2   W. James, *The Principles of Psychology* (New York: Dover Publications, 1950), pp. 291-401.

3   M. Weber, *The Protestant Ethic and the Spirit of Capitalism*, trans. T. Parsons (New York: Charles Scribner's Sons, 1958).

4   R. Benedict, *Patterns of Culture* (Boston: Houghton Mifflin Co., 1934).

5   F. Dostoevsky, *The Gambler*, trans. A. R. MacAndrew (New York: Bantam Books, 1964).

6   J. Barr, "Biblical Words for Time," in *Studies in Biblical Theology*, Vol. XXXIII (Naperville, Ill.: Alec R. Allenson, 1962).

7   H. Feifel, "Attitudes Toward Death in Some Normal and Mentally Ill Populations," in H. Feifel, (ed.), *The Meaning of Death* (New York: McGraw-Hill Book Co., 1959), p. 121.

8   Meister Eckhart as quoted in W. T. Stace, *The Teachings of the Mystics* (New York: New American Library, 1960), pp. 153, 155.

9   W. James, *The Varieties of Religious Experience* (London: Longmans, Green & Co., 1945), p. 68.

10   A. Huxley, *The Doors of Perception* (New York: Harper & Brothers, 1954), p. 21.

11   A. T. Boisen, "Economic Distress and Religious Experience—a Study of the Holy Rollers," *Psychiatry*, II (1939), 185-194.

12   L. Feuerbach, *The Essence of Christianity*, trans. G. Eliot (New York: Harper & Brothers, 1957), pp. 29-30.

13   E. H. Erikson, *Young Man Luther, a Study in Psychoanalysis and History* (New York: W. W. Norton & Co., 1958).

14   K. Menninger, "Toward the Understanding of Violence," *Journal of Human Relations*, XIII (1965), 418-426.

15   G. Winter, "The Church in Suburban Captivity," in *The Christian Century Reader* (New York: Association Press, 1962), pp. 59-65.

16   W. James as quoted in *The Concise Oxford Dictionary of Quotations* (London: Oxford University Press, 1964), p. 113.

17   S. W. Ginsburg, "The Role of Work—a Contribution to Ego-Psychology," *Samiksa*, VIII (1954), 1-13.

18   I. Hendrick, *Facts and Theories of Psychoanalysis* (New York: Alfred Knopf, 1958).

19   D. J. Maitland, "Vocation," in *A Handbook of Christian Theology* (New York: Meridian Books, 1958), pp. 371-372.

20   J. Fletcher, *Moral Responsibility—Situation Ethics at Work* (Philadelphia: Westminster Press, 1967), p. 43.

21   M. Rokeach, *The Open and Closed Mind* (New York: Basic Books, 1960).

22   J. B. Pratt, "The Psychology of Religion," in O. Strunk, Jr. (ed.), *Readings of the Psychology of Religion* (New York: Abingdon Press, 1959), p. 29.

23   M. Luther, "Short Preface to the Large Catechism," in *Concordia, or Book of Concord—the Symbols of the Evangelical Lutheran Church* (St. Louis: Concordia Publishing House, 1952), p. 168.

24   Z. Ursinus and C. Olevianus, "The Heidelberg Catechism, (1563)," in *Reformed Standards of Unity* (Grand Rapids: Society for Reformed Publications, 1957).

25   "The Westminster Catechism (1643–1649)," in *The Constitution of the United Presbyterian Church in the United States of America* (Philadelphia: Office of the General Assembly of the United Presbyterian Church in the United States of America, 1961).

26   O. Pfister, *Christianity and Fear,* trans. W. H. Johnston (London: George Allen & Unwin, 1948), p. 551.

27   Pfister, *op. cit.,* p. 22, Preface.

28   T. Reik, *Dogma and Compulsion: Psychoanalytic Studies of Religion and Myths* (New York: International Universities Press, 1951).

29   Pratt, *op. cit.*

30   E. Fromm, *Psychoanalysis and Religion* (New Haven: Yale University Press, 1950), pp. 34 ff.

31   Pfister, *op. cit.,* pp. 540 ff.

32   K. Lewin, R. Lippitt, and R. K. White, "Patterns of Aggressive Behavior in Experimentally Created Social Climates," *Journal of Social Psychology,* X (1939), 271-299.

33   R. Lippitt, "An Experimental Study of Democratic and Authoritarian Group Atmospheres" (Studies in Topological and Vector Psychology I, Vol. XVI, No. 3 in University of Iowa Studies in Child Welfare [Iowa City: University of Iowa Press, 1940]), pp. 145-193.

34   E. R. Goodenough, *The Psychology of Religious Experiences* (New York: Basic Books, 1965), pp. 89-90.

35   *Ibid.,* p. 100.

36   *Ibid.,* p. 120.

37   G. W. Allport, "Prejudice: Is It Societal or Personal?" *Journal of Social Issues,* XVIII (1962), pp. 120, 125.

38   S. A. Stouffer, *Communism, Conformity and Civil Liberties* (Garden City, N.Y.: Doubleday & Co., 1955), p. 147.

39   Allport, *op. cit.,* pp. 126-127.

40   *Ibid.,* p. 131.

41   G. W. Allport, "The Religious Context of Prejudice," *Journal for the Scientific Study of Religion,* V (1966), 447-457.

42   G. M. Stratton, *Man, Creator or Destroyer* (London: George Allen & Unwin, 1952), p. 57.

43   James, *Varieties,* op. cit., p. 41.

44   L. White, Jr., "The Historical Roots of our Ecologic Crisis," *Science* CLV (1967), 1203-1207.

45   L. Mumford, "The Fulfillment of Man," in *This Is My Philosophy,* ed. W. Burnett (New York: Harper & Brothers, 1957), p. 31.

46   P. Tillich, *Systematic Theology,* III (Chicago: University of Chicago Press, 1963), 197-198.

47   Goodenough, *op. cit.,* pp. 142-143.

X: RELATIONS TO THE SELF

1   K. Jaspers, *Allgemeine Psychopathologie* (Berlin-Heidelberg: Springer Verlag, 1948), pp. 101-109.

2   W. James, *The Principles of Psychology* (New York: Dover Publications, 1950), pp. 291-401.

3   Gregory of Nyssa, "An Address on Religious Instruction," trans. C. C. Richardson in *Christology of the Later Fathers* (Philadelphia: Westminster Press, 1954), pp. 268–325.

4   Irenaeus, "Against Heresies," trans. E. R. Hardy in *Early Christian Fathers* (Philadelphia: Westminster Press, 1953), pp. 387, 390, 391, 397.

5   J. Pelikan, *The Shape of Death: Life, Death and Immortality in the Early Fathers* (New York: Abingdon Press, 1961), pp. 103 ff.

6   F. Pfeiffer, *Meister Eckhart,* trans. C. de B. Evans (London: John M. Watkins, 1924), p. 164.

7   Pfeiffer, *op. cit.,* p. 117.

8   S. Freud, "Civilization and Its Discontents," in J. Strachey (ed.) *The Standard Edition of the Complete Psychological Works of Sigmund Freud,* Vol. XXI (London: Hogarth Press, 1961), p. 65.

9   C. K. Barrett, *From First Adam to Last; A Study in Pauline Theology* (New York: Charles Scribner's Sons, 1962).

10   C. Beers, *A Mind That Found Itself* (Garden City, N.Y.: Doubleday, Doran & Co., 1928), p. 86.

11   A. T. Boisen, *Out of the Depths* (New York: Harper & Brothers, 1960), p. 99.

12   *Ibid.,* p. 204.

13   *Ibid.,* p. 119.

14   W. James, *The Varieties of Religious Experience* (London: Longmans, Green & Co., 1945), pp. 163-185.

15   K. Menninger, M. Mayman, and P. W. Pruyser, *The Vital Balance* (New York: Viking Press, 1963), pp. 76-152.

16   J. C. Smuts, *Holism and Evolution* (New York: Macmillan, 1926), p. 299.

17   E. H. Erikson, *Young Man Luther, a Study in Psychoanalysis and History* (New York: W. W. Norton & Co., 1958), p. 21.

18   F. Pfeiffer, *Meister Eckhart*, trans. C. de B. Evans (London: John M. Watkins, 1924), p. 246.

19   "The Bohemian Hymn," in *The Complete Works of R. W. Emerson* (New York: Sully & Kleinteich, n.d.), pp. 298-299.

20   K. Bühler, *The Mental Development of the Child* (New York: Harcourt, Brace & Co., 1930).

21   H. Hartmann, *Ego Psychology and the Problem of Adaptation*, trans. D. Rapaport (New York: International Universities Press, 1958).

22   *The Table Talk of Martin Luther*, ed. T. S. Kepler (New York: World Publishing Co., 1952), p. 158, no. 224.

23   E. R. Goodenough, *The Psychology of Religious Experiences* (New York: Basic Books, 1965), p. 20.

24   P. W. Pruyser, "Nathan and David: a Psychological Footnote," *Pastoral Psychology*, XIII (1962), 14-18.

25   W. Cannon, "Voodoo Death," *Psychosomatic Medicine*, XIX (1957), 182-190.

26   R. Schafer, "The Loving and Beloved Superego in Freud's Structural Theory," in *The Psychoanalytic Study of the Child*, XV (New York: International Universities Press, 1960), 163-188.

27   Goodenough, *op. cit.*, pp. 88-158.

28   J. K. Mozley, *The Doctrine of the Atonement* (London: Gerald Duckworth & Co., 1915).

29   P. W. Pruyser, "Anxiety, Guilt and Shame in the Atonement," *Theology Today*, XXI (1964), 15-33. The following pages are an adaptation of this article, with the publisher's permission.

30   M. Heidegger, *Being and Time*, trans. J. MacQuarrie and E. Robinson (New York: Harper & Brothers, 1962).

31   Anselm of Canterbury, "Cur Deus Homo," in *A Scholastic Miscellany: Anselm to Ockham*, trans. and ed. E. R. Fairweather (Philadelphia: Westminster Press, 1956), pp. 100-183.

32   C. G. Jung, *Answer to Job*, trans. R. F. C. Hull (London: Routledge & Kegan Paul, 1954).

33   N. Soederblom, "Introductory Article on Incarnation," in J. Hastings (ed.) *Encyclopedia of Religion and Ethics*, VII (New York: Charles Scribner's Sons, 1955), 183-184.

34   Irenaeus, "Against Heresies," as quoted from W. Walker, *A History of the Christian Church*, revised C. C. Richardson, W. Pauck, and R. T. Handy (New York: Charles Scribner's Sons, 1959), p. 63.

XI: SOME PERENNIAL PROBLEMS

1   J. H. Leuba, *The Psychological Study of Religion: Its Origin, Its Function, Its Future* (New York: Macmillan, 1912).

2   W. James, *The Varieties of Religious Experience* (London: Longmans, Green & Co., 1945), pp. 58 ff.

3   *An Encyclopedia of Religion,* ed. V. Ferm (New York: The Philosophical Library, 1945), pp. 646-647.

4   S. Freud, *The Future of an Illusion,* trans. W. D. Robson-Scott (Garden City, N.Y.: Doubleday & Co., n.d.), pp. 56-57.

5   James, *op. cit.,* p. 449.

6   E. R. Goodenough, *The Psychology of Religious Experiences* (New York: Basic Books, 1965), p. 2.

7   James, *op. cit.,* p. 502.

8   R. Otto, *The Idea of the Holy,* trans. J. W. Harvey (London: Oxford University Press, 1928), pp. 119 ff. The notion of a talent for numinous experience is more clearly expressed in pp. 140 ff. of the German edition, revised in 1936: *Das Heilige,* 23-25 Auflage, (München: C. H. Beck'sche Verlagsbuchhandlung).

9   Goodenough, *op. cit.,* p. 8.

10   *Ibid.,* pp. 179 ff.

11   P. Tillich, *Systematic Theology,* I (Chicago: University of Chicago Press, 1959), 211 ff.

12   "Goodness of fit," a statistical term indicating "the degree to which a set of empirical observations conforms to a standard or an expected (or theoretical) distribution . . . ," as defined in H. B. English and A. C. English, *A Comprehensive Dictionary of Psychological and Psychoanalytical Terms* (New York: Longmans, Green & Co., 1958), p. 209.

Index